No Jim Crow Church

UNIVERSITY PRESS OF FLORIDA

Florida A&M University, Tallahassee
Florida Atlantic University, Boca Raton
Florida Gulf Coast University, Ft. Myers
Florida International University, Miami
Florida State University, Tallahassee
New College of Florida, Sarasota
University of Central Florida, Orlando
University of Florida, Gainesville
University of North Florida, Jacksonville
University of South Florida, Tampa
University of West Florida, Pensacola

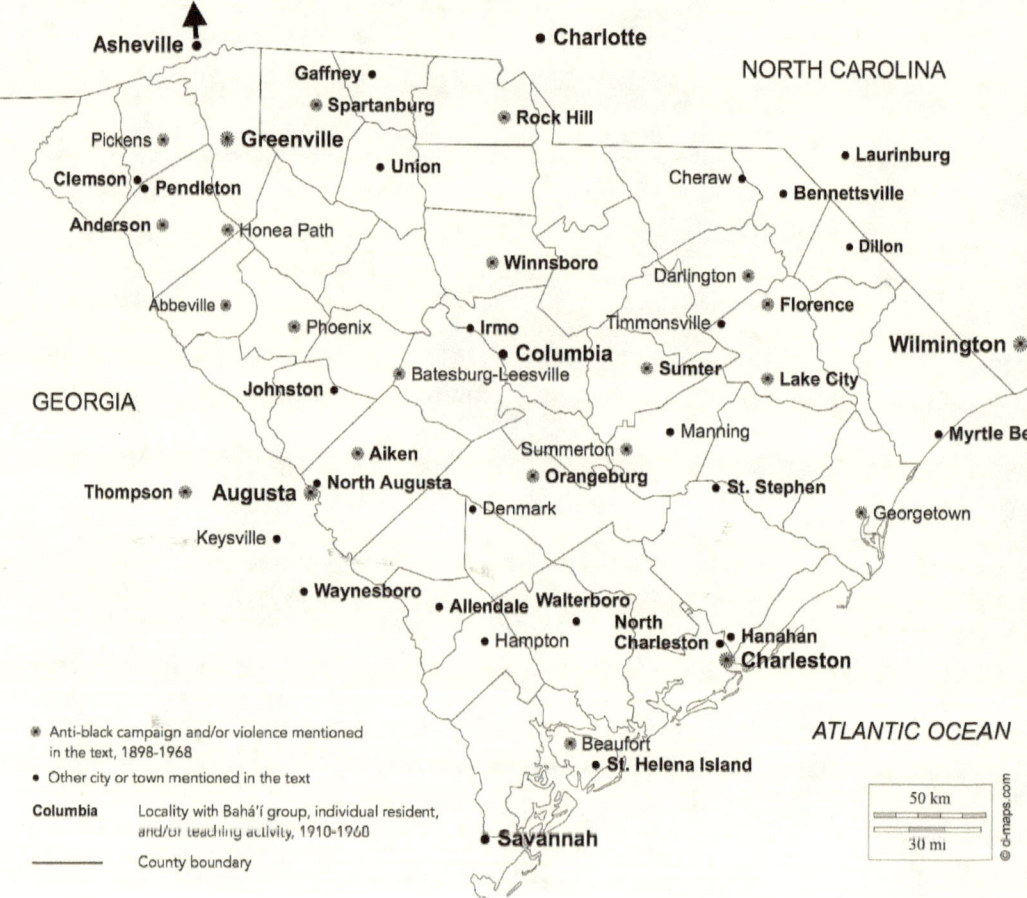

NO JIM CROW CHURCH

The Origins of South Carolina's
Bahá'í Community

Louis Venters

University Press of Florida
Gainesville Tallahassee Tampa Boca Raton Pensacola Orlando
Miami Jacksonville Ft. Myers Sarasota

Frontispiece: Localities mentioned in the text. Prepared by author. Outline courtesy of d-maps.com (http://d-maps.com/m/america/usa/carolinesud/carolinesud/carolinesud20.pdf).

COPYRIGHT 2015 BY LOUIS VENTERS
All rights reserved
Printed in the United States of America on acid-free paper

This book may be available in an electronic edition.

21 20 19 18 17 16   6 5 4 3 2 1

First cloth printing, 2015
First paperback printing, 2016

LIBRARY OF CONGRESS CATALOGING-IN-PUBLICATION DATA
Venters, Louis, author.
No Jim Crow church : the origins of South Carolina's Bahá'í community / Louis Venters.
pages cm
Includes bibliographical references and index.
ISBN 978-0-8130-6107-8 (cloth)
ISBN 978-0-8130-5407-0 (pbk.)
1. Bahai Faith—South Carolina—History—20th century. 2. Bahais—South Carolina.
3. South Carolina—History. I. Title.
BP352.S6V46 2015
297.9'309757—dc23   2015006614

The University Press of Florida is the scholarly publishing agency for the State University System of Florida, comprising Florida A&M University, Florida Atlantic University, Florida Gulf Coast University, Florida International University, Florida State University, New College of Florida, University of Central Florida, University of Florida, University of North Florida, University of South Florida, and University of West Florida.

UNIVERSITY PRESS OF FLORIDA
15 Northwest 15th Street
Gainesville, FL 32611-2079
http://www.upf.com

For Isaiah and Micah

Some movements appear, manifest a brief period of activity, then discontinue. Others show forth a greater measure of growth and strength, but before attaining mature development, weaken, disintegrate and are lost in oblivion. . . .

There is still another kind of movement or cause which from a very small, inconspicuous beginning goes forward with sure and steady progress, gradually broadening and widening until it has assumed universal dimensions. The Bahá'í Movement is of this nature.

'Abdu'l-Bahá in Washington, D.C., April 22, 1912

Contents

List of Figures x
Preface xi
Acknowledgments xix

Introduction 1

1. First Contacts, 1898–1916 16

2. The Divine Plan, the Great War, and Progressive-Era Racial Politics, 1914–1921 55

3. Building a Bahá'í Community in Augusta and North Augusta, 1911–1939 91

4. The Great Depression, the Second World War, and the First Seven Year Plan, 1935–1945 129

5. Postwar Opportunities, Cold War Challenges, and the Second Seven Year Plan, 1944–1953 172

6. The Ten Year Plan and the Fall of Jim Crow, 1950–1965 199

Coda: Toward a Bahá'í Mass Movement, 1963–1968 243

Notes 251
Bibliography 287
Index 303

Figures

1.1. Louis George Gregory, ca. 1896 19
1.2. Joseph and Pauline Hannen, ca. 1895 25
1.3. Parker Building, South Carolina State Hospital for the Insane, ca. 1905 39
2.1. Rev. I. E. Lowery, ca. 1911 84
3.1. Margaret Klebs at Green Acre Baháʼí School, date unknown 94
3.2. Hampton Terrace Hotel, North Augusta, ca. 1915 102
4.1. Greenville Baháʼís and friends, 1944 164
4.2. All-America Convention, Chicago, May 1944 170
5.1. Louis Gregory with Columbia Baháʼís and friends, ca. 1940s 186
6.1. First Local Spiritual Assembly of Florence, 1961 222
6.2. Southeastern Baháʼí Summer School, St. Helena Island, 1961 225
6.3. Greenville Baháʼís and friends, 1964 237

Preface

I started to hear the stories as a young teenager, shortly after I first encountered the Bahá'í Faith. During a series of growth campaigns from the late 1960s to the mid-1980s, thousands of my fellow South Carolinians, from all parts of the state and from all walks of life, had become Bahá'ís. Diverse teams of young Bahá'ís had fanned out across cities and hamlets, talking with people on street corners and front porches, singing in folk and gospel styles, distributing literature, and conducting evening mass meetings in tents and rented halls. Their message was as simple as it was radical, and it was the same one that had attracted me: in the Orient in the middle of the nineteenth century, Christ had returned. His new name, as prophesied in the Bible, was Bahá'u'lláh, the "Glory of God," and he had come with a new divine revelation that would bring the long-awaited millennium of universal justice and peace. They had found many ready listeners, with African Americans in rural areas constituting the largest number of new believers. Some people, old and young, had dreamed dreams telling them that the Bahá'ís would come with a new message from God. In this modern-day Pentecost, the South Carolina Bahá'í community had grown from some two hundred members in a handful of cities and towns to some twenty thousand in hundreds of localities almost overnight. It was the first such rapid expansion of the Bahá'í Faith in an industrialized country, a major development for a young world religion most of whose growth outside its native Iran had been slow and measured. Although it still represented only a small portion of the population, the community had become South Carolina's largest religious minority. Moreover, its emergence had permanently changed the face of the Bahá'í Faith in the United States. In ways that most Bahá'ís around the country could hardly have predicted a few years earlier, the growth in South Carolina catapulted a small, poor, southern state into the front ranks of the national Bahá'í movement, confronting a faith community that already prided itself on its diversity with new and often subtle challenges in the "post–civil rights" era. I was fascinated. As I met more Bahá'ís, particularly at the Louis Gregory Institute, a training center near the Lowcountry town of Hemingway, my father's family home, I asked everyone I could about the heady days of the 1970s. Here was a story, I thought, that needed to be told. Little did I know that I was not only exploring the history of my native state and of my newfound religion but also setting the course of my professional career.[1]

As I began formal research, the picture that quickly emerged was of a South Carolina Bahá'í movement that was much older, and even more interesting, than I had imagined. The community's origins lay not in the 1960s and 1970s, or even in the 1950s, as some of the older Bahá'ís told me, but far earlier, at the turn of the twentieth century. South Carolina expatriates had first encountered the religion in urban areas of the Northeast, Midwest, and Upper South in the late 1890s, shortly after its arrival in the United States from the Middle East, and Bahá'í teachers had first come to South Carolina at least as early as 1910. It soon became clear that the warm interracial fellowship I saw in every Bahá'í gathering during the 1990s had not emerged suddenly, as a natural result of the civil rights movement. Rather, the foundations had been laid during the long decades of Jim Crow, as tiny groups of Bahá'ís in South Carolina had struggled, often at their own peril, to build an interracial faith community within a racially segregated and religiously orthodox society. I realized I needed to start at the beginning, not with the thousands who became Bahá'ís in South Carolina during the 1970s but with the initial two hundred who were their spiritual forbears.

This book, then, represents my effort to reconstruct the earliest development of the Bahá'í Faith in South Carolina and, in so doing, to uncover the hidden history of what may well be the oldest genuinely interracial religious body in the state. It covers what may be considered the movement's critical formative period, from the earliest known contacts in 1898 until 1968, when a statewide community of some two hundred stood on the precipice of large-scale expansion. Not coincidentally, this formative period coincides almost exactly with the lifespan of South Carolina's Jim Crow regime. Indeed, the first documented encounter of an expatriate South Carolinian with the faith took place in 1898, a critical year in the violent enforcement of the disfranchisement provisions of the state's Jim Crow constitution, passed just three years earlier. And of the large-scale growth that took shape after 1968, the most dramatic campaign took place during 1970 and 1971, just as mandatory desegregation ended South Carolina's dual school system, the last and largest vestige of the Jim Crow order. During this period, by far the most challenging issue confronting South Carolina's nascent Bahá'í community, shaping indelibly the ways in which it grew and developed, was a legal and social system that enshrined racial prejudice and oppression—attitudes and structures that ran directly counter to the faith's cardinal principle of the oneness of humanity. I argue that from its arrival in South Carolina early in the Jim Crow era, the Bahá'í Faith represented a significant, sustained, spiritually based, and deceptively subtle challenge to the ideology and structures of white male supremacy and to the Protestant orthodoxy with which they were inextricably linked.

Although numerically insignificant and apparently powerless during the period under review, South Carolina's Bahá'í community accomplished a remarkable feat that was without real parallel: in the midst of a political and religious culture that denied the humanity of people of African descent in virtually every department of life, they created an interracial religious fellowship in which blacks and whites participated fully, unitedly, and as complete equals, from the local level up. The very existence of such a community, forged in the interstices of Jim Crow South Carolina, undermined both the practical mechanisms and the spiritual underpinnings of white supremacy. For it must be said that while other religious bodies in South Carolina had histories of *biracialism* (that is, comprising both black and white members but maintaining various forms of segregation and discrimination at the level of the congregation, the denomination, or both) going back in some cases to the colonial period, among the state's Protestant churches there was precious little experience of *interracialism* (that is, maintaining a commitment to racial equality, both ideologically and structurally) prior to the civil rights movement. South Carolina's Roman Catholic and Jewish communities, both of them old and well assimilated to the substantial Protestant majority, largely followed suit.[2]

While the laws and practices of their society often forced them to conduct their community activities at night, in secret, or otherwise far removed from the gaze of the white public, the Bahá'ís in South Carolina boldly and consistently proclaimed their faith's teachings to politicians and leaders of thought, in schools and churches, through the mass media, and in lectures and other meetings in public and private establishments. Even as they focused on building their own model of interracial fellowship (eventually securing legal protection from the state for their activities), they sought to encourage or collaborate with other individuals and organizations, both religious and secular, who were working for civil rights and interracial reconciliation. And if one gauge of the effectiveness of a radical organization is the opposition it engenders, then South Carolina's Bahá'ís played a much larger role than their numbers alone would suggest, for they were frequent targets of intimidation (and, occasionally, of violence) by neighbors, the Ku Klux Klan, law enforcement agencies, government officials, and conservative Christian clergymen. Through it all, they deliberately sought converts from diverse backgrounds, forging bonds of shared religious identity across traditional social boundaries. By the late 1960s, as a combination of federal legislation, judicial rulings, and ad hoc arrangements at the state and local levels dismantled the Jim Crow regime, South Carolina's Bahá'í community, small as it was, represented a cross-section of the state's population. During the difficult decades of segregation and disfranchisement, they had accumulated invaluable experience in creating an alternative arena of interracial spiritual democracy.

In the context of the long and sordid history of racial prejudice and oppression in the United States, virtually any organization, however small or short-lived, that made sincere efforts at interracial cooperation and fellowship prior to the civil rights revolution is probably worthy of study. But the story of the Bahá'ís in Jim Crow South Carolina deserves attention as well for their movement's durability: the structures and sensibilities of interracial community that they worked to build in such an inhospitable environment were precisely the foundation for their movement's remarkable expansion after Jim Crow's demise. After 1968, with the major legal barriers to interracial association removed, forces inside and outside the religion combined to produce unprecedented growth, centered in South Carolina, that redefined the Bahá'í Faith in the United States. By 1973, perhaps as many as twenty thousand South Carolinians, mostly rural African Americans, had identified themselves as Bahá'ís, constituting up to one-third of the faith's adherents in the United States.[3]

Ideally, this book might have included one or more chapters on the larger-scale growth of the South Carolina Bahá'í community during the 1970s and 1980s. However, there are two reasons why I have chosen to end the narrative in 1968. From a conceptual point of view, 1968 is something of a turning point, both inside and outside of the Bahá'í Faith. In the Bahá'ís' own perceptions of time, 1967–1968 was a significant centennial year that the faith's supreme body said would mark the beginning of a new period of world history, one characterized both by increasing signs of chaos in the society at large and by a greater responsiveness of the world's peoples to the faith's teachings. The prediction of growth was certainly borne out in

South Carolina in the twenty years or so after 1968. Moreover, historians of the twentieth century widely describe 1968 as a watershed year of rather unprecedented violence and turmoil in the United States (and around the world), heralding the long-term political, economic, and social changes of the 1970s and beyond.

The other, more practical reason that this study ends when it does is quite simply the volume of Baháʼí source material for the post-1968 period in South Carolina. The processed archival material alone is staggering, and I suspect there is a great deal more that remains as yet uncollected and unprocessed, inside and outside the state. The number of living participants in this period remains quite high, requiring an extensive effort to collect oral histories from people both nearby in South Carolina and now scattered across the globe. Because the South Carolina Baháʼís experimented with a variety of techniques in their expansion and consolidation programs, consideration of the post-1968 period will also require the collection and analysis of songs, films, and other forms of media, a formidable undertaking by itself. All things considered, then, it seems to me that the larger-scale growth of the Baháʼí Faith in South Carolina in the 1970s and subsequent decades can best be treated in a future volume of its own.

For now, then, just a few words about those developments. In 1969, the national Baháʼí administration began to position the community to take advantage of new opportunities for the spread of the faith that seemed to be opening up in the South. Encouraged by the religion's highest global leaders, an emboldened cadre of mostly young Baháʼís developed new approaches to growth that borrowed elements of the language, music, and organizing strategies of the civil rights movement and the emerging youth culture. During the winter of 1970–1971, a three-month regional campaign yielded results the likes of which Baháʼís in the United States had never witnessed, with South Carolina leading the way.[4]

Based in Dillon in the northeast corner of the state, teams of resident Baháʼís and young visitors from across the country fanned out across South Carolina's cities and towns every morning. They shared the message of the faith wherever they found listeners; according to one colorful report, they talked with people "in laundromats, restaurants, night-clubs, on the streets, in yards, in the rain, in the mud, in the snow." With those who were interested they shared prayers from the Baháʼí scriptures or left copies of the "*Ebony* reprint," a large, full-color booklet based on an article on the faith from the popular African American magazine. Often they enrolled new believers on the spot:

One lady looked out her window and saw two Baháʼís singing. She opened the door and yelled to them that if it was their music she heard she wanted them to come and sing for her. She insisted that they come inside her house and "set awhile." Next moment all her children were becoming Baháʼís. A few days later some more of us visited her again and she gave us all the warmest welcome. We talked awhile and then spent most of the time with her in prayer—each child, with the exception of one who was just too shy, read from the prayer book.

In evening mass meetings at rented halls, the Baháʼí teachers made more in-depth presentations, in word and song, to new Baháʼís and their friends and family members, often with active participation from the audience. According to a report of one meeting:

> During the night almost all of the 80 people there became Baháʼís and those who'd already declared [their belief] experienced their first deepening class. . . . Some of the audience joined us up front. Some of them sang for us, and we parted only after all forming a big unity circle and sharing prayers for unity and thanksgiving.[5]

Even before the close of the three-month campaign, the faith's highest council announced to the worldwide Baháʼí community the enrollment of eight thousand new believers in South Carolina. Almost overnight, the Baháʼí Faith in South Carolina had gone from a tiny community in a handful of localities to a mass movement with members in every county. In 1970, there were 8 of the faith's local governing councils in South Carolina; the following year, there were 108, more than any other state in the country. By 1973, perhaps as many as twenty thousand people—most of them African Americans in rural areas but also hundreds of whites and Native Americans—had become Baháʼís in South Carolina.[6]

While Baháʼís across the United States initially greeted the rapid expansion with enthusiasm, the task of consolidating the gains, in dozens of towns and hamlets across South Carolina, proved more challenging than most supporters of the campaign had imagined. For example, the relative remoteness of many of the new believers from the handful of established local communities, and the acute poverty and limited literacy that many of them faced, made for serious logistical obstacles as a core group of teachers sought to nurture new Baháʼí communities in hundreds of localities at once. At the national level, the swelling membership in South Carolina and other states tested the ability of the Baháʼí administrative system to maintain a unified vision and to marshal the necessary resources, human and financial, to support continued growth. The daunting challenges associated with rapid growth launched the entire national movement—in concert with the faith's continental and global institutions and with other national communities facing similar circumstances—on a period of experimentation, consolidation, disappointment, and learning that lasted until nearly the turn of the twenty-first century.[7]

By then, although numerical growth had slowed considerably, the South Carolina Bahá'í community remained among the largest and strongest in the country, with local organizations in some forty localities and adherents in more than a hundred more. The Bahá'í Faith was increasingly recognized in academia and the media as the largest non-Christian religious body in South Carolina, and it was relatively well known around the state for its commitment to promoting interracial harmony, interfaith dialogue, and the moral education of children and youth, as well as for the adherence of several prominent individuals. The Louis G. Gregory Bahá'í Institute in rural Georgetown County, founded in 1972 and named for the native son who first brought the faith to the state, was a focal point of Bahá'í education and identity in the state and region. A community-service radio station, inaugurated in 1985, broadcast to a large area of northeastern South Carolina and neighboring North Carolina from the institute's campus, bringing awareness of the faith and its teachings to a substantial portion of the population. In 2003 in the heart of downtown Charleston, with the dedication of Louis Gregory's boyhood home as a museum—in a virtual city of museums, the first dedicated to the life of a single individual—the statewide movement successfully preserved and opened to the public a historic site associated with its own rise.[8]

The community for which small groups of black and white South Carolinians had laid the foundation during the Jim Crow era had grown to play an outsized role in the cultural and structural evolution of a new world religion. But the Bahá'ís' long-term and fundamentally radical goal—to engage ever-larger numbers of fellow South Carolinians from all walks of life in the work of establishing a just, peaceful, spiritual world order—had barely begun. In the mid-1990s, based on some thirty years' worth of trial and error in South Carolina and in a number of countries around the world, the faith's global institutions launched what they said would be a concerted, decades-long effort to develop the human resources and institutional capacity needed to revive and sustain the large-scale growth of the community and accelerate the process of social transformation. The central element of the strategy was a new grassroots system of distance education. With an initial focus on training groups of youth to conduct simple devotional meetings, home study visits, and children's classes in their own neighborhoods and villages, the aims of the system were to lay the foundations of the Bahá'í community more broadly and solidly than before and to equip rising generations to foster the profound cultural, political, and economic changes called for in the faith's scriptures. And in the state where that religious vision had, over the course of a century, begun to affect the lives of a larger portion of the population than it had anywhere else in the country, the South Carolina Bahá'í community seemed well positioned to revive and sustain the growth that it had helped to pioneer a generation before.[9]

Acknowledgments

Far from being the product of one mind alone, this book represents the collaborative efforts of a diverse community of teachers, students, and practitioners. The seeds for this project were sown more than twenty years ago, and during that time I have become deeply and pleasantly indebted—spiritually, intellectually, and materially—to more people than I could possibly recount. In that sense, I think of this book as ours, not mine. Nevertheless, I take responsibility for all errors and shortcomings herein.

Special thanks to my colleagues in the Department of History of the University of South Carolina, a bright constellation of scholars with whom it was my great pleasure to interact and exchange ideas. Eric Bargeron, Nancy Brown, Becky Miller Davis, Bobby Donaldson, Kathryn Edwards, Adam Ewing, Veronica Gerald, Larry Glickman, Wanda Hendricks, Wesley Joyner, Thomas Lekan, Valinda Littlefield, Barry Malone, Preston McKever-Floyd, Stephanie Mitchem, Connie Schultz, Cleveland Sellers, Kathryn Silva, Patricia Sullivan, and Bob Weyeneth, among others, helped to broaden my mind, sharpen my thinking, and make me a better reader and writer. Several of them read all or part of this work, improving it beyond measure with their insightful comments and probing questions. Interactions, however brief, with the late John Hope Franklin, Henry Louis Gates, Leon Litwack, Waldo Martin, and the late Judge Matthew Perry, all guests of the department, were immensely encouraging. Walter Conser at the University of North Carolina, Wilmington, read an earlier version of this work and shed light on some important aspects of national and regional religious culture.

A host of librarians and archivists, the intrepid heroes of the historical profession, did much to make this work possible. In addition to all those whose institutions are mentioned in the notes and photo credits, my special thanks to Roger Dahl and Lewis Walker at the National Baháʼí Archives of the United States; Beth Bilderback and Robin Copp at the South Caroliniana Library, University of South Carolina; Georgette Mayo and Deborah Wright at the Avery Research Center for African American History and Culture, College of Charleston; and during the final stages of the project, the circulation, interlibrary loan, and acquisitions staff of Rogers Library, Francis Marion University. Although the credit lines do not reflect it, Aisha Johnson, special collections librarian at the Franklin Library, Fisk University; Tewodros Abebe, senior archivist at the Moorland-Spingarn Research Center, Howard University; and Helia Ighani at the Washington, D.C., Baháʼí Archives responded readily to my requests for help in identifying the provenance of one photograph. Janie Williams in the Office of Public and Community Affairs at Francis Marion University provided generous assistance in reproducing another.

Also at Francis Marion University, President Fred Carter and Provost Richard Chapman; my colleagues in the Department of History (especially three successive chairs, Larry Nelson, John Britton, and Christopher Kennedy); and Bob Barrett, former executive director of the Francis Marion Trail Commission, were extraordinarily patient, providing a congenial environment in which to complete this project. A generous summer stipend and several rounds of travel assistance from the Professional Development Committee greatly advanced my research and scholarly engagement, and I found both the Humanities and Social Sciences Symposium and the Phi Alpha Theta History Lecture Series to be excellent spaces for thoughtful cross-disciplinary exchange on campus. Special thanks to all my current and former students, some of whose families are part of the story told in these pages. Their curiosity and courage in confronting the history of South Carolina and the nation, their spirit of encouragement and striving, and their disarming good humor have kept me going through the final stages of this project.

My sincere gratitude to Sian Hunter, Marthe Walters, and the rest of the staff at the University Press of Florida; two anonymous reviewers; and my copy editor, Jesse Arost. Their professionalism and warmth at every step of the way reflected the best of the academic tradition and made preparing this work for publication a surprisingly pleasant process.

Several mentors, inside and outside of the academy, either helped mold my thinking or provided guidance and encouragement at critical moments (or both): Farzam and Sona Arbab, Kenneth Bowers, William Collins, Tod Ewing, Betty Fisher, Hoda Mahmoudi, Gayle Morrison, Karen Pritchard,

Behrooz Sabet, Nader Saeidi, Martha Schweitz, Moshe Sharon, Nancy Songer, Robert Stockman, Michael Penn, and Richard and June Manning Thomas. My gratitude to the members of the Executive Committee of the Association for Bahá'í Studies North America for their moral and material support. There are simply no words for Penny Walker, who made all the difference in the world during my brief service to the Auxiliary Board for Protection. My thanks as well to Gene Andrews, who understood my need to step down from that position in order to complete this project, and to Windi Burgess and Becky Dibble Louis, who took up my slack without missing a beat.

I am particularly grateful to the many Bahá'ís and other friends, in South Carolina and elsewhere, who shared so generously of their time and treasures during the course of this project. I hope that all those who have been associated in some way with the Bahá'í Faith in South Carolina will find here a true and honest reflection of that which is so close to their hearts. Special thanks to several elders who taught me much about the principles and practices of the Bahá'í community—among them Charles Abercrombie, Juanita Battle, Mary Beckmon, Walter Davis, Rafael Fiamo, David Gordon, Jannie Green, Heloise Herbert, Debbie Jackson, Josephine McFadden, Richard Pratt, Ruth Pringle, Ursula Richardson, Katya Sousa, Charles Thomas, Isaac Thompson, Trudy White, Goli Collestan Young, and Jordan Young—but who passed away before they saw the publication of this book.

Finally, my deepest gratitude goes to my biological/marital/adoptive/fictive/white/black/brown/Northern/Southern/Midwestern/Western/West African/West Indian/East Indian/South American/Central American/Central European/Iranian/urban/rural/Jewish/Eastern Orthodox/Roman Catholic/Protestant/Muslim/former Communist/Bahá'í family, which could not exist in its variegated fullness but for the profound social changes described in this book. Thanks and praise to my parents, Ed and Martha Venters; my surrogate parents, Phillip and Dorcus Abercrombie; my sister, Emily Venters Wannemacher; my wife's parents, Barry and Marilyn Smith; her surrogate parents, Taiwo and Betsy Ayankoya; my sister-in-law, Amy Smith, her husband, Vesal Dini, and all of the Dini family; my paternal and maternal aunts and uncles, Woody and Becky Palmore, Joe and Nancy Zurawski, and George Nicholson; and some very special friends, Marcy Bernbaum, the late Susie Clay, Ashwin Deshmukh, and Julie Porch, for the abundant material and spiritual sustenance they have provided. Among the additional siblings I have been fortunate to acquire over the years, Mihael

Arežina, Nawo Fiamo, Jessica Gaines, Jay Green, Damien-Adia Marassa, Alison Milston, Oak Ritchie, Greg Schweitz, Carlos Serrano, Ravi Starr, Tim Wood, Aaron Yates, Bahiyyih Young, and Rebecca Young were each there at just the right time, over and over again. Aaron's parents, Dick and Melodie Yates, were our port in an especially difficult storm. *Merci beaucoup*, *hvala liepo*, and *muchas gracias* to loved ones too many to name in Togo and Côte d'Ivoire, Bosnia, and Honduras and Nicaragua, respectively, for formative experiences that nourished my heart and profoundly shaped my priorities in life. Of our many loved ones in the Florence and Hemingway areas, Cathy Birchmore, the late Dallas Charles II, Jimmy Chinnes, CJ Cohen, Ray and Beverly Collins, Liz Ellis, Mark and Gabrielle Griggs and our godson Paul Adib Griggs, Shahin Hemat, Ernest and Nellie Hilton, Maggie Laursen, the late Rebecca Powell Lewis, Vincent and Jennie Pezé, Annette Reynolds, and Chuck and Nancy Thomas have been particular wellsprings of support and fellowship. And *muito obrigado* to Diego Silveira, Steve Kotwa, the students of Diego Silveira Capoeira Group, and Diego's family and friends in Niterói and Rio de Janeiro for doing so much over the last few years to help keep my body strong, my head clear, and my heart happy.

My paternal grandmother, Rebecca Glymph Venters, who first set my South Carolina kinfolks on their encounter with the Bahá'í Faith before I was born, did not quite live to see the end of this project, but her unfailing love was a solid rock and her utterly unreasoning confidence in my abilities a welcome balm during some of its most difficult phases. My sons, *mes anges*, *mes chéris*, Isaiah Ali Venters and Micah Amin Venters, each came at the perfect time, bringing indescribable joy to their papa during the final stages of writing and editing. It turns out that it is they, two of the choicest fruits of the community depicted in these pages, for whom I was laboring all along. Above all, I thank my wife, Melissa Smith-Venters, a worthy heir of the many extraordinary women in this story. That she was able to provide so much practical, intellectual, and spiritual support while occupying a succession of demanding positions at the regional, national, and continental levels over the past decade—and, most recently, the intensely local and most demanding position of mothering two energetic children—is nothing short of miraculous. Her masterful attention to both detail and process, her uncommon wisdom and patience, her unceasing encouragement, and the exceptional example of her life of service have made this work hers in ways that only she and I can know.

Introduction

I

In 1903, as a virulent new system of white supremacy grew and consolidated itself across the United States, the Harvard-trained African American scholar W.E.B. Du Bois sounded an alarm-bell of warning. In *The Souls of Black Folk*, he predicted that the essential problem of the twentieth century would be "the problem of the color-line,—the relation of the darker to the lighter races of men in Asia and Africa, in America and the islands of the sea." Claiming a power of insight not unlike that of the Hebrew prophets of old, he identified racial prejudice and oppression as a fundamentally spiritual problem and arraigned an ostensibly Christian America for its hypocrisy in denying people of African descent their full humanity.[1]

At the moment Du Bois wrote, the seeds were just being sown for the American branch of a new religious community that, during the life of the Jim Crow regime and afterward, within the United States and around the world, would distinguish itself perhaps more than any other for successfully and systematically addressing "the problem of the color-line." The Baháʼí Faith, the innovative religious movement that emerged amid the messianic expectations of mid-nineteenth-century Iran, was first brought to the United States in the 1890s by young converts of Syrian Christian heritage. During its first decade on American shores, the faith attracted new adherents from diverse ethnic, religious, political, and class backgrounds, from Boston to San Francisco and from Kenosha, Wisconsin, to Fairhope, Alabama. Within a few short years, Du Bois himself would laud the young movement's contribution to the cause of racial reconciliation and world peace in the pages of the *Crisis*, the magazine of the new National Association for the Advancement of Colored People (NAACP).[2]

At the heart of this distinctive emerging community was the principle of the oneness of humanity, the central theme of the faith's scriptures and the foundation of its organized life. Bahá'u'lláh ("the Glory of God," 1817–1892), the religion's founder, and the Báb ("the Gate," 1819–1850), his prophetic herald, claimed to represent the fulfillment of the prophecies of all the great faiths of the past, a fresh outpouring of the divine will for the dawning age of human maturity. Their successive revelations, they said, had infused the collective body of humanity with a new life, and the application of their teachings would, over the course of the next several hundred years, weld all the peoples of the world into an organic, interdependent global commonwealth, the culmination of human evolution on this planet. This startlingly original vision of radical spiritual and social change—bearing little resemblance to any of the other political or religious ideologies of the day, in the Islamic world or elsewhere—was perhaps best summarized in Bahá'u'lláh's famous formulation: "The earth is but one country, and mankind its citizens."[3]

From the outset, Bahá'ís took the oneness of humanity not simply as a pious hope but as the bedrock of a new identity and as a mandate for individual and collective action. Adopting the "world-embracing" vision to which their faith called them, they set out to carry its message beyond the borders of Iran and enroll an ever-widening diversity of people as believers. By the time of Bahá'u'lláh's passing in 1892, the religion had spread to Egypt and Sudan in the west and Burma and China in the east, and after its establishment in the United States, American Bahá'ís quickly took the lead in its establishment throughout their own continent, Europe, sub-Saharan Africa, Australia, and the Pacific. During the course of the twentieth century, men and women from virtually every conceivable social, economic, political, and religious background helped to build the faith's highly democratic and egalitarian system of governance, conceiving of themselves as fellow citizens in a new worldwide religious polity and builders of a new global civilization.[4]

By the evening of W.E.B. Du Bois's life, the Bahá'í Faith had made good on its claim to be a world religion (a fact he likely would have verified for himself as an observer at an international Bahá'í conference in New Delhi in 1953 had the U.S. government not denied him a passport for alleged Communist activities). Not only had the faith spread to virtually every corner of the globe in little more than a century, but a few months before Du Bois's death in the summer of 1963 its far-flung adherents had, in what was likely the first worldwide democratic election, brought into being the crowing unit of their administrative system, the nine-member council that Bahá'u'lláh had promised would carry humanity into its golden age. As if to underscore the progress the American branch of the faith had come toward realizing within its own ranks Du Bois's long-held dream of a nation purged of racial prejudice was the fact that of the four Americans first elected to that body (in a process that was completely free of nominations, campaigning, or backroom dealing), one was a black southerner.[5]

II

This book is the first attempt by a professional historian to reconstruct and analyze the formative period of the Bahá'í Faith in South Carolina, a state where it eventually gained among its most important followings in the Western world, and the only one in the United States where it is today, by at least one reliable count, the largest religious minority. It is the story of a small, unusually diverse group of people—white and black; women and men; native-born and immigrant; southerners and northerners; young, middle-aged, and elderly; housewives, domestic workers, blue-collar and white-collar workers, professionals, wealthy scions of the antebellum plantation elite—who, inspired by a radical religious vision, began to transcend the pervasive provincialism, racialism, and obscurantism of the society around them and imagine themselves as part of a new spiritual polity that embraced the whole of humanity. It is the story of the origins and early development of the first genuinely interracial religious community in a state known more for white male supremacy and Protestant orthodoxy than for egalitarianism or religious innovation. As a case study in the early development of a spiritual community that was fundamentally open, outward-looking, and collaborative, it is the story of how the South Carolina Bahá'í movement was shaped by contemporaneous social and political currents and attempted to reshape them in turn, especially regarding race relations and an emerging civil rights movement. And as a contribution to the cultural, intellectual, and organizational history of an emerging young religion, it is the story of how the South Carolina Bahá'í movement shaped developments at the regional, national, and international levels and vice versa. It situates the Bahá'í Faith as an integral part of the history of South Carolina and the United States in the twentieth century, particularly in the critical arenas of religion, race, and social transformation.

One would think that the boldness and intellectual innovation of Bahá'u'lláh's program alone would be enough to commend the American Bahá'í movement to the attention of contemporary historians, who have tended to be attracted to the radical (even if relatively obscure) in the nation's past. On the contrary, so far the Bahá'í Faith has remained nearly invisible to historians of religion and race in the United States. Several factors seem to explain this. First, with few exceptions, academic presses and journals have been most receptive to works treating the Bahá'í Faith as a subset of Islamic or Middle Eastern Studies. Scholars who have taken the faith on its own terms, assuming it to be a social and religious phenomenon with its own conceptual categories, have often resorted to publishing by official or independent Bahá'í presses and journals, where their work has received smaller circulation and remained on the periphery of academic discourse. Unfortunately, the persistence of the Middle Eastern Studies view of the Bahá'í Faith has, perhaps inadvertently, overlooked essential aspects of the phenomenon. For one thing, it minimizes the creative genius of its founders. While the Báb and Bahá'u'lláh were born and reared as Muslims and a conceptual dialogue with Islam runs throughout their writings, they consistently claimed to have brought a new and independent world religion quite apart from any of the traditional religions. It also marginalizes the lived experiences and worldviews of most of the faith's adherents. By the last quarter of the twentieth century, nearly 90 percent of the world's Bahá'ís lived in the "Third World," with the highest concentrations in South Asia, sub-Saharan Africa, and Latin America, while those in the Islamic heartland constituted less than 7 percent of the total, and few if any of them saw their faith in culturally or historically particular terms. As such, whatever usefulness it may hold for explaining the origins of the Bahá'í Faith in Iran, the Middle Eastern Studies frame is largely irrelevant in considering its historical development in the United States or most anywhere else in the world.[6]

A second possible reason for the Bahá'í Faith's relative invisibility is that it is extraordinarily difficult to label. In its origins not a sect of Christianity or of any other world religion, not a faith primarily of immigrants to the United States, and not a typical "new religious movement" that avoids contemporary social concerns, it defies the most common scholarly categories of American religious bodies. Moreover, the Bahá'í Faith has largely eschewed the factors that tend to bring otherwise obscure religious movements to the attention of scholars and the media, such as bizarre theology, charismatic leaders, financial controversy, withdrawal from society, and unusual sexual or other personal practices, to name a few. Nor does it fit neatly with other organizations, religious or secular, that have been concerned with issues of racial justice. The social and theological radicalism of the Bahá'í program is tempered by various scriptural injunctions (against aggressive proselytizing, involvement in political controversy, disloyalty to the state, membership in parties, and civil disobedience, for example) that sometimes limited the ways Baháʼís in the early twentieth century could engage with mainstream civil rights groups and contributed to a somewhat reserved public image, then and now. The Baháʼís' small numbers during most of the century, their refusal to engage in traditional forms of protest, their egalitarianism and lack of any form of clergy, even their consistent preference for building human relationships over physical structures—all may have helped to disguise the religion's significance to many observers, including most historians.[7]

This book follows others that have attempted to situate the Baháʼí Faith within American social and religious history. Most notably, Gayle Morrison's pioneering biography of Louis Gregory, the son of South Carolina freedpeople who became one of the foremost national and international Baháʼí leaders in the first half of the twentieth century, and Robert Stockman's several works examining the development of the American Baháʼí movement from 1892 to 1921 plowed much of the ground from which this study grows. Specifically, it represents an effort to relate the Baháʼí Faith to the rich historiography of race, religion, and social change in the post–Civil War South. It is a beneficiary of, and contributes to, a growing literature on the roles of interracial movements, religious motivations and identities, and the appeal of different visions of America's racial future in the profound social transformations of the twentieth century. It follows important recent works that explore the promises and limitations of moments of interracial cooperation from Reconstruction to the civil rights movement, manifesting themselves in, for example, labor and women's organizations, the Democratic Party, and the Popular Front. By highlighting an organization that sought to foster interracialism as a matter of spiritual principle (rather than primarily of economic or political reasoning), this book joins other recent works that argue that the religious worldviews of black and white southerners, and the various religious organizations through which many of them channeled their energies, are of central importance to understanding the struggle for (and, for that matter, against) racial justice.[8]

This book differs from most others at the intersection of religion and race in the Jim Crow South in that the community on which it focuses lay far outside the region's Protestant mainstream. While few scholars have questioned the uniquely pervasive role of evangelical Protestantism in the region's post–Civil War cultural and political life, the literature suggests that religious diversity and dissent have been constant, widespread phenomena. Beyond the obvious cleavages within Protestantism over race, class, and theology and the presence of sizeable Roman Catholic and Jewish minorities in many areas, a number of factors complicate the long-held notion of a regional "Baptist-Methodist hegemony." The struggles of black and white women for greater power in church governance; the growth of new denominations and nondenominational churches that experimented with degrees of interracialism; the modernist-fundamentalist cleavages within the mainline denominations; the criticism by academics, ministers, and laypeople of churches' relative quiescence in areas of race relations and social justice; and the emergence of nondenominational, interdenominational, and essentially secular agencies for social service and reform, to name some of the more salient—all indicate a broad spectrum of religious dissent, both from outside the traditional Protestant denominations and, perhaps more significantly, from those who remained within them.[9]

The Bahá'í Faith represents perhaps the most radical wing of this spectrum of dissent. The Bahá'ís were hardly the only religious transgressors in the early-twentieth century South, but they were certainly among the most consistently interracial in character, and they were arguably the farthest from the Protestant mainstream. Decades before the proliferation of nondenominational churches across South Carolina and the appearance of Buddhist, Hindu, and Islamic houses of worship in the state's urban areas, small groups of Bahá'ís quietly but insistently pushed the bounds of religious respectability. The Pentecostal movement, which emerged as a conscious critique of mainstream Protestantism roughly contemporaneously with the Bahá'í Faith in the United States, provides a useful comparison. Originating with a racially diverse, millennialist revival in Los Angeles in 1906, early Pentecostals stood apart from the rest of society and from the mainstream churches, which they held had strayed from biblical Christianity, with a mission to prepare the way for Christ's imminent return. As the movement spread in the South, however, it bowed to regional racial mores, splintering into a welter of separate black and white congregations and denominational structures, some of which maintained occasional interracial contacts. Incomplete as it was, the interracialism of the Pentecostal movement largely surpassed that of any other branch of southern Protestantism in the first half of the century, and it was one of a number of factors that placed the movement outside the religious mainstream—in the minds of both its own members and their fellow southerners. In contrast to Pentecostalism, as the Bahá'í Faith spread in South Carolina and other southern states, it became more, not less, explicitly and completely interracial in character. Combined with their theological radicalism (unlike Pentecostals, Bahá'ís believe that Christ has *already* returned, in the appearance of the Báb and Bahá'u'lláh), the interracial radicalism of the Baháʼís in South Carolina placed them about as far away from the religious orthodoxy of their state and region as possible.[10]

Nor were these the only ways Baháʼís in the Jim Crow South set themselves apart. Indeed, this book examines their simultaneous transgression of regional racial, gender, class, and religious orthodoxies and the difficulties that often arose from such a position. It has become almost axiomatic in the U.S. historical profession that race, class, and gender, far from being essential or discrete categories, are and have been socially constructed, mutually constitutive of each other, and shifting. Of particular relevance to this study, all of these categories have been closely bound up with Americans' understandings and practices of religion. The Baháʼís in South Carolina sought to build a religious community that was interracial but also one that crossed class boundaries and made women equal partners with men. The progressive economic teachings of the Baháʼí Faith, emphasizing rural development, the elimination of extremes of wealth and poverty, and international economic coordination, were certainly threatening in theory to South Carolina's political and economic elite. Indeed, to the extent that the state and federal governments implemented programs along those lines, from the Progressive era through the 1960s, they often proved destabilizing to the Jim Crow economic order. However, other than voluntary contributions to the Baháʼí funds, during the early twentieth century there was little incentive or opportunity for numerically small local Baháʼí communities in the United States to implement any of the faith's economic prescriptions. However, there were more subtle ways in which they undermined the system. In an era of rapid urbanization and pervasive spatial segregation, in religious bodies as much as in other social institutions and by social class as well as by race, the Baháʼís deliberately sought to bring their message to diverse segments of the population. Because all the believers in a city or town constituted a single local organization (rather than a number of autonomous congregations), participation in Baháʼí community life often involved people who differed markedly from each other in wealth, occupational status, and educational attainment moving back and forth across otherwise segregated neighborhoods, enjoying intimate social interactions with new friends with whom they would previously have been unlikely to share a church pew.

Even a casual student of the Baháʼí Faith in South Carolina (and in the United States as a whole) during the Jim Crow era would notice both the large number and prominent roles of women in a movement that explicitly proclaimed the equality of the sexes as one of its core principles. The founding member and guiding force of the state's earliest local Baháʼí community, for example, was a woman, and during the 1940s and 1950s the groups in Greenville and Columbia appear to have been mostly or entirely composed of women. Bahá'u'lláh specifically forbade any form of clergy, the main vehicle of patriarchal power in other religious communities, and instead prescribed corporate leadership for the community. As the Bahá'ís in South Carolina established their local governing councils beginning in the mid-1930s, women often formed a majority of both electors and those elected. As these pages show, South Carolina Bahá'í women were not only fundraisers, caregivers, and behind-the-scenes organizers in their communities—the most common roles for women in late nineteenth- and early twentieth-century American religious practice—but also founders, teachers, public speakers, and administrative leaders who in some ways outshone their male counterparts.[11]

Although specific local circumstances sometimes differed and the constraints that affected them were not constant or fixed over the whole period of Jim Crow, it is fair to say that the South Carolina Bahá'ís' radical revisioning of their region's religious, racial, class, and gender norms made for difficulties at every turn. Comparisons with a number of other reform movements in the state and region during the Jim Crow era highlight the precariousness of the Bahá'ís' position. Put simply, in the face of these intertwining orthodoxies, any reform-minded organization with good sense made efforts to transgress in only one category at a time. Those that openly worked for change in two or more categories at once exposed themselves to various forms of attack—and often proved short-lived. For example, the Commission on Interracial Cooperation, a post–World War I regional body with representatives at the state and local levels, was careful to promote a reduction in racial violence and the amelioration of some economic conditions for blacks without calling the Jim Crow system itself into question. While officially secular, the organization clothed itself in Protestantism: it was closely allied with nondenominational Christian organizations such as the YMCA and YWCA, and its leaders, black and white, tended to be ministers and prominent laypeople. They also tended to be men. Consequently, the organization never came under serious attack from the upholders of the Jim Crow order. To take another example, in the Alabama coal and iron region in the early twentieth century, black and white miners found the "breathing room" to collaborate in the labor movement, sometimes in integrated union locals, because of the single-gender nature of their job and their explicit adherence to other key elements of white supremacy. In other words, interracial union organizing in northern Alabama was less viscerally threatening to the Jim Crow order than it might otherwise have been because it did not raise the specter of sexual liaisons between black men and white women. When interracial labor movements did appear to promote social equality or eschew Christianity—as, for example, in the Communist Party and associated organizations in northern Alabama during the New Deal era, or the Communist-inspired union organizing that took place in Greenville, South Carolina, at the same time (discussed in chapter 4)—they invited serious opposition and often violence.[12]

Even thoroughly Protestant organizations courted disaster if they pushed in too many directions. During the 1930s and 1940s at Koinonia Farm, a Christian commune in rural southwest Georgia, the residents—all of whom were white, southern, and Baptist—won acceptance from their white neighbors only to the extent that they couched their interracial activities in a traditional language of Christian charity and restricted their contact with blacks to agricultural extension services. When they engaged in public displays of social equality—such as conducting an interracial children's summer camp or simply inviting black neighbors to eat and worship with them—opposition became intense and the Koinonians backed down. Similarly, the Greenville County Council for Community Development in South Carolina, a consortium spearheaded by Baptist-affiliated Furman University and designed to stimulate a carefully segregated local New Deal, collapsed when university trustees and local Baptist clergymen accused its leader (himself a prominent fellow Baptist) of conspiring with the NAACP, promoting interracial mixing, and turning Furman into a center of biblical modernism and social-gospel liberalism (as discussed in chapter 4).[13]

By advocating unity and equality across traditional lines of race, class, and gender, as well as what many of their neighbors regarded as religious heresy, the Baháʼís in Jim Crow South Carolina placed themselves entirely outside the pale of white male supremacy and its Protestant trappings. Despite their miniscule numbers in the period under consideration, multiple examples in this book make clear that the Baháʼís' simultaneous transgression of so many of the region's cultural norms exposed them to various forms of opposition by neighbors, local police, elected officials, the FBI, Christian ministers, the Ku Klux Klan, and employers and business associates. In fact, some aspects of the Baháʼís' approach may have helped them to avoid even more serious trouble. For example, cooperation among black and white southern churchwomen—although hedged about with limitations—was hardly unheard of during the Jim Crow era, so perhaps the preponderance of women in the early South Carolina Baháʼí community played a part in tempering the community's radical image. Moreover, the faith's rather strict standards of personal morality may have protected the Bahá'ís from widespread charges of interracial sexual liaisons, which, at least through the 1940s in South Carolina, tended to have deadly consequences. Similarly, the community's undermining of class differences was rather subtle, which probably protected it from the violence that often attended union organizing, particularly the interracial variety, in the state. Even so, the Bahá'ís' consistent promotion of social equality among whites and blacks did open them, like interracial unions, to withering accusations of Communism and miscegenation, and (as discussed in chapter 3) in the one significant example from this period of the faith attracting a large black working-class audience, in North Augusta during the 1930s, suppression by white authorities was swift and effective.

III

Perhaps most critical to the modest successes that attended their ambitious project during the Jim Crow era was the fact that the Bahá'ís in South Carolina saw themselves as part of a global movement whose inspiration, coherence, and relevance derived not primarily from parochial sources or concerns but from universal ones. For them, the Bahá'í Faith was the arrowhead of a worldwide spiritual and social revolution that both encompassed and transcended the issue of racial injustice in the United States. Like W.E.B. Du Bois, they linked the resolution of America's racial problem with the establishment of order and justice the world over, and they saw themselves as local actors on a national and international stage. During the New Deal era, Charleston-born Louis Gregory, among the most prolific Bahá'í writers and traveling teachers in the first half of the twentieth century, employed an evocative analogy from an earlier generation of American history to describe the supranational origins and impact of the faith: "This Most Great Reconstruction which the majestic Revelation of Bahá'u'lláh brings to view, is not black or white or yellow or brown or red, yet all of these. It is the power of divine outpouring and endless perfections for mankind."[14]

Gregory knew whereof he spoke. As a member of South Carolina's first generation born after the Civil War, he was the product of Reconstruction and its substantial legacies for African American education, entrepreneurship, and political awareness. Even more importantly for the theme of this book, he was heir to Reconstruction's venture in interracial community. Gregory's people, the Gullah of South Carolina's Lowcountry, had greeted emancipation as the "Day of Jubilo," the long-awaited day when God would intervene to right the wrongs of the world. During Reconstruction, they had committed the truly radical: with northern teachers and missionaries and a few native white South Carolinians, they had dared to imagine and work to realize a new nation in which blacks and whites could live, work, study, and worship together as one people. By 1898, the year that the United States took up the "white man's burden" in its war with Spain (and, somewhat ironically, that the Baháʼí Faith first arrived in the South), such notions had largely faded from public discourse—replaced by a militant new nationalism that reunited northern and southern whites, sanctified the social and spiritual segregation of the races, and drove the country's new venture in overseas imperialism.[15]

But the Reconstruction-era dream of a just and equitable interracial community never entirely faded among black southerners, even during the long decades of Jim Crow. When Louis Gregory invoked the powerful historical metaphor of the "Most Great Reconstruction," he was simultaneously reviving, expanding, and re-sacralizing that dream. For Gregory and other South Carolina Baháʼís in the early twentieth century, their movement was destined not to simply remake the South in the image of the North as in the first Reconstruction but to remake the whole planet in the image of Paradise. Indeed, the fact that the lives and ministries of the Báb and Baháʼu'lláh on the other side of the world had coincided with the convulsions of the abolitionist movement, the Civil War, and Reconstruction at home seemed to many early-twentieth century American Baháʼís to lend additional significance to their country's long struggle over slavery and its legacies. Moreover, the leaders of their faith indicated that their work to promote racial reconciliation within the United States would have world-shaking effects.

With a purpose that thus extended far beyond their own country, Baháʼís in South Carolina and the United States came to view themselves not only as Americans but also as members of a new religious polity the only boundaries of which were those of the planet itself. At the heart of their distinctive identity was the Baháʼí system of covenant, a system of institutional relationships, from the local level to the global, designed to give practical expression to Baháʼu'lláh's fundamental teaching of the oneness and equality of all human beings. The covenant required that American Baháʼís adhere to the guidance of a succession of supranational institutions—ʻAbdu'l-Bahá, the Center of the Covenant, from 1892 to 1921; Shoghi Effendi, the Guardian, and his appointed deputies, the Hands of the Cause, from 1921 to 1963; and, from its first election in 1963, the Universal House of Justice—all believed to derive their inspiration and authority from Baháʼu'lláh himself. Charged with protecting the unity and integrity of the worldwide movement as well as with setting the direction of its growth and development, the influence of the successive global heads of the faith was indispensable to making interracial fellowship a hallmark of the American Bahá'í community. While ultimate responsibility for its execution lay with the American Bahá'ís themselves, primary initiative came from the covenantal authority, which at every stage of the movement's development in the United States made interracial unity a matter of moral and spiritual principle, insisted on its importance regardless of opposition from inside or outside the community, and prevented any schism in the body of the believers over such a potentially divisive issue. Thus, any study of the formative decades of the Bahá'í movement in South Carolina (or anywhere else in the United States) necessarily involves careful consideration not only of the issues, concerns, and personalities at work in a collection of localities but also of influences from the regional, national, and especially global levels.

Moreover, South Carolina Bahá'ís were not simply recipients of instructions and influences from above but active participants in shaping the faith in the South, the United States, and the world during its first two centuries—a critical time in the life of any emerging religion. In particular, this book is an account of the essential place of South Carolina in understanding the development of the American Bahá'í community as a whole, for the decades under consideration here were not the earliest ones for the faith in South Carolina alone. In fact, the emergence of Bahá'í communities in South Carolina and other Deep South states began only a handful of years after its first arrival on American shores. The "national" Bahá'í movement (that is, one centered on a few urban areas in the Northeast and Midwest) that early on took steps to foster the establishment of the faith in the South was itself in the initial stages of its cultural and organizational development. Not only was the imperative for expansion in the South a major precipitating cause for the emergence of a national-level Bahá'í organization, but the expectations and concerns and talents of southern Bahá'ís played essential roles in the emergence of an American Bahá'í movement that was truly nationwide in scope.

This was perhaps nowhere truer than in the matter of race. Because the vast majority of African Americans during most of the early twentieth century lived in the South, and because the global covenantal authority at every stage insisted on the importance of interracial fellowship, any plan for growth in the South became almost synonymous with confronting the realities of Jim Crow and creating new alternatives. Since this effort was undertaken in the critical formative years of the American movement as a whole, it meant that the challenges and rewards of building interracial community in the South were kneaded into the very clay from which American Bahá'í identity, priorities, and institutions were formed.

An accurate account of the early South Carolina Bahá'í movement requires attention not only to the regional, national, and global levels of the faith but also to the broader social realities in which the Bahá'ís found themselves. No new religion grows and develops in a cultural vacuum, and the worldwide Bahá'í community has been particularly sensitive to this reality since its inception. The Báb and Bahá'u'lláh claimed that the divine outpouring associated with their missions had set in motion dramatic social processes that belonged to the world at large, processes with which the growing community of their followers and the generality of humankind would necessarily interact for hundreds or thousands of years to come. "The summons and the message which We gave," Bahá'u'lláh wrote, "were never intended to reach or to benefit one land or one people only. . . . The whole earth is illuminated with the resplendent glory of God's Revelation." These pages thus depict an embryonic faith community for which a dynamic social consciousness was part and parcel of belief and practice. That is, the Bahá'ís had an understanding of being *in* the world and *of* the world while working creatively and collaboratively, and often with like-minded individuals and groups, to *reshape* the world in what they saw as a long-term civilizing process on an ultimately global scale. This sensibility is perhaps best summarized in Bahá'u'lláh's exhortation: "Be anxiously concerned with the needs of the age ye live in, and center your deliberations on its exigencies and requirements."[16]

In South Carolina (and, for that matter, probably in the United States as a whole) during the early twentieth century, the single greatest structural and intellectual barrier to the realization of the Bahá'ís' project was racism, a ubiquitous reality with which they had every reason to be "anxiously concerned." More than any other factor, it was the Jim Crow system in all its manifestations that shaped the South Carolina Bahá'í movement in the critical formative decades of its existence; the "exigencies and requirements" of living in a segregated society affected everything from the Bahá'ís' public discourse and teaching methods to their conception of their own community and of their personal and family lives. Specifically, the Bahá'ís were profoundly affected by the specific contours of Jim Crow at the state and local levels (for it was not a monolithic system), by the various challenges to the system mounted by blacks and sympathetic whites, and by the quality and strength of conservative white responses. Small as it was, the community also managed to exert some influence in return. For these reasons, this book attempts to explain the development of South Carolina's Baháʼí movement in relation to, and in dialogue with, the broader struggles for and against civil rights and racial justice. Not only does doing so reflect accurately the lived experiences of early South Carolina Baháʼís, but this dimension of the book will also, I hope, have the benefit of bringing South Carolina's long, dramatic, and important civil rights history to new audiences in a fresh and coherent way.[17]

As historian Adam Fairclough has noted in reference to study of the long civil rights struggle in Louisiana, a state-level analysis provides the scope both to compare a number of local movements with each other and to place them in regional and national contexts. While much local and state Baháʼí history, in the South and elsewhere, has yet to be written, a similar approach (with the significant addition of the global context) has seemed appropriate here. The chapter divisions reflect a rather straightforward chronological approach, primarily following the contours of the formal planning process that ʻAbdu'l-Bahá initiated during World War I for the community's worldwide growth and development. Each chapter moves both "up" and "down," across different levels of geographic scope, and "inside" and "outside," from the Baháʼís themselves to the broader currents of social change around them and back again. The book concentrates on the four urban areas in South Carolina that were the focus of Baháʼí activity during the Jim Crow era: Charleston, the state's "first city" and main port; Columbia, the capital, located in the geographic center of the state; Greenville, a textile manufacturing center in the foothills of the Appalachians; and, especially in chapter 3, Augusta–North Augusta, a commercial and industrial hub on the western border with Georgia. (While Augusta proper is located entirely within Georgia, the large suburb of North Augusta is directly across the Savannah River in South Carolina, and together they and a number of other municipalities form, for all practical purposes, one city straddling two states. Because of the area's crucial role in the early development of other local Baháʼí communities in South Carolina, I believe it makes a great deal of sense to include it here.) In addition, there is treatment in chapter 1 of the early Baháʼí community of Washington, D.C., which formed the basis, both practically and conceptually, for the establishment of the faith in South Carolina and the rest of the Deep South, and chapter 6 introduces the Florence and Beaufort areas that were to become crucial to its development in South Carolina after 1968.[18]

For each area, I have mined Baháʼí community membership lists, newsletters, and other official documents; oral interviews and personal correspondence of individual Baháʼís and others; and U.S. census data, city directories, newspaper accounts, and local histories. I have attempted to uncover something of the social, economic, and religious background of Bahá'í members; their relationships with each other and with the larger society, especially the various phases of the civil rights movement; the changing methods by which Bahá'ís taught their religion to others and the content of their message; the processes by which Bahá'í institutions and community practices developed; and the motivations and aspirations of those who took part. As much as possible, I have attempted to let the Bahá'ís speak for themselves and for the remarkable religious movement with which they were associated.

On that note, a brief mention of terminology. Bahá'ís in South Carolina and elsewhere worked long and hard during the period under consideration here so that they and their faith would be correctly identified by governments, the media, and so forth. This book employs the nomenclature and system of transliteration adopted by Shoghi Effendi in the early twentieth century and used by Bahá'ís worldwide since then. The Arabic/Farsi word "Bahá'í" is an adjective, as in "the Bahá'í community" and "Bahá'í books." It can also be used with an article ("a Bahá'í in Greenville") to refer to a follower of Bahá'u'lláh. The plural is formed by adding an *s* ("the Bahá'ís in Greenville"). The correct name in English for the religion (also standardized by Shoghi Effendi) is "the Bahá'í Faith" with a capital *f*, a compound noun that is equivalent to, for example, "Christianity" or "Buddhism" (although in this book general references to, for example, "the faith," "the religion," or "the movement" are not capitalized). The exception to all the foregoing is quotes from older sources, where generally the original usages and spellings have been retained. Other Bahá'í terms and phrases that may be unfamiliar to most readers (as well as otherwise familiar ones that have a specific meaning in a Bahá'í context, e.g., "pioneer") are defined at their first occurrence in the text.

First Contacts, 1898–1916

In early November 1910, a dignified but unassuming visitor returned to his native city of Charleston, South Carolina. A son of former slaves, Louis George Gregory had risen from a childhood of poverty, misfortune, and social upheaval to achieve a measure of success that few black men of his day could hope for. Gregory made his home in Washington, D.C., the country's leading center of African American cultural, political, and economic life. In the prime of his life at thirty-six and lauded by the local black press as "one of the most gifted writers and speakers in this country," he was a member of the capital city's African American elite. With an undergraduate degree from Fisk University in Nashville and a law degree from Howard University in Washington, he held a comfortable position in the U.S. Treasury Department. During his recent tenure as president of the Bethel Literary and Historical Society, he had breathed "new life" into one of the oldest and most prestigious black cultural organizations in the city. Until recently, he had counted himself an ardent Republican Party activist, and he had supported the Niagara Movement, formed by W.E.B. Du Bois and other race leaders in 1905 to press for full civil and political rights for African Americans. Quite unexpectedly, however, events over the previous three years had profoundly altered his approach to addressing the nation's social problems. Louis Gregory was returning to the city of his birth not for business nor politics nor pleasure but on a mission of a different order altogether. He was on fire with the spirit of a new religion, and he had undertaken a journey into the heartland of the country's Jim Crow racial order to spread its message among his own kith and kin.[1]

Louis Gregory's trip heralded the arrival in earnest of the Bahá'í Faith, a radical new religion that taught the unity and equality of all people, in the South. Other black and white southern expatriates had become Bahá'ís in the northern and western cities where the faith had first taken root in the United States, but on the eve of Gregory's tour it had barely spread south of the Potomac. In Washington, D.C., where it had recently attracted its first substantial following among African Americans, the local Bahá'ís were struggling over whether to bow to the city's pervasive racial segregation or to identify themselves publicly as an interracial organization. Wielding the clear guidance of the religion's international head as well as his own considerable qualities of leadership, Gregory was already playing a central role in a process that, by the end of the World War I, would forge the Washington Bahá'ís into what was likely the first fully and explicitly interracial local religious body in the United States. With such a living laboratory of interracial community to back his claims for the transforming power of the Bahá'í Faith, Gregory set out for Virginia, the Carolinas, and Georgia in the autumn of 1910. By introducing its revolutionary teachings to larger audiences in the South—the region where more than nine in ten of all African Americans still lived and, not coincidentally, home to the country's most virulent form of racial oppression—Gregory hoped to reinforce the interracial character of the national Bahá'í movement and broaden its social foundations. The region's racial and religious conservatism, combined with the rudimentary state of the national Bahá'í organization, initially left new converts in the Deep South perilously isolated—as a harrowing case from Charleston indicates. Gregory's trip proved to be only the initial act in a long and difficult effort to establish the Bahá'í Faith in the South, but it set important precedents. For at least the following two decades, Washington would be the primary staging ground for the religion's southern expansion. As the main source of funding, labor, and organization for growth in the region and, perhaps just as critically, as a successful example of interracial fellowship in a major southern city, the local community of Washington became both the source and the template for the Bahá'í Faith in the South as an interracial movement. In practical terms, the origins of the faith in South Carolina thus lie principally in Washington. And from his 1910 trip until the end of his life some forty years later, the principal link between the nascent community in South Carolina and the main centers of Bahá'í activity in Washington and elsewhere was Louis Gregory.

Finding Fulfillment

Louis Gregory first heard of the Bahá'í Faith in late 1907 when one of his officemates at the Treasury Department, an elderly white Civil War veteran, suggested that the new religion might appeal to his young coworker. Gregory, however, was disinclined to investigate. After "seeking, but not finding Truth," he had "given up" on the Congregationalism of his youth—indeed, on any and all religion—as a means to solve the pressing issues of the day. Rather, he believed, with Du Bois and others, that the remedies African Americans most needed were comprehensive education and complete civil and political rights. To those ends, Gregory lent his support to various educational and cultural ventures in the capital city, organized for Republican Party candidates, denounced lynching in the local press, and worked to stem the tide of racial segregation. In 1904, for example, while in private practice with James A. Cobb, another young Howard-trained attorney, he had argued the case of Barney McKay, a black former cavalry soldier, newspaper editor, and Republican activist, who had accused a white saloonkeeper of assault and violation of the District of Columbia's civil rights law. Later, after taking a position in the law division of the Treasury Department, he and another black attorney, former justice of the peace Emanuel M. Hewlett, had put their bodies on the line, staging a protest at a whites-only lunchroom in Washington's city hall. Having placed his faith in essentially secular approaches to combating racial oppression, Gregory finally agreed to attend a Bahá'í meeting only out of courtesy to his coworker. What he found there, however, would challenge his previous understanding of religion and ultimately change his life's course.[2]

The address his coworker gave him was a rented room in the Corcoran office building, on 15th Street just opposite the Treasury Department. It was a "cold, blustery, extremely unpleasant night," and only one other person was present when Gregory arrived. Pauline Hannen, a white woman born in Washington and raised in Wilmington, North Carolina, was the host for the evening. She gave Gregory "an unusually cordial welcome" and proceeded to tell him that tonight he "would hear something wonderful, though difficult," a message that would afford him an opportunity similar to that which would have been his had he "lived on earth as a contemporary of Jesus Christ." She also gave him three Bahá'í books.[3]

The next to arrive was another white woman, Lua Getsinger, whom Hannen introduced as "our teacher." Although she held no particular rank in the religion, which had no clergy, she was among the most knowledgeable Bahá'ís in the United States. Just before the turn of the century, Getsinger and her husband had been among the first Americans to encounter the faith. They had attended a series of classes in Chicago taught by Ibrahim George Kheiralla, a Lebanese of Christian background and himself

Figure 1.1. Louis George Gregory (1874–1951), probably on his graduation from Fisk University, 1896. An attorney and civil servant who was a son of former slaves, he became one of the most accomplished teachers and administrators in the early American Bahá'í movement and introduced the faith to much of the Deep South, including his native South Carolina. Used with permission of the National Bahá'í Archives, United States.

a recent Bahá'í convert, who had been the first person to bring the new religion to the United States. Of the thousand or so people in Chicago and other northern cities who had already embraced the faith—mostly old-stock whites of evangelical Protestant background—the Getsingers had become some of the most active in its propagation. The last to arrive were two working-class black women with family roots in North Carolina: Mildred York, a twenty-nine-year-old seamstress, and her younger cousin Nellie

Gray. They were among more than a dozen black Washingtonians who had recently joined the faith as a result of meetings organized by Hannen and her family. Small as it was due to the inclement weather, the gathering was unusually diverse for a city largely bound by hierarchies of race, class, and gender.[4]

Getsinger gave a "brief but vivid" introduction to the Bahá'í Faith, with a historical account of the "appearances of the Bab and Baha'u'llah and of the great persecutions and martyrdoms in Persia." The story was dramatic indeed. Gregory learned that the new religion traced its origins to the early nineteenth century, when religious revivals, millennial expectations, and reform movements had stirred both Christian and Islamic countries from the United States to India. In 1844, Siyyid 'Alí-Muhammad, a young merchant of Shiraz, Iran, had declared that he was a Manifestation of God sent to prepare the people for the imminent coming of another divine teacher even greater than himself. Taking the title of the Báb ("the Gate" in Arabic), he had revealed a profusion of divine verses that radically redefined essential elements of Islamic thought and practice and overturned the authority of Iran's Shia clerical establishment. The Báb himself had been executed for heresy in 1850, and in the reign of terror that followed, some twenty thousand of his followers across the country had been slaughtered. Only one of his prominent followers, a nobleman by birth, had escaped the maelstrom. With his death sentence commuted to lifelong exile, Mírzá Husayn-'Alí of Núr had rebuilt the Bábí movement while under house arrest in the neighboring Ottoman province of Iraq. In 1863, on the eve of a further banishment to the Ottoman capital, he had announced that he was the Messenger foretold by the Báb and the Promised One of all the world's religions and had assumed the title of Bahá'u'lláh ("the Glory of God" in Arabic). In his writings addressed to Christian audiences, Bahá'u'lláh had identified himself as the return of the spirit of Christ, come to establish the Kingdom of God on earth as prophesied in the Bible. The central theme of his teaching was the oneness of the whole human race, and his voluminous writings, revealed over a forty-year ministry, identified both the spiritual conditions and the practical means for establishing a just and peaceful global commonwealth. Bahá'u'lláh's final exile had been to the Ottoman prison-city of 'Akká, on the plain of Sharon in northern Palestine, where he had passed away in 1892. His son and appointed successor, 'Abdu'l-Bahá, the living head of the faith, remained a prisoner there.[5]

Gregory was intrigued by what he heard. He read the three books that Pauline Hannen had given him: two introductory works written by American Baháʾís and an English translation of the Hidden Words, Baháʾuʾlláh's summary, in short poetic verses, of the moral and spiritual essence of religion. He soon attended a second Baháʾí meeting, this time "among poor people" at the home of Gray and York, where Pauline Hannen was the teacher. Then Hannen and her husband, Joseph, also a white southerner, invited him to their home. For more than a year Gregory visited the Hannens on Sunday evenings, often bringing black friends and associates, to learn more about the Baháʾí Faith. "The light they unfolded was so wonderful," he later recalled, "that for about a year we sat in dumb amazement, listening to their patient, loving talks, not knowing whether to advance or retreat, yet held by supernal power."[6]

In the teachings of Baháʾuʾlláh, Louis Gregory found his social and political concerns broadened and refined and, quite to his surprise, harmonized with the deepest longings of his ancestral faith—the prophetic promise of a reign of justice and righteousness on earth. For the intellectual committed to secular activism, his encounter with the Baháʾí Faith inspired a rekindling of personal religious feeling. His "mental veils were cleared away, and the light of assurance mercifully appeared within," Gregory recalled, as the Hannens taught him "how to pray." Moreover, the Baháʾí teachings brought him "an entirely new conception of Christianity and of all religion." With it, he said, his "whole nature seem[ed] changed for the better."[7]

At the heart of this new conception of religion was Baháʾuʾlláh's claim to be the Promised One of the world's great faiths. As Pauline Hannen had indicated at their first meeting, the Baháʾís believed they were living at the dawn of the great Day of God. As the earliest adherents of a new divine revelation, theirs was the opportunity and the responsibility to lay the groundwork for an unprecedented spiritual civilization destined to take shape over the course of a thousand-year dispensation. The implication for America's seemingly intractable racial problems were profound. For Louis Gregory the activist, here was a sophisticated vision of social change that was both universal in scope and rooted in the deepest wellsprings of personal spiritual transformation. "The appearance of Bahaʾuʾllah," Gregory testified, "is the direct fulfillment of the Lord's Prayer in the establishment on earth of the Kingdom of the Father. The Manifestation of the Father, Bahaʾuʾllah, heralded by all the prophets, comes to unite the souls of His creatures. His Divine utterances reveal the means of harmony for all religions and all peoples." In the Baháʾí telling, the actual coming of the Kingdom of God on earth would be a far cry from the fantastic events depicted in popular Christianity. Baháʾuʾlláh's divine revelation constituted the "new heavens" promised in the Gospels, while the "new earth" would take shape as the peoples of the world and their leaders put into practice the specific social and political arrangements he prescribed. Among such practical measures, as Gregory summarized them, were "cessation of war, a universal language, to be taught in all the schools of the world, a universal calendar, the education of all classes and of both sexes, [and] religious tolerance." While unity and peace were the explicit will of God, their realization was dependent on the practical efforts of human beings. Gregory noted that Bahá'u'lláh encouraged "commerce, the arts, science, agriculture and scientific discovery." "The people," Gregory said, "are commanded to bring forth fruit upon the earth."[8]

In addition to Bahá'u'lláh's teachings for the individual and society, the Hannens introduced Gregory to the figure of 'Abdu'l-Bahá ("Servant of Glory"), his eldest son and appointed successor. In written documents, Bahá'u'lláh had named him as the "Center of the Covenant," the head of the faith and authoritative interpreter of its sacred scriptures after Bahá'u'lláh's own passing, and the perfect exemplar of its teachings. Still under nominal house arrest in Haifa, the modern town across the Bay of Haifa from the prison-city of 'Akká, 'Abdu'l-Bahá was the living focal point for the faith of the Bahá'ís, who called him "the Master" or "Our Lord." He guided and encouraged them through a steady stream of letters (called "tablets" from the Arabic *alwáh*) and, despite the conditions of his confinement, by interacting personally with the pilgrims who came to pay their respects at Bahá'u'lláh's resting place outside 'Akká. In the words of one such early American pilgrim, 'Abdu'l-Bahá was "the Example and Leader of all mankind in service, sacrifice, love and peace, fulfilling before all the Law of the Kingdom as declared by the Great Manifestation Baha'u'llah."[9]

Early in 1909 Joseph and Pauline Hannen made their own pilgrimage to Palestine, and they mentioned Louis Gregory to 'Abdu'l-Bahá. He encouraged them to continue teaching Gregory, predicting that he would become an enthusiastic believer. When they returned home in April, the Sunday evening visits resumed. "At length," Gregory remembered, "as the lesson of humility took effect and every hope vanished save the Will of God, Abdu'l-Baha . . . revealed himself." In June 1909, Gregory became a "confirmed believer" and, in keeping with a practice among new American Bahá'ís begun by Ibrahim Kheiralla, he wrote a personal confession of faith and sent it to 'Abdu'l-Bahá.[10]

Washington Origins

When Louis Gregory became a Baháʼí, the religion had only been in the United States about fifteen years. With a few dozen believers, the Washington Baháʼí community of which he became a member was one of the largest and most successful such groups in the country, but it, like those in other cities, was still in a critical formative phase. Gregory came to play a decisive role in the creation of a single, racially integrated local Baháʼí community in Washington, the first American city with a significant black Baháʼí population. The Washington example set the standard of complete and uncompromising integration for the entire American Baháʼí movement, and as the Washington community became the main staging ground for expansion into the Deep South, it had a profound impact on the faith's development in the heartland of the Jim Crow system. To understand the early history of the Baháʼí Faith in South Carolina and other southern states, then, requires first an understanding of Washington.

Washington was one of the first centers of Baháʼí activity in the United States and an important early laboratory for putting Baháʼí teachings into collective practice. The first person to bring the faith to the nation's capital was Charlotte Brittingham Dixon. Her family, middle-class Episcopalians from the Eastern Shore of Maryland, had been seeking the return of Christ for generations: her father and grandfather had attended the revivals of the Millerites, who expected Christ's second coming in 1843–1844, and Dixon herself was strongly influenced by the Holiness movement in Methodism. Like Lua Getsinger, she attended Ibrahim Kheiralla's classes in Chicago and, convinced that Baháʼu'lláh had come "to establish the glorious reign of Peace, and the *Millennium*," she became a Baháʼí in September 1897. The next year, she returned east, teaching friends and members of her extended family in her hometown before settling in Washington. By late September 1899, there were seven Baháʼís in the city. Over the next few years, the faith gained a more substantial following in Washington, largely through the efforts of a handful of new believers from the city's white elite, including Phoebe Apperson Hearst (the wealthy widow of mining magnate and U.S. senator George Hearst and mother of newspaper publisher William Randolph Hearst), who had become a Baháʼí in California two years before and hosted Baháʼí meetings in her Washington residence; Alice Pike Barney, a successful painter whose husband was from a family of Ohio industrialists, and her daughter, Laura Clifford Barney; and Charles Mason

Remey, wealthy son of a U.S. navy rear admiral. The latter three had all become Baháʼís while living in Paris. Through the personal contacts of these prominent individuals, meetings for inquirers began to draw hundreds of people.[11]

From early on, the Washington Baháʼís were closely connected with other local communities in the United States and with the faith's world center in Palestine. From 1902 to 1904 they hosted Mírzá Abu'l-Fadl Gulpaygání, the most prominent in a series of Iranian teachers sent by ʻAbdu'l-Bahá to consolidate the fledgling Baháʼí movement in the United States. A professor of Islamic jurisprudence at Cairo's al-Azhar University, he was the foremost scholar of the Baháʼí Faith in the world. During his stay he wrote extensively and was a frequent speaker at public meetings, making the Washington Baháʼís perhaps the best-informed in the country. Encouraged in part by Mírzá Abu'l-Fadl, a few Washington Baháʼís began publishing introductory pamphlets on the faith and circulating English translations of ʻAbdu'l-Bahá's tablets. Also, by 1904 the growing Washington community had adopted the practice of the Chicago believers of holding a devotional gathering, called a "Unity Feast," on the first day of each Baháʼí month according to Baháʼu'lláh's instructions.[12]

In this dynamic Washington community, one of the most important new members was Pauline Knobloch Hannen. Along with members of her extended family, she spearheaded the first concerted efforts in the country to teach the faith to African Americans. The only American-born child of Lutheran immigrants from Saxony, Pauline Hannen had spent many of her formative years in Wilmington, North Carolina. Convinced that the new religion fulfilled the prophecies of the Bible, she became a Baháʼí in 1902. She was quickly followed by her husband, Joseph Hannen, an executive in a medical products company; her mother-in-law, Mary Alexander, a Virginia native who lived with them in Washington; her mother, Amelia Knobloch; and her older sisters, Alma and Fanny Knobloch.[13]

While a handful of African Americans had already become Baháʼís in other cities, the Hannens and Knoblochs were among the first white believers in the United States to appreciate the implications of the teaching of the oneness of humanity for the country's racial dilemma and to translate their understanding into concrete action. Pauline Hannen later admitted that while she had imbibed attitudes of racial prejudice in the divisive atmosphere of post-Reconstruction North Carolina, a passage from Baháʼu'lláh's Hidden Words had called her to account:

O children of men! Know ye not why We created you all from the same dust? That no one should exalt himself over the other. Ponder at all times in your hearts how ye were created. Since We have created you all from one same substance it is incumbent on you to be even as one soul, to walk with the same feet, eat with the same mouth and dwell in the same land, that from your inmost being, by your deeds and actions, the signs of oneness and the essence of detachment may be made manifest. Such is My counsel to you, O concourse of light! Heed ye this counsel that ye may obtain the fruit of holiness from the tree of wondrous glory.

After reading and reflecting on the passage, Hannen resolved to share the faith with blacks, and she started with those with whom she had the most immediate contact: Carrie York, her washerwoman, and Pocahontas Pope, her sister's seamstress. York, a sixty-year-old North Carolina native, was a

Figure 1.2. Joseph Hannen (1872–1921) and Pauline Hannen (1874–1939), probably shortly after their marriage, ca. 1895. Both of southern origin, they were outspoken proponents of racial integration in the early Washington, D.C., Bahá'í community and were primarily responsible for nurturing Louis Gregory's interest in the faith. Used with permission of the National Bahá'í Archives, United States.

widow with several grown children, a son-in-law, and young grandchildren at home. Two of her daughters worked as domestic servants and another was a schoolteacher. Pope, who had moved to Washington from North Carolina with her husband in the 1890s, conducted her tailoring business from her home. York and Pope both embraced the faith and, edified by correspondence with 'Abdu'l-Bahá, took steps to share it with their friends and family members. They held meetings for inquirers—often attracting twenty to forty people and cutting across the class lines in black Washington—at their own homes, with Joseph or Pauline Hannen, one of her sisters, or Bahá'í visitors from other cities as teachers. When Louis Gregory became interested in the faith, he arranged for Joseph Hannen to speak twice to the Literary Club at Howard University, opening additional contact with the city's black intellectual class. By the middle of 1908, some fifteen black Washingtonians had become Bahá'ís.[14]

With intimate gatherings in homes and formal encounters at Howard University, the Hannens and their friends, black and white, were beginning to forge links between the Bahá'í Faith and the largest and most influential black urban population in turn-of-the-century America and to cement the American Bahá'í movement's early commitment to interracial fellowship. The unique characteristics of black Washington made it both the ideal testing ground for Bahá'í interracial community and the most effective gateway for reaching African Americans in South Carolina and other southern states. Of the cities and towns where the faith first spread in the United States, Washington had the largest proportion of black inhabitants, some 30 percent during the first decade of the twentieth century. Compared to most cities in the country, it had a reputation as a haven of security and opportunity for African Americans, due in part to congressional oversight of the District of Columbia. In the 1880s and 1890s, as an upsurge of anti-black violence and discrimination rolled back many of the political and economic gains of Reconstruction, Washington's black population swelled. The migrants included skilled tradesmen and artisans, teachers and other professionals, and politicians pushed out of office in their home states and hoping for federal appointments. With an excellent system of black public schools, the literacy rate among the burgeoning African American population increased rapidly, from approximately 60 percent in 1890 to 83 percent in 1910. For black professionals in particular, federal agencies, the public schools, and Howard University represented unparalleled employment opportunities. Indeed, such a high concentration of well-educated, politically savvy African Americans made Washington the intellectual capital of turn-of-the-century black

America, with the Bethel Literary and Historical Society and the American Negro Academy heading a long list of cultural, social, and philanthropic organizations.[15]

Even in such a citadel of black achievement, building a religious community across racial lines was difficult. While a local civil rights law remained on the books, Washington was hardly immune to the nationwide trend toward racial segregation. The city's schools and churches had been separate since the era of the Civil War. Restaurants, hotels, and barber shops served only one race or the other, and black theatergoers were segregated in balconies. During the first decade of the twentieth century, the number of black employees in federal agencies and in city government declined, segregated work spaces, washrooms, and dining facilities emerged in several federal offices, and southern congressmen began a legislative campaign to segregate the city's streetcar system. In private social life, racial segregation was the unwritten rule. As one social worker observed in 1908, the "better class" of white and black Washingtonians knew "absolutely nothing of each other." In such a context, the Bahá'í meetings organized by the Hannens, Carrie York, and Pocahontas Pope—bringing together black and white, rich and poor, male and female around an explicitly egalitarian message, in both public and private settings—were most unusual affairs.[16]

However, interracial activities did not represent the standard practice of the Washington Bahá'ís. Indeed, most of the city's white believers probably found interracial association distasteful or detrimental to the good name of their religion. For a time, the mixed meetings constituted something of a community within a community—the larger one effectively all-white and conducting its activities without regard to the existence of the other. Seeing two groups, one white and one interracial, emerging in one of the leading centers of the faith in the United States, 'Abdu'l-Bahá took advantage of Joseph and Pauline Hannen's 1909 pilgrimage to encourage them to continue the interracial meetings. Expressing the hope that they would be "the means of bringing about peace between the Blacks and the Whites," he told the Hannens to convey to the entire community his desire for even more efforts to cross racial lines. As Joseph Hannen recounted in the national newsletter, 'Abdu'l-Bahá told them that in order "to prove the validity of our Teachings and as a means of removing existing prejudices between the races," additional white Bahá'ís should open their homes to interracial meetings.[17]

The Hannens apparently did not press the issue among their white fellow believers, however, until Louis Gregory began to teach his peers in Washington's black elite and received criticism for the community's segregation.

In the fall of 1909 and spring of 1910, Gregory arranged for a series of lectures on the Baháʼí Faith before the Bethel Literary and Historical Society, of which he was serving as president. The talks drew large audiences and coverage by the *Washington Bee*, a local black newspaper with a national reach, which announced the "power" of the "new teachings" as a "solvent of racial and religious differences." But the praise among Washington's black intelligentsia was hardly unanimous. "As soon as I became a believer and began to teach . . . ," Gregory recalled, "my colored friends got on my back and began to press me with troublous questions. If this were a New religion which stood for unity, why were its devotees divided? Why did they not meet altogether in one place? Were the Baha'is not full of prejudice like other people?"[18]

Clearly, the Washington community was falling short of the faith's professed teachings, placing Gregory in an embarrassing position. His hopes for his new religion might have been dashed but for the direct encouragement he received from ʻAbdu'l-Bahá. The latter's reply to Gregory's declaration of faith arrived in November 1909. Rather than retreat in understandable disappointment, ʻAbdu'l-Bahá directed Gregory to step into the breach. He wrote: "I hope that thou mayest become . . . the means whereby the white and colored people shall close their eyes to racial differences and behold the reality of humanity, that is the universal unity which is the oneness of the kingdom of the human race. . . . Rely as much as thou canst on the True One, and be thou resigned to the Will of God, so that like unto a candle thou mayest be enkindled in the world of humanity and like unto a star thou mayest shine and gleam from the Horizon of Reality and become the cause of the guidance of both races."[19]

Gregory took the tablet as a mandate to continue teaching African Americans and to press for the full integration of the local Baháʼí community. He asked to meet with the "Working Committee," the community's fledgling executive committee (of which Joseph Hannen was a member), about the issue of integration. At least two developments seem to have emerged from the meeting. Early in 1910, Gregory and the Hannens initiated a new, fully integrated monthly teaching meeting at their home. As Joseph Hannen reported for the first issue of a new national Baháʼí newsletter: "On the evening of March 6th, an important gathering assembled at the home of Mr. and Mrs. Hannen, representing the joining in one meeting of the white and the colored Bahais and friends of this city. . . . This is the first [such] meeting . . . , and is to be repeated monthly. There were present about 35 persons, one-third of whom were colored, and nearly all believers." At about the same time, the Working Committee began to desegregate the Unity Feast, the community's central worship service. Hannen continued: "It is also planned that every fourth Unity Feast, beginning April 9, should be held in such manner that both races can join. This is a radical step in this part of the country, and is in reality making history." As the Unity Feast was usually held in a rented hall, the inclusion of black believers likely involved changing the regular venue or making special arrangements with the landlord. Of course, the opening of only every fourth Unity Feast to interracial worship meant that the rest of the time the gathering was effectively all-white. Such a compromise, while preventing a complete splintering of the community, did not meet 'Abdu'l-Bahá's expectations. Through correspondence and conversations with pilgrims, he continued to insist on the complete integration of all the Washington community's activities, while for several years some of the white believers persistently misunderstood or ignored his instructions.[20]

For Louis Gregory, these steps, while incomplete, represented unmistakable progress toward an inevitable outcome of full interracial fellowship. Even in such a "partially integrated" state, the small Washington Bahá'í community stood out from the city's other religious groups as the meeting ground of a virtual cross-section of the diverse city—black and white; male and female; northern and southern; native-born and immigrant; working-class, middle-class, and elite; conservative and activist. Their unity was still tentative and partial, but Gregory believed that if even a handful of white Bahá'ís, whose own backgrounds and social positions made them otherwise very unlikely radicals, were willing to overcome their prejudices and associate intimately with blacks, the rest would follow. Heartened by the progress in Washington and determined to bring the message of the faith to larger numbers of blacks, he set out in the fall of 1910 for a speaking tour through the southern heart of segregated America.

When Louis Gregory left the District of Columbia for points south, he was coming home to a region beset by an agricultural economy in steep decline, rapid and uneven industrialization, brutal racial oppression of one-third of the population, and astonishing levels of legal and extralegal violence. Since the rise and rapid fall of the Populist movement of the 1890s, an alliance of conservative white political and business leaders, buttressed in large part by Protestant clergymen, had consolidated their control of every state of the former Confederacy and energetically promoted an ethos of white male supremacy. For concerned Bahá'ís like Gregory and the Hannens, such conditions called out for application of Bahá'u'lláh's moral and social teachings. But they also meant that bringing his religion to the South would be a difficult, lonely, and potentially dangerous undertaking. Beyond Washington and Baltimore, the South remained virtually untouched by the faith, with only half a dozen scattered believers and one small and isolated group anywhere south of the Potomac. Louis Gregory's trip would represent a major advance in establishing the Bahá'í Faith in an enormous region. As a native southerner and member of the country's black elite, he took full advantage of his personal and professional connections to speak to hundreds of people in churches, schools, social organizations, and private homes in eight cities and towns, including Richmond, Virginia; Durham, Enfield, and Wilmington, North Carolina; Charleston, South Carolina; and Macon, Georgia. He may also have spoken in Augusta, Georgia, and the neighboring city of North Augusta, South Carolina. While there were already a handful of believers in Virginia, it was likely the first time anyone had spoken publicly on the Bahá'í Faith in the Carolinas and Georgia.[21]

Home in Charleston

When Louis Gregory's parents moved to Charleston in the early 1870s, the city meant hope for a brighter future. Ebenezer and Mary Elizabeth George had grown up as slaves in Darlington District, some 120 miles north of Charleston in the Pee Dee section of South Carolina. Now in their twenties, they came to the city with their infant son, Theodore, and Mary Elizabeth's mother, Mary Bacot, to make a new life. They were hardly alone. As soon as Union forces entered Charleston in March 1865, freedpeople from across the state's Lowcountry began to stream in, hoping to find loved ones separated through the vagaries of the internal slave trade, seeking security from white violence and distance from their former masters, pursuing opportunities in employment, education, and community life far beyond what was available in the countryside, and feeling the first flush of freedom. For the first time in its two hundred years, the city's sizeable black minority became a decisive majority. Black laborers, skilled and unskilled, formed the backbone of the city's economy. Along with a coterie of black businesspeople and professionals, they built a network of vibrant institutions—churches, schools, social and benevolent societies—to serve their needs.[22]

As for many other families, it was as much the miserable conditions in the postwar countryside as the opportunities of urban life that drew the Georges to Charleston. During the early 1870s, white insurgents seeking to topple South Carolina's Reconstruction government wreaked havoc among rural freedpeople, including Mary Elizabeth's family. Her natural father was her late former master, George Washington Dargan, a judge on South Carolina's highest court, but after the war her mother's husband had been a newly freed blacksmith who achieved some success in business. White paramilitaries in Darlington had marked him as a threat, and one night, a band of masked men had called him out of his house and shot him dead. In Charleston, by contrast, the Georges could live and work in relative peace, Ebenezer as a blacksmith like his late father-in-law and Mary Elizabeth as a seamstress. Their second son, Louis, was born in 1874, and soon both boys became students in South Carolina's first system of free public education, set up under the Reconstruction state constitution of 1868.[23]

While Charleston offered certain advantages over the plantation districts, urban life was hard on many black migrants, who tended to suffer most from the city's postwar economic woes. During its antebellum heyday, Charleston had been an important city, but after the Civil War, with the Lowcountry's agricultural system in disarray, new railroads competing for port traffic, and chronically ineffective municipal leadership, the area began a long period of decline. With a burgeoning population, housing in the city was inadequate and crowded, the streets unpaved and filled with garbage and animals, and the drinking water unclean. Construction of a modern sewer system did not begin until 1909, and for decades it would bypass the poorest black neighborhoods. Even the forces of nature seemed bent on compounding Charleston's woes. In August 1885, when young Louis George was eleven years old, a powerful hurricane damaged or destroyed 90 percent of the houses in the city. Barely a year later, a major earthquake killed more than a hundred people and destroyed some two thousand buildings. In 1893 another major hurricane struck, killing thousands of blacks in the isolated Sea Islands to the south of Charleston and devastating the phosphate industry, the city's largest employer of African Americans. Some black carpenters and laborers benefitted from a building boom that followed these disasters, but during the late 1880s and 1890s most black workers experienced a decline in real wages and had a hard time achieving economic security.[24]

At the same time, the city's political climate became almost as poisonous as its water. In 1876, two years after Louis George was born, South Carolina's Republican-dominated state government, which rested on the votes of newly enfranchised black men, fell to a white paramilitary campaign; the following year, the biracial, reform-minded local government of Charleston was toppled. Over the next two decades, conservative Democrats chipped away at black political rights at both the state and local levels, and in 1895, the provisions of a new state constitution all but completed the removal of African American men from the voting rolls, the jury box, and state and local elective offices. After that, Charleston whites even blocked the appointment of blacks to a handful of federal posts in the city, the last chance for a few loyal Republicans to play a minor political role. In Charleston as across the South, black disfranchisement opened the door to systematic racial segregation. When Charleston's first electric streetcar system opened in 1897, just a year after the U.S. Supreme Court enunciated the "separate but equal" doctrine in *Plessy v. Ferguson*, it was on a segregated basis. By the first decade of the twentieth century, most public accommodations in the city were segregated, and, in a particularly galling blow to the morale and upward mobility of the black population, the local school board even barred blacks from teaching in the segregated public schools. Racial prejudice compounded the city's economic distress in other ways as well. With few exceptions, wealthy Charleston whites preferred to invest in cotton textile mills in the South Carolina Piedmont, which employed almost exclusively white laborers, over any venture that depended on their own city's abundant black workforce. Even concerted attempts to revive the city's fortunes suffered from racial myopia. In the winter of 1901–1902, for example, the white organizers of Charleston's Interstate and West Indian Exposition alienated blacks through the prominent placement of a statue depicting them only as manual laborers. Black leaders organized a successful boycott, and the fair ended a dismal failure.[25]

The squalor of Charleston's black neighborhoods and the limitations imposed by poverty took a terrible toll on the George family. In 1879, Ebenezer died of tuberculosis, the leading killer of black Charlestonians. In 1881, after struggling for two years to support her children alone, Mary Elizabeth George married George Gregory. He adopted the boys and raised them as his own; Louis George became Louis George Gregory. Before the Civil War, the Gregory family had been part of Charleston's sizeable free black community and had owned property. George Gregory was literate, a carpenter by trade, and a veteran of the Union army. He had served for about a year in the 104th Regiment U.S. Colored Infantry, one of two regiments raised from the area at the close of the conflict to augment the Union's occupation forces. Along with literacy and relative financial security, as a veteran George Gregory likely brought to his new family some of the benefits that came with military service, including greater political sophistication, a sense of pride and self-worth, stature within the black community, and an insatiable taste for education. He built the family a modest house in the Radcliffeborough section of the city's lower peninsula, a neighborhood mostly inhabited by freedpeople. The boys continued their education at the missionary-run Avery Normal Institute, the city's only black school with a college-preparatory program. But misfortune was not far away. In 1890, Theodore died of typhopneumonia. The following year, just as Louis was finishing high school, Mary Elizabeth died of spinal meningitis.[26]

For young Louis, the key emotional and practical support in the face of such blows came from his stepfather, who remained a caring father figure for the rest of his life. George Gregory was able to finance Louis's first year of college at Fisk University in Nashville, one of the premier institutions of higher learning for blacks in the country; after that, Louis paid his own way by tailoring for other students and working summer jobs back in Charleston. Between graduating from Fisk in 1896 and entering the law school at Howard University in 1900, Louis Gregory returned again to the family home, teaching at his alma mater, Avery Institute, and editing a weekly newspaper, the *Afro-American Citizen*.[27]

When Gregory returned as a Bahá'í in November 1910, it was thus to a community rich with family ties and social and professional connections. He was among his people, and he found plenty of friends, associates, and family members who were receptive to the message he had come to share. "Am just having the time of my life!" he wrote to Joseph Hannen from a relative's house on Coming Street. He had "numerous engagements to speak in churches, halls, and . . . parties" and to the Colored Ministerial Union. He reported a meeting with an Episcopal priest who, it turned out, already knew something of the Bahá'í Faith. The priest had attended sessions at Green Acre, a summer colony on the southern coast of Maine that attracted liberals and freethinkers and was owned by a Bahá'í. There he had met and been favorably impressed with Mírzá 'Abu'l-Fadl, who lectured frequently at Green Acre during his Washington-based American sojourn of 1901 to 1904. On November 8, Gregory was the featured speaker at a "Lecture and Musicale" at the Carpenters' Hall on Line Street. As a carpenter, Gregory's stepfather was probably responsible for the arrangements at the union local's meeting place. Gregory was to have shared the podium with three ministers, but none of them showed up. Instead, Gregory "had the attentive audience to face alone, yet not alone, for the Spirit was powerful." Altogether, he told Hannen, "the whole city seems interested."[28]

Gregory also shared the news of his meeting with some or all of Charleston's six black attorneys, most of whom he probably already knew. According to Gregory, all the lawyers at the meeting "seem[ed] favorable" to the Bahá'í message. One of them, Alonzo Edgar Twine, identified himself as a believer, based in part on Gregory's exposition of biblical prophecy: "One of them has accepted [the faith], saying that he was particularly impressed with the explanation concerning 'clouds.' He added that if Christ were to come thru the literal clouds, he certainly would be hidden from half the earth, in view of its roundness." Twine became Gregory's close companion during the rest of the latter's stay in the city, arranging for at least one additional speaking engagement. On Sunday, November 20, Twine gave a moving introduction to Gregory's talk before the Young People's Union, an organization of which he was a member, at New Tabernacle Fourth Baptist Church. Twine attested to his own "faithfulness and fidelity to the Union," lending added legitimacy to Gregory's message. A local newspaper noted that Twine was "at his best" and that he "touched the hearts of the people." The next night, Twine probably accompanied Gregory for his talk at Morris Brown African Methodist Episcopal Church.[29]

Gregory and Twine had remarkably similar backgrounds. Born three years apart—Gregory in 1874 and Twine in 1877—both men grew up after the fall of Reconstruction and came of age in a period of steadily worsening race relations. Alonzo Twine's father, Charles Twine, was probably born a slave in eastern North Carolina. During the Civil War, he served in the Twenty-First Regiment U.S. Colored Infantry, which took part in operations against Charleston during 1864 and was one of the regiments that occupied the city after the Confederate surrender. After the war, he remained in Charleston and worked in a saw mill. He married a South Carolina–born freedwoman named Phillipa, who worked as a nurse and housemaid. The couple raised a family in a rented house on Montague Court, an enclave of freedpeople in the Harleston Village neighborhood, and they sent at least one of their children to school at Avery Institute, only a short walk down Bull Street. Sometimes they took in boarders for extra income. The Twine and Gregory families had likely crossed paths well before Louis Gregory's visit in 1910. While Charles Twine and George Gregory had served in different army regiments, they may have known each other after the war as members of the carpenters' union, one of the strongest locals in the city's active labor movement. The families lived only three blocks away from each other, and their children overlapped at Avery Institute. In 1900, when Louis Gregory returned to Avery to teach, he probably had Joseph Twine, Alonzo's younger brother, in his eighth grade class.[30]

Alonzo Twine continued his education at Claflin University, a school in Orangeburg, South Carolina, founded by northern Methodist missionaries during Reconstruction. Admitted to the bar by the state supreme court in May 1899, Twine began practicing law in Charleston. He partnered with Eugene R. Hayne, another young black attorney who had attended law school at Allen University in Columbia, until 1903, when Hayne moved to New Jersey to practice there. For several years Twine partnered with Robert C. Brown, a black attorney some thirty years his senior, and from at least 1909 he practiced on his own. In 1909 and 1910 he argued three minor criminal appeals before the South Carolina Supreme Court, losing all three. Twine and his parents were members of Old Bethel Methodist Church on Calhoun Street, part of the northern branch of Methodism and one of the oldest and most prestigious black congregations in the city. Twine also served as one of the congregation's trustees. An astute political observer at a time when opportunities for blacks in public service and the professions seemed under attack in South Carolina, Twine was a member and officer of the Aurorean Coterie, a men's club of local black professionals and entrepreneurs. The group enriched black Charleston's cultural and intellectual life by welcoming such guests as Mary Church Terrell, national leader in the black women's club movement, and sponsoring concerts featuring the works of African American composers. Unfortunately, like many of his black peers in South Carolina in the early twentieth century, Twine's educational, professional, and social leadership did not always translate into financial success. In 1910, unmarried at age thirty-three, he lived at home with his parents, two younger adopted sisters, and a boarder.[31]

The Perils of Conversion

When Louis Gregory embraced the Bahá'í Faith in the intellectual capital of black America, he experienced opposition and pity from his friends and associates and ridicule in the press. Alonzo Twine's circumstances were far worse: in the more conservative atmosphere of Charleston, his conversion led him down a road of isolation, incarceration, and death. The stories of Gregory and Twine suggest that in the early twentieth century, religious orthodoxy remained an important marker of black respectability, with powerful defenders among the black elite. Even young men as promising and capable as Gregory and Twine could not seriously question traditional Protestantism and the clerical establishment without risking their careers and class status.

While some of Louis Gregory's African American associates questioned his decision to become a Bahá'í because of the community's mixed record on race, others criticized him solely on religious grounds. As he recalled in his memoir: "By far the majority of my friends thought I had become mentally unbalanced. One of my old teachers, a professor of international law and a very affectionate friend, almost wept over my departure from orthodoxy and with others warned me that I was blasting all hopes of a career. The *Washington Bee*, a well-known colored newspaper, on one occasion gave me two columns of ridicule which remained unanswered. Others, knowing my controversial habits of the past said, 'He must have religion since he does not answer that!'" For Gregory, who was accustomed to coverage of his political, professional, and cultural activities in the local press, the attacks in the pages of the *Bee* must have been particularly embarrassing. His critic was Roscoe Conkling Bruce, who wrote a regular column in the *Bee* under a nom de plume, the "Sage of the Potomac." Bruce, the only son of the late Blanche K. Bruce, one of Mississippi's two black U.S. senators during Reconstruction, was a Harvard-educated school administrator and political climber who had started his career as academic director at Booker T. Washington's Tuskegee Institute. With Washington's help, he had secured positions in the national capital, first as a principal, then as assistant superintendent for black schools. Like his patron in Alabama, Bruce was a strong advocate of manual training, and his disdain for classical education alienated many in the city's black elite. As the "Sage of the Potomac," he vented his rage against others in his class.[32]

Bruce devoted large parts of two columns, in January and June 1911, to scathing attacks on Louis Gregory and the Bahá'í Faith. In the first, he described the faith as "that Baha substitute for orthodox religion," "a lot of dope that was popular just before Christ came," and "chloroform." "I never could see anything," he stated, "in conditions in India and the Orient to make their religion, or any religion that came from such environments, appeal to me." He also implied that Gregory's attraction to the faith was unmanly. While calling him "one of the most studious, pious, and gentlemanly young men in Washington," Bruce attributed Gregory's aberrant behavior to the fact that he was not yet married. He opined: "A fellow who does not get around with one of Adam's lost ribs is bound to take up with some mummified, prehistoric pinch-hitter like Buddha or Confucius or a minor leaguer like Baha.... I will guarantee that if he gets the right [woman], ... he will forget that Baha ever wore a turban."

The second column was even less charitable. In it he ridiculed the Bahá'í Faith as one of a number of "Oriental get-rich-quick creeds" attracting "highbrows and faddists" who were no longer satisfied with traditional Protestantism. In one passage, he indicated that study of the faith would lead to both damnation and insanity:

About a year ago I started to study this Bahaismatic fifteen-block puzzle, but I hadn't got far into the mysteries of it until I found that if a fellow finished out the nine innings of the game he would be dippy for sure. So I just dropped it. These old fashioned creeds will do for me to worry along with. And I'll bet the fellow that is a good batter in the old fashion league will come nearer getting by St. Peter, who is on first base, than most of these fellows who rattle off a lot of jargon on which some Oriental fakir holds the copyright. I was born and bred and reared in that submarine boat they named Baptist, and I guess I can make port in her. Believe me, I can't afford to dally with Louie's Bahaism, his godman substitute for the old creeds, for fear I'll wake up some morning over at St. Elizabeth's [Hospital].[33]

While Gregory chose not to answer Bruce's ridicule, he did have a chance to try and set the record straight. In November 1911, the *Bee* published a front-page article by Gregory outlining the teachings, objectives, and history of the Baháʾí Faith, including a discussion of religious unity surely meant to emphasize its harmony with Christianity. "The Revelation of Bahaʾoʾllah is not a new Religion," he stated. "It is rather a renewal of the Spirit of Religion. It comes to antagonize no existing church, sect, or religion, but rather to unite all." In contrast to Bruce's portrayal, in his own account Gregory and the religion he espoused appeared both warm and reasonable.[34]

Two weeks after the article's publication, the *Bee* reprinted shocking news from a Charleston paper. Under the provocative banner "He Had Wrong Religion," the article stated that Alonzo Twine had been arrested and taken to a mental hospital in Columbia. According to sources in Charleston, the cause of his illness was his having forsaken "the faith of his fathers" and accepting the "new and . . . strange kind of religion" called the "religion of Bahai." In February, a Savannah paper carried a similar story and offered the same conclusion. Something terrible had happened to the faith's lone adherent in South Carolina, and it was being associated with insanity in the black press.[35]

It is unclear exactly what circumstances led to Twine's confinement. According to the legal and medical record and to press accounts, the Baháʾí Faith made him insane. Clearly, Twine experienced painful opposition to his new religious beliefs and a profound sense of isolation that may well have contributed to a mental breakdown. At the same time, he lived in the heart of a society with a long record of labeling troublesome blacks as insane. It is unclear whether or not Twine was actually mentally ill, but opposition by his former pastor and by his immediate family seems to have contributed directly to his institutionalization.

When white doctors first examined Alonzo Twine on October 2, 1911, he was being held in a cell of the psychiatric ward of Roper Hospital, an area Charlestonians referred to as "the Black Hole of Calcutta." "Patient stands at window," they reported, "and grips the iron bars and sings continually, 'Shine on bright star, Shine on,' and then turns and curses as we walk in the room." According to Phillipa Twine's testimony to the local probate court, her son's attack had come on suddenly the week before. Its cause, she indicated, was "religion." There had been "indications of [the] present attack of insanity" for some six months in the form of "religious [obsession]." She testified that the disease was exhibited as "religious excitement," that her son was suffering religious "delusions," and that he was "deranged" on the subject of "religion." In response to a series of questions, Phillipa Twine testified that her son had remained regular in his work and was not destructive of himself or others. Asked whether he was "irritable, quarrelsome, or noisy," she indicated only that her son was "noisy." Nevertheless, the probate judge found Alonzo Twine a danger to society. He signed a commitment order on October 5, and the next day Twine was transported by train to Columbia and admitted to the South Carolina Hospital for the Insane. Shortly after his arrival, he was diagnosed with manic-depressive disorder, but like most black patients in the facility, he apparently received little or no treatment.[36]

Even if Twine was of perfectly sound mind when he entered the state hospital, a short time there certainly would have been enough to undo him. When it was founded in the 1820s as the South Carolina Lunatic Asylum, it had been at the forefront of treatment for the mentally ill. By the turn of the twentieth century, however, it was a pesthole that did little more than warehouse broken men and women. A legislative investigation in 1909 documented overflowing toilets and wards crawling with lice and bedbugs, an inadequate and poorly trained staff that were quick to use violence and mechanical restraints to maintain order, and unwashed patients often wearing little more than rags. Between 1890 and 1913, some 14 percent of patients in the facility died each year, a far higher rate than at comparable institutions around the country. The two leading causes of death across the hospital were tuberculosis, which was easily transmitted in the crowded and filthy conditions, and pellagra, a debilitating niacin deficiency caused by overconsumption of corn. Untreated, victims of pellagra developed painful skin lesions; swelling of the mouth and tongue; abdominal swelling, vomiting, and diarrhea; mental deterioration and dementia; and, within four or five years, death. In the late nineteenth and early twentieth centuries, as a declining agricultural economy led to impoverished diets, pellagra became a major killer in the rural South. It was also rife in the state hospital, where patients subsisted on grits, cornbread, fatback, and coffee.[37]

For black patients in particular, the state hospital was a living hell. Alonzo Twine lived in the Parker Building, which housed black men. Designed for 200 patients, it held some 330 in 1909. It was infested with vermin, and patients slept on straw on the floor of their cells. Between 1903 and 1908, more than a quarter of the patients in Parker died each year. An assistant physician was appointed in 1905 specifically for black patients, but he did not reside on campus and spent only one to four hours a day at the hospital. Even white patients complained that they seldom saw doctors; surviving records give no indication that black patients received psychological or medical treatment beyond a perfunctory examination upon their arrival. The death rate for black patients was twice as high as for whites. While the black patients were judged unfit for free society, they were apparently competent enough to keep the hospital running at significant cost savings to South Carolina's taxpayers. Some 80 percent of black inmates were healthy

Figure 1.3. Parker Building, South Carolina State Hospital for the Insane, Columbia, ca. 1905. Built by and for African American inmates, it is almost certainly the spot where Alonzo Edgar Twine, alone and persecuted for his embrace of the Bahá'í Faith, succumbed to pellagra in 1914. No photograph of Twine has survived. Courtesy of Richland Library, Columbia, S.C.

enough to build new hospital buildings, maintain the extensive grounds, milk the cows, and do the laundry. Hospital administrators complained that with so many black patients working at menial tasks, it was hard to get the whites to do the same. Instead, white inmates were provided with minimal recreational opportunities.[38]

Since antebellum times, the subject of blacks' mental health had been intimately connected to social control in South Carolina. There was a long and well-documented history, on the one hand, of slaves suffering legitimate mental illness, mostly in conditions of neglect and isolation. On the other, slaves who exhibited too much self-confidence or independence—especially by running away—were often labeled as insane. In the early twentieth century, the state hospital was one part of an ad hoc system of social control that minimized the threat of troublesome blacks to the state's white minority. The chief means of controlling poor young black men were the state penitentiary and the county chain gangs, which housed vastly disproportionate numbers of blacks and worked them—in many cases to death—for public profit. Voluntary out-migration and forced exile often removed from the state educated and self-confident black men who could not hold their tongues in the midst of galling injustice. In Alonzo Twine's case, perhaps the Hospital for the Insane performed the same function.[39]

The institutions of social control found a willing, if perhaps unwitting, accomplice in Twine's former pastor at Old Bethel, Rev. I. E. Lowery. Driven to enforce religious orthodoxy, Lowery took away what was likely Twine's only solace in the oppressive and pestilential surroundings of the state hospital, reinforcing his profound isolation. In comments published more than a decade later, Lowery wrote that when he was transferred to a church in Columbia, he had come to visit Twine in the state hospital. "The first time we called to see him," Lowery recalled, "he held in his hand a little pamphlet, and we asked him for it. He readily gave it to us, and we found it to be a book on the Bahai religion. We took it from him and brought it home, knowing that it was this that caused him to lose his mind." Alonzo Twine survived three years in the abominable conditions of the asylum before succumbing to pellagra. He died on October 26, 1914, probably alone and completely demented in the last stages of the disease. At his parents' request, Lowery brought the broken body back to Charleston for a funeral at Old Bethel.[40]

A comparison of the opposition that Louis Gregory and Alonzo Twine faced is instructive. When Gregory became a Bahá'í in Washington, his friends thought he had become "mentally unbalanced"; a prominent mentor, among others, thought he was "blasting all hopes of a career"; and a newspaper columnist implied that he was risking his soul, his mind, and his manhood. With strong connections to friends in the city's Bahá'í community, however, Gregory weathered the storm of criticism and did not abate his Bahá'í activities. By the next year, the tone in the local press had changed, and the community continued to grow. When Alonzo Twine became a Bahá'í in Charleston, he apparently experienced similar opposition. In both cases, peers and mentors in the black community judged that it was "insanity" for a promising young professional to abandon traditional Protestantism. The substantial difference between the two is that Twine was alone and unable to defend himself. If even a few other members of Twine's family, church, or profession had become believers with him and begun to identify themselves as a Bahá'í community, perhaps they could have afforded each other some measure of protection and support.

Southern Diffusion of the Bahá'í Faith

The fate of Alonzo Twine, while unusually grim, is but one example of the range of challenges American Bahá'ís faced as they first sought to propagate their religion in the South. From the earliest days of the Bahá'í Faith in the United States, many of the believers seem to have sensed a need for the movement not only to gain new adherents but also to spread geographically. Indeed, for such a numerically small community, the Bahá'ís achieved a remarkable degree of dispersion in their first decade and a half. However, they were heavily influenced by social and economic factors that severely hampered their penetration of the former Confederacy, giving the faith a decidedly regional tilt and initially limiting its spread among African Americans in the region where the vast majority of them lived. Twine's case illustrated most dramatically the need for a stronger national Bahá'í organization and for more systematic attention to expansion in the South.

When Louis Gregory traveled through the South in 1910 there were about twelve hundred Bahá'ís in the country, and they lived in localities stretching from Boston to San Francisco. As Thornton Chase, one of the first Chicago converts and a prominent teacher of the faith, observed, mobility "seems to be the *way* of this Cause." Indeed, mobility was increasingly the way of America as a whole. In part, the successful dispersion of the faith was due to the fact that it arrived in the United States during an era of rapid industrialization and urbanization, when a burgeoning railroad network facilitated unprecedented movement of goods and people. Bahá'ís from the first group in Chicago, often prompted at least in part by family ties or employment opportunities in the new national economy, were able to travel or settle in other areas and teach. They quickly established the faith in urban areas of the Northeast and Midwest, with outposts on the West Coast. In more than twenty larger towns or cities, the number of believers necessitated renting spaces for worship, study, and teaching activities and hence some form of local community organization. Most local Baháʼí communities had organized themselves as typical American voluntary associations, with elected officers, a treasury supported by the members, and regular activities. Through a stream of tablets, discussions with pilgrims, and the dispatch of a series of knowledgeable Iranian teachers to the United States, ʻAbduʼl-Bahá began to introduce features of the Baháʼí model of governance. He encouraged the election in each locality of an executive board the members of which would have corporate, but not individual, authority and would operate through consultation and consensus. While they differed from city to city in number of members, operating procedures, and even name, ʻAbduʼl-Bahá indicated that each fledgling body was as a forerunner of the local House of Justice (*baytuʼl-adl*) that Baháʼuʼlláh had ordained in his writings as the future governing body of every city and village.[41]

If the modern economy afforded the Baháʼís opportunities to spread their religion, in certain respects it also constrained their movement. For decades, the faith would remain a mostly northern, urban phenomenon concentrated in the densely populated, highly interconnected urban core of the Midwest and Northeast. Even within these regions, the small towns and farms had few believers. In 1905, in addition to the twenty or so large, organized groups, there were some 150 localities with only one or two believers each, accounting for perhaps a third of the country's Baháʼís. "All these scattered souls," Chase wrote optimistically, "are kindling little fires all over the land," but with no organization above the local level, it was unclear how to ensure their full participation in the movement. One early experience illustrates the difficulty. In 1897, a woman in the tiny town of Enterprise, Kansas, heard about the Baháʼí classes in Chicago and invited Ibrahim Kheiralla to come teach her family and friends. A dozen or more people became believers during and after Kheirallaʼs visit, making Enterprise the second locality in the United States where Baháʼís resided. Thornton Chase and perhaps some of the other Chicago Baháʼís attempted to keep up correspondence, but no other teachers visited Enterprise, leaving the new group essentially alone with beginners' knowledge of the faith. Initial reaction to Kheirallaʼs visit in the local and statewide press was negative, and the new converts, many of whom were from the town's upper class, likely experienced a painful social rift with their churchgoing neighbors. They never organized regular activities, even though they were all related or knew each other well, and many apparently lost interest over the next several years. While isolated believers in Enterprise and other similar localities may have been "kindling little fires" in theory, Chase knew that they were not having much success. "It seems an impossibility," he admitted of such areas, "to establish an Assembly of any size."[42]

If the Midwestern countryside was hard to consolidate, by 1910 the vast West and South had been virtually impossible even to penetrate. In the West, demography was largely responsible for the faith's slow growth. Large areas of the region were sparsely settled, and mirroring the region's population at large, few Bahá'ís lived outside of California. The South, too, was a mostly rural region, but compared to much of the West it was heavily populated and thickly laced with transportation and communication networks. Bahá'í teachers leaving Chicago and its daughter communities in the North would not have had serious problems of physical access to the region and its people. Rather, it was primarily social and cultural factors that inhibited the growth of the faith in the South. A comparative lack of employment opportunities; high rates of poverty, illiteracy, and disease in both urban and rural areas; an atmosphere of cultural and intellectual torpor; a widespread suspicion of outsiders; a dominant theology concerned more with personal salvation than social transformation; a crippling racial divide; and a leadership class that relied on violence and fear to maintain its hold on power—all made it difficult for Bahá'ís from the Northeast and the Midwest to penetrate the region.

Somewhat better suited to introduce the faith in the South were the southern expatriates among the first generation of American Bahá'ís, a small handful of the nearly two million people, black and white, who left the South in the three decades following the collapse of Reconstruction. In such Northeastern and Midwestern urban centers as Chicago, Philadelphia, New York, and Boston, a few of them embraced the Bahá'í Faith. Many southern-born believers became active teachers and administrators of the faith, and several made efforts to spread it in their home region. In Chicago, for example, Corinne Knight True, the eldest daughter of an abolitionist minister and a Kentucky plantation heiress, became a Bahá'í in 1899, played a leading role in organizing the early community, and, beginning in 1909, spearheaded a major project to build the first Bahá'í temple in the Western world. South Carolina–born Julia Elizabeth Diggett, who became a Bahá'í in 1904, served with True as a member of Chicago's first Women's Assembly of Teaching, a precursor of the community's first executive body, and she traveled "from Coast to Coast and from the Gulf to the Great Lakes" in the interests of the faith. In Washington, D.C., at the southern extremity of the country's urban-industrial core, a steady stream of southerners encountered the faith, including the Hannen and Knobloch families from North Carolina and probably the majority of the African Americans they taught, among them Louis Gregory. Claudia Stuart Coles, a white Charleston native who moved to Washington with her family during Reconstruction, served on the community's Working Committee beginning in 1907. Through her public and private associations with African Americans, including speaking on the faith in the series that Louis Gregory organized for the Bethel Literary Society, Coles came down in support of the full equality and integration of black Bahá'ís.[43]

All things being equal, such a talented pool of native southerners could have constituted the vanguard of Bahá'í traveling teachers and settlers in their home region. While individuals such as Julia Diggett and Louis Gregory traveled extensively, outside of Baltimore and Washington only a few Bahá'ís were able to make their homes in the South during the first decade of the twentieth century. The earliest students of the faith in Chicago had included two people from Virginia, one from Kentucky, and one from Georgia, but they may not have become believers or remained connected to the faith after they returned to their homes. The lone Bahá'í in Tennessee, who had studied the faith in Sandusky, Ohio, died in 1908. One potential South Carolina connection misfired. Pearl Battee Doty, an Ohio native with an alternative healing practice in Baltimore, became a Bahá'í in 1898 and soon became the nucleus of a community of about fifty people. Her husband, Henry "Harry" Archer Doty, a white Charleston native, was certainly one of the first South Carolinians to encounter the Bahá'í Faith and may have become a believer himself. Unfortunately, however, Pearle's interest in the religion seems to have coincided with the couple's separation. By 1900, Harry Doty was living with his widowed mother just a few blocks from Louis Gregory's family home in Charleston, while Pearle and the couple's young son remained with her father in Baltimore. Three years later, Pearle Doty died, and with her, apparently, the remaining family's only link with the faith. In a tablet written to the Baltimore community after Pearle's death, 'Abdu'l-Bahá expressed the hope that her son, as well as the boy's two living grandparents, would become Bahá'ís: "I hope her noble son may seek the Path wherein his mother walked, and may become better and more illustrious; nay, rather, the lights of his love may also take effect in his grandparents." However, there is no evidence that any other member of the family, either in Charleston or in Baltimore, maintained any connection to the Bahá'í Faith, or that Harry

Doty and Louis Gregory were aware of each other during the latter's visit to Charleston in 1910.[44]

When Louis Gregory came south in 1910, not only Charleston but a vast region was virtually untouched by the Bahá'í Faith. There were four Bahá'ís in Virginia, one in Richmond and three in rural Fauquier County southeast of Washington; two in Florida, both in the Jacksonville area; and one in Texas near Austin. South of the Potomac, the only fledgling group in the South was in Fairhope, Alabama. Located on the eastern shore of Mobile Bay, Fairhope was a model community founded in 1894 by members of the Single-Tax Club of Des Moines, Iowa. It was intended to put into practice the economic philosophy of Henry George, whose 1879 magnum opus, *Progress and Poverty*, proposed to promote economic equity by abolishing all taxes except on the unimproved value of land. Here, two of the earliest Bahá'ís in Chicago, Paul and Adelaide Dealy, moved with their children in 1898–1899. Paul Kingston Dealy, New Brunswick–born son of Irish immigrants, was a self-educated businessman, an ardent student of the Bible, and a Populist activist before he and his wife attended Ibrahim Kheiralla's classes and became Bahá'ís in Chicago in 1897. Dealy quickly became Kheiralla's chief assistant, teaching classes to new sets of seekers. In 1898, only a year after embracing the faith, he moved to Fairhope, where he leased land and began to farm; the rest of the family joined him the following year. The Dealys apparently attracted dozens of new believers, black and white, in Fairhope and in the nearby county seat of Bay Minette, and for several years they maintained close contact with the rest of the American Bahá'í movement even from so far away. For example, Paul Dealy wrote a widely used introduction to the faith that went through several editions and was one of the three books that Pauline Hannen gave to Louis Gregory at his first Bahá'í meeting in 1907. Even in Fairhope, however, with Bahá'í settlers who were exceptionally knowledgeable and a relatively progressive social environment in which to work, poverty and geographic isolation seem to have inhibited the development of a strong local community. The colony itself was located on land that was too poor for farming, and for years the Dealys suffered financially along with their neighbors. It would have been time-consuming and relatively expensive for the Fairhope Bahá'ís to travel to Chicago or Washington, the closest major centers of activity, and the same factors meant that Bahá'í visitors who might have lent support to the struggling group were rare. For example, while the Gulf Coast is a relatively short distance from Macon, Georgia, Louis Gregory's last stop on his 1910 trip, there is no indication that he visited the town on that or any other occasion. For some reason, the Fairhope group seems to have not followed the national trend of forming a local executive board, establishing a treasury, and holding regular activities. Most of the local converts appear to have drifted away from the faith, and even the Dealys' children apparently did not remain believers after their parents' deaths.[45]

From Enterprise to Charleston to Fairhope, the experience of isolated believers and small groups highlighted important problems for the nascent American Bahá'í movement. No matter the degree of sincerity and enthusiasm of the new believers, it was not clear how to nurture the faith and deepen the understanding of a few scattered individuals—perhaps only one or two in a city—who were so far away from the existing Bahá'í population centers. In a religion that specifically banned both clergy and professional missionaries, who had the responsibility for teaching and encouraging new believers and groups? When the only organization that had emerged was at the local level, how could a regional or national consciousness be fostered and resources coordinated? Who would travel to teach the faith in new areas and strengthen new communities? Who would produce and distribute literature? Who would direct such efforts? Who would finance them?

The answer to such questions was the creation of a national Bahá'í organization, a development that would have far-reaching effects on the movement's ability to establish itself in South Carolina. During the first decade of the twentieth century, local executive boards in Chicago, Washington, and New York were already attempting to foster closer communication and collaboration across the country, circulating news bulletins and group letters to 'Abdu'l-Bahá, and in 1902 a group of believers in Chicago incorporated the Bahai Publishing Society. The movement's first truly national organization was an outgrowth of another Chicago effort, the initiative to build a Bahá'í house of worship (*mashriqu'l-adhkár*, "dawning-place of the mention of God"). Inspired by a similar project undertaken by Bahá'ís in Russian Turkestan, just outside the borders of Iran, a group of Chicago women led by Corinne True asked 'Abdu'l-Bahá if they, too, could build a temple. 'Abdu'l-Bahá agreed, but he insisted that all the believers in the country should work together for its construction. In March 1909, delegates from across the country attended a national convention in Chicago, called to devise means for erecting the house of worship. They created a national organization, called the Bahai Temple Unity, to consist of representatives of each local community in North America, with an Executive Board elected annually to oversee the organization's affairs. Within the first few years of its existence the Executive Board assumed responsibility for the Bahai Publishing Society and began to coordinate teaching efforts around the country in addition to supervising the temple project. In late 1910, however, it was still a new and weak institution, with no experience and little administrative capacity to assist traveling teachers or to maintain correspondence with isolated believers.[46]

Against this backdrop of the national Bahá'í movement's rudimentary organization and its lack of substantial progress in the South for more than a decade, Louis Gregory's 1910 tour was a critical step forward. As an initial foray into a large and difficult region of the country, the trip was an unqualified success. Gregory spoke to hundreds of people about the Bahá'í Faith, secured positive press coverage on the road and at home in Washington, and reported finding many interested listeners. According to Gregory's memoir, written decades later with the experience of a seasoned traveler and speaker, people embraced the faith everywhere he went: "In every city, people were found who accepted the great Message, however crudely and abruptly given, and the spirit was powerful." A summary of the trip in the national newsletter included an assessment of black southerners' spiritual receptivity and of the prospects for growth in the region: "Eight cities or towns were visited, and in the form of free public lectures the glad-tidings were heralded directly to about nine hundred souls. Indications are that the colored people of the south will be very deeply and vitally interested. The oppression of centuries having made many of them live very close to God, to them the Holy Spirit is a reality, and if the Message is presented with fragrance, their hearts respond and often yield." But the trip also highlighted the need for a more systematic approach to the religion's expansion and consolidation. "Unfortunately," Gregory noted in his memoir with poignant hindsight, "the system of follow-up work was not then developed." Indeed, without a systematic approach to deepening new believers, those Gregory had taught were more or less on their own, as the story of Alonzo Twine indicates. If a young and relatively unorganized Bahá'í movement could not even consolidate its foothold among the Midwestern radicals at Fairhope, it is hard to imagine the herculean effort that would have been required to establish a new community in Charleston—closer by rail to Washington but socially and culturally much farther from the Bahá'í mainstream. Gregory apparently left Twine with some Bahá'í books and may have kept up correspondence with him for a time, but he would not return to Charleston in person for another six years. Given Twine's extreme isolation, it appears all the more remarkable that he stayed true to his new faith to the very end.[47]

Louis Gregory, Bahá'í Leader

For Louis Gregory, the nearly four years between his first teaching trip and the outbreak of the World War I in Europe were a time of growth, change, and pain during which he became more deeply involved in the affairs of his faith, the national Bahá'í movement made important new inroads among African Americans, and the Washington community solidified its interracial character. By the time he returned to his native South Carolina in the autumn of 1916, there was no doubt that interracial fellowship had become a permanent feature of the American Bahá'í community, nor that Louis Gregory had come to occupy a central place as an administrator, teacher, and thought leader in the movement.

In February 1911, just months after returning from the Deep South, Louis Gregory was elected to fill a vacancy in the Washington community's Working Committee. Gregory's election, by black and white believers in a local community that was still not entirely settled on an interracial identity, made him the first person of African descent to serve on a Bahá'í administrative body in the United States. It was the beginning of decades of leadership in the American Bahá'í movement. Little more than a year later, at the national convention of the Bahai Temple Unity in April 1912, he was elected to that organization's Executive Board. Although not reelected for several years afterward, he was asked to serve in additional national administrative capacities, including as a member of a committee to audit the Board's finances and a reporter on the proceedings of the annual convention. Such tasks nurtured in him a strong regional and national perspective on the progress of the Bahá'í movement, exposed him to all segments of the community, and made him well known to believers across the country—all factors that he brought to bear in subsequent teaching efforts in South Carolina and elsewhere.[48]

During 1911 and 1912, a series of profound encounters with 'Abdu'l-Bahá strengthened Louis Gregory's bond with the center of the faith and cemented him in his life's work of promoting interracial unity. In the spring of 1911, Gregory went on pilgrimage to Palestine, stopping first to meet 'Abdu'l-Bahá at his temporary residence in Alexandria. 'Abdu'l-Bahá, a political prisoner for more than half a century, had been released from confinement in 1908 after the Young Turk revolution. Now free to travel in the interests of the faith, he first sought to regain his health in Egypt, where he introduced Bahá'í history and teachings to the Arabic-language press and to Sunni Muslim intellectuals and received pilgrims en route to 'Akká. During the course of Gregory's nearly two weeks in Alexandria, 'Abdu'l-Bahá showered him with affection, answered his questions, and encouraged him to continue to teach the faith in the United States and abroad. In contrast to European imperialist scholarship, which held that Africa was a continent outside of history, 'Abdu'l-Bahá extolled the ancient black civilizations of Egypt and Ethiopia. In a further subversion of Western pseudoscience, which argued that racial mixing resulted in degeneration, 'Abdu'l-Bahá stated that blacks and whites should intermarry, indicating that it would produce strong and beautiful children and help remove misunderstandings between the groups. He inquired repeatedly about race relations in the American Bahá'í community, stating in strong terms that all Bahá'í meetings must be open to all, and that in the Bahá'í teachings above all else African Americans would find both spiritual and material progress. As if to underscore his points about the worth of people of African descent and the importance of interracial and intercultural harmony, 'Abdu'l-Bahá asked Gregory to change the route of his return trip so that he could visit the Bahá'í communities in Germany.[49]

Within the year, 'Abdu'l-Bahá had left Egypt for an extended journey to Europe and North America. From February to September 1912, he traveled by rail across the United States, addressing an astonishing number and variety of audiences, large and small, public and private. The world, he said, was on the brink of war, and the remedy to humanity's suffering was the teachings of his father. The press gave extensive coverage to his appearances, and he spoke to thousands of people of a variety of backgrounds. His greatest impact, however, was on the Bahá'ís themselves. He encouraged them, answered their questions, and clarified their understanding of important Bahá'í concepts. In particular, he stressed the importance of interracial unity and insisted that the Bahá'ís, who were as yet mostly white and northern, should spread the religion among all segments of society and in all parts of the country.[50]

'Abdu'l-Bahá's itinerary took him almost exclusively to localities where Bahá'í communities could host him and secure advance publicity, so he only skirted the South. He visited Baltimore and Washington, but an already-full schedule prevented him from responding to an invitation from the chamber of commerce in Atlanta, where a lone white believer lived. Even so, 'Abdu'l-Bahá's public and private interactions, particularly in Chicago and Washington, reinforced the Bahá'ís' commitment to building an interracial fellowship, significantly raised the religion's profile among African Americans nationally, and made the pages of southern newspapers. Louis Gregory interacted closely with 'Abdu'l-Bahá on several occasions. In Chicago, Gregory was present for 'Abdu'l-Bahá's address to the fourth annual conference of the

NAACP, which was later reprinted, with favorable commentary by W.E.B. Du Bois, in the association's widely distributed organ, the *Crisis*. In Washington, Gregory was instrumental in arranging for 'Abdu'l-Bahá to speak to large mixed audiences at Howard University's Rankin Chapel and, under the auspices of the Bethel Literary Society, at Metropolitan African Methodist Episcopal Church. 'Abdu'l-Bahá also spoke to gatherings of various sizes in the homes of several Washington Bahá'ís, black and white.[51]

In his talks, 'Abdu'l-Bahá subverted contemporary racial theory by boldly asserting the oneness of humanity and predicted that unity between blacks and whites in the United States would be a "sign of the Most Great Peace." He also turned American color imagery on its head, frequently associating African Americans with the qualities of light and purity and extolling the beauty of mixed-race gatherings. "In the clustered jewels of the races," he said to one such group, "may the blacks be as sapphires and rubies and the whites as diamonds and pearls. The composite beauty of humanity will be witnessed in their unity and blending. How glorious the spectacle of real unity among mankind!" On another occasion, as the guest of honor at a luncheon with some of Washington's white elite, 'Abdu'l-Bahá brushed aside race and class conventions by rearranging the place cards at the table and inviting Louis Gregory to sit at his right hand. One witness recalled: "He stated He was very pleased to have Mr. Gregory there, and then, in the most natural way as if nothing unusual had happened, proceeded to give a talk on the oneness of mankind." Although he did not venture in person south of the Potomac, black and white southern newspapers ensured that news of 'Abdu'l-Bahá's tour, and of the Bahá'í teachings on the oneness of humanity, reached such cities as Greensboro, Charlotte, Augusta, and Savannah.[52]

'Abdu'l-Bahá's visit also brought about a profound change in Louis Gregory's personal life, as he discovered that 'Abdu'l-Bahá's advocacy of interracial marriage was more than theoretical. During his pilgrimage the previous year, 'Abdu'l-Bahá had encouraged a friendship between Gregory and English fellow pilgrim Louisa Mathew, "a lady," Gregory later recalled, "whose long range of accomplishments and great devotion to the Faith claimed admiration." Mathew, called Louise by her friends, was now among the small group of Bahá'ís who had accompanied 'Abdu'l-Bahá to North America, and he gently suggested that the two should marry. In September 1912, while 'Abdu'l-Bahá was visiting the West Coast, Gregory and Mathew were joined in the first interracial marriage in the American Bahá'í community, and they took up residence together in Washington. The District of Columbia, along with eighteen of the forty-eight states, had no restriction on interracial marriage, but the practice was far from accepted. Only three months after the Gregorys' wedding, black prizefighter Jack Johnson's highly publicized marriage to a white woman in Chicago stirred a national controversy. In its wake, eleven additional states and the District of Columbia attempted to pass anti-miscegenation laws, and the NAACP mounted an energetic lobbying campaign to ensure the bills' defeat. Other forms of interracial association were becoming increasingly difficult as well. In 1913, under the new presidential administration of southern-born Democrat Woodrow Wilson, the trend of segregating black and white federal employees, already underway in some departments during previous Republican administrations, accelerated. Louis Gregory appears to have been among the large number of black employees who resigned from the Treasury Department in protest. Gregory went back to private law practice and started a real estate business, neither of which proved particularly successful.[53]

As the federal government and the states sought to extend and consolidate Jim Crow, within Washington's Bahá'í community the Gregorys found themselves in the middle of a renewed conflict over issues of race and class. According to explicit instructions received from 'Abdu'l-Bahá, every Unity Feast—not just every fourth one—was now conducted on a completely integrated basis. That is, the official monthly meeting of Bahá'í believers in the city brooked no racial distinction. Disagreement remained, however, over how to conduct meetings for inquirers, both in public halls and in private homes. One group of black and white believers, encouraged by 'Abdu'l-Bahá's bold demonstrations of social equality during his visits to the city, wanted all Bahá'í meetings to be open to everyone. A small group of whites, insisting that "mixed meetings were the one serious obstacle to the growth of the Cause in this locality," wanted to be able to have teaching meetings—including those held in public spaces and advertised in the papers—for whites only. A larger group of whites was unsure how to proceed. As Louise Gregory confided to another Washington believer, she and her husband often acted "the difficult part of peacemaker, explaining the difficulties of the white people to the colored & the point of view of the colored people to the white." Louis Gregory recalled some of the challenges—social, practical, and conceptual—surrounding the issue:

> Some of the friends, reading the command of Baha'u'llah which read: "Close your eyes to racial differences and welcome all with the light of oneness," interpreted it to mean that all barriers of race should be put aside in every meeting that was planned for teaching the Faith.

Others knew the principle was wise and just, but felt that the time was not yet ripe for its application. One difficulty was finding places, either private or public, that were willing to welcome all races. In the same family, one or more members being Baha'i and the others not believers, the mixing of races would cause a family disturbance. Even where all the believers were free from prejudices some felt that it would upset inquirers after the truth if they were confronted too soon with signs of racial equality. One of the friends went so far as to state that some of the Baha'i principles would not be operative for a full thousand years! On the other hand, others were [insistent] that such principles should be upheld and applied even though the world should go to smash.[54]

In May 1914, one of the Washington Bahá'ís received a tablet from 'Abdu'l-Bahá addressing the situation. "I know about everything that is happening in Washington," he wrote. "The sad, somber news is the difference between the white and the colored people." He suggested the creation of three public meetings for seekers: one for whites, one for blacks, and a mixed one for "those who do not wish to bind themselves either way." In the absence of unity among the believers, he said, "I can see no better solution to this problem."[55]

'Abdu'l-Bahá's intervention failed immediately to create a consensus, and for a few months several separate meetings for inquirers threatened to degenerate into virtually autonomous Bahá'í communities. Then, late in the year, when the Ottoman Empire entered the Great War on the side of the Central Powers, communication with 'Abdu'l-Bahá in Palestine was abruptly severed. Without further instructions from the head of the faith, the Washington believers were left to resolve the crisis themselves. The impasse continued for more than a year until, in the spring of 1916, the community adopted a new policy. As Louis Gregory put it: "The decision was reached that meetings for teaching which were publicly advertised through the press should welcome and teach any who responded, regardless of race. On the other hand those holding private meetings for contacting and teaching their friends might use their own discretion about bringing the races together where such a step seemed premature." By requiring that all advertised meetings for inquirers be held on an interracial basis (despite the practical difficulty of securing venues for mixed gatherings), the plan ensured that the official stance of the Washington Bahá'í community—and not just a particular segment of it—would be one of commitment to interracial fellowship. At the same time, it provided for flexibility in the face of the realities of living in a Jim Crow city. When individual believers wished to invite their personal acquaintances to their own homes to share the faith, they could "use their own discretion about bringing the races together" based on their own family circumstances and knowledge of the seeker's background and expectations. In effect, the Bahá'ís would continue to identify themselves clearly as an interracial community, while providing for the fact that not every interested seeker (white or black) would be comfortable in mixed settings *prior* to having encountered the faith and being transformed by it. While unresolved feelings likely persisted after implementation of the new policy, the Washington Bahá'ís had passed through a severe test and come out firmly on the side of social equality and complete integration. In subsequent decades, the model they pioneered of how to build an interracial fellowship within a segregated city would be applied in localities in South Carolina and across the South. Indeed, Louis Gregory did not wait for the situation in Washington to be completely resolved before embarking on his second teaching trip to the South, spending about two weeks in the autumn of 1915 in Nashville and Atlanta. In Nashville, where he had been an undergraduate student at Fisk, Gregory introduced the faith to his many professional and personal contacts, and in Atlanta, he supported the efforts of the city's lone believer, a young white man from Minneapolis who had begun to attract a circle of black and white seekers.[56]

From the perspective of the post–civil rights movement era, the achievement of the early Washington Bahá'ís might seem modest, but it should not be underestimated. That it took some of the white Bahá'ís several years to fully embrace the idea of interracial fellowship should come as no surprise: the Washington believers were struggling to create an interracial faith community at a time when majority public opinion and governmental policy at all levels were both running in precisely the opposite direction. Given the pervasiveness of white supremacy, nothing but the persistence of 'Abdu'l-Bahá and the consciences of individual Bahá'ís kept Jim Crow ideas and practices from taking hold in a nascent faith community. 'Abdu'l-Bahá's vision, supported by those of his followers who understood his instructions and were willing to act on them, was to make of the Washington believers an organization that was without real precedent in American religious history. Rather than promoting limited or occasional contact between autonomous white and black congregations (such as working on a common charitable project) as was the practice in some Christian denominations, 'Abdu'l-Bahá insisted that all the Bahá'ís in the city constitute a single, unified body, in which members of diverse racial backgrounds would interact on terms of complete equality in all their public and private affairs: worship, study, teaching, community governance, social activities, service, and even the personal domains of marriage and family life. In an era bound by hierarchies of race, class, and gender, he was calling the Baháʼís of Washington to be an example of the erasure of such distinctions, to forge a new collective identity based on ultimate loyalty to the whole human race. As a diverse and cosmopolitan urban center with a large black population, Washington was perhaps an ideal location for the faith's first attempts at interracial community-building. As it resolved questions of how to grow on an interracial basis within a segregated society, the Washington community became home to the American Baháʼí movement's first black man elected to an administrative body, its first interracial marriage, and its first fully integrated Feasts, teaching activities, and social and economic development initiatives, including a weekly Sunday school for children, an annual summer conference at nearby Colonial Beach, Virginia, and the Persian-American Educational Society, a charitable organization that sent teachers and health professionals to assist the persecuted Baháʼí community in Iran. Neither black nor white believers in Washington had any direct social or material benefits to gain from integration; indeed, there could be much to lose. They were venturing into uncomfortable, uncharted territory essentially out of devotion to the head of their religion, who insisted that interracial unity was a vital matter of spiritual principle. Their responses to the demands of their faith resulted in a collective understanding of essential Baháʼí teachings and practices that indelibly shaped the character of the national Baháʼí movement and set important precedents for the religion's expansion in South Carolina and other southern states.[57]

The Divine Plan, the Great War, and Progressive-Era Racial Politics, 1914–1921

During the years surrounding World War I, Baháʾí teachers across the United States sensed a heightened receptivity to their message. Inspired by the Tablets of the Divine Plan, a fresh mandate from ʿAbduʾl-Bahá for spreading the faith throughout North America, they worked with more urgency and better coordination than before along several lines at once: teaching the faith and attempting to establish local Baháʾí communities in the South; promoting the Baháʾí vision of interracial unity to broad national audiences; and supporting the work of other emerging interracial organizations, in the South and across the country. Due primarily to the efforts of Louis Gregory, South Carolina figured in all three developments. During the war years, Gregory and other traveling teachers in South Carolina encountered an African American community energized by wartime upheavals to press for full citizenship rights as well as a tentative new interracial movement that sought to mitigate the worst abuses of the Jim Crow system. They cultivated important relationships in both areas, initiating Baháʾí efforts to influence public discourse and to effect social change in South Carolina that would continue for many years. In the Augusta metropolitan area on the South Carolina–Georgia border, where a lone believer had taken up residence in 1910 and where Louis Gregory probably visited the same year, the wartime era was a time of slow, persistent community-building (discussed in chapter 3), but beyond the Augusta suburbs of North Augusta and Aiken, the war years appear to not have witnessed the emergence of new Baháʾí groups in South Carolina, despite repeated and extensive visits by Louis Gregory and others. Indeed, many of the same factors that resulted in a violent backlash against black political activists and made the incipient interracial movement quite cautious in its demands also hardened the state's soil against the growth of an indigenous Bahá'í movement. Nevertheless, during the war years Bahá'í traveling teachers built important relationships that would bear fruit in subsequent decades.

Introducing the Divine Plan

The proper framework for understanding the Bahá'ís' wartime efforts in teaching, community-building, and public discourse—and the place of South Carolina in such efforts—comes from 'Abdu'l-Bahá's influence on the priorities of the American Bahá'í movement. In the years leading up to the outbreak of the Great War in Europe, one of the dominant themes in 'Abdu'l-Bahá's relationship with the American Bahá'ís was teaching the faith. He repeatedly emphasized the subject of teaching in countless tablets to individual believers, groups, and fledgling local executive bodies, and he frequently discussed it with American pilgrims, whose notes were often circulated widely upon their return home. In addition, 'Abdu'l-Bahá's extended visit in 1912 provided a major impetus to the growth of the faith in the United States. In his public addresses, he articulated a compelling summary of the social and spiritual teachings of the faith and accelerated the Bahá'ís' contact with liberal religious groups and progressive organizations. By closely observing their leader's approach, many Bahá'ís gained greater proficiency in teaching, and through his encouragement, many individuals were inspired to make greater efforts of their own. Between 1906 and 1916, the number of Bahá'ís in the United States more than doubled to nearly three thousand, with most of the increase occurring in the wake of 'Abdu'l-Bahá's visit. And the size of the Bahá'í community itself did not tell the whole story. There were also "large numbers," the Bahá'ís reported to the census bureau, "who attend Bahá'í meetings and are closely identified with the movement, but have not discontinued their connection with the churches."[1]

'Abdu'l-Bahá counseled urgency in spreading the faith, in part, he said, because the world was perilously close to a disastrous conflict and needed desperately the remedy of Bahá'u'lláh's teachings. During his stay in California, for example, 'Abdu'l-Bahá described Europe as "a storehouse of explosives ready for ignition," for which agitation in the Balkans would provide the probable first spark. In a talk at Stanford University, he associated the coming war with the apocalyptic vision of Christian scripture: "We are on the eve of the battle of Armageddon, referred to in the 16th chapter of Revelation. The time is two years hence, when only a spark will set aflame the whole of Europe. The social unrest in all countries, the growing religious skepticism, antecedent to the millennium, are already here. Only a spark will set aflame the whole of Europe as is prophesied in the verses of Daniel and in the Book of John." But 'Abdu'l-Bahá did not dwell on ancient prophecies. To a Montreal journalist he stated that war in Europe was a practical certainty: "All Europe is an armed camp. These warlike preparations will necessarily culminate in a great war. The very armaments themselves are productive of war. This great arsenal must go ablaze. There is nothing of the nature of prophecy about such a view. . . . It is based on reasoning solely." In March 1914, the editors of *Star of the West*, the national Bahá'í magazine, echoed 'Abdu'l-Bahá's concern. They associated 1914, "the seventieth year of the Millennium" (i.e., since the Báb's declaration of his mission in 1844), with the seventieth year of the Christian era, when the Temple of Jerusalem was destroyed and the Jews scattered. They said it would be a significant year in the "culmination of the old order of things," and humanity would be "swept by conflicting emotions and tend to go to extremes." The responsibility of the Bahá'ís, they held, was to teach: "In the midst of such crucial conditions the Bahais are called upon to proclaim the glad tidings of the Kingdom come on earth, and to manifest the characteristics of the people of the Most Great Peace. The Center of the Covenant, Abdu'l Baha, is calling souls to travel and spread the Message of the Kingdom far and wide. It is the spirit of the hour."[2]

Within months, 'Abdu'l-Bahá's dire predictions seemed to be materializing. The assassination of the heir to the Austro-Hungarian throne in Sarajevo provided the "spark" to which he had referred, and by August, the whole continent was "ablaze" with a conflict of awesome destructiveness that shocked the world. In the United States, the administration of President Woodrow Wilson sought to maintain a difficult neutrality as both British and German naval forces targeted American civilian vessels in the North Sea, and the disruption of trade with Europe brought an economic downturn and fears of a depression. The American Bahá'ís felt the economic effects of the war immediately. In early 1915, for example, the national convention of the Bahai Temple Unity approved a new plan to finance part-time traveling teachers, but a lack of funds prevented its full implementation; that fall, when Louis Gregory set out on his second teaching trip to the South, it was, like the first, at his own expense. While the economy soon recovered with the beginning of wartime production for the Allies, a far more devastating effect of the war on the American Bahá'ís was the virtual severing of communication with 'Abdu'l-Bahá. When the Ottoman Empire joined the Central Powers in the autumn of 1914, 'Abdu'l-Bahá's imprisonment was renewed. For a period of nearly four years, only a few letters found their way in or out of Haifa, and the flow of pilgrims came to a halt. Only after September 1918, when British forces captured Haifa in the Battle of Megiddo, could the Bahá'ís communicate regularly with their leader.[3]

Given these circumstances, it was a welcome surprise when, in the summer of 1916, five individuals received tablets from 'Abdu'l-Bahá addressed to the Bahá'ís of the northeastern, central, western, and southern regions of the United States and of Canada, respectively. They were quickly published in *Star of the West* under the title "Tablets of the Divine Plan." The letters represented a further intervention by the head of the faith to accelerate the process of growth, calling the believers in North America to spare no effort in spreading their religion to all parts of the continent. In each of the five tablets, 'Abdu'l-Bahá specifically named states and provinces with few or no Bahá'ís and directed teachers to travel to those parts to establish the faith. Throughout the tablets he mentioned the spiritual qualities that the teachers must have and promised divine assistance in their efforts. He also reminded the believers that he had urged them to action well before the outbreak of the world war; in his tablet to the western states he directed them to refer to his published talks on the subject so that they might "fully realize that *this is the time* for the diffusion of the fragrances."[4]

'Abdu'l-Bahá's tablet for the South was sent in the care of Joseph Hannen in Washington. While addressed to "the friends and maid-servants of God in the Southern States," for all practical purposes it was meant for the region's only two functioning local Bahá'í communities, in Washington and Baltimore. Calling the believers "heralds of the Kingdom of God," 'Abdu'l-Bahá assured them of divine assistance in the work of spreading the faith throughout the South. They would certainly need it. Unlike the tablets to some of the other regions, 'Abdu'l-Bahá named all sixteen states in the South as requiring attention, and he left little ambiguity that the Washington community—by far the largest and best organized in the region and the one to which the tablet had been mailed—would be responsible for a concerted effort: "In the southern states of the United States, the friends are few, that is, in Delaware, Maryland, Virginia, West Virginia, North Carolina, South Carolina, Georgia, Florida, Alabama, Mississippi, Tennessee, Kentucky, Louisiana, Arkansas, Oklahoma, and Texas. Consequently, you must either go yourselves or send a number of blessed souls to those states, so that they may guide the people to the kingdom of heaven." Joseph Hannen, the secretary of the Washington community's Working Committee, became the regional teaching coordinator, and within a few weeks of the tablets' publication Louis Gregory and two other believers were on the road.[5]

Between late October and late December 1916, Gregory visited fourteen of the sixteen southern states, including South Carolina, speaking mainly in churches, schools, and colleges. Back home in Washington, he reported that during the entire trip "probably more than fifteen thousand people were reached directly, most of them students, representing many sections and communities." Receptivity to the message was high. "So slight was the opposition," Gregory wrote, "even in the ranks of the clergy, as to be not worthy of mention." In a Memphis meeting, for example, "over fifty persons, all in sight save one, after hearing the message and proofs, arose and said the Greatest Name." "Without exception," Gregory added, "souls were found ready in cities where the message was given." One result of his trip, he noted, was an invitation to return to Charleston, South Carolina, on January 1 to make the keynote speech for the city's Emancipation Day celebration. "This will be an opportunity," he wrote, "to tell them of real freedom."[6]

As Gregory's experience indicates, during the early twentieth century many black southerners were receptive to the Bahá'í message; apparently individuals became Bahá'ís in every city he visited, including Charleston and elsewhere in South Carolina. Yet, as in the case of Alonzo Twine following Gregory's 1910 trip, serious cultural and structural impediments remained that stalled the emergence of local Bahá'í communities in South Carolina. The key to understanding these apparently contradictory phenomena—individual spiritual receptivity on the one hand and slowness of group formation on the other—is the Jim Crow system. When Louis Gregory visited South Carolina during and after World War I, he encountered a white supremacist regime at the height of its power and tenacity. Aimed at keeping political and economic control in the hands of the state's white elite, the system rested on the pillars of political disfranchisement, racial segregation, and violence. By the time the war had begun, Jim Crow's most important legal provisions were in place and a host of associated social practices firmly entrenched. In such a stifling environment, the Bahá'í message represented—at least to the largely urban, educated African American audiences to which Louis Gregory had the readiest and safest access—both an affirmation of their ancestral religious impulses and an encouragement of their contemporary strivings for racial justice, even if they did not become believers as Alonzo Twine had. Aspects of the faith's teachings appealed to some white Progressives as well. But in wartime South Carolina, the faith's uncompromising interracialism—already on display in the Washington, D.C., Bahá'í community—probably limited its opportunities for substantial growth and local community-building. What little positive interracial contact there was in the state took place on terms almost exclusively dictated by whites, and when black and white community leaders did work together it was to advocate a moderation of the system's cruelest features, not to question its fundamental assumptions as the Bahá'ís did. Even though Louis Gregory asserted after his fall 1916 trip that "souls were found ready" and accepted the faith in Charleston and the other cities he visited, in the context of pervasive racial polarization and violence apparently few South Carolinians, black or white, could be found willing to identify themselves openly with the Bahá'í Faith's radicalism or, if they did, to withstand the intense social pressures that would have attended such a stand. Moreover, as the circumstances of American involvement in the Great War stimulated black South Carolinians to a new wave of political organizing, the nonpartisan and nonconfrontational character of Bahá'í activism may have limited its immediate appeal to the socially conscious audiences who heard Gregory and other Bahá'í teachers.

White Supremacy and Black Accommodation in South Carolina

As challenging as it had been to create and sustain an interracial fellowship in the relatively cosmopolitan, reasonably safe atmosphere of turn-of-the-century Washington, Bahá'í teachers in wartime South Carolina faced a Jim Crow regime that was powerful, pervasive, and violent. Born in the late nineteenth century amid the upheavals associated with urbanization, industrialization, and rural decline, South Carolina's Jim Crow system was still relatively new during the era of the Great War, but its defenders were many and confident, its effects broad and deep. In the face of such militant and effective white supremacy, black leaders in South Carolina during the early twentieth century could often do little more than hold their communities together while attempting to mitigate the effects of segregation, discrimination, and violence. In such an environment, there was precious little room for the Bahá'ís—or anyone else brash enough to attempt it—to establish and nurture meaningful, egalitarian bonds across the racial divide. To understand the slowness with which the Bahá'ís established new communities in South Carolina in the decade or more after Louis Gregory's 1910 teaching trip—and to appreciate the progress, however limited, that Bahá'í teachers were able to make despite great difficulties—a closer look at the shape of the Jim Crow system that they faced in South Carolina is indispensable.

The immediate background for the emergence of Jim Crow in South Carolina was wrenching social and economic change. During the 1880s and 1890s, falling cotton prices, spiraling debts, and depleted and eroded soils drove hard-pressed farm families to leave the land. Local boosters, particularly in the hard-hit Piedmont, invested in textile mills as a sure means of economic development, civic improvement, and sustenance for impoverished rural folk—whites only, with few exceptions. New towns sprang up overnight, and existing ones grew, as textile companies built housing for workers—called "operatives"—around the factories. While they offered former farming families many advantages over life in the countryside, the mill villages became the locus of rising tensions of race, class, and gender that had far-reaching social and political consequences. Many men in mill communities felt an acute loss of personal autonomy as they watched their wives and children become wage earners, and as families were increasingly exposed to consumer culture and the mass media. For well-to-do whites, the rapid shift of so many white families from agriculture to industry was a mixed blessing. "Town people," many of whom had invested in the development of the textile industry in the first place, came to see "mill people" as a potential threat to social order, whose interests as a class might differ markedly from those of the wealthy farmers and businessmen who, regardless of factional disputes within the Democratic Party, dominated local and state politics. During the early twentieth century, under the banner of a nationwide Progressive movement, South Carolina's town people campaigned to "clean up" the mill villages, while many operatives resented what they perceived as meddling in their families' affairs.[7]

As a wrenching urban-industrial transformation exposed cleavages among white South Carolinians, any evidence of black progress or political influence was particularly galling. African Americans were hit harder than whites by the regionwide agricultural downturn and shut out of most textile employment, but rates of black landownership and literacy, while low overall, increased steadily during the late nineteenth century. Blacks were a numerical majority in three-fourths of the state's counties, and in the larger towns, a proliferation of black churches, schools, colleges, businesses, and fraternal and benevolent societies provided a vibrant community life. In the main cities of Charleston and Columbia, blacks enjoyed substantially equal access to public accommodations such as street cars and theaters. Despite the fall of the state's Reconstruction government in 1876–1877 and the imposition of voting restrictions and gerrymandering during the 1880s, black voters still turned out at the polls, and a few black men continued to hold elected or appointed offices. Against such conspicuous evidence of black social and economic progress and political tenacity, the need to establish and defend white supremacy was one of the few points on which South Carolina's white mill people, town people, and planter elites could all agree, and white men worked energetically to shore up their authority over their own wives and children as much as over African Americans.[8]

In fact, issues of gender and sexuality were intimately intertwined with public discussions of race. During the late nineteenth and early twentieth centuries, white South Carolinians became increasingly preoccupied with what they perceived as an upsurge of black insolence, vice, and crime, especially sexual assault against white women. Although South Carolina's black majority surely made the white population more nervous than their counterparts in states with different demographics, their basic racial assumptions were shared by most white Americans. According to popular discourse—propagated nationwide by the Dunning School of historical scholarship centered at Columbia University, for example—under slavery, when the foundations of the South's racial hierarchy were secure, sexual assault by blacks had been nonexistent. Only during Reconstruction, when the natural order was temporarily reversed by extending the franchise to black men, had they begun to desire "social equality" with whites, that is, informal mixing in public or private settings such as schools, churches, entertainment venues, and public transportation. Social equality had supposedly aroused in black men the desire for sexual access to white women—the ultimate challenge to white male supremacy. Indeed, in the late nineteenth and early twentieth centuries, the term "social equality" was usually a euphemism for forced sexual liaisons between black men and white women. Borrowing from popular social Darwinist thought, many white opinion leaders believed that "miscegenation" or race-mixing would degrade the Anglo-Saxon people and undermine American civilization itself. In scholarly literature, the press, and popular entertainment, black men were increasingly portrayed as incapable of disciplining their carnal desires. In such a charged environment, virtually any kind of transgression (real or imagined) by a black man could be construed as having sexual overtones, regardless of the actual victim.[9]

All these factors help explain the emergence of a new white supremacy campaign in South Carolina during the 1890s. The principal architect of the state's Jim Crow order was Benjamin Ryan Tillman, a prosperous Edgefield County farmer and politician who rose to prominence through leadership of the state's Farmers' Alliance. In 1890, Tillman used his control over the farmers' movement to wrest control of the Democratic Party from the Lowcountry planter elite, which had run South Carolina virtually unchallenged since the colonial period. Although he handily won the governorship, the old guard's last-ditch appeal to the state's remaining black voters had left Tillman with a determination to eliminate blacks from public life once and for all. In 1895, after the legislature had elected him to the U.S. Senate, Tillman arranged for a state constitutional convention with the principal objective of disfranchising blacks. Over the objections of a handful of black delegates, the convention produced a document that included additional suffrage restrictions—a strict residency requirement, a poll tax, and a literacy test—that leaned most heavily on rural African Americans without directly running afoul of the Fifteenth Amendment. In elections the following year, black voting declined precipitously. As effective as the suffrage restrictions were, however, violence—sponsored or condoned by the state and supported by white leaders of thought—was necessary to eliminate blacks from politics completely. In 1898, the next election year, a white mob in Lake City, a hamlet in the Pee Dee, assassinated their black postmaster and one of his children and twice burned down the post office; on Election Day in the Piedmont county of Greenwood, rampaging whites left at least seven blacks and one white dead around the hamlet of Phoenix after a local white Republican attempted to collect the signatures of black men who had been prevented from voting. In 1900, whites in coastal Georgetown County, supported by state militia units from Sumter and Charleston, staged a coup that brought down the state's last biracial local government, a "fusion" arrangement in which white Democrats and black and white Republicans had agreed to share city and county offices. The year of the Georgetown violence, only ten thousand black men in the state, about a tenth of those eligible, were registered voters; of these, only two thousand or so dared to go to the polls. South Carolina's last black legislator for three-quarters of a century, a representative from Georgetown County, left office when his term expired two years later.[10]

With South Carolina's black citizens shut out of politics, whites of various class backgrounds united in an effort to expand and codify racial segregation. Often couched in the language of the Progressive movement, segregation was accomplished through a patchwork of unwritten codes of interpersonal behavior, official and unofficial business practices, and state and local ordinances. In particular, segregation laws and practices policed the behavior of black men, discouraging any expressions of social equality with white men and minimizing opportunities for contact with white women, particularly in urban and industrial environments. South Carolina's Constitution of 1895 codified the state's already universal practice of segregating public schools (otherwise, whites feared, friendships in childhood would lead to sexual liaisons later) and confirmed an earlier statutory prohibition of interracial marriage. With the blessing of the U.S. Supreme Court in *Plessy v. Ferguson* (1896), a host of other state and local laws followed that required, for example, segregated railway cars and train stations, steamboats and ferries, city streetcars, and state militia units. In 1912 in the Piedmont textile center of Greenville, the city council mandated residential and commercial segregation by designating all-white and all-black blocks; in other towns, blacks were confined to separate neighborhoods, often in the least desirable locations, by informal means. In 1915, the South Carolina General Assembly passed the Factory Law, which effectively shut textile mill production rooms—already full of white women and children employees—to blacks, making it clear that the state's leading industry and surest route to the middle class was for whites only.[11]

While the rhetoric of South Carolina's Progressives appealed to reason, order, and good governance, in fact the maintenance of white social and economic dominance depended on corruption and violence. The legal system provided one means of control. State and local laws regarding vagrancy, civil disorder, contracts, crop liens, and mortgages strongly disfavored blacks, and black men—mostly those who were young, rural, poor, and marginally literate—were disproportionately convicted for misdemeanors and felonies and sentenced more harshly than their white counterparts. Prisoners were routinely subjected to inadequate food, shelter, and medical care; overwork; and brutal corporal punishment. Nor was official violence alone sufficient. Between 1900 and 1915, at least sixty blacks—mostly men who demonstrated political or economic independence or violated racial mores—died at the hands of lynch mobs in the state, an average of one nearly every four months, and there were almost as many reported lynching attempts. In other words, in a state as small as South Carolina most blacks in the early twentieth century must have known, or at least known of, someone who had been the victim of racial violence. Lynching and rioting received the blessing—overt or tacit—of South Carolina's white politicians, newspaper editors, prominent businessmen, and Christian clergymen. Governor Coleman Livingston Blease, one of the state's most prominent and vocal advocates of lynching, once pledged to resign his office and lead the mob himself if local whites in the Piedmont town of Honea Path failed to lynch the supposed attacker of a white girl. Even on the floor of the U.S. Senate, Ben Tillman defended lynching in provocative terms that placed an alleged black rapist outside the pale of humanity, saying that he had "sinned against the Holy Ghost," "invaded the holy of holies," and struck the "most deadly and cruel" blow to civilization. When a white leader did speak out against lynching, it was usually less out of concern for the black victims than for what extralegal violence might do to the moral fiber—and the reputation abroad—of white South Carolinians. In 1906, for example, Governor Duncan Clinch Heyward, easily the most refined of the state's Progressive-era governors, arrived on the scene of the impending lynching of Bob Davis, who was accused of assaulting two teenage girls (one black and one white) in Greenwood County. Even Heyward agreed that Davis was a "black devil and fiend of hell"; it was only for the sake of "the supremacy and the majesty of the law" that he appealed to the local whites to allow a proper trial. Out of consideration for the governor, the mob decided to shoot Davis rather than burn him alive.[12]

Faced with disfranchisement, segregation, and overwhelming violence, black leaders in South Carolina in the two decades between the advent of Jim Crow and the beginning of World War I had precious little room to maneuver. Caught between the social, economic, and political needs of their people and the necessity of cooperation with the regime in power, most African American community leaders adopted a public stance of deference to whites and acceptance of the system while emphasizing blacks' responsibility to improve their own lot. Taking their cue from Booker T. Washington, the charismatic founder of Tuskegee Institute in Alabama and the most prominent black public figure in the country, most of South Carolina's black leaders in the early twentieth century articulated a doctrine of racial uplift that held up self-discipline, practical education, and economic development as moral and religious duties—and the surest way to ensure fair treatment from whites. Of these, the most influential was Rev. Richard Carroll of Columbia (ca. 1859–1929), whom whites sometimes referred to as South Carolina's Booker T. Washington. Like Washington, Carroll's philosophy was a potent combination of Protestant orthodoxy, materialism, and racial accommodation, making him a bulwark, if partially unwitting and unwilling, of white supremacy. Also like Washington, Carroll's life embodied the story of racial uplift. Born a slave in Barnwell County just before the Civil War, Carroll worked his way through school at Benedict Institute (later Benedict College) in Columbia and went on to become an itinerant minister for the Home Mission Board of the Southern Baptist Convention, the largest white denomination in the region, and to found an industrial home for orphaned and wayward black children, a newspaper, and an employment agency. In 1907 he inaugurated a series of annual "race conferences" that, for more than a decade, would draw representatives of South Carolina's black elite to Columbia to hear black and white speakers discuss the amelioration of the "Negro problem." Throughout his career, he was a frequent contributor to white newspapers. Indeed, Carroll held the ear of white South Carolina as did no other black man in the state, often making it necessary for other black leaders to curry his favor and constraining their ability to openly criticize the Jim Crow regime.[13]

Richard Carroll and his allies encouraged black South Carolinians to make the best of segregation by building up their own farms, businesses, and community institutions—and by staying clear of politics, legal challenges to Jim Crow, and "friction with the white race." Sometimes Carroll was even more frank than Washington in his disavowal of civil rights and his embrace of materialism. In 1905, for example, he advised blacks: "If voting antagonizes the white man, if voting will retard the progress of the race, then do not vote. Let the white man do the voting. Let us get the cash." Against a backdrop of widespread racial violence, Carroll disavowed any claim to social equality with whites, blaming lynching on "colored and white lawbreakers, who practice 'social equality' in the darkness." Race riots, he argued, could be traced to "the dens, dives, gambling places, and houses of ill-fame, where negroes and white men meet." Addressing whites on the occasion of the opening of his children's home in 1899, Carroll succinctly linked the concepts of political, economic, and social equality—and renounced black South Carolinians' claims to all three: "We do not ask you to put us in your homes, but to help us get homes. We do not ask to get into your church pews, but to help us build churches. We do not ask to get into your school houses, but want you to help us build schools. We do not want intermarriage with your race, but want you to help us produce women of our race. (They are all colors, and we are satisfied.) We do not ask you to let us run the government, but ask you to see that the government gives us justice. We do not ask you to give us '40 acres and a mule,' but a chance to buy and time to pay." Carroll was not the only church leader who put a religious stamp on Booker T. Washington's doctrine of racial uplift. Many black ministers and prominent laypeople were quick to blame their own communities for crime, lawlessness, drinking, and sexual immorality and loath to criticize whites or the Jim Crow system they had created. Even when they denounced lynching, denominational leaders pointed the finger at blacks, not whites. In 1904, for example, a committee of the state conference of the African Methodist Episcopal Church urged black South Carolinians to "deplore both lynching and the crime which sometimes provokes it, rid ourselves of the fiends, and help to promote better relations between the races." According to these leading churchmen, the cause of lynching was not white paranoia and viciousness but a moral failure of the entire African American population.[14]

At best, black leaders—including clergymen, schoolteachers, college professors, clubwomen, and businesspeople—had to ply an uneasy course between accommodation and protest, choosing their issues and their language carefully. For example, the South Carolina Federation of Colored Women's Clubs, formed in 1909, placed itself firmly within the sphere of racial uplift ideology with the motto "Lifting as We Climb" and focused its attention inward, on education and health care programs in African American communities. In 1910, when a group of prominent educators appealed to the South Carolina Department of Education for modest improvements in the state's underfunded black schools, they were careful to assure white officials of their "conservative spirit and judgment." Their modest petition requested more money for libraries and school buildings, more vocational education, additional summer schools for black teachers, and a black supervisor of rural schools who, they insisted, would work "by permission, and under the control of the state superintendent." In sum, during the early twentieth century South Carolina's black leaders, religious and secular, sought minor adjustments to the white supremacist industrial order rather than calling the system itself into question.[15]

Conciliatory rhetoric aside, the harsh realities of African American life in Progressive-era South Carolina eventually forced even Richard Carroll to admit the futility of his self-help theology. He expressed disillusionment with white South Carolinians' opposition to voting rights even for black men (such as himself) who could meet the stringent registration requirements, and he was alarmed at the lack of personal safety afforded blacks, high and low alike. One graphic demonstration of the limits of Carroll's brand of racial uplift was the lynching of Anthony Crawford in 1916. Born to slaves in the last year of the Civil War, Crawford was a husband and father, a successful cotton farmer, and the secretary of his local church congregation near Abbeville in South Carolina's lower Piedmont. As one contemporary observer noted, "Anthony Crawford's life and character embodied everything that Booker T. Washington held to be virtuous in a Negro." In the autumn of 1916, however, those very qualities became Crawford's undoing. After arguing with a white storeowner over the price of cotton, Crawford was arrested and put in jail, supposedly for his own protection, but a white mob broke into the jail and beat him to death. Tying a rope around the neck, they dragged Crawford's corpse through the black sections of town, hung it from a tree at the county fairgrounds, and finally emptied some two hundred rounds of ammunition into the lifeless form. A meeting of white citizens ordered Crawford's family to leave town within three weeks, but "cooler heads" prevailed and the family remained. A coroner's jury found that Crawford had died "at the hands of parties unknown."[16]

Some leading Progressives condemned the Crawford lynching, but in his justification of the mob's actions the editor of the *Abbeville Scimitar* probably came closer to capturing the mood across white South Carolina: "The 'best people' of South Carolina know that when white men cease to whip, or kill negroes who become obnoxious, that they will take advantage of the laxity, and soon make this state untenable for whites of ALL kinds. . . . The point here made is, that no matter who actually killed Crawford, the responsibility for his death rests upon us ALL ALIKE, and because of his own reckless course, due to chest inflation from wealth, it was inevitable and RACIALLY JUSTIFIABLE." For Richard Carroll and other blacks, the Crawford lynching—and whites' energetic defense of it—made it clear that no black person, regardless of wealth, education, or moral uprightness, was safe in South Carolina. Indeed, Anthony Crawford's death showed that these very markers of respectability, not supposed sexual aggression, were often the real causes of white violence. "Our people," Richard Carroll told the editor of the *State* in the wake of the Crawford lynching, "are restless, more so now, than I have ever known them."[17]

Wartime Black Activism and White Reactions

The "restlessness" that Richard Carroll identified in the autumn of 1916 only increased with U.S. involvement in the Great War. Many black South Carolinians saw in wartime mobilization their greatest opportunity in a generation to press for full citizenship rights and to dismantle the Jim Crow system. Economic dislocation, persistent discrimination in the state's war industries and preparedness efforts, participation by thousands of young black men in military service overseas, and the stirring rhetoric of fighting a war "to make the world safe for democracy" all combined to contribute to a new wave of protest by black South Carolinians. For their part, whites were anxious to harness black energies for the war effort but adamant about preserving Jim Crow. "Truth is," the editor of the *State* confided to his diary just prior to the U.S. declaration of war, "the people of the South—and of the United States—have no idea of conceding to the negroes the full rights of American freedmen in this year of our Lord 1917." Indeed, black organizing and protest during and immediately after the war prompted a violent white crackdown in defense of Jim Crow. In turn, the violence inspired moderate whites to organize an interracial effort to mitigate the worst effects of the system. For the Bahá'í movement in the United States, both the orgy of anti-black violence and the emergence of a tentative southern interracial movement helped to spur a new nationwide teaching campaign and a concerted effort to affect the national discourse on race. Traveling teachers in South Carolina in the immediate postwar years pursued both objectives, bringing the Bahá'í message to a larger segment of the African American population and attempting to cultivate closer relations with black and moderate white leaders.[18]

Even before U.S. entry into the war, a reduction in the flow of immigrant workers from Europe and an increased demand for manufactured goods to supply the belligerent nations led northern factories to open their doors to black laborers for the first time, and African Americans left South Carolina to pursue industrial jobs in dramatic numbers. Early in 1917, Charleston undertaker and activist Richard Mickey called the movement an "exodus" and predicted it would only accelerate. Indeed, the 1920 census revealed that some seventy-five thousand black South Carolinians—some 4 percent of the state's black population—had moved away during the previous decade. Those who remained at home fought for full participation in the state's wartime mobilization. Early on, most black organizations and opinion leaders in South Carolina came out strongly in support of the war effort, but white authorities rejected any proposal that they feared would undermine Jim Crow. In April 1917, for example, when Richard Carroll led a delegation of black leaders to meet with Governor Richard Manning, the Progressive governor turned down their offer to raise black troops—with black officers—for the state's National Guard. Instead, Manning said that the best place for blacks was in the fields, and he offered a reward for the arrest and conviction of labor agents who, he said, were enticing blacks away to northern factory jobs using false claims. Throughout the state, discrimination in wartime employment was widespread, taking various forms according to local conditions. In May 1918, for example, when the Navy Yard in North Charleston announced six hundred jobs at a new clothing factory, it specified that "only white women" should apply. On the other hand, in October the Greenville city council, facing a shortage of workers, considered a measure to force black women (but not white) to go to work in wartime industries.[19]

Aside from threats to the economic order, the mobilization of black men as soldiers during the war revived many whites' fears of "social equality." At Richard Carroll's annual race conference in March 1918, Gov. Manning warned blacks that wartime cooperation between the races would not lead to social equality, saying that such an outcome would "not be tolerated by the southern whites, and wouldn't be good for the negroes." When black soldiers began arriving at army training camps in South Carolina and other southern states, they experienced both a strictly segregated military and local white communities hostile to their presence. At Camp Wadsworth near Spartanburg, a textile center in the upper Piedmont, tensions between local storeowners and black troops from the Fifteenth New York Regiment nearly led to rioting in the fall of 1917. The army quickly sent the Fifteenth to France to avoid further trouble; by the time Erwin Harris, an eighteen-year-old white Baháʼí from New York City, arrived at Camp Wadsworth for training in early 1918, it was a whites-only facility.[20]

Black South Carolinians' wartime restlessness expressed itself in new organizations with new demands. On January 1, 1917, Louis Gregory's Emancipation Day speech at Charleston's Morris Street Baptist Church, the keynote address in a day-long program that included a "grand parade" through the city, opened a year of increased activism and self-confidence among blacks across the state. While reports of the speech have apparently not survived, it surely made reference to the Baháʼí teachings on interracial unity and justice. Just a month later, James Weldon Johnson, the new field secretary of the NAACP, arrived in South Carolina as part of his first southern organizing tour, and he found audiences who were ready to act. Johnson's strategy was to connect older institutions of racial uplift—churches, schools and colleges, fraternal organizations, and women's clubs—to the NAACP, in effect pushing Tuskegee-inspired community leaders such as Richard Carroll toward a more activist agenda. By the time the United States entered the Great War in April, the NAACP included a new "Dixie District" or "Southern Empire" with new branches in ten of the region's important cities, including Columbia and Charleston in South Carolina. In both of the new South Carolina branches, influential black laypeople—many with ties to Avery Institute or otherwise acquaintances of Louis Gregory—initially took the lead. Gregory appears to have had a particularly close, decades-long relationship with leaders of the Charleston branch. Edwin A. "Teddy" Harleston, an accomplished art student in Atlanta and Boston who had returned home to take over his family's undertaking business, was the Charleston branch's first president, and his sister, Eloise Harleston Jenkins, the wife of a prominent local minister, was another founding member. Both had been students at Avery while Louis Gregory was a teacher there, and they became quite familiar with the Baháʼí Faith from his visits to their home during his subsequent trips to the city. Under the leadership of the Harlestons and others, the Charleston branch quickly mounted a letter-writing campaign to secure jobs for 250 black women at the new Navy Yard Clothing Factory, which had initially advertised positions for white women only; following this success, it mounted a much larger campaign to force city officials to employ black teachers in black schools, where they had been virtually excluded since the 1880s. In Columbia, the new branch's first project was a voter registration campaign.[21]

The initial successes in Charleston and Columbia spurred the formation of additional NAACP branches in towns across the state. During 1918 and 1919, new branches emerged in Aiken, Anderson, Beaufort, Darlington, Florence, and Orangeburg. In addition, some of the state's leading black ministers—perhaps spurred by the growth of a bold new civil rights organization with an essentially secular approach—began to demonstrate a new outspokenness. In February 1919, as the Charleston branch prepared to launch its own voting rights campaign, Bishop William D. Chappelle, the president of Allen University in Columbia, convened a statewide conference on black political mobilization. Participants committed to forming local clubs to register new black voters and passed resolutions demanding a place for blacks on local school boards, the elimination of the disfranchisement provisions of the state constitution, and equality in segregated public facilities. Later the same month, when the all-black 371st Regiment, which had distinguished itself in battle in France, returned to Camp Jackson outside Columbia, prominent ministers found another occasion to press black political demands. After a victory parade through the streets of town, a succession of speakers at a rally at Benedict College called for wider political roles for black citizens. Dr. Nathaniel F. Haygood, minister of Sidney Park Colored Methodist Episcopal Church in Columbia, insisted on securing a "man's place" for returning soldiers, including on juries and as policemen. Turning the Wilson administration's wartime rhetoric onto the situation of blacks at home, Bishop Chappelle said: "The war was fought for democracy. We want democracy in our own country."[22]

Despite blacks' cogent arguments for civil rights, as the war drew to a close most whites in South Carolina still had no intention of extending democracy to their black fellow citizens. They were hardly alone in their attempts to maintain the status quo. During the war, as more than half a million black southerners moved to the Northeast and Midwest to take industrial jobs previously held by whites, white mobs lashed out at black communities and uniformed black soldiers from Illinois to Pennsylvania. In 1919, a massive wave of industrial strikes across the country stoked fears of radical activity.

U.S. Attorney General A. Mitchell Palmer and the Federal Bureau of Investigation led a nationwide crackdown on labor unions, Communists, socialists, anarchists, and black activists, while a resurgent Ku Klux Klan—decrying the influence not only of blacks but of immigrants, Jews, and radicals—gained followers in every state. In this volatile environment, an unprecedented outburst of racial violence shook the country. During 1919 at least seventy black southerners, some still in military uniform, fell prey to lynch mobs, and from late spring to early fall more than two dozen cities and towns, mostly outside the South, erupted in anti-black riots. James Weldon Johnson of the NAACP termed the bloodbath the "Red Summer." The first riot began late on a Saturday night in May in a pool hall in downtown Charleston, South Carolina, when a verbal altercation between white sailors and a group of unarmed black men spilled into the street and turned violent. During several hours of mayhem, a mob of white servicemen and civilians rampaged across downtown Charleston, shooting indiscriminately into crowds of black people, pulling at least two black passengers from streetcars and assaulting them, and ransacking at least one black-owned business. Three blacks were killed and perhaps forty injured.[23]

Mob action, unplanned and uncoordinated, was only the most dramatic aspect of white postwar reaction. In South Carolina and across the South, local and state governments, allied with the new Klan and the FBI, launched a campaign of violence and intimidation to roll back the limited gains that blacks had made during the war. Most opposition took shape at the local level, but the highest public officials often inspired and condoned the campaign. In August 1919, for example, Rep. James F. Byrnes of South Carolina's Second District gave tacit permission to act from the floor of Congress. In effect denying the existence of a local branch of the NAACP in his own hometown, Byrnes asserted that blacks in his district did not "seek to participate in politics." He blamed the violence of the Red Summer on the "criminal class" of blacks, whose "passions" had been aroused by the "radical" publications of the NAACP and its alleged supporters: the Industrial Workers of the World, Russian Communists, and the "misguided theorist of the North." Implicitly acknowledging how the war had stoked black political activism, he assured his colleagues that white supremacy was still strong: "The war has in no way changed the attitude of the white man toward the social and political equality of the negro ... because this is a white man's country, and will always remain a white man's country."[24]

In South Carolina, white citizens organized to make good on Byrnes's assertions, both by intimidating the black population in general and by dismembering the state's NAACP. The Ku Klux Klan spread, openly and confidently, to towns across the state, often with official sanction. In Spartanburg, for example, organizers held the inaugural meeting of the local Klan on the steps of the county courthouse. In large newspaper ads explaining the purpose of the organization, Klan leaders cloaked their campaign of intimidation, threats, and violence with a defense of "our pure womanhood" and preventing "the causes of mob violence" (namely, sexual aggression by black men). Political leaders provided additional rhetorical cover, as in 1921 when Rep. Byrnes explained to his colleagues in Washington that "rape is responsible directly and indirectly for most of the lynching in America." Between 1919 and 1927, at least fourteen blacks fell victim to lynch mobs in South Carolina, with five killed in 1921 alone. In addition, the Klan, local officials, and newspaper editors specifically targeted the NAACP and its leadership for silencing or elimination. After the Charleston riot in May 1919, local branch president Teddy Harelston's life was threatened repeatedly, and membership in the Charleston and Columbia branches plummeted. Outside the state's two main urban centers, the situation was even worse. In mid-1919 in the Piedmont textile town of Anderson, the local newspaper editor waged a two-month war of words to silence M. H. Gassaway, NAACP branch president and principal of the local black high school. When the written attacks failed to get Gassaway fired, the editor printed death threats. Gassaway and two other local NAACP leaders fled for the North, and the branch folded. By 1923 the branch in Aiken, James F. Byrnes's hometown, had ceased its activities, and the following year the local Klan ordered the Florence branch to disband. By mid-decade, the NAACP in South Carolina was little more than an empty shell.[25]

As effective as the Klan and its allies were in dismantling the NAACP in South Carolina and other southern states, misinformation, intimidation, and violence were not whites' only responses to the rise in racial tensions during and after World War I. A very different outcome was the emergence of a southern interracial movement that aimed to diffuse racial conflict and ameliorate the situation of blacks under Jim Crow. Early in 1919, a group of black and white community leaders formed the Commission on Interracial Cooperation. With a small appropriation from a federal agency, they organized conferences of social workers from across the region—one for whites at Blue Ridge Assembly, a YMCA retreat center in North Carolina, and one for blacks at Gammon Theological Seminary in Atlanta—to make plans for the peaceful reintegration of returning black soldiers into their local communities. Following the Red Summer of 1919, what began as a temporary network developed into a permanent regional organization that sought to promote interracial harmony and to improve the situation of blacks within segregation. Commonly known as the Interracial Commission, it spawned some eight hundred local, county, and state committees across the region—some white, some black, and some biracial—that worked with differing degrees of success to address specific problems in their communities. Under the leadership of Will W. Alexander of Nashville, a white former Methodist minister and community organizer, one of the Interracial Commission's primary concerns was lynching. State and local committees often attempted to prevent lynchings before they happened and, when they did, to secure indictments against the perpetrators. The Interracial Commission's efforts complemented those of the national-level NAACP, which launched a major anti-lynching campaign in 1919. At the national conference to launch the campaign, the NAACP released a comprehensive report that noted that fewer than one-sixth of lynching cases involved an accusation of rape or attempted rape. Armed with such data, a 1920 conference of white Methodists at Blue Ridge formed the Interracial Commission's Division of Women's Work, which began to mobilize mostly white southern women—the purported beneficiaries of lynching—in the fight to end racial violence.[26]

Because most of the Interracial Commission's funding came from northern philanthropists and church groups, it could afford to take a cautiously liberal approach to race relations. However, for all its opposition to lynching, debt peonage, and the Klan, it was hardly a force for systemic change in the region. Some of the organization's white leaders believed that Jim Crow was unjust, but neither they nor their northern benefactors sought to challenge the system's underlying assumptions. Rather, they sought to ameliorate conditions for blacks and promote fairness within the framework of "separate but equal." In fact, commitment to maintaining segregation was a key to most whites' participation in the organization. As one white leader admitted, "unless those forms of separation which are meant to safeguard the purity of the races are present, the majority of the white people flatly refuse to cooperate with the Negroes." Another critical factor in the organization's limited success was maintaining its orthodox Protestant credentials. While officially secular, the Interracial Commission's regional and local leadership included large numbers of Protestant clergymen and prominent laypeople, and it operated in close cooperation with such organizations as the YMCA and YWCA. Coupled with its official commitment to segregation, these Protestant ties gave the organization's work on behalf of blacks the protection of conservatism. White Methodist leaders who gathered at Blue Ridge in 1920 captured both these aspects of the Commission's orientation in a report of their meeting. On the one hand, they asserted that "the real responsibility for the solution of inter-racial problems in the South rests directly upon the hearts and consciences of the Christian forces of our land." On the other, they affirmed their "absolute loyal[ty] to the . . . principle of racial integrity." While they believed that the Jim Crow system needed modification, these leaders of the southern interracial movement left no doubt that the "Christian forces" they represented bore no relationship with social equality or integration.[27]

In the experiences of the NAACP and of the Interracial Commission can be seen some of the practical problems that Bahá'ís in South Carolina and other southern states faced in the immediate postwar years. The organization that stood squarely for racial integration and full civil rights for blacks—the position closest to that of the Bahá'ís—was the target of a concerted campaign of terror that virtually exterminated it in South Carolina and across the region, while the organization that relied on the blessing of the Protestant establishment and maintained a public commitment to the fundamentals of Jim Crow—neither one of which was possible for the Bahá'ís—avoided violence but made only limited gains. In this atmosphere of fear and compromise, it is perhaps unsurprising that Bahá'í communities were slow to emerge in South Carolina during the period. Bahá'í teachers visiting the state, however, still found receptive audiences for their message, and they made efforts to share the faith with moderate white leaders. They took a pragmatic approach to the interracial movement, limited as it was, seeking to encourage those who were working to soften white public opinion and promote harmony and cooperation across racial lines. In these efforts, which largely took shape between 1919 and 1921, the Bahá'ís were guided and encouraged by further interventions by 'Abdu'l-Bahá.

Completing the Divine Plan

For the American Bahá'í movement, the racial violence of the war and its aftermath coincided with two important new developments, both initiatives of 'Abdu'l-Bahá. One was a new wave of teaching activity in all parts of the country, with special attention on the South. The other was a concerted effort to bring the faith's teachings on interracial unity to the attention of leaders of thought and the general public, which included reaching out to leaders of the emerging southern interracial movement. Louis Gregory was an important participant in both these lines of action, promoting coherence and connection between them. Primarily because of his efforts, South Carolina had a place in both domains.

In early 1919, not long after the statewide black political conference and the triumphal welcome for the 371st in Columbia, Louis Gregory was back home in South Carolina teaching the faith. After a stay in Wilmington, North Carolina, Gregory made a two-week visit to unspecified "points in S.C.," using a relative's house in Charleston as his base of operations. In late April, some three weeks before his old neighborhood erupted in the first riot of the Red Summer, he took a ship from Charleston to New York City for the eleventh annual national Bahá'í convention, a gathering that would lend new momentum to teaching across the South. With some six hundred believers from across the country in attendance, the 1919 convention was the first since the end of the war and the largest in the movement's history. Now that communication with Palestine was restored, they had come to witness formal delivery of all fourteen of 'Abdu'l-Bahá's Tablets of the Divine Plan—the five that had reached the community in 1916 plus three written that year and six written in early 1917 that had previously remained undelivered. Taken as a whole, the collection of letters outlined a worldwide mission that the North American believers would undertake in the wake of the war and for decades to come. 'Abdu'l-Bahá called them to spread the faith not only in the United States and Canada but throughout Latin America and the Caribbean and beyond them to the rest of the globe:

> It is the hope of Abdul-Baha that just as ye are confirmed and assisted on the continent of America, ye may also be confirmed and assisted on other continents of the globe—that is, ye may carry the fame of the Cause of God to the East and to the West and spread the glad-tidings of the appearance of the Kingdom of the Lord of Hosts throughout the five continents of the world.
>
> When this divine call travels from the continent of America to Europe, Asia, Africa, Australia and the islands of the Pacific, the American believers shall be established on the throne of everlasting glory, the fame of their illumination and guidance shall reach to all regions and the renown of their greatness become worldwide.

In addition to general exhortations, he named some 120 countries, territories, and islands to which the American believers should travel.[28]

The world war, 'Abdu'l-Bahá indicated in the tablets, was part of God's plan for humanity. As the peoples of the world turned away from outworn institutions, and as governments took steps to implement, however unwittingly, elements of Bahá'u'lláh's program for world order, the Bahá'ís would find new opportunities to teach their faith:

> This world consuming war has set such a conflagration to the hearts that no word can describe it. In all the countries of the world the longing for universal peace is taking possession of the consciousness of men. There is not a soul who does not yearn for concord and peace. A most wonderful state of receptivity is being realized. This is through the consummate wisdom of God, so that capacity may be created, the standard of the oneness of the world of humanity be upraised, and the fundamentals of universal peace and the divine principles be promoted in the East and the West.

For the assembled Bahá'ís, current events seemed to confirm the mandate 'Abdu'l-Bahá had given them. They noted that their own gathering, "discussing plans for spiritual union and harmony throughout the world," was taking place at the same time as the Paris Peace Conference, where world leaders were "meeting to establish the new world conditions politically, economically and socially." As Joseph Hannen observed in his report of the convention: "It is within the ready recollection of many of us, that the Bahai teachings were called 'ahead of the times' and termed a dream philosophy, perhaps adapted to some future age of the world. And now, how rapidly 'the times' have caught up with The Message, so that today men talk the world over in terms of internationalism and world unity, strange to their minds and tongues, but familiar to the Bahais."[29]

Like the original set from 1916, the newly arrived tablets included messages addressed to each geographic region of North America. In his second tablet to the southern states, 'Abdu'l-Bahá observed that as the region's moderate climate and physical beauty were conducive to the development of material civilization, so must the South excel in spiritual civilization. "Unquestionably," he said, "the divine teachings must reveal themselves with a brighter effulgence ... and the fragrances of holiness be diffused with swiftness and rapidity." He urged his followers to action, lamenting the fact that "no adequate and befitting motion ha[d] been realized, and no great acclamation and acceleration ha[d] been witnessed" in the region since the introduction of the faith to the United States more than twenty years earlier. He pointed to the story of St. Gregory the Illuminator, in Christian tradition the first apostle to Armenia: "Nearly 2,000 years ago, Armenia was enveloped with impenetrable darkness. One blessed soul from among the disciples of Christ hastened to that part, and through his efforts, ere long that province became illumined." Alluding to the problem of racial prejudice, he called on the Baháʼís to put forth an effort similar to that of St. Gregory to establish the oneness of humanity in the South, indicating that their achievement would have a transforming impact on the United States and the world: "With a firm resolution, a pure heart, a rejoiced spirit, and an eloquent tongue, engage your time in the promulgation of the divine principles; so that the oneness of the world of humanity may pitch her canopy in the apex of America and all the nations of the world may follow the divine policy. This is certain, that the divine policy is justice and kindness toward all mankind."[30]

In response to ʻAbduʼl-Baháʼs mandate, the convention voted to appoint a national "Teaching Committee of Nineteen." Compared to the virtually nonexistent support network at the time of Louis Gregory's first teaching trip, this action proved to be a major step forward in the organization of teaching, across the country and in the South in particular. Among the members of the new committee were Joseph Hannen and Louis Gregory, two of the most experienced believers in the country in teaching and administration. Hannen stayed in Washington to coordinate a new "Central Bureau for the South," charged with distributing literature to seekers and to libraries, publishing articles on the faith in the region's newspapers, identifying "all the liberal organizations, clubs and churches who would be willing to have Bahai lecturers," coordinating teaching circuits and follow-up visits, promoting the establishment of Baháʼí study groups in "all the larger towns," and keeping an index of all the believers in the region. Under the new effort the number and range of itinerant teachers increased, and Hannen supported them by forwarding mail and financial contributions from other believers. Through the circulation of typewritten bulletins, the Teaching Committee sought to involve all the believers in the nationwide enterprise, not just the relative few able to travel "but all who give what time they can in their own localities and who help in the way of contributing to the expenses of the teaching work."[31]

Louis Gregory returned to the field, resuming what would become a nearly three-year period of uninterrupted travel throughout the South. From 1919 to 1921, he crisscrossed the region, often in tandem with Roy Williams, an African American believer from New York City. The two were particularly active in South Carolina. Williams later recalled that he and Gregory "taught together in 30 towns and cities in South Carolina" during the period, noting especially their engagements "in many churches in Greenville and Anderson Count[ies]," violence-prone areas with substantial black minorities in the heart of the Piedmont textile manufacturing belt. Sometime during a nine-month period in 1919, Williams, a highly skilled carpenter, stayed in Charleston long enough to find temporary employment, perhaps with the help of Louis Gregory's stepfather; he reported earning fifteen dollars there to help finance his continued travels. During the winter of 1920–1921, Gregory toured Georgia and the Carolinas on the last leg of his extended journey. From engagements in Atlanta he traveled to Augusta, Georgia, and its sister city of North Augusta, South Carolina; to Columbia and Charleston; and finally to several towns in North Carolina before returning to Washington. Surviving documentation of their engagements during the period is limited, but if Gregory and Williams indeed visited "30 towns and cities" in the relatively compact territory of South Carolina, then their efforts must have touched all parts of the state, including many of the smaller towns.[32]

While the American Bahá'ís worked to increase the size and scope of their community in all parts of the country, they also attempted to influence public attitudes about race. Like many of their fellow citizens, the Bahá'ís were appalled at the racial violence of the Red Summer, and in several localities, especially Washington and Chicago, the outbreaks directly or indirectly touched local Bahá'í communities. In the latter city, one Bahá'í home was firebombed, two members of another Bahá'í family were jailed briefly, and another believer, an Iranian physician named Zia Bagdadi, aided relief efforts in black neighborhoods. During the summer and fall, the Executive Board of the Bahai Temple Unity consulted about "the best means of promulgating and promoting [the] principle of human unity," and Louis Gregory and Harlan Ober, a white Bahá'í, discussed plans to hold "mass meetings" to bring blacks and whites of all classes together to alleviate racial tension.[33]

However, it was an initiative of 'Abdu'l-Bahá that finally led to an increased public role for the Bahá'í movement. Early in 1920, Agnes Parsons, a wealthy white Bahá'í from Washington, went on pilgrimage to Palestine. Parsons recounted that one evening at dinner, 'Abdu'l-Bahá turned "quite out of the blue" to her and said "'I want you to arrange a convention in Washington for amity between the colored and the white.'" Though doubting her own ability to arrange such a gathering—she had never planned a large event and she had barely moved outside the elite circles of white Washington before becoming a Bahá'í in middle age—Parsons returned to the United States with a mission. Enlisting the help of friends both inside and outside of the Bahá'í community, Parsons worked for almost a year to develop an approach and to plan the convention. One of her confidants, a former Republican U.S. senator from Minnesota named Moses E. Clapp, suggested that the convention should avoid protest over specific grievances or a tone of political polarization. "'Do not make a protest about anything,'" Parsons recalled him as saying. "'Lift the whole matter up into the spiritual realm and work for the creation of sentiment.'"[34]

Louis Gregory agreed. In December 1920, after more than two years traveling to bring "the Glorious Message of the Kingdom to the oppressed and broken-hearted" across the South, he wrote to Parsons with his advice. While he said he was encouraged by the work of the Interracial Commission, he was well aware of its limitations of scope and purpose: "There are many, many souls throughout the South today who are working and longing for a better day. But without the Light of Abhá ['Most Glorious,' a form of the Greatest Name] their efforts seem infantile and helpless. Even some members of the state inter-racial committee, earnest, thoughtful, hard-working men, have voiced to me despair." Rather than imitate the approach of the Interracial Commission, Gregory said that the Bahá'ís should involve a broader cross-section of the population, openly advocate integration and unity, and directly share the faith's teachings on race: "If the Washington inter-racial congress is along these conventional lines I fear it will like the others, be fruitless. But if it be aflame with the Fire of Divine Love, the hearts will be powerfully influenced and the effect will be great in all the years to come." The heart of the matter, he suggested, was not to address this or that baneful effect of racial prejudice but to foster a sense of the oneness of humanity. "Nothing short of a change of hearts will do," he wrote. "Unless the speakers are able to make the power of love felt, the occasion will lose its chief value."[35]

The Race Amity Convention, held over three days in May 1921 at Washington's First Congregational Church, was the first large interracial gathering in the capital city since the Red Summer less than two years before. The printed program stated the purpose of the gathering, calling "all the inhabitants of these United States" to participate in a new crusade to "establish amity between the white and colored people of our land." It succinctly placed the current effort in historical context, at the same time aligning the Bahá'ís with the legacy of emancipation: "Half a century ago in America slavery was abolished. Now there has arisen need for another great effort in order that prejudice may be overcome." Bahá'ís and prominent guests, black and white, served as session chairs, speakers, and artistic presenters. Diverse crowds of at least fifteen hundred people attended each of the evening sessions, while advance distribution of some nineteen thousand of the printed programs in churches, stores, schools, and other public places and widespread coverage by newspapers in Washington and other southern cities ensured an even larger indirect reach.[36]

While it is difficult to gauge the practical impact of an event focused on "the creation of sentiment" rather than specific action items, the Bahá'ís took the very fact of such a large and well-publicized interracial event in the nation's capital—cutting across lines of political affiliation, religion, and class—as a victory. Gregory later pointed out that the convention spurred members of other Washington churches to start organizing interracial committees. It also encouraged Bahá'ís in other areas to organize their own conventions. During the rest of the 1920s and the 1930s, Race Amity Conventions and related activities were held in various cities of the Northeast, Midwest, and West. In the process, local Bahá'í communities collaborated with organizations such as the NAACP, the National Urban League, and the League of Women Voters and developed relationships with leading intellectuals and activists. As a result of such explicit public efforts, the Bahá'í Faith became more widely known as an interracial movement. At the same time, the membership of local Bahá'í communities increasingly reflected the religion's interracial commitment. According to one survey, by the mid-1930s blacks were found in at least thirty-three local communities and constituted at least 5 percent of the American Bahá'í population. That was less than the percentage of blacks in the total national population, but compared only to the black population of the states where the faith was established (mostly outside the South, and thus having relatively smaller black populations) they were more nearly at par or even overrepresented within the Bahá'í community.[37]

As a practical effort to influence public discourse on race in the United States, the Race Amity Conventions also helped the Bahá'ís forge links with the southern interracial movement. During the 1920s, Louis Gregory and other teachers in the South saw interracial workers as important contacts, both for the purpose of encouraging what they regarded as a more or less positive development in the region and, potentially, for teaching the faith directly. In the southern interracial movement Gregory saw "the Hand of Divine Bounty, the emanation of which more and more links the living elements of humanity into a worldwide fellowship." Suggesting that the "Bahai Spirit has revealed its Light to many hearts still unaware of its Name," he recommended that other traveling teachers in the South approach these "servants of humanity," the leaders of the interracial movement, as potentially receptive to the Bahá'í message.[38]

Gregory energetically publicized the efforts of the southern interracial movement among the Bahá'ís, and of the Bahá'ís among southern interracial workers. In South Carolina at the end of his 1919–1921 teaching trips, for example, while visiting Columbia to speak in several churches and schools, he sought out Josiah Morse, a professor of philosophy and psychology at the University of South Carolina. Morse, a Virginia-born Jew, was an early supporter of the Interracial Commission who embodied the contradictions of the organization. Morse opposed calls for social equality and the NAACP's approach of organizing only African Americans in its southern branches, but his outspoken criticism of lynching and support of black education and welfare brought accusations of Communism and race-mixing from fellow whites. Shortly before Gregory's visit, Morse had arranged a conference of students from his own institution and its two nearby black counterparts, Benedict College and Allen University, to discuss current social issues. Morse's effort presaged the establishment of an educational department of the Interracial Commission, which spurred the holding of a variety of interracial forums for college students across the region. Gregory's positive contact with Morse may have encouraged the latter's interracial activities, which lasted well into the 1930s; it certainly disposed him to welcome other Bahá'í teachers to campus in subsequent years.[39]

On several occasions Louis Gregory shared with Bahá'í audiences the example of Samuel Chiles Mitchell, a respected white southern educator, for whom an encounter with 'Abdu'l-Bahá during the latter's visit to the United States provided decades' worth of inspiration for his interracial work. Born in Mississippi and raised in Texas, Mitchell was an ordained Baptist minister, history professor, social reformer, and university administrator. In addition to serving as president of the University of South Carolina and other institutions, he worked with various northern philanthropies dedicated to improving education for black and white southerners. In 1912, during his tenure at the University of South Carolina, Mitchell attended the annual Lake Mohonk Conference on International Arbitration in New York, where 'Abdu'l-Bahá was the special guest speaker. The following year, Mitchell's progressive attitude on black education provoked his most bitter professional experience. As a consultant to the Peabody Education Fund, he recommended that the organization focus its resources in South Carolina on State College in Orangeburg, a black institution. In response, the president of Winthrop College, the state's institution for white women in Rock Hill, appealed to Gov. Coleman Blease. The governor, eager to discredit his "elite" opponents, accused Mitchell of favoring the education of blacks over that of white women and insisted on an embarrassing legislative hearing. While both the board of trustees of the University of South Carolina and the state legislature vindicated Mitchell, he accepted a timely offer to head the Medical College of Virginia and never returned to South Carolina.[40]

According to Louis Gregory, who visited and corresponded with Mitchell during the 1920s and 1930s, 'Abdu'l-Bahá's talk on the oneness of humanity at Lake Mohonk had had a direct and lasting impact on Mitchell's interracial work, causing him to resolve never to draw lines of racial division between his fellow human beings. Apparently alluding to the image from Baháʼí scripture of the Manifestation of God as the sun, Gregory reported that "the great horizon line which covers all mankind is sufficient for him." Since Lake Mohonk, Gregory said, Mitchell had repeated the teachings of 'Abdu'l-Bahá "upon many platforms."[41]

Louis Gregory, Rev. I. E. Lowery, and Uplift Theology

Another incident from Louis Gregory's early 1921 visit to Columbia illustrates that some conservative southern leaders seem to have recognized in the new religion—numerically insignificant as it was—a potential threat to their authority. In the first documented public attack on the Baháʼí Faith by a South Carolina clergyman, prominent black Methodist minister, journalist, and racial uplift ideologue Rev. I. E. Lowery devoted an entire weekly column to a scathing denunciation of Louis Gregory and the religion he espoused. The column appeared in at least two black newspapers, the *Watchman and Defender* of Timmonsville and the *Southern Indicator* of Columbia, the second of which was distributed statewide. While there is no evidence of a response by Gregory, further contact between him and Lowery, or continued public debate about the Baháʼí Faith in the state's press, the publication of the column likely brought the faith to the attention of a substantial portion of the state's black reading public for the first time. The substance of Lowery's objections sheds light on the relationship between the Baháʼí teachings and elements of racial uplift theology.[42]

If Richard Carroll was the most powerful proponent of racial uplift in early twentieth-century South Carolina, perhaps its most eloquent and prolific apologist was Rev. Irving E. Lowery (1850–1929), Alonzo Twine's former pastor. Born a slave in Sumter County, after emancipation Lowery went from a makeshift school near the plantation he grew up on to become an influential minister and journalist. His membership in the Methodist Episcopal Church, which created a substantial branch among black southerners after the Civil War, led him to attend a series of three schools sponsored by the denomination: Baker Bible Institute, a new seminary for freedpeople in Charleston; Claflin University in Orangeburg, which initially offered only grammar and normal school training; and Wesleyan

Figure 2.1. Rev. Irving E. Lowery (1850–1929), Methodist minister, prolific journalist and writer, racial uplift ideologue, and vociferous early opponent of the Bahá'í Faith in South Carolina, ca. 1911. Lowery was instrumental in having Alonzo Twine removed from free society in 1911, and in 1921 he used the incident to attack Louis Gregory in the press. Courtesy of the South Caroliniana Library, University of South Carolina, Columbia, S.C.

Academy, a college-preparatory school in Wilbraham, Massachusetts. After returning to South Carolina in 1874, he served as pastor for Methodist congregations across the state and became a prolific writer, at various times reporting for or editing at least five newspapers, black and white. In 1909, he helped organize Booker T. Washington's two-week speaking tour through South Carolina.[43]

In 1911, Lowery published a book that summarized his racial and religious worldviews. Entitled *Life on the Old Plantation in Ante-Bellum Days, or A Story Based on Facts*, the work combined autobiographical vignettes and journalistic essays in an exposition of racial uplift theology. In the narrative, Lowery portrayed what he called the "better side" of slavery through a series of vignettes from the idyllic plantation of his childhood. And in a lengthy appendix comprising essays originally published in the Columbia *Daily Record*, a white newspaper, Lowery presented contemporary evidence for the success of racial uplift ideology. Lowery argued that while most blacks dwelled on "lynchings, burnings, murders and . . . outrages" and were therefore pessimistic about the future, the "best white people" and the newspapers were opposed to anti-black violence. Like Booker T. Washington and Richard Carroll, Lowery tacitly accepted white justifications for lynching, suggesting that as "the brutal offense against the purity of womanhood" was decreasing, so was anti-black violence. Lowery also argued that it was blacks' Christian duty to accept segregation, pointing to vocational education and traditional Protestantism as the twin keys to black advancement. Through his own words and those of the prominent whites he frequently quoted, Lowery made clear his view: that white supremacy was essentially benevolent and that by learning the virtues of capitalism, eschewing social equality and citizenship rights, and holding fast to Protestant orthodoxy, blacks could indeed achieve progress within Jim Crow.[44]

During U.S. involvement in World War I, Lowery, along with other black ministers in South Carolina, supported mobilization efforts and joined calls for black political rights. But when he heard Louis Gregory speak in Columbia in early 1921, nothing had changed his basic religious conservatism and the intense antagonism with which he had responded to the Bahá'í Faith in Charleston more than a decade before. According to Lowery's account, Louis Gregory spoke in the afternoon of January 30 at Sidney Park Colored Methodist Episcopal Church, a fashionable congregation housed in an impressive Gothic revival structure on Blanding Street in downtown Columbia. Sidney Park's minister, the Rev. Nathaniel F. Haygood, was an activist who had spoken publicly for black political rights at Columbia's welcome celebration for the 371st Regiment in 1919. With a concern for contemporary social problems, Haygood was exactly the kind of minister who would open his church to speakers from progressive causes, including the Bahá'í Faith. At Haygood's invitation, Louis Gregory attended Sidney Park's Sunday morning service and from the podium invited the congregation to his lecture, which would take place at the church that afternoon. Lowery, also a visitor at Sidney Park's morning service (probably because January 30 fell on the fifth Sunday of the month, when kindred churches in an area often held joint services), recognized Gregory from his talks "on the Bahai Religion in some of the churches and halls" of Charleston in 1910 and decided to attend the afternoon talk.[45]

In his column, published three weeks later, Lowery condemned the Baháʼí Faith as unchristian and devoid of spirit. He called it "a head religion, and not a heart religion," incorrectly but repeatedly referring to Gregory as "professor" and comparing him to Nicodemus, the Pharisee who, because of his attachment to his worldly learning, could not understand Jesus's teaching of the second birth. The Baháʼí Faith, Lowery said, was the same religion that Nicodemus followed, in other words, a sterile and legalistic form without divine inspiration. To underline his point, he listed the principles of the faith as Gregory taught them: "The Search for Truth; The Oneness of Humanity; The Unity of Religions; Religion and Science Agree; Equality of Men and Women; Abandonment of Prejudice; A Universal Language; Universal Education; Universal Peace; An International Tribunal; Solution of the Economic Problem; The Power of the Holy Spirit." While Lowery had no quarrel with such teachings, he asserted that they were not grounded in a personal belief in Jesus Christ: "The principles seem to be all right, but the Lord Jesus Christ is not recognized in them, and any religion that has no Christ in it, is not worthy of the attention of intelligent Christian people. And any attempt to teach, enforce and build up a religion without Christ will be an utter failure. The Bahai religion teaches love, but it is not the love that Christ taught. It is not the love that the Apostles taught. It is not the love that is promulgated by Christianity."

To underline the danger of the Baháʼí Faith, Lowery recounted a cautionary tale. Though he never mentioned the young man's name, he was clearly telling the story of Alonzo Twine. Lowery recalled that some years earlier, when he was pastor of Old Bethel Methodist Church in Charleston, Gregory had spoken in the city, and that one of his congregants, a "brilliant young lawyer" who had grown up at Old Bethel, "took hold of this new religion, and tried to master it." According to Lowery, as a result of his struggle to understand the Baháʼí Faith, the young man had "lost his mind" and been committed to the insane asylum in Columbia. Later, when Lowery was transferred to a church in Columbia, the young man's parents had asked him to visit their son often. He had taken away the man's Baháʼí literature, and finally he had escorted the body home for a church funeral. "This," he dramatically concluded the story, "is what the Bahai religion did for a brillian[t] young lawyer."[46]

Lowery's primary argument was that, as attractive as the new religion might seem, and as eloquently as Gregory presented it, there was "no Christ in it." As the Baháʼís understood it, however—and as Gregory certainly expressed it in Columbia—there was plenty of Christ in the Baháʼí Faith. This is an important theological point that bears directly on both the appeal of the faith to black and white South Carolinians and the opposition it sometimes garnered. Bahá'u'lláh was forthright in his identification with Christ's return in the glory of the Father—and his writings, as well as the writings and recorded public addresses of 'Abdu'l-Bahá, abounded with biblical references, extensive interpretation of Christian prophecies and theological concepts, praise for the person and station of Jesus Christ, and explanations of the relationship between him and Bahá'u'lláh. Among American Bahá'ís, most of whom came from evangelical Protestant backgrounds, such claims and scriptural discussions were widely known and openly shared with friends and seekers. In particular, Louis Gregory's published writings, letters, and talks indicate that he had studied extensively the relationship between Christianity and the Bahá'í Faith, was very conversant in the scriptures of both religions, and was able to explain the Bahá'í teachings in language that was familiar to Christian audiences. Gregory himself had become a Bahá'í because he believed it was an expression of precisely "the love that Christ taught" and the fulfillment of Christian eschatology, and it would have been uncharacteristic of him to not have said so in his Columbia engagements.

A short, unpublished essay, distributed by the Teaching Committee of Nineteen as part of its regular bulletin in early 1922, provides an indication of Gregory's thinking at the time. Entitled "A Brief Answer to Questions on the Fulfillment of Some Bible Prophecies Concerning This Day," the essay appears to have been prepared by Gregory for distribution to interested Christian seekers during his southern teaching trips, and it likely reflected some of the content of many of his talks. Gregory either included many of these arguments in his talk at Sidney Park or interacted personally with Lowery afterward (or both), for the paper is clearly the source of the twelve principles Lowery quoted, down to the identical wording and capitalization. In the essay, Gregory asserted that "pride and arrogance," attachment to worldly learning, and faulty interpretation of prophecies caused people to reject the "Divine Messengers" from age to age. He quoted from Jesus's lengthy condemnation of the Jewish religious leaders who opposed him: "Ye search the Scriptures for out of them ye think ye have Eternal Life. These also testify of me." The same veils that had caused the "scribes and Pharisees" to reject the Son of God, Gregory implicitly warned, might keep contemporary Christians from recognizing "BAHA'O'LLAH, His Greatest Manifestation, and ABDUL BAHA, the Servant of God and the Center of His Covenant" in this "Day of God," the day of Christ's "second appearance." Gregory mentioned twelve principles that Bahá'u'lláh and 'Abdu'l-Bahá proclaimed for the "healing of the nations" and the "pacification of the world." Gregory's discussion put the principles, a version of 'Abdu'l-Bahá's summary of the Bahá'í teachings from his talks in the United States, in the context of Christian millennial expectation, far from the legalism of which Lowery accused him. He linked the twelve principles to the "new Jerusalem," the city of God associated in Christian prophecy with Christ's return. "If a man will accept it," he said, "these twelve great principles are symbolized by the Tree, in the Book of Revelation, bearing twelve manner of fruits, and the leaves of this tree are for the healing of the nations." In the remainder of the essay, Gregory treated some dozen additional Christian prophecies, explaining the meaning of Bahá'u'lláh's title, the manner of his coming, the relationship between the "Son" and the "Father," and the station of 'Abdu'l-Bahá. In closing, he asserted that a pure-hearted Christian, investigating the prophecies of the Bible "in the light of the Bahai Revelation" would find "that the whole Bible was written for this great day of God, in which we are now living, and that all these prophecies . . . are now fulfilled."[47]

Even if Gregory mentioned only a few such ideas in his Sidney Park talk, it appears that Lowery deliberately misrepresented Gregory's exposition of the Bahá'í teachings on Jesus and Christianity. Further, he strongly implied that Gregory had malevolent intentions. In his account, Lowery complimented Gregory for his "good, clear voice," and called his oratory "really eloquent and forceful," but he added that Gregory "displayed considerable sagacious judgment in the wording and presentation of his new doctrine" and "was shrewd enough to conceal his real purposes." By misrepresenting the Bahá'í Faith as devoid of spirit and anti-Christian, implying that Gregory had evil intent, and including the harrowing tale of Alonzo Twine, it seems clear that Lowery was attempting to scare his readers away from the Bahá'í Faith.[48]

The reasons for Lowery's rather energetic denunciation of the new religion are a matter of some speculation. Lowery may well have called into question Gregory's integrity in order to conceal other aspects of the faith that he found more troubling. For a racial accommodationist such as Lowery, who had made his career as an intermediary between his black constituents and the white elite, the Bahá'í teachings and practices on race may have highlighted some of the shortcomings of his own program. It is unknown how much Louis Gregory referred to race in his Sidney Park talk or subsequent discussions with the ministers in attendance, beyond the references to "The Oneness of Humanity" and "Abandonment of Prejudice." Gregory may have discussed his interaction with Josiah Morse and the work of the southern interracial movement or the Bahá'í-sponsored Race Amity Conventions, but relatively mild interracial contact of this sort would not have been enough to rankle Lowery. It is unlikely that Gregory mentioned publicly his own marriage to a white woman, an egregious violation of white supremacist racial mores. More likely is that Gregory mentioned 'Abdu'l-Bahá's insistence on the social equality of the races during his North American sojourn or the integrated practice of the Washington Bahá'í community, neither of which was compatible with Lowery's cautious version of racial uplift.

Lowery might also have had a problem with the pronounced anti-clericalism of the new religion. Bahá'u'lláh's extensive teachings on the spiritual sovereignty of the individual (summarized in Gregory's list as "The Search for Truth") included, in language remarkably like that of Jesus's rebuke of the Jewish sectarians, a strong condemnation of clerics who would arrogate spiritual authority to themselves. These teachings formed part of the usual framework for Gregory's presentations of the Bahá'í Faith to Christian audiences, and he referred to them in his essay. While Jesus's treatment of the subject accused clergymen of susceptibility to spiritual blindness, Lowery reversed the analogy to paint Gregory, a layman, not himself, a minister, as a latter-day Pharisee. His churchgoing readers would certainly have understood the intent of the accusation, but if they failed to recall the details of the original story, they might not have noticed Lowery's rhetorical sleight of hand.[49]

Bahá'í anti-clericalism had practical implications. Bahá'u'lláh expressly prohibited the creation of a Bahá'í clergy, providing instead for a system of elected, corporate leadership. By the early 1920s, under 'Abdu'l-Bahá's guidance, the fledgling Bahá'í executive bodies at the local and national levels in the United States had taken on many of the basic pastoral functions—protecting and propagating the faith, educating and nurturing the community, arbitrating disputes among members, and collecting and administering funds—traditionally associated with clergy. Even full- and part-time Bahá'í traveling teachers usually paid their own way, and they held no official status in the body of believers. In the racial uplift theology shared by I. E. Lowery, Richard Carroll, and Booker T. Washington, material attainments and Christian moral development were closely intertwined, and upright, prosperous ministers were potent symbols (as well as arbiters) of the race's aspirations. Lowery may well have concluded that if the egalitarian Bahá'í system were to win over too many of his congregants, he risked losing his privileged status or even his livelihood. In the context of the rise of new centers of power inside and outside the black church, such as women's denominational auxiliaries and clubs and the NAACP, the democratic structure of the Bahá'í Faith (not to mention its full inclusion of women in positions of leadership) might have appeared to Lowery as one more potential blow to the clerical class.

While Lowery may have seen in the Bahá'í Faith a potentially potent theological and social force—defying at once the orthodoxies of race, religion, class, and gender that lay at the heart of white supremacist ideology, his own version of racial uplift, and the position of ministers in the black community—the fact that (in Lowery's mind at least) the faith had destroyed Alonzo Twine, a promising young fruit of uplift theology, was alone enough to have ensured his negative public reaction to Gregory in 1921. His personal animus and his unusually conservative theology may have made his an extreme case; indeed, Haygood's invitation for Gregory to address his congregation indicates an entirely different kind of clerical response to the Bahá'í Faith. Across the United States and in many southern cities and towns, Bahá'í teachers found Christian ministers—black and white, and from traditionally liberal and conservative denominations—who were warm to their message. Many opened their pulpits to Bahá'í visitors, and a handful even became Bahá'ís and propagated their new faith openly (including Albert Vail, a white former Unitarian minister who was one of Louis Gregory's fellow travelers during 1919–1921). As for the rank and file of black churchgoers, Lowery was at pains to downplay the impact of Gregory's talks on Columbia audiences: "While the people admired his oratory, they failed to accept his teaching. The impression he seemed to have made was short lived, and soon passed away. But there may be a few . . . like the young lawyer referred to above, who will follow the professor." Judging by responses in other southern cities during Gregory's 1919–1921 tours, however, his presentation of the Bahá'í Faith—a new religion that was socially and theologically progressive, united black and white in intimate fellowship and common purpose, and claimed to fulfill Christian expectation of the Kingdom of God on earth—would likely have been intriguing, if not deeply compelling, to at least a few of those in attendance at the Sidney Park talk. While he may have been out of step with progressive ministers such as Haygood and with the aspirations of an increasingly assertive African American community, Lowery's opposition to Gregory and the Bahá'í Faith and his attempt to reinforce Protestant orthodoxy in his readers indicate some of the difficulties that conservative clergymen might face when confronted with a new religion that defied their traditional social and intellectual categories. It also indicates that in South Carolina in the era of the Great War, defenders of the racial order and its Protestant trappings could come in all colors, making the task of Bahá'í community-building challenging indeed.[50]

Building a Bahá'í Community in Augusta and North Augusta, 1911–1939

While the first person to introduce the Bahá'í Faith to South Carolina was a native son, the founder of the state's first Bahá'í community came from half a world away in the medieval city of Königsberg, East Prussia. A vocal instructor who immigrated to New York in 1895, Margaret Klebs became a Bahá'í in New England. In 1912, two years after Louis Gregory's first teaching trip, Klebs settled permanently in the Augusta area, a New South urban-industrial center that spanned the border of South Carolina and Georgia. Her move to the Augusta area was critical to the development of the Bahá'í Faith in the Deep South. With only a scattering of Bahá'ís in the region—one in Austin, two in Jacksonville, a struggling little group on Mobile Bay, and perhaps a handful of isolated new believers as a result of Gregory's 1910 foray—Klebs's arrival represented an additional outpost of the religion and the beginning of a new local community that would eventually serve as a base of expansion into other nearby cities and towns, especially in South Carolina.

During more than a quarter century that Klebs spent in the Augusta area, the American Bahá'í movement underwent dramatic changes, as the final decade of 'Abdu'l-Bahá's ministry gave way to a new period of administrative development under his immediate successor, Shoghi Effendi, the Guardian of the Bahá'í Faith. In terms of both administrative development and approaches to race, the Augusta-area community is a useful lens for viewing an important moment in American Bahá'í history. Far from distant outliers, Margaret Klebs and the Augusta-area Bahá'í community she built and nurtured became active participants in this critical transitional period, both shaping and being shaped by developments at the national and regional levels. By the mid-1930s, the Augusta-area community was larger and better organized than most in the South and reflected many of the changes in the national movement, with a local governing council functioning according to standards introduced by Shoghi Effendi, a regular schedule of activities for members and seekers, a dedicated meeting facility, and a growing roster of members. Such a well-developed local community stood in stark contrast to the situation in the rest of South Carolina. During the same quarter century, despite repeated visits by traveling teachers, the lack of experienced Bahá'í settlers elsewhere in the state severely impeded the emergence of additional local communities.

In terms of race, the work of Klebs and others in the Augusta area indicated a relatively high degree of receptivity to the faith not only among southern blacks, as Louis Gregory had already demonstrated, but among whites of various class backgrounds as well. However, unlike the early Washington community described in chapter 1, by the middle of the 1930s the Augusta-area Bahá'ís had achieved at best only partial racial integration. Along with the experiences of others in the region, the struggle with race in the first local Bahá'í community in South Carolina (and Georgia) helped inform a new approach to teaching, introduced by the faith's international leadership and subsequently adopted across the South, which in turn spurred the emergence of more thoroughly integrated local communities elsewhere in South Carolina during the 1940s. As both an administrative base and a contributor to the faith's regional racial policy, then, Augusta was not just the first local Bahá'í community in South Carolina but its "mother community."

From Unified Germany to the United States

When Margarethe Sophia Klebs was born there in June 1862, the Baltic Sea port city of Königsberg was a cosmopolitan provincial capital in the Kingdom of Prussia, an industrializing, militaristic, and authoritarian state with grand ambitions in Europe. During Margarethe Klebs's early childhood, her country led the fractious German-speaking states of north-central Europe toward economic and political unification. As Klebs grew to adulthood, the confident new German Empire rose as a world political and economic power, and the more fortunate among its citizens enjoyed unprecedented degrees of material prosperity. Klebs was part of a "distinguished and cultured" family in the empire's leading state; one of her brothers became a prominent surgeon in Munich, and one of her uncles, a bacteriologist, discovered the bacillus that causes diphtheria. Klebs herself received an excellent education, studying piano and voice with some of the best teachers in Germany,

France, and Italy. Possessed of self-confidence and an independent spirit, Margarethe Klebs made her own living as a vocalist and music teacher. In 1895, unmarried at age thirty-three, she left Europe for the United States. Her bacteriologist uncle had already resettled there, practicing medicine at a sanatorium in Asheville, North Carolina, before accepting a teaching position at Rush Medical College in Chicago; a cousin, also a physician, followed the next year, treating tuberculosis in Alabama and then also in Chicago. But unlike her relatives, Margarethe Klebs did not gravitate to the Midwest or, initially, to the South. Striking out on her own, she settled in New York City and adopted an anglicized spelling of her first name, Margaret.[1]

In her new country, Margaret Klebs continued to teach music, sometimes as a private instructor and sometimes in academic settings, and she often ventured far from New York. Around the turn of the century, for example, she held a teaching position at the Presbyterian College for Women in Columbia, South Carolina, and was a member of the Southern Educational Association. At least by 1911, she had returned to South Carolina and was living and working among the wealthy northerners who wintered at the luxury hotels, golf courses, and polo grounds of Aiken and North Augusta, South Carolina, and nearby Augusta, Georgia. She was also an early and regular patron of Green Acre, an unusual summer colony in southern Maine. Founded in 1890 as a resort hotel by Sarah J. Farmer, a daughter of New England transcendentalists, Green Acre was billed as a nonsectarian oasis for the comparative study of religion and philosophy. With speakers ranging from Swami Vivekananda to W.E.B. Du Bois, it attracted a diverse array of poets, artists, intellectuals, freethinkers, and spiritual seekers from Boston, New York, and other cities of the Eastern Seaboard. Margaret Klebs was right at home. She routinely spent her summers in one of Green Acre's rustic cottages, teaching private students, arranging musical programs for the other guests, attending lectures, and enjoying the natural beauty of the riverside setting.[2]

Green Acre also provided Klebs with her first encounter with the Bahá'í Faith. Early in 1900, faced with financial difficulties and ill health, Sarah Farmer took a cruise on the Mediterranean. On the ship she met two old friends who had become Bahá'ís and were on their way to Palestine to meet 'Abdu'l-Bahá, and they encouraged her to join them. Farmer did so, and was immediately transformed by the experience. "Heart too full for speech," she wrote in her diary after her first audience with 'Abdu'l-Bahá, "—received by my Lord." During the 1900 summer season at Green Acre, she taught a class on "The Persian Revelation," and one of her early and enthusiastic students was Margaret Klebs. It is unclear whether or not Klebs identified herself as a

Bahá'í as early as 1901, when she was working at Presbyterian College in Columbia, but she certainly did so by the time of her return to South Carolina in 1911, when she sent a contribution from North Augusta to the building fund for the Bahá'í temple in Chicago. During 'Abdu'l-Bahá's visit to the United States the following year, Klebs was one of the five hundred people who met him at Green Acre, where he spoke on Bahá'í concepts of education and human development, predicted that the first Bahá'í university and the second temple in the United States would be built on the property, and engaged in intimate conversation with many individuals. More than twenty years later, Margaret Klebs recalled fondly her time with "Him who walked with holy feet on the ground of our cherished Green Acre." "Never to be forgotten," she said, was the sight of 'Abdu'l-Bahá with Sarah Farmer, permanently disabled after a fall and unable to continue her life's work, "driving slowly around the Green Acre fields. Blessed are we who could witness it."[3]

As with many early North American Bahá'ís who interacted personally with him, Margaret Klebs's encounters with 'Abdu'l-Bahá had a profound effect, setting the course of her life's work and fueling her personal faith for years to come. Either at Green Acre in August 1912 or later that fall during his

Figure 3.1. Margaret Klebs (1862–1939) on the porch of her cabin at Green Acre Bahá'í School, Eliot, Maine, date unknown. During her quarter century of residence in the Augusta metropolitan area, Klebs remained closely connected with the mainstream of the national Bahá'í movement in part through summers spent at Green Acre. Used with permission of the Eliot Bahá'í Archives, Eliot, Maine.

second visit to Washington, D.C., Margaret Klebs had a personal interview with 'Abdu'l-Bahá in which he directed her to return to the South and dedicate her life to teaching the faith there. By the winter of 1912–1913, Klebs was back in Aiken and North Augusta, South Carolina, and she followed 'Abdu'l-Bahá's instructions until the end of her life more than a quarter century later. Her pattern was to spend the summers at Green Acre, where lectures, study groups, and interactions with other believers kept her connected to the main currents of American Bahá'í thought and practice, and the remaining nine months or so in the Augusta area, teaching music classes and private students, staging recitals and concerts to benefit local charities, and attempting to build a new Bahá'í community from scratch.[4]

Louis Gregory appears to have introduced the faith in the Augusta area for the first time during his 1910 tour. He probably spoke at Haines Normal and Industrial Institute, a private school for black children, and Paine College, both in Augusta, and he may have also spoken at Schofield Normal and Industrial School, another black institution, in Aiken. Even so, Klebs's move was a step forward for the faith in the Augusta area. Even as Gregory's trip through the Carolinas and Georgia had indicated the potential receptivity of the region's people, especially African Americans, to the Bahá'í message, its aftermath had also highlighted the limitations of an approach to teaching that relied on itinerant lecturers without some method of following up with interested individuals and groups. Klebs's move provided part of an answer, at least for one of the metropolitan areas Gregory had visited. By pursuing her livelihood and making friends and acquaintances in Augusta, North Augusta, and Aiken, Klebs could come in contact with seekers on her own and teach them individually, nurturing a new Bahá'í community through interpersonal contact over an extended period of time. When other Bahá'í teachers did visit, she could greatly enhance their effectiveness by making arrangements and securing publicity in advance and by maintaining contact with those who had expressed an interest in the faith.[5]

Sister Cities on the Savannah

When Margaret Klebs moved to the environs of Augusta, she was making her home in an old city that embodied all the contradictions of the New South. Located on the Savannah River at the Fall Line, the rocky shoals marking the transition from the Piedmont to the broad Coastal Plain, the area had been inhabited by Native Americans for at least four thousand years, and in the early decades of the Carolina colony the native settlement of Savannah

Town on the east bank of the river was an important trading center. The new colony of Georgia was chartered in the 1730s with the Savannah River as its border with South Carolina, and a new settlement on the west bank, named Augusta, was designed to usurp the Carolinians' Indian trade. During the late colonial period, the new town prospered as a regional tobacco market, and after the invention of the cotton gin in 1793, as a center of a rapidly expanding backcountry cotton trade. The cotton boom brought a rise in population—including large numbers of African slaves—and a culture of entrepreneurship. In 1819 Henry Shultz, an immigrant from Germany who already had Augusta's new wharf, a bridge across the river, a bank, and the first steamboat service to the city of Savannah to his credit, decided to build a new town on the east side of the river. He laid out streets where his bridge crossed into South Carolina—not far from the site of Savannah Town—and called it Hamburg after his native city. In 1834, Hamburg became the western terminus of what was at the time the longest railroad in the world, from Charleston, and a little more than a decade later a canal bypassing the rapids on the Savannah River opened. These developments in infrastructure brought new cotton textile factories, powered by the swiftly flowing waters of Horse Creek, a tributary on the South Carolina side, making the area what one scholar has called "the cradle of southern industrialization." The railroad also brought the area's first tourist industry, with the new town of Aiken, laid out along the railroad some fifteen miles east of Hamburg, attracting wealthy visitors from the Lowcountry seeking relief from tuberculosis or from the heat of summer.[6]

After the Civil War, which largely bypassed the area, whites on both sides of the river fought to maintain political and economic control over a substantial black population. In Georgia, where whites made up a slight majority, white conservatives were able to oust the state's Republican regime at the ballot box in 1871, and Reconstruction in Georgia was over. In South Carolina, where blacks outnumbered whites two to one, the task of white conservatives was much harder, and during the pivotal election season of 1876 the town of Hamburg became a pivotal flashpoint in the struggle between the Republican-led government and an emerging white paramilitary movement. The Hamburg Riot of July 8, 1876, in which a former Confederate general led hundreds of armed white men from both sides of the river in an assault on Hamburg and its all-black militia unit, unleashed "Redemption," a wave of intimidation and violence that swept the state, resulting in claims of victory by two rival governments and—because it was not clear which party's candidate would take the electoral votes of South Carolina and two other disputed southern states—an inconclusive national presidential election. Dealmakers in Washington awarded all the electoral votes in question to the Republican candidate, Rutherford B. Hayes of Ohio, with an understanding that the last Republican strongholds in the South would be allowed to return to local Democratic control. In April 1877, the last federal troops left South Carolina, and Reconstruction in that state was over, too.[7]

In the Augusta area, the demise of Reconstruction opened a new wave of violence and oppression for black people on both sides of the border. In the rural districts, corruption and manipulation of the legal system ensured the virtual reenslavement of thousands, mostly men, through debt peonage, county chain gangs, and—in Georgia from 1868 to 1908—the brutal convict lease system. For the rest, extralegal violence became a constant threat. Much as Louis Gregory's family moved from Darlington to Charleston, blacks from Augusta's Georgia and South Carolina hinterland migrated to the city in search of education, employment, and safety. By the first decade of the twentieth century, black Augusta boasted a number of churches, lodges, and mutual aid societies; two high schools, one public and one private; a Methodist-supported college; a nursing school; and a host of businesses. Black professionals hailed the city's positive racial climate; in 1894 the editor of one of the city's black newspapers declared it "the garden spot of the country as far as the relations of the races go." But the success of a small minority masked deteriorating conditions in the city's black working-class neighborhoods. In the Territories, or the "Terri," the sprawling slum south of Gwinnett Street, limited employment opportunities and a lack of city services spawned disease, crime, and drug use. Nor were urban African Americans entirely immune from white violence. In the spring of 1900, for example, a mob lynched a black painter who was accused of killing a wealthy cotton broker's son in a fight over a seat on one of the city's streetcars. In the wake of the lynching, neighbors narrowly prevented another white mob from burning down the office of an outspoken black newspaper editor.[8]

Augusta-area whites did not act to defend white supremacy entirely on their own. Beginning in the 1880s, the area's politicians played important roles in the erection and violent maintenance of the Jim Crow regime. Benjamin Ryan Tillman, the chief architect of Jim Crow in South Carolina, was a native of Edgefield County just across the river from Augusta; he often trumpeted his participation as a youth in the 1876 violence at Hamburg as proof of his white supremacist credentials. On the Georgia side of the river, sometime Farmers' Alliance and Populist Party leader Thomas E. Watson of Thomson, some thirty-five miles west of Augusta, turned increasingly hostile to African Americans after his run for the vice presidency in 1896, when the Populists went down to disastrous defeat. Much as Tillman used his platform in the U.S. Senate to advance nationwide support for disfranchisement, segregation, and lynching, Watson disseminated his ideas through a national journal he published. His anti-black, anti-Catholic, anti-Semitic, anti-immigrant, and anti-radical invective encouraged the emergence of an anti-Catholic faction in the area's Democratic Party, which held power in the city of Augusta until the 1940s; spurred the Georgia disfranchisement movement, which by 1910 had decimated the ranks of black voters; and helped contribute to the lynching of Jewish factory manager Leo Frank in Atlanta in 1915 and the subsequent national revival of the Ku Klux Klan.[9]

The Jacksons of North Augusta

Across the region during the decades after Reconstruction, a new generation of ambitious young men came to embody the New South spirit of economic development. One such entrepreneur was James Urquhart Jackson, whose contributions to the Augusta metropolitan area's commercial, infrastructure, and cultural development included construction of the suburb of North Augusta, South Carolina, where the area's early Bahá'í community was centered. Following Margaret Klebs's arrival, Jackson and his family developed long and close associations with her and with the Bahá'í Faith. For better or for worse, the Jacksons probably did much to set the tone for the development of the Augusta-area Bahá'í community, particularly in matters of race and class.

James U. Jackson was born in 1856 and grew up on the family farm just outside Augusta. The large household included several members of the extended family and up to a dozen enslaved house servants and farm hands; after emancipation, many of these same African Americans stayed on to work as free laborers. Jackson's extended family was part of the Augusta area's political and commercial elite both before and after the Civil War. One of his uncles, a general during the war, was an attorney; another uncle was president of a local bank and of one of the area's first textile mills; and his father, a local militia leader during the war, was a stock and bond broker and the owner or director of a granite mill, a grain processor, two textile factories, and the Georgia Railroad and Banking Company. The Jacksons were members of Augusta's First Presbyterian Church on Telfair Street, where Joseph R. Wilson, father of future U.S. president Thomas Woodrow Wilson, was pastor from 1858 to 1870. James Jackson and the younger Wilson were born in the same year and likely attended Sunday school together. After he graduated from the University of Georgia in 1876, Jackson returned to Augusta and continued the family tradition of entrepreneurship, partnering with his cousin and adopted brother, Marion Jackson Verdery, in a brokerage business; becoming involved in the postwar railroad-building boom; helping to organize the Augusta National Exposition, an annual fair designed to draw visitors and boost the area's economy; and investing in a new resort hotel, the Bon Air, on the sandy hills of Summerville just northwest of the city.[10]

James Jackson's crowning achievement was the establishment of North Augusta, a new garden suburb on the South Carolina side of the river that epitomized the social, economic, and political ideologies of the New South. To begin with, North Augusta could have no association with the deteriorating black town of Hamburg. Surveying the slum on the flood plain near the river, Jackson planned his town for higher ground. In 1890 he purchased fifty-six hundred acres on the bluffs just northwest of Hamburg and, with tax incentives from the Augusta city council, built a new bridge at 13th Street that would bypass Hamburg completely. Under no illusion about competing with Augusta for business, Jackson planned North Augusta primarily as a residential suburb. The Delaware civil engineering firm he hired produced an innovative town plan: manufacturing and businesses were concentrated on the floodplain and residences above, with parks and greenways that followed the natural contours of the land interspersed among otherwise regular city blocks. The town's two principal squares, named Calhoun Place and Hampton Place, commemorated John C. Calhoun, the ideological father of South Carolina's secessionist movement, and Wade Hampton, the former Confederate general and leader of Redemption in 1876, respectively. Its two main thoroughfares, named Carolina and Georgia avenues, symbolized the economic joining of the two states. In 1897 the streetcar system, and with it electricity, were extended from Augusta to North Augusta, and by 1902 Jackson had created the South's first inter-urban electric railroad, linking the resort hotels west of Augusta with North Augusta and Aiken, a distance of some twenty miles. It is not an exaggeration, then, to say that North Augusta embodied the spirit of the New South: its physical situation provided for a steady supply of black laborers while simultaneously effacing African Americans from historical memory and placing them at the bottom of the new social and economic order; it was designed to be prosperous, orderly, and beautiful, taking advantage of state-of-the-art planning and the latest technologies; and its landmarks and infrastructure joined economic development with white supremacy.[11]

If North Augusta itself was Jackson's crowning achievement, then the jewel in his crown was the Hampton Terrace Hotel. A new resort financed by Jackson, the Hampton Terrace opened for business in 1903. Built atop a hill overlooking North Augusta and named, like one of the town's squares, for Wade Hampton, the imposing five-story building had three hundred guest rooms in two massive wings, with a ballroom, sunrooms, and other amusements in the center around the entryway. An eighteen-hole golf course, horseback riding, and a game preserve provided additional entertainment. For the next dozen years, many of the country's wealthiest and most powerful people—including Marshall Fields, Harvey Firestone, John D. Rockefeller, and William Howard Taft—spent their winters at the Hampton Terrace. Like North Augusta itself, Jackson's grand hotel symbolized the contradictions of the South in the Progressive Era: simultaneously forward- and backward-looking, it was a whites-only island of wealth and leisure in a sea of sharecropping, debt, forced labor, low-wage industry, political corruption, and endemic violence. It was, to say the least, an unexpected location from which to first proclaim the Bahá'í principle of the oneness of humanity.[12]

"Ere Long in that City"

From her arrival in the Augusta area, Margaret Klebs sought through her profession to integrate into the social life of her new home. As she shared her faith with a growing network of students, friends, and acquaintances, a small group of Bahá'ís emerged. Klebs's work necessarily put her in contact with the area's middle- and upper-class white residents—those most interested in and able to afford private voice instruction and most likely to attend performances of classical music—and those who aspired to such status, and it was primarily among this segment of the population that she initially attempted to share the Bahá'í message. Klebs's close association with the Jackson family, one of the most prominent in the area, began early, providing a variety of openings for teaching and likely lending the Bahá'í Faith an air of legitimacy in the eyes of the general public.

As a member of a wealthy German family with impressive training in European classical music, Margaret Klebs enjoyed an elite cultural status in the United States, but she lived simply, usually boarding in a home or renting a small apartment for the nine months each year she spent in the Augusta area. While her own circumstances were modest, early on Klebs began to make a mark on the cultural life of the area, hosting several public performances by her students each year, often to raise funds for local charities. In early March 1912, for example, Klebs arranged a musical program at the Hampton Terrace attended by hotel guests as well as local residents. The evening featured twenty students, performing solos and as a chorus, to benefit Augusta's YWCA. In May 1913, Klebs's students from Augusta, North Augusta, and Aiken performed at a school auditorium in North Augusta to benefit both the school and a local Methodist church. Several of Klebs's musical contacts were among the first people in the area to embrace the Bahá'í Faith, and their varied backgrounds give an indication of how Klebs's work offered social connections across middle- and upper-class white Augusta. Mary Anne Bracey, a teenage student whose father was a traveling salesman, became a Bahá'í. So did Robert Irvin, a local music teacher who participated in Klebs's concerts as an accompanist and performer. In his early thirties and single, Irvin lived at home with his mother, a widowed older brother who was an attorney, a younger brother who was city editor at the *Augusta Chronicle*, a younger sister who was a stenographer in a cotton warehouse, and his older brother's young son. Another student who became a Bahá'í was Daisy King Jackson, daughter of James U. Jackson and his second wife, Edith Barrington King of Savannah. A scion of Augusta's business elite on her father's side, Daisy Jackson descended from the coastal planter aristocracy on her mother's. Other contacts studied the faith and remained friendly to it but did not make it their own. Julia Moore, society editor at the *Augusta Herald*, readily publicized Bahá'í events and participated in the group's activities for years, apparently without ever identifying as a believer. Frank Hulse, a small-business owner in his early twenties with a wife and young child, was another of Klebs's students who attended Bahá'í activities but never joined.[13]

While Margaret Klebs was able to teach the faith effectively on an individual basis and was comfortable organizing large events, she seems to never have considered herself a public speaker. To attract larger numbers of people to the faith and capitalize on her own teaching successes, she needed the assistance of other experienced believers. In 1914, Klebs invited Joseph Hannen, Louis Gregory's mentor and one of the strongest proponents of interracial fellowship in the Washington Bahá'í community, to come to the Augusta area for a series of speaking engagements. Hannen, who often traveled as far south as North Carolina in his work as a salesman of medical instruments, likely combined his Augusta engagements with a work trip, and Klebs appears to have paid his train fare from either Charlotte or Asheville to Augusta and back. During his visit Hannen spoke in North Augusta and Aiken on at least three occasions. The first talk was held the evening of March 8, 1914, at James U. Jackson's mansion in North Augusta. The following evening,

Hannen was on the program of a concert at the Hampton Terrace "for the benefit of the Children's Home and the Mashrak-el-Azkar," the Bahá'í temple in Chicago. Frank Hulse, Daisy Jackson, and another student, Mabel Rogers, performed two sets of selections with Robert Irvin and Klebs at the piano. Between sets, Hannen addressed an audience of about two hundred people about the faith. Hannen also addressed students at the Schofield Normal and Industrial School in Aiken, one of the oldest and most respected schools for African Americans in South Carolina. Founded by the Freedman's Bureau just after the Civil War, the school was named for its principal, a Pennsylvania Quaker named Martha Schofield, and had produced numerous African American teachers and professionals. The Schofield School was supported by local blacks as well as some influential white patrons, both Aiken natives and winter colony regulars. Klebs had arranged the lecture through an association with John H. Landes, the school's business manager.[14]

After he returned to Washington, Joseph Hannen reported to 'Abdu'l-Bahá about his trip. 'Abdu'l-Bahá's tablet in reply began by praising Hannen's teaching efforts—particularly the "delivery of an eloquent talk," probably referring to the large gathering at the Hampton Terrace—and assuring him of

Figure 3.2. Hampton Terrace Hotel, North Augusta, South Carolina, postcard ca. 1915. The site of Joseph Hannen's "eloquent talk" on the Bahá'í Faith in March 1914, the Hampton Terrace was the centerpiece of entrepreneur James U. Jackson's vision for a prosperous garden suburb across the Savannah River from Augusta. It burned to the ground in 1916. Courtesy of the South Caroliniana Library, University of South Carolina, Columbia, S.C.

divine assistance: "Thy detailed letter was received. It was the incarnation of pure joy for it contained the particulars of thy trip to Augusta, Georgia. It explained the delivery of an eloquent talk by thee; that thou hast summoned the people to the Kingdom of God and hast spread the Divine Teachings. Consider how every soul who has arisen to serve the Word of God will be confirmed with the heavenly Cohorts. Therefore, be thou happy, because thou art assisted with such service." The tablet continued with a prophecy about the future of the Augusta area:

> Ere long in that city a great multitude shall enter in the Kingdom of God, the Flag of the oneness of the world of humanity will cast its shade over that state and the Song of the Supreme Concourse will be raised from its glens and dales. The fountain of the Water of Life will gush forth and the birds of the rose-garden of God will break into the rapturous songs of the glorification of the Kingdom of Holiness in the most wonderful melody. This trace will become eternal and will be continued throughout the future ages and cycles.

Predicting the spiritual transformation of the area, including the growth of the Baháʼí community and the removal of racial prejudice, the letter was as much a confirmation of Klebs's move as it was of Hannen's brief visit, and it inspired her to continue her work in Augusta and North Augusta for another quarter century.[15]

Over the next few years, the area's Baháʼí community grew, but slowly. By 1918 the circle of believers and seekers included at least half a dozen people in addition to Margaret Klebs. Julia Moore, the newspaper reporter, continued to associate with the Baháʼís but did not consider herself a believer. Among those who appear to have committed to the faith were G. P. Talbot, advertising manager for one of the local white newspapers (who may have learned about the faith from Julia Moore), and his wife, Louise Biggar Talbot, a nurse, both of whom had Georgia roots. Another was Ann McKennie Verdery, who was also a Georgia native and related to the Jackson family by marriage; her husband was a former railroad executive and president of a textile mill on Horse Creek. Another, Myrtis Tinsley, a South Carolinian born to parents from Georgia, was one of Margaret Klebs's voice students. Other believers moved away. Daisy Jackson married in 1915 and moved to Savannah, her husband's home, and young Mary Anne Bracey moved with her family to Savannah as well. Robert Irvin, among the first in the city to embrace the faith, spent three years working for the YMCA in Chicago and in Europe during the war years but had returned to Augusta by 1918. While in Chicago, he had taken part in local Baháʼí activities and been a frequent visitor to the home of Zia Bagdadi, an immigrant from Palestine who was one of the leaders of the national movement. Around 1920 a new Baháʼí, Esther Sego, moved to the city. Sego was an Augusta native born to parents from South Carolina, but she had recently embraced the faith while living in Jacksonville, Florida, where Charles Mason Remey of Washington had made a teaching trip. When Sego and her husband, a schoolteacher and later a principal, returned to Augusta with their children, she became an active member of the small Baháʼí community. At least by the immediate postwar years, the little group was sufficiently organized to name delegates to the annual national convention of the Bahai Temple Unity and, perhaps, to help fund their travel. Such participation was probably important in the group's consolidation. Meeting believers from all parts of the country, consulting on matters of importance to the national movement, and helping to elect the members of the Executive Board surely helped consolidate the Baháʼí identity of those who attended. Louise Talbot, for example, was the Augusta-area community's delegate to the landmark 1919 convention in New York. Robert Irvin was the delegate the following year. Both years, Margaret Klebs served as alternate delegate and presumably attended the convention with her spiritual children.[16]

During the era of World War I, Margaret Klebs continued to invite prominent Baháʼís from other parts of the country to come to the Augusta area to speak. Among them were Charles Mason Remey and John Bassett of Washington, who came in 1918 and again in 1919. On one occasion, they spoke at the Jackson home in North Augusta, and on another at Klebs's music studio on Greene Street in Augusta. Around 1920, Mírzá Asaduʼlláh Fádil-i-Mázandarání, an Iranian Baháʼí scholar whom ʻAbduʼl-Bahá sent on a tour of the United States, visited the area and spoke to an audience of "about sixty-five of the outstanding colored men" at the YMCA in downtown Augusta. Accompanied by Esther Sego, Jináb-i-Fádil (as the American Baháʼís usually called him) spoke to the group about the elimination of prejudices and distributed Baháʼí literature. "There were tears in their eyes as he left," Sego recalled. In April 1921, Martha Root, a journalist from Pennsylvania who would become the most widely traveled teacher in the Baháʼí world community, visited the Augusta area as part of an extensive southern tour. Fresh from an interview with labor leader and Socialist Party presidential candidate Eugene V. Debs in the Atlanta Federal Penitentiary, Root gave three talks in the area, one of which was at the home of Esther Sego and another at the home of Louise Talbot's sister, Nellie F. Baird, and her husband, neither of whom were believers. Root's main impact may have been on the small group of Bahá'ís themselves rather than on seekers; Esther Sego recalled that the visit increased "the enthusiasm and faith in the hearts of her hearers." Other Bahá'ís stopped in the area on their way to and from winter homes in Florida, some on an annual basis.[17]

Small as the Augusta-area Bahá'í community was, the local believers pursued their own teaching efforts and sought publicity in the local press. In January 1917, for example, the *Augusta Chronicle* noted that Margaret Klebs, Louise Talbot, and Julia Moore had called on conservative ideologue Thomas E. Watson at his estate outside Thomson. Guests for the day of Watson, his wife, and his secretary and magazine editor, Alice Louise Lytle, the Bahá'ís had presumably asked for the meeting in order to present the faith to a nationally prominent politician. While no other record of the meeting indicates the nature of their exchange, a visit with one of the area's most controversial public figures indicates that sometimes the local Bahá'ís could be rather bold in their outreach. More commonly, they were able to ensure that national and international news of the faith was printed in the local newspapers. In June 1915, for example, the *Chronicle* noted that 'Abdu'l-Bahá, "the leader of the worldwide Bahai movement for the unifying of all humanity in stronger social and religious ties," had sent a personal representative to the religious congress at the Panama-Pacific International Exposition in San Francisco. In April 1917, it announced the opening of the national Bahá'í convention in Boston as one of "Today's Events"—along with the postponement of a trade dinner in Chicago and a meeting of the Intercollegiate Association of Amateur Athletics in Philadelphia. Such "routine" coverage conveyed the message that the faith was a normal, nonthreatening part of the life of metropolitan Augusta, the nation, and the world—no small feat for a foreign, radical, non-Christian religion in the heartland of the new Ku Klux Klan.[18]

According to Margaret Klebs, even opposition from local clergy was an indication of the little Bahá'í community's growing influence in the area. "The interest in the Bahá'í Cause," she told delegates to the movement's 1925 National Convention, "has been manifested in a most wonderful way. Every year it is increasing, and perhaps the best proof that the Cause has been spreading is that from the various churches the Bahá'í movement has been denounced." While Klebs's comments provide little indication of the specific nature or motivation of the criticism in the Augusta-area churches, they suggest that I. E. Lowery's rhetorical attack on the Bahá'í Faith in Columbia in 1921 may not have been an isolated incident. Apparently, some conservative white clergymen, as well, felt threatened enough by the emergence of the new religion to denounce it in public.[19]

Formative Age

On November 28, 1921, the secretary of the Bahai Temple Unity's Executive Board received a shocking telegram that would have far-reaching effects on the believers in the Augusta area, across the country, and around the world. Signed by 'Abdu'l-Bahá's sister, Bahíyyih Khánum, it read simply: "His Holiness Abdul-Baha ascended to Abha Kingdom." With the passing of 'Abdu'l-Bahá, the Bahá'í Faith in the United States entered a new stage of its development. Under the leadership of his successor, Shoghi Effendi, in little more than a decade the American movement would grow from a loose association of local groups into a closely knit national community pursuing systematic plans for expansion of the faith. The transformation had a profound effect on the development of the Augusta-area community and on subsequent efforts to establish the faith in other localities in South Carolina. Shoghi Effendi linked two major themes in the ministry of 'Abdu'l-Bahá—teaching the faith and the development of its administrative institutions—into a framework that would guide the Bahá'ís' efforts in South Carolina and elsewhere around the world for decades to come.[20]

The devastating news of 'Abdu'l-Bahá's death was quickly disseminated to Bahá'í communities across the country. The Augusta-area group probably followed closely the next several issues of *Star of the West*, the national movement's magazine, which were filled with letters from members of 'Abdu'l-Bahá's household and from American pilgrims explaining the nature of his brief illness, photographs of his remarkable funeral in Haifa, and extracts from his tablets and addresses meant to strengthen the solidarity of the believers in their grief. "Be firm," he had told a group of pilgrims in 1905, "whether I am in this world or not." Nevertheless, mourning was mixed with anxiety as Bahá'ís in the United States and elsewhere wondered who would lead them. News arrived slowly. On December 22, a second telegram from Bahíyyih Khánum stated that 'Abdu'l-Bahá had "left full instructions in His Will and Testament" for the organization of the faith after his passing. A third message, dated January 16, 1922, and printed on the first page of the subsequent issue of *Star of the West*, conveyed the first indications of his plans for a dual succession: "In will, Shoghi Effendi appointed Guardian of Cause and Head of House of Justice. Inform American friends." Above the text was a photograph of a young, olive-skinned man with large, round eyes and a short moustache, wearing a black fez and Middle Eastern garments. A caption read, "Shoghi Effendi Rabbani, Grandson of His Holiness Abdul-Baha, Guardian of the Bahai Cause and Head of the House of Justice." For most of the Baháʾís in the United States, probably including all those in the Augusta-area group, it was their first introduction to the unassuming individual who would have far-reaching effects on their religion's expansion and development.[21]

The American Baháʾís were already familiar with the idea of the House of Justice. In several of Baháʾuʾlláh's tablets he had mentioned an international institution that would be the supreme organ of the Kingdom of God on earth, describing its members as "the Trustees of God among His servants and the daysprings of authority in His countries." And as early as the turn of the century, ʿAbduʾl-Bahá had sometimes used the term to refer to the local executive boards in the United States. During his 1912 visit to North America, he had discussed in some detail the central place of these local and international Houses of Justice in Baháʾuʾlláh's vision for a new global order:

> He has ordained and established the [local] House of Justice, which is endowed with a political as well as a religious function, the consummate union and blending of church and state. This institution is under the protecting power of Baháʾuʾlláh Himself. A universal, or international, House of Justice shall also be organized. Its rulings shall be in accordance with the commands and teachings of Baháʾuʾlláh, and that which the Universal House of Justice ordains shall be obeyed by all mankind. This international House of Justice shall be appointed and organized from the Houses of Justice of the whole world, and all the world shall come under its administration.

Unlike the House of Justice, however, the institution of the "Guardian of the Cause" (*valíyuʾl-amruʾlláh*), while based on the principle of hereditary succession that Baháʾuʾlláh had also mentioned in his writings, was entirely new. Even Shoghi Effendi, the holder of the new office, was surprised. At age twenty-four, Shoghi Effendi was the oldest of the children of ʿAbduʾl-Bahá's four daughters, and he had served as ʿAbduʾl-Bahá's primary English secretary during his youth. At the time of his grandfather's death, Shoghi Effendi was studying English and the humanities at Oxford University, and public reading of ʿAbduʾl-Bahá's will (and thus transmission of complete details to the Baháʾís around the world) was delayed until after his return to Haifa in late December. He later confided that he had imagined that ʿAbduʾl-Bahá might have given him, as the oldest grandson, the task of convening a gathering to elect the Universal House of Justice.[22]

Instead, ʿAbduʾl-Bahá had appointed him as "the sign of God, the chosen branch, the Guardian of the Cause of God," to whom all the relatives of the Báb and Bahá'u'lláh and the rest of the Bahá'ís must turn. After 'Abdu'l-Bahá, he was "the Interpreter of the Word of God," charged with resolving questions of doctrine and ensuring the integrity of the faith's scriptures. Further, 'Abdu'l-Bahá had named him as "the sacred head and the distinguished member for life" of the Universal House of Justice, which would have the power to legislate on matters not explicitly covered in the sacred texts. 'Abdu'l-Bahá had essentially extended Bahá'u'lláh's Covenant into the future, specifying the twin institutions that would operate in concert to protect the faith from schism and ensure its worldwide development. Both of them, he wrote, would be under the "care and protection" of Bahá'u'lláh and the "shelter and unerring guidance" of the Báb, and their decisions would be inspired by God.[23]

Most of the American Bahá'ís had never met Shoghi Effendi, but in the Bahá'í New Year (March 21) issue of *Star of the West*, under the banner "Resurrection," his first general letter to the American community gave some indication of the intellectual and spiritual qualities he would bring to his new office. After mentioning 'Abdu'l-Bahá's premonitions of his passing and quoting one of his tablets about the future growth of the faith, Shoghi Effendi asked:

> With such assuring utterances and the unmistakable evidences of his sure and clear knowledge that his own end was nigh, is there any reason why the followers of his Faith, the world over, should be perturbed? Are not the prayers he revealed for us sufficient source of inspiration to every worker in his Cause? Have not his instructions paved before us the broad and straight path of teaching? Will not his now doubly effective power of grace sustain us, strengthen us and confirm us in our work for him? Ours is the duty to strive, by day and night, to fulfill our own obligations and then trust in his guidance and never failing grace.[24]

With such stirring communications, most American Bahá'ís were able to quickly transfer their intense feelings of personal loyalty for 'Abdu'l-Bahá to his young successor. A handful of experienced believers, some with South Carolina connections, helped ease the transition. Emogene Hoagg, one of the earliest believers in the country and the first native Californian to become a Bahá'í, would later help establish local communities in Charleston and Greenville, but she was in Haifa with members of 'Abdu'l-Bahá's family shortly after his passing. In subsequent months she addressed letters to friends in the United States about his will and testament and the appointment of Shoghi Effendi as Guardian. "How wonderfully the Beloved provided for the protection of the Cause," she wrote to one member of the Executive Board. "Let us pray that the friends in America will arise with strength and goodwill to obey and to serve." One of the small minority of American believers who was already personally acquainted with Shoghi Effendi was Louis Gregory, who had met the young man during his pilgrimage in 1911. Gregory fondly recalled "a youth of about fifteen, keenly intelligent, diligent in his work, all reverence and devotion to the Master." He wholeheartedly embraced the new institution of the Guardianship, and during his teaching circuits across the country he counseled the American Bahá'ís to do the same.[25]

Shoghi Effendi's first concern as Guardian was establishment of the second institution mentioned in 'Abdu'l-Bahá's will, the Universal House of Justice. 'Abdu'l-Bahá had specified that the international body should be formed through "universal suffrage" of the Bahá'ís in a staged election process: a new institution, called the secondary or national House of Justice, should be elected "in all countries," and the members of the secondary Houses of Justice would then "elect the members of the Universal one." In March 1922, Shoghi Effendi invited a group of respected and well-informed believers from the United States, Europe, Iran, and India to his home in Haifa to discuss preparations for the elections. However, the consultation revealed a bleak picture of the worldwide movement's chances of fulfilling 'Abdu'l-Bahá's instructions any time soon. There were only a few dozen rudimentary local executive bodies—the practical prerequisites for establishing the national ones that 'Abdu'l-Bahá had called for—in the United States, and barely more than a handful in all of the Middle East. Each functioned largely autonomously, with little consistency between them in such essential matters as the number of members, voting procedures, modes of operation, and even name. The only body anywhere in the world that approximated a secondary House of Justice was the Executive Board of the Bahai Temple Unity in the United States, a relatively weak institution that existed only to carry out the decisions of the American movement's annual convention.[26]

Without the necessary structure of local and national bodies, election of the Universal House of Justice according to 'Abdu'l-Bahá's instructions was impossible; without a pool of believers experienced in administering the affairs of the community, Shoghi Effendi concluded that it was also simply impractical. As one American pilgrim who was visiting Palestine at the time of the consultation put it succinctly in a letter home: "It seems that before the Universal House can be established the Local and National Houses of Justice must be functioning in those countries where there are Bahá'ís." In effect, before the worldwide Bahá'í community could carry out this essential provision of their departed leader's will, its members faced a preliminary stage of administrative development. Shoghi Effendi sent his consultants home to inform their respective communities of the imperative of forming local and national bodies in preparation for the election of the Universal House of Justice. (Following 'Abdu'l-Bahá's usage, he settled on the temporary title of "Spiritual Assemblies" to avoid any appearance that the Bahá'ís were attempting to usurp civil governments.) At the time, perhaps only Shoghi Effendi himself suspected how long and difficult the task would prove to be.[27]

Two members of the Executive Board who had participated in the discussions in Haifa were to report the results of the meeting to the annual convention in the United States, planned for April 1922 in Chicago, and a lengthy letter from Shoghi Effendi, forwarded to all the local communities in the country shortly before the convention, outlined his instructions. He called for the direct election of a "local Spiritual Assembly in every locality where the number of adult declared believers exceeds nine" and for the "indirect election of a Body that shall adequately represent the interest of all the friends and Assemblies throughout the American Continent." To replace the previous system of ad hoc national working groups, he specified that the new body would appoint and directly supervise committees for such matters as publishing, teaching, the temple project, archives, membership, and "the racial question in relation to the Cause." At the convention, the testimonials of those who had just returned from Haifa helped cement the loyalty of the delegates to their new Guardian. "All the complex problems of the great statesmen of the world," said one, "are as child's play in comparison with the great problems of this youth. . . . He is indeed young in face, form and manner, yet his heart is the center of the world today." Responding to Shoghi Effendi's written and verbal instructions, the delegates voted to dissolve the Executive Board and replace it with a new nine-member body, the National Spiritual Assembly of the Bahá'ís of the United States and Canada.[28]

It was the beginning of an intensive period of institutional development, lasting more than a decade, that would reshape the Bahá'í movement in the United States and around the world. As Louis Gregory put it in his report of the 1922 convention: "It became apparent to all that the time of the organization of the Divine Kingdom on earth ha[d] come." Indeed, until the middle of the 1930s Shoghi Effendi and the American Bahá'ís wove together the strands of a distinctive Bahá'í system of governance. Then, as the American community began in earnest to fulfill its worldwide mission under 'Abdu'l-Bahá's

Tablets of the Divine Plan, that system served as the principal template for Bahá'í administration in other countries. In this sense, South Carolina's first local Bahá'í community in the Augusta area was one actor in a process with global ramifications.[29]

In their writings, Bahá'u'lláh and 'Abdu'l-Bahá had already delineated the founding principles that set the Bahá'í administration apart from other political systems, among them the fundamental unity of the body politic; avoidance of schism, partisanship, or special interests; obedience to and love of individuals for their institutions; the importance of collaborative decision-making and unified action; and the essential role of such spiritual qualities as selflessness, humility, and courtesy. Specific practices and procedures, however, were left to the Bahá'ís themselves to work out. Generally, Shoghi Effendi adopted a flexible approach, deferring to the legislative authority of the future Universal House of Justice for the establishment of definite rules and in the meantime allowing the American believers to reach their own conclusions about best practices. Through extensive correspondence with institutions and individuals and through personal interaction with pilgrims (essentially the same tools that had been at 'Abdu'l-Bahá's disposal), Shoghi Effendi kept abreast of every development, providing encouragement, raising questions, referring to relevant principles, or gently directing as necessary.[30]

During the 1920s and early 1930s, Shoghi Effendi and the American Bahá'ís tackled a variety of issues, some of them rather complex. The beginning of the administrative year, for example, was set at the Festival of Ridván (April 21–May 2), the anniversary of Bahá'u'lláh's public declaration of his mission in 1863, and all Local Spiritual Assemblies would be elected then. The movement's annual convention, a tradition since 1909, evolved into the Bahá'í National Convention, a temporary institution that met (also during the Ridván Festival) to elect the new National Spiritual Assembly and provide it with counsel about the national affairs of the faith. Delegates to the National Convention were reapportioned based on the populations of local Bahá'í communities, which required the maintenance of reliable lists of believers and the introduction of a formal process for enrolling new members. Local and national voting procedures were refined to ensure the full freedom of the electors, for example eliminating the practice of nominations. The consolidation of national committees under the National Spiritual Assembly required introduction of a single National Fund; to ensure the independence of the faith from special interests and underline the spiritual nature of giving, financial contributions could come only from members of the faith. Green

Acre in Maine, previously under the direction of a private board of trustees, gradually came under the direction of the National Spiritual Assembly, and two additional summer school campuses, in Michigan and California, were acquired. National and local constitutions and bylaws were adopted, and the National Spiritual Assembly and strong Local Spiritual Assemblies secured legal incorporation. The Nineteen Day Feast, a central activity at the grassroots of the movement since the turn of the century, was refined as local groups added a period of community consultation and information-sharing to the gathering's devotional and social portions.[31]

Throughout the period, Shoghi Effendi worked to place such administrative matters in their proper context. As challenging and time-consuming as it was to build, Shoghi Effendi repeatedly reminded the American community that the fundamental purpose of the system outlined in 'Abdu'l-Bahá's will was to harmonize the efforts of the Bahá'ís and to canalize the transformative spiritual powers inherent in their faith. In his lengthy "World Order Letters" written between 1929 and 1936 and a host of shorter communications, he explained that the "Administrative Order" that the Bahá'ís were constructing was not simply a system for the organization of one tiny religious faction among many in the world but the structural basis of the Christ-promised Kingdom of God on earth, the "nucleus" and "pattern" of the "New World Order" brought by the promised one, Bahá'u'lláh. With the passing of 'Abdu'l-Bahá, Shoghi Effendi explained, the faith had entered a "stage of transition," a "Formative Period" or "Iron Age" of institution-building. He called the local and national Spiritual Assemblies the "bedrock" of the Universal House of Justice, which Bahá'u'lláh had named as the supreme governing authority for the coming "Golden Age" of humanity. The local and national bodies the Bahá'ís were building, then, were essential to the faith's mission. Shoghi Effendi's compelling articulation of Bahá'u'lláh's vision for the future invested every believer's actions, however small, with both immediate spiritual import and far-reaching consequences for the world. Moreover, such a vision was indispensable to enabling individuals raised in a divisive political culture—one often characterized by skepticism of government, intense partisanship, pursuit of narrow interests, and a coarse and manipulative public discourse—to create an alternative system with distinctly Bahá'í characteristics.[32]

While Shoghi Effendi's part in the process could often seem gentle and indirect, he concerned himself with the intimate workings of each part in the new system, and his guiding presence was felt early on even among the tiny group of Bahá'ís in the Augusta area. In January 1923, he wrote collectively to them and to thirty other local communities in North America—from Santa Rosa, California, and Bisbee, Arizona, to Ithaca, New York, and St. John's, New Brunswick—whose numbers were not large enough to form a Local Spiritual Assembly. The letter is exemplary of his leadership style for its care and specificity; its elevated language; its messages of encouragement, urgency, and confidence in the abilities of the believers and in the power of divine assistance; and its reliance on passages of scripture for inspiration and reflection. Listing each city and town by name, Shoghi Effendi encouraged the small groups of believers to rely on the heavenly forces at their disposal, to persevere in teaching the faith, and to remain focused on the long-term goal of the regeneration of the world. He wrote that although their numbers were "small and limited," through the "Celestial Potency bequeathed" to them by the departed 'Abdu'l-Bahá, each "small company" would "expand and wield such power and influence as no earthly power can ever hope for or attain." Quoting the words of 'Abdu'l-Bahá, he wrote that the faith was at the "'beginning of its growth,'" but the powers within it would "'gradually appear and be made manifest.'" It marched inexorably forward according to the will of God, "lead[ing] humanity to its glorious destiny." In the midst of widespread pessimism about the state of the world, he said the duty of each Bahá'í was to "arise with greater confidence than ever before, endeavoring to clear the mists of hate and prejudice that have dimmed the vision of mankind and . . . point out to a weary world the Way of True Salvation." Finally, he enumerated specific goals for each locality: "I very eagerly await the news of the progress of the Movement in your cities and shall be grateful and delighted to hear that you have reinforced your numbers, extended your activities, established a centre and founded a Spiritual Assembly that shall direct and co-ordinate your efforts for the promotion of the Cause." Through letters such as these, Shoghi Effendi sought to stimulate the grassroots of the American community and to impart a sense of shared responsibility for the development of the religion's institutions. In effect, he was letting the small circle of believers in Augusta and the other localities know that the head of their faith knew who they were, loved them, and had great expectations for them.[33]

Teaching Methods

While the development of the Bahá'í administrative structure during the 1920s and 1930s included certain elements of centralization and standardization, in the essential work of teaching the period was characterized more by decentralization. At the same time that the faith's local and national institutions developed into a coherent structure, the American Bahá'í community was developing new teaching methods and learning to involve a larger number of believers in carrying them out. These new approaches to teaching had a profound impact on activities in South Carolina. In the Augusta area, the community grew more steadily than before, and by the mid-1930s it was large and strong enough to elect the first Local Spiritual Assembly anywhere in the Carolinas and Georgia. Traveling teachers in other parts of South Carolina employed the new methods as well, but the absence of experienced resident believers meant that their effects were less pronounced.

From its inception in the early 1920s, the National Spiritual Assembly and its agencies tried a variety of approaches to stimulating, organizing, and carrying out teaching activities. Throughout the period, the National Assembly charged its National Teaching Committee (the heir to the Committee of Nineteen formed in 1919 in response to the Tablets of the Divine Plan) with coordinating teaching around the country. The committee in turn was usually structured as one executive chair and five regional chairs (corresponding to the four U.S. census regions and Canada), each responsible for arranging teaching conferences, public meetings, and circuits for traveling teachers. At the same time, the National Assembly's two "Plans of Unified Action" (for 1926–1928 and 1931–1934, respectively) called for local communities to take the lead in teaching. Local Spiritual Assemblies were asked to appoint their own teaching committees, to train more believers as teachers, and by the late 1920s, to initiate "extension teaching projects" in which Bahá'ís from an existing community systematically visited a nearby locality to establish a new community there.[34]

While the decentralization of teaching began during the 1920s, it was the onset of the Great Depression that forced a larger number of Bahá'ís at the local level to take on responsibility for propagating the faith. In the midst of unprecedented financial straits, with construction of the house of worship in Chicago commanding the lion's share of the movement's national budget, the National Spiritual Assembly and its agencies could no longer fund traveling teachers and large public meetings as they had before. If the faith was to grow during the Great Depression, it would largely depend on initiative at the grassroots. Crucial to this change in the community's culture was the thought and influence of Leroy Ioas, a member of the National Teaching Committee beginning in 1932 and its chair for fourteen years. Ioas, whose German immigrant parents had embraced the faith in Chicago in 1898, was a railway manager by profession, and he brought a businessperson's energy, efficiency, and vision to the work of the committee. In particular, Ioas championed two methods of teaching: the fireside meeting and the study group.

In a "fireside meeting," or simply "fireside" (a name perhaps influenced by President Franklin D. Roosevelt's famous "fireside chats," begun in March 1933), a Bahá'í invited one or more prospective seekers to his or her home, showed warm hospitality, and shared the faith in a conversational fashion. Leroy Ioas believed that the fireside would enable every Bahá'í to become a teacher, increase the pool of interested contacts in each locality, and broaden the audience for other forms of teaching, such as public talks. Previously, traveling lecturers had tended to receive the most attention in Bahá'í publications, perhaps contributing to a sense among some in the national community that only good public speakers could be considered teachers of the faith. For example, as Louise Talbott of Augusta had written to Joseph Hannen in 1917, "We sincerely hope to have you here to speak on the Bahai Cause later in the spring. We try in a quiet way to interest people, but are poor talkers generally in large gatherings." For Ioas, such a dependence on skilled public speakers not only artificially limited the pool of teachers in the community, but it ran contrary to the call in Bahá'u'lláh's writings for every believer, not a specific class of ministers or missionaries, to share the message. It also missed the point that most of the previous growth of the faith in the United States—as in the cases of Washington and Augusta, for example—had been as a result of the kind of intimate, home-based teaching of friends, family members, and neighbors that Ioas was now calling the fireside. Writing for the National Teaching Committee in a 1936 bulletin, Ioas called for "a number of these intimate, conversational gatherings" in each locality.[35]

Once attracted to the faith in a fireside, seekers could be invited to regular study classes. Like the fireside, the study class was another long-standing teaching method that was to some extent formalized in the 1920s and 1930s. By 1932, the National Teaching Committee reported that most local communities had some type of study class, which it described as "a versatile and effective medium of teaching." Also like firesides, study groups could be tailored to individual circumstances: "Probably very few study groups are of the same type. They are large and small, public and private, for inquirers, new believers and confirmed Bahá'ís of long standing. They are usually based on one or more of the study outlines distributed by the National Bahá'í Study Committee or upon some Bahá'í book. They have resulted in a deeper knowledge of the teachings, the development of active workers and teachers, and many new believers." As part of its efforts to define Bahá'í membership as necessitated by the electoral process, the National Spiritual Assembly's policy, at least from 1935 on, was that seekers' initial education on the fundamentals of the faith should happen before their formal enrollment in the community. Study classes, then, became an important route for cultivating new believers.[36]

Across the country, the number of firesides and study classes increased during the 1930s. Combined with a more widespread observance of the Nineteen Day Feast and of the faith's Holy Days (and, in some localities, activities for children and youth), they made for a more robust local Bahá'í organization and a broader reach into the life of the community at large. In some areas, they received a boost from or were started as a result of visits by traveling teachers, who could often reach a wider audience through public talks and then channel the most interested to regular firesides and study groups. A handful of American believers specialized in what they called "teaching campaigns," visiting one city for a week or more to give a well-planned series of public lectures that culminated in the formation of a study group. All these approaches increasingly characterized Bahá'ís' efforts throughout South Carolina.[37]

Trying New Approaches across South Carolina

During the 1920s and 1930s, national developments in teaching and administration were reflected in the activities of Bahá'ís in South Carolina, from the Augusta metropolitan area to the cities of Charleston and Columbia and the smaller towns of Orangeburg and Sumter. However, the absence of long-term settlers outside of Augusta and North Augusta meant that the gains elsewhere were mostly short-lived. The experiences of Bahá'í visitors in several South Carolina localities during the period provide an instructive counterpoint to the relatively robust growth of the Augusta-area community. Indeed, the contrast appears to not have been lost on Shoghi Effendi. In the mid-1930s, when he introduced his own plans for the expansion and consolidation of the faith in North America and beyond, there was an emphasis on the settlement of experienced Bahá'ís in new localities, the very piece that had been missing from efforts in most of South Carolina since Louis Gregory's first foray in 1910.

After the passing of 'Abdu'l-Bahá, Louis Gregory continued unabated his travels through the South and other parts of the country, and he adapted his long-standing practices to new developments in teaching and administration. For example, in December 1931 he helped start a Bahá'í study class during a brief visit to Atlanta, and in the winter and spring of 1934, he resided for several months in Nashville, where he taught a study class on the Fisk University campus, confirmed six new believers, and enabled the community to elect its first Local Spiritual Assembly. He tried similar methods in South Carolina, but in localities with no resident Bahá'ís he met with less success than in Atlanta or Nashville. During a fall 1924 tour of Virginia, the Carolinas, Alabama, and Tennessee, Gregory spent twelve days in Sumter, South Carolina, a town some sixty miles east of Columbia. He reported speaking to about five hundred students at Morris College, founded in 1908 by the state's black Baptists, and to some fourteen hundred students at Lincoln Public School. He also spoke at an African Methodist Episcopal church, two white Baptist churches, and a Presbyterian school. A report of his visit to Sumter stated that there were enough "deeply interested" people there to form a "small reading circle," but it is unclear whether a group ever actually formed.[38]

From Sumter, Gregory returned to his hometown of Charleston. In the space of eight days, he spoke to five churches, six schools, and two "small interested groups." It was probably also during his 1924 visit to Charleston that Gregory called at the home of Clarence W. Westendorff. A white South Carolina native, Westendorff owned a gas station on St. Philip Street, just two blocks from Gregory's childhood home. He lived nearby with his wife, their five children, and several boarders. While it is unclear how Westendorff first came to his attention, Gregory had previously written to him about the faith and included a Bahá'í text. At the 1925 national convention, the National Teaching Committee's regional chair for the South recounted the story of Westendorff's response:

> Mr. Gregory had written to this name and he went to the address and asked if any Bahais lived there, and a voice responded, "Yes, I got the letter, and I am a Bahai." He had been given the Word and had set forth immediately to spread the teachings that the little book taught him, and he said: "This is the best thing in the world." He began to preach on the street corners, until finally the mayor sent for him. He said the mayor said it was not permissible for him to preach on the main street. He was imprisoned several times. He said he told them, "When I was among you as a Christian, you let me alone; but now I am rising you put me in jail." It was for the sake of his children that he stopped this propaganda in the streets of Charleston. It seems they began to be persecuted in the streets, and then our good friend Gregory advised him not to work in that way, not so melodramatic.

More than a decade after they condemned Alonzo Twine to the insane asylum, Charleston's white authorities silenced Clarence Westendorff's outspoken public advocacy of the Bahá'í Faith. In contrast to Twine's plight, however, the administrative development of the American Bahá'í movement in the intervening years meant that Westendorff did not remain completely isolated in his new belief. After Gregory's visit, he was apparently listed as a Bahá'í and began to receive the national newsletter. Yet there was still no local community—indeed, no other single believer—with whom he could associate and form bonds. Despite an apparently sizeable pool of interested people in Charleston, for some reason Gregory did not stay long, nor did he recommend the creation of a study group there, as he did in Sumter.[39]

Louis Gregory visited Charleston at least two more times in the next several years, but still no local Bahá'í community emerged. One trip was unplanned. In October 1929, Louis Gregory was called to Charleston for the funeral of his beloved stepfather, George Gregory. The elder Gregory, aged just shy of eighty-seven years, had died after being accidentally struck by a truck one morning before dawn. He had long been a supporter of his son's work for the Bahá'í Faith and of his marriage. "I am glad to hear from you all your travels," he had written early in 1914. "You seem to be going all over the Country. . . . I hope you may live long to do good for the Master. . . . God bless you and wife. I am praying for you both." After the funeral, Louis Gregory wrote that "more of the spirit and understanding [of the Bahá'í Faith] had penetrated him than his son had dared to hope for in one so advanced in years." He had taken a "deep interest in the Cause, distributed the literature" to friends in Charleston, and helped to arrange teaching meetings during his son's visits. The funeral itself gave an indication of George Gregory's standing in the community and the extensive social network he was able to draw on to promote the faith. About a thousand people, both black and white, attended, and seven clergymen took part in the service. The Mickey Funeral Home, owned by local NAACP founders Richard and Edward Mickey, handled the arrangements. Louis Gregory read Bahá'í prayers as part of the program. Only a year and a half after his stepfather's death, in early 1931, Louis Gregory returned to Charleston as part of an extended trip through Maryland, Virginia, and the Carolinas. He spoke at five churches, a Catholic high school, and the Book Lovers' Club, a black women's literary and service society. Still, however, there was no indication that he found any opening to start a study class in the city. Perhaps a class would have emerged if Gregory had stayed longer. Indeed, the faith might have developed quite differently in South Carolina if he had been able to reside in Charleston for several months and confirm a group of new believers.[40]

Also in 1931, the National Spiritual Assembly's Racial Amity Committee began sending interracial teams on teaching tours to southern colleges and schools, an idea suggested by Shoghi Effendi some time before. Perhaps the committee was also encouraged by growing evidence of racial liberalism and student activism on the region's college campuses, brought on in part by the social and economic dislocation of the Great Depression. In preparation for deploying interracial teams, the committee consulted with Will W. Alexander of the Interracial Commission. He predicted that the participants in such a plan "would meet with many agreeable surprises," and the committee solicited volunteers at the next National Convention. The first team to make a trip consisted of Chauncey Northern of New York City and Philip Marangella of Portsmouth, New Hampshire. Together they embodied a great deal of the country's diversity. Northern, a twenty-seven-year-old black man whose family had migrated north from Hampton, Virginia, was a professional singer. He lived at home on the edge of Harlem with his parents, six siblings, his wife, and a sister-in-law. Marangella's family had migrated from their village in the Potenza region of southern Italy to New York when he was an infant. Married and the father of two children at age thirty-six, he was an accountant and an amateur poet who frequently contributed to artistic programs at Green Acre. The two developed a presentation of the Bahá'í teachings using song, poetry, and speech and traveled by car together in the autumn of 1931, first to Washington and Baltimore and then through Virginia and the Carolinas.[41]

In Richmond, they were "happily received" by Louis Gregory's friend Samuel C. Mitchell, professor of history at the University of Richmond and former president of the University of South Carolina, who had heard 'Abdu'l-Bahá speak at the Lake Mohonk conference in 1912. In Columbia, South Carolina, Northern and Marangella spoke at the University of South Carolina "through the courtesy of Professors in ethics and educational philosophy." They also met Josiah Morse, chair of the Department of Psychology and Philosophy, whom Louis Gregory had met a decade earlier and who had been an early advocate of interracial student exchanges. Morse's colleagues and students respected him as "a pioneer in the field of racial relationships in the South" and as a person who was concerned with "the oppressed, underprivileged and neglected classes of Society." The university's student newspaper, usually silent on racial issues, carried no news of the activities of Northern and Marangella. But about the time of their visit it did report public remarks by Morse that closely resembled Bahá'í teachings. The "campus philosopher" told his ethics class: "Justice is represented as blindfolded. She has no regard for race, relation, or wealth. The world today is being weighed and I am afraid it will be found wanting. We have come to a turning point in the history of man. The time has come for the young people to think clearly and put an end to these age-old hatreds or there will be an end to mankind. It is up to you to think broadly and put an end to patriotism that carries a chip on its shoulder all the time! Put an end to hatred—national, religious, and racial!" Also in Columbia, Marangella and Northern spoke at Benedict College and Allen University. Located on adjacent campuses in the heart of Columbia's main black commercial and residential neighborhood and long centers of the state's black cultural and political life, Allen and Benedict had likely received Louis Gregory and Roy Williams during their 1919–1921 teaching trips through the region.[42]

In Orangeburg, Northern and Marangella visited two more black institutions, the Colored Normal, Industrial, Agricultural, and Mechanical College (known as "State College") and Claflin University, the alma mater of I. E. Lowery and Alonzo Twine. Located on adjacent campuses like Allen and Benedict in Columbia, State College and Claflin formed the cultural and intellectual hub of black Orangeburg. The duo found receptive audiences of "theologians and students" in Orangeburg, and several of their listeners recalled "previous visits of other teachers of the Bahá'í Cause," probably Gregory and Williams. A dean at one of the colleges said he would start a Bahá'í study group "as soon as literature was received for it." However, as in Sumter, it is unclear whether the national movement responded to the opportunity and, if it did, what became of the group.[43]

Teaching and Community Development in Augusta and North Augusta

In contrast to the situation in the rest of South Carolina, the Augusta metropolitan area had a small group of resident believers, at least a few of whom were relatively well deepened in the Bahá'í teachings and connected to the mainstream of the American movement, and during the 1920s and early 1930s they were able to employ new teaching methods to achieve a more sustained pattern of growth. They continued to pursue their own means of spreading the faith locally, often advertising their activities in the press. For example, Margaret Klebs hosted firesides at her studio, and she met new people to teach when she started music classes in nearby small towns, including Waynesboro, the seat of Burke County, Georgia, some thirty miles from Augusta, and Johnston, South Carolina, a black-majority town in Edgefield County some twenty-five miles from North Augusta. Esther Sego met people through participation in several local choirs. They were also able to capitalize on the assistance of traveling teachers by inviting their own contacts to lectures, securing venues and advance publicity, arranging smaller meetings in homes, and following up when the visitors had departed. For example, Lorol Schopflocher, a believer from Montreal who had traveled widely for the League of Nations Union, visited the area in April 1933. She combined a lecture with moving pictures from her most recent world tour, including scenes of California and Hawaii; war-torn Manchuria, Burma, and other sites in Europe and Asia; and the Bahá'í holy places in Palestine. Margaret Klebs and one of her students provided music. A "large and appreciative audience," including many who responded to advance advertising and whom the local believers had not invited personally, came to the YMCA for the evening's program.[44]

Another traveling teacher had an even greater impact on the local community's development. Stanwood Cobb, a child of New England intellectuals and a prominent educator in the Washington area, visited the Augusta area in 1934 to conduct a "teaching campaign." Cobb was one of the country's most knowledgeable and experienced Bahá'ís, having met 'Abdu'l-Bahá five times in Palestine and the United States, been an editor of *Star of the West* and its successor magazine, *World Order*, and served as a member of the Local Spiritual Assembly of Washington. Cobb was traveling under the auspices of the National Teaching Committee, and the Bahá'ís and their friends in the Augusta area arranged at least seven public lectures for his stay during late March and early April. His topics were wide ranging, reflecting both his own interests and background and a desire among many American Bahá'ís, heightened during the Great Depression, to relate the teachings of the faith to contemporary social issues. These included "Constantinople Days" (an allusion to his time as a college professor in Turkey and his writings presenting Islam to Western audiences), "Education in the Future Baha'i State," "The Unity of Science and Religion," "A Planned Society" (about Bahá'u'lláh's prescriptions for world order), and "The New Deal in Washington" (certainly a timely topic but unusual given the Bahá'í prohibition on giving any appearance of political partisanship). In North Augusta, Cobb spoke to the high school parent-teacher association and to the local American Legion. In

Augusta, he spoke at the YMCA and in the auditorium of the Georgia Power Company building.[45]

After the Georgia Power meeting, "well attended by many teachers and Theosophists, as well as representatives of various clubs and organizations," the local Baháʼís invited some of the guests who were "more than casually interested" to join a study group. It met at the North Augusta home of one of the seekers, Marie Kershaw, the area's only female physician. The group represented a virtual cross-section of the Augusta area's white middle and working classes, including its relatively large immigrant population; many of the participants were neighbors or already had social ties to each other. It also included individuals with deep roots in the Baháʼí Faith, relatively new believers, and seekers who had just discovered the religion. Daisy Jackson Moore, who had returned to North Augusta after living in Savannah, and Esther Sego were the most experienced believers in the group. William and Christine Bidwell had recently become Baháʼís while living in Miami. He was a naturopathic physician originally from Tennessee, and she was a native of Pendleton in South Carolina's upper Piedmont. They had not had a chance to study the faith in depth, so they joined the group along with their friend Marie Kershaw, whom they had invited to Cobb's talks. Another participant who was already familiar with the faith was Mary Biggar Andrews. Her sister, Louise Biggar Talbott, who had moved away to New York, had been one of the early believers in the Augusta area; she may have attended the talk given by traveling teacher Martha Root at the home of another of their sisters, Nellie Baird, in 1921. A recent widow and the mother of two teenage girls, Andrews ran an antique business.[46]

There were other professionals in the class besides Marie Kershaw and William Bidwell. Josephine MacDonald was an attorney. A South Carolina native, she lived in downtown Augusta with her husband, also an attorney, and teenaged children. Elkin Vogt was a physician and instructor at the University of Georgia Medical School. The son of immigrants from Alsace-Lorraine and Germany, Vogt was born and raised in Atlanta and had come to Augusta as a student. At age thirty, he and his wife, Dorothea, were just starting a family; both of them joined the study group. Anna Krogius was a massage therapist who lived in the Summerville neighborhood west of downtown. A Finnish immigrant, she was single at age fifty-six.[47]

Others in the group were lower-middle-class or working-class. Sophie Wallace, a Georgia native, was a housewife with two children at home on Greene Street in downtown Augusta; her husband was a locomotive engineer. Ailene Fletcher, also a Georgia native, lived on Broad Street only a few blocks from the Wallaces. A widow with two teenage children, Fletcher ran a beauty salon in her home. Her nineteen-year-old son Clay also joined the study group. Another Georgia native, Vivian Hoffman, age twenty-three, lived at home on Reynolds Street downtown with her father, an automobile machinist, and her mother, a housewife. She worked as a secretary in an eyeglass store. Claire Glover, in her mid-thirties and single, lived in the countryside outside North Augusta but worked as a clerk for the post office in downtown Augusta. Morgan Barton, a railroad machinist, lived in a working-class neighborhood outside North Augusta. He was a Georgia native, but his father was a New Yorker and his mother a South Carolinian born to German immigrants. In his mid-thirties, Barton was married and the father of two young children.[48]

Several members of the study group evidently identified themselves as Baháʼís immediately; by the time of the Ridván Festival at the end of April, less than a month after Cobb's lectures, the group expected to elect a Local Spiritual Assembly. The National Spiritual Assembly, however, apparently concerned by most of the participants' inexperience, informed them in a letter that, as one participant recalled, they "would have to stay a Study Group for a whole year in order to be deepened in the Teachings." Over the next year, between fifteen and twenty-three believers and seekers met each Wednesday night at Marie Kershaw's house in North Augusta. Their topics of study, including progressive revelation, the life of Baháʼuʼlláh, and health and healing, were reported in the local press, usually with extensive factual coverage or a complete reproduction of the lesson. After a year of study, the National Spiritual Assembly recognized the group's participants as believers and gave permission to form a Local Spiritual Assembly. In April 1935, the community met at Kershaw's home and conducted an election to form the first Baháʼí administrative institution in either South Carolina or Georgia. Two of the new Local Assembly's nine members were veteran Baháʼís, seven new; five members lived in North Augusta, four in Augusta.[49]

Notably absent from the study class and from the new Local Assembly was Margaret Klebs, the founder of the community and by far its most experienced believer. Apparently Klebs was uncomfortable with the class for some reason, because she attempted to organize her own group on Friday evenings. Perhaps she questioned the group's grounding in the teachings, or felt sidelined or unappreciated as the community grew. Whatever her personal feelings, Stanwood Cobb's visit, the formation of the study group, and the election of the first Local Spiritual Assembly coincided with a period of declining mental and physical health and financial insecurity for Klebs that limited her involvement in community activities. One of the newer believers simply recalled that "Miss Klebs did not associate with our group." But the divide was not total. In April 1935, just before the election, Klebs fell and broke her hip. The injury necessitated a long convalescence, and other members of the community, including Esther Sego and Marie Kershaw, attempted to take care of Klebs at home and solicited financial assistance from her other Bahá'í friends around the country. In 1936, Klebs suffered again from a "trying and serious illness" and spent many weeks in the hospital. She rallied by the end of the year, preparing a Thanksgiving concert in appreciation for the doctors and nurses who had cared for her and announcing the opening of a "Baha'i Reading Room" on Telfair Street—even though the community had already opened a Bahá'í Center on 13th Street. During the summer of 1938 the Local Spiritual Assembly of Eliot, Maine, tried to care for Klebs as local residents and Green Acre guests complained about her increasingly erratic and disruptive behavior. She returned to the Augusta area the following autumn and died of pneumonia in January 1939. The Local Spiritual Assembly of Augusta conducted the funeral service, the Eliot Bahá'ís paid for flowers, and Edith Jackson (Daisy Jackson Moore's mother and the wife of North Augusta's founder) donated a family cemetery plot in the town for her burial.[50]

Despite the discomfort Margaret Klebs may have had with the study group, it proved an effective means of attracting seekers and confirming new believers in the faith. Meeting consistently over the course of several years, the participants ranged over Bahá'í introductory texts, works of scripture, and the stories of the faith's apostolic age. The class was a venue for participants not only to familiarize themselves with the history and teachings of the faith but also to form or strengthen bonds of friendship and shared identity. It was also a regular activity to which new seekers could be easily invited. According to one participant, between 1934 and 1938, the class completed study of *Bahá'u'lláh and the New Era*, a widely used introductory text; *Bahá'í Administration*, a compilation of letters of Shoghi Effendi; *The Kitáb-i-Iqán*, Bahá'u'lláh's exposition of the prophecies of the Bible and the Qur'án; *Some Answered Questions*, compiled from a series of table talks by 'Abdu'l-Bahá, mostly on Christian topics; *Tablets of Abdul-Baha Abbas*, a three-volume compilation; and *The Dawn-Breakers*, Shoghi Effendi's translation of a lengthy history of the birth and rise of the faith in Iran.[51]

Late in 1936, the community was further augmented when an experienced Bahá'í family moved to Augusta from Chicago. Zia Bagdadi initially visited the area as a traveling teacher. Of Iranian background but born and raised in the Arab world of Lebanon and Palestine, Bagdadi had been a part of

'Abdu'l-Bahá's retinue during his 1911–1912 visits to the West, a member of the Executive Board of Bahai Temple Unity, a champion of the temple project, and editor of the Farsi section of *Star of the West*. A physician, he was one of the most active teachers of African Americans in the Chicago Bahá'í community. He already had some links with the Augusta area, having befriended Robert Irvin during the latter's stay in Chicago during World War I and known Margaret Klebs from many years at the National Convention. In August 1936 Bagdadi made a two-week visit to Augusta, speaking, for example, to a white women's luncheon club about the role of women in establishing world peace. During his trip, members of the Augusta-area community evidently persuaded Bagdadi to move. He returned later in the fall with his wife, Zeenat, who had grown up in the household of 'Abdu'l-Bahá in Haifa, and their young daughter. The Bagdadis and the Local Assembly agreed to rent jointly a building on 13th Street in the heart of downtown Augusta that would serve at once as the community's Bahá'í Center, Bagdadi's professional office, and a residence for him and his family. Soon the new center filled with activities: the Nineteen Day Feast, Holy Day observances, meetings of the Local Assembly, study group every Wednesday night, lecture series, and informal dinners. One believer recalled that the Bagdadis "baked delicious chicken" and served Persian rice dishes. Other meetings, including firesides and Esperanto classes, took place in the homes of believers and seekers.[52]

By 1937 the community numbered more than thirty members and perhaps at least that many friends and seekers. Many of the new believers were friends, neighbors, and family members of the original 1934 study group participants, and many accepted the faith through Zia Bagdadi's teaching efforts. Vivian Hoffman's mother, Emma B. Hoffman, a housewife, became a Bahá'í. So did Pawnee Barton, Morgan Barton's wife. Effird Lynch, a young clerk at a bakery and delicatessen, was Josephine MacDonald's next-door neighbor in Augusta. Carlton Sample had taken singing lessons from Margaret Klebs. Age thirty-five and single, he was a draftsman at an iron factory and lived in North Augusta. The personal connections of some of the other new believers are less clear. George Stevens Frain, age thirty-seven and single, lived on West Avenue in North Augusta and owned a radio repair shop on 8th Avenue in Augusta. He and Marie Kershaw would marry a few years later. Ruth Johnson and Martina S. Wise, both widows, shared a house just down the street from Frain. Mabelle Cartledge was a bookkeeper at the J. B. White & Company department store downtown. Donald Radford had grown up in Keysville in rural Burke County south of Augusta, where his father ran a hardware store. Age twenty-two and single, he was the membership secretary (and a resident) at Augusta's YMCA, which had hosted several Bahá'í speakers.[53]

At least two members of the Augusta community were African Americans. Della Scott lived on Gwinnett Street a few blocks from white believers Josephine MacDonald and Effird Lynch, but her personal connection with the Bahá'í Faith was from a different source. Marie Kershaw identified Scott as Esther Sego's "old nurse." Although Scott was only eight years older than Sego, the age difference was enough that when Scott was a young teenager she could indeed have served as a babysitter for Sego. By the late 1930s, Scott was married with grown children, only one of whom was still at home. Her husband, Joseph Scott, was a railroad porter. They lived on a mostly black, mostly working-class block; a few of their neighbors were black professionals. Kershaw recalled that Sego had introduced Scott to the faith and that she "often carried the Message to her and took a few Friends in order to have Prayers and Readings." Another black believer was Fannie Gadson Toombs. A widow, she had three grown children, one from her first husband and two from her second. She owned her own home on Camille Street in Bethlehem, a black neighborhood built on land formerly owned in part by the Jackson family. Toombs had worked as a domestic servant, but she was also a midwife. It is unclear how she learned of the faith and became a Bahá'í.[54]

It is difficult to evaluate the extent to which Della Scott and Fannie Toombs participated in the activities of the local Bahá'í community. When Toombs died around 1939, her passing was noted in the "In Memoriam" section of *The Bahá'í World*, a volume compiled and published by the National Spiritual Assembly, indicating that she was officially enrolled as a believer and that she probably received newsletters and other mail from the national movement. Marie Kershaw's recollections of the relationship between Esther Sego and Della Scott may shed light on the situation. Kershaw indicated that at least a few white Bahá'ís in addition to Sego knew Scott and visited her house for devotional or study meetings, but in an otherwise rather detailed account of the community's activities she gave no indication that Scott ever came to the Bahá'í Center or to the homes of white believers.[55]

The best that can be assumed is that by 1937 the Augusta Bahá'í community was only "partially integrated." Beginning at least with the visit of Joseph Hannen and Margaret Klebs to the Schofield School in 1914, white Bahá'ís had made attempts to teach the faith to African Americans, but apparently inconsistently and with little tangible result. White believers may have visited the small number of black believers in their homes for purposes of religious practice, but blacks were probably functionally excluded from the other activities of the community. That is, individual whites were relatively free to discreetly cross lines of residential segregation by visiting the homes of African Americans whom they knew, but the same freedom did not usually apply in reverse. Both black and white Bahá'ís could face adverse social, economic, or even physical consequences if blacks visited white homes in any capacity other than that of servant. Even the sight of black and white Bahá'ís worshiping or socializing together in the Bahá'í Center, a private establishment in the city's central business district, could have brought unwelcome attention. Like Washington early in the century, the Augusta community could not be characterized as truly interracial; rather, it was essentially a white organization with a few black members. Unlike Washington, however, in its first two decades the Augusta community had no figure like the Hannens or Louis Gregory to champion teaching among African Americans and insist on full integration. In the absence of such a champion, it was easy for white Bahá'ís to remain complacent, and interaction among white and black believers in the Augusta area thus seems not to have contravened regional racial norms.

The believer who almost became such a champion in Augusta was Zia Bagdadi. Previously, Bagdadi had been one of the most energetic proponents of interracialism in the Chicago Bahá'í community. After the Chicago race riot in the Red Summer of 1919, for example, he had been among the few whites to enter affected black neighborhoods with relief supplies. And he had forged a friendship with Robert S. Abbott, the Georgia native who was founding publisher of the *Chicago Defender*, one of the country's most influential black newspapers. After years of association with the Chicago Bahá'í community, Abbott had publicly declared his faith in 1934. True to form, in the few months that he lived in the Augusta area, Bagdadi seems to have lost no time in efforts to teach African Americans. Based on contacts Daisy Jackson Moore had made during her previous residence there, he and two other believers traveled to Savannah, speaking at Georgia State College (formerly Georgia State Industrial College for Colored Youth) and befriending Augustus Harris, a prominent black physician, and his wife. Closer to home, Bagdadi spoke to "several hundred" people at one of Augusta's black Methodist churches. He also pursued an opening among working-class African Americans at the home of Marie Kershaw's washerwoman in North Augusta. Kershaw recalled that things started quite well: "Zia made Thursday evening talks to first a handful of colored friends . . . , then to a houseful, then to a house and porch and yard full, and then to a tremendous gathering." The meetings ended abruptly, however. Kershaw believed that the problem was local law enforcement. "Evidently the authorities were displeased with such large groups of colored people gathering," she wrote, "because after this the house became dark and closed to us."[56]

When Zia Bagdadi died suddenly in April 1937, barely six months after arriving in Augusta, the community lost its one potential champion of teaching African Americans. In a subsequent telegram, Shoghi Effendi praised Bagdadi's "exemplary faith, audacity, unquestioning loyalty, [and] indefatigable exertions." After the crackdown on Bahá'í activity in black North Augusta, however, no other believer arose to take his place. The episode helps to illustrate some of the external limitations faced by southern Bahá'ís when they attempted to enlarge and diversify their membership. While the dearth of African American believers and of sustained teaching among blacks in the Augusta area were at least in part the result of attitudes among the white Bahá'ís themselves, there were other factors at work. In the first quarter century of its presence in South Carolina, the guardians of white supremacy seem to have ignored the Bahá'í movement as long as it remained unthreatening: numerically small, culturally marginal, geographically circumscribed, and (at least in the case of Augusta) functionally monoracial. However, outspokenness on the part of individuals such as Louis Gregory, Alonzo Twine, and Clarence Westendorff, or hints that the faith had mass appeal across racial lines as in the meetings at the home of the North Augusta washerwoman, brought swift reaction. Whether in the form of police action, other opposition from local whites, criticism by conservative power-brokers within the black community, or some combination thereof, the Jim Crow system severely constrained the growth of the faith, dampening whatever efforts the Bahá'ís made to breach the color line.[57]

The Great Depression, the Second World War, and the First Seven Year Plan, 1935–1945

By the mid-1930s, after more than a decade of institution-building, Shoghi Effendi judged that the Bahá'í administrative system in the United States was effective enough for the believers there to return in earnest to the global mandate for teaching that 'Abdu'l-Bahá had assigned to them in the Tablets of the Divine Plan. During a seven-year campaign of expansion and consolidation designed by Shoghi Effendi and executed by the National Spiritual Assembly, the Bahá'ís of the United States thrust outward into entirely new territory, establishing outposts of the faith throughout Latin America and the Caribbean, and broadened the geographic scope of their movement at home with new local communities in every state and province of North America. Within the United States, the lion's share of the work was devoted to spreading the faith in the states of the former Confederacy where, despite recent growth in Augusta and a few other cities, progress had been painfully slow since the first of the Tablets of the Divine Plan had been received in 1916.

In South Carolina, the Augusta-area community served as the initial base for expansion into other localities. During the seven-year campaign, Bahá'ís settled in the state's three largest population centers of Charleston, Columbia, and Greenville, laying the foundations for new local communities that were more thoroughly and, particularly in the case of Columbia, more fearlessly integrated than the one in Augusta had initially been. Such advances, however, did not come easily. The campaign's focus on expansion in South Carolina and other southern states raised important questions for a religious community that professed to be interracial. A quarter century after Louis Gregory's first teaching trip through the Deep South, with hard-won community-building experience in a handful of southern cities, the national Bahá'í movement faced the daunting task of founding new interracial communities throughout the South in multiple localities at once. Early on, Shoghi Effendi set the tone and expectations for expansion in the region by guiding the formulation of a new policy for holding teaching meetings and by addressing a major letter that reaffirmed the faith's commitment to interracial fellowship. But not all the Bahá'ís were clear about Shoghi Effendi's instructions, and the work of interracial community-building in many southern cities and towns proved to be hard and slow. By 1945 an interracial Bahá'í movement had indeed taken root in more than one South Carolina locality—but only barely. The experiences of the Bahá'ís in South Carolina during the era of the New Deal and World War II—part of the national community's effort to develop and pursue a safe and effective approach to expansion in the South—illustrated not only the structural challenges faced by any would-be interracial organization in the region but also the extent to which the attitudes and understandings of individual Bahá'ís could help or hinder the development of nascent interracial communities.

Systematic Action amidst Global Crisis

During the mid-1930s, Shoghi Effendi began to indicate that the Bahá'í movement in the United States was entering a new stage in its development. In this "phase of concentrated teaching activity," the Administrative Order erected in the United States since 'Abdu'l-Bahá's passing would have to be strengthened at home and established in the rest of the world. In a cablegram to the National Convention in 1936, Shoghi Effendi recalled the "historic appeal voiced by 'Abdu'l-Bahá in [the] Tablets of the Divine Plan" and announced a new campaign of geographic expansion in the Americas that would conclude in 1944, the centenary of the Báb's declaration of his prophetic mission to his first disciple in Shiraz. "Would to God," Shoghi Effendi pleaded, "every State within [the] American Republic and every Republic in [the] American continent might ere [the] termination of this glorious century embrace the light of the Faith of Bahá'u'lláh and establish [the] structural basis of His World Order." In a follow-up letter to the newly elected National Spiritual Assembly less than a month later, he specifically called for the "permanent establishment of at least one center"—in other words, a locality with a group of believers—in every state of the United States and every country in Latin America. In addition, he added that the plan should "gradually be extended" to European countries where no Bahá'ís yet resided.[1]

Even leaving Europe for a future phase of the project, it was no small task to which Shoghi Effendi was calling the Bahá'ís of the United States, who were still heavily concentrated in the eastern urban core. Twenty-six states of the United States and seven provinces or territories of Canada—huge swaths of the continent encompassing most of the South, the Great Plains, the mountain West, Alaska, and the Far North—held a few scattered believers or none at all. In Latin America the situation was even more daunting: barely half a dozen Bahá'ís had ever set foot in all the vast territory south of the Rio Grande. The task before the American movement, Shoghi Effendi acknowledged, was "gigantic," and he stressed the need both for effective leadership by the national executive body and for the complete support of each individual: "A systematic, carefully conceived, and well-established plan should be devised, rigorously pursued and continuously extended. Initiated by the National representatives of the American believers, the vanguard and standard-bearers of the radiant army of Bahá'u'lláh, this plan should receive the wholehearted, the sustained and ever-increasing support, both moral and financial, of the entire body of His followers in that continent." Clearly, to extend the reach of the faith so broadly and so quickly would dwarf all previous expansion efforts and tax the resources and commitment of the movement in America.[2]

While the tasks before the Bahá'ís were challenging in themselves, world events gave Shoghi Effendi's call an unmistakable note of urgency. In a January 1936 letter, he predicted that the teaching campaign would synchronize with "a period of deepening gloom, of universal impotence, of ever-increasing destitution and wide-spread disillusionment in the fortunes of a declining age." In his cablegram to the 1936 National Convention, he said that as the faith's first century drew to a close humanity as a whole was "entering [the] outer fringes [of the] most perilous stage [of] its existence." "The present opportunity [for teaching] is unutterably precious," he wrote a few months later. "It may not recur again." Few observers would have disagreed with his gloomy assessment of the domestic and international scene. As the American Bahá'ís gathered for their annual convention in the spring of 1936, the global economy was in a shambles and the international political order erected after World War I was rapidly collapsing. At home, the Great Depression had brought massive unemployment, widespread hunger, and the dislocation of countless families. The country's hardest-hit region was the South, where so much of the work of the teaching campaign would necessarily focus. As state and local governments throughout the South faced bankruptcy and local charities foundered, only massive federal relief programs staved off starvation. Overseas, aggressively expansionist regimes in Germany, Italy, and Japan were severely destabilizing the fragile world order. Just a month before the National Convention, the German military—emboldened by Italy's successful invasion of Ethiopia, a fellow member of the League of Nations, the year before—had reoccupied the Rhineland in brazen violation of the Versailles settlement. Events seemed to confirm 'Abdu'l-Bahá's predictions, voiced shortly after the end of the Great War, of a second global conflict.[3]

Against such a chaotic background, the National Spiritual Assembly acted quickly to launch the new teaching campaign. Following the 1936 National Convention, it created ten new Regional Teaching Committees in the United States and Canada, established a special teaching fund of $30,000, and appointed an Inter-America Committee to coordinate expansion into Latin America. During the year, nine individuals made teaching trips of various lengths to Mexico, the Caribbean, and several countries in South America. Another dozen moved to cities in New Mexico, North Carolina, North Dakota, Oklahoma, Saskatchewan, Texas, Virginia, and Wyoming—all of them territories with few or no Bahá'ís. That fall, moved by a further appeal from Shoghi Effendi for the American believers to "intensify their teaching work a thousand fold and extend its ramifications beyond the confines of their native land," Louis and Louise Gregory spent three months in Haiti, attracting a sizeable group of seekers, many of them young people, to firesides and a study group. The Gregorys intended to stay longer, but opposition by Haitian government officials to the spread of the faith forced their early return.[4]

The Seven Year Plan

In the spring of 1937, at the urging of Shoghi Effendi, the National Spiritual Assembly formally launched a new Seven Year Plan for the Bahá'ís of the United States. Its twin objectives were completion of the exterior ornamentation of the temple in Chicago and establishment of the faith throughout North and South America and the Caribbean. "No triumph," Shoghi Effendi cabled to that year's National Convention, "can more befittingly signalize [the] termination of [the] first century of [the] Bahá'í era than accomplishment of this twofold task." The ambitious goals would necessitate both a major financial commitment and a significant redistribution of the Bahá'í population.[5]

The plan's first and more straightforward objective—completion of the temple's exterior—was the latest step in an undertaking with important symbolic and practical consequences. Initiated nearly thirty years earlier during the movement's infancy in the United States, the temple project was of a scale and complexity, and the anticipated result of such a grandeur and beauty, as to make it more like the construction of a medieval cathedral than of a neighborhood church. On the eve of the plan, the temple's massive concrete-and-steel superstructure, erected at great cost during the first terrible years of the Great Depression, stood complete but far from lovely on the shore of Lake Michigan. The next phase of the project—implementing the architect's vision for the building's outer ornamentation, an intricate fretwork interlaced with sacred symbols of the world's great religions—was unfinished. Using exposed-aggregate architectural concrete, a new method that would adorn the temple in a glittering white layer of crushed quartz, a contractor had fabricated and installed the ornamentation of the dome and clerestory levels—until, buffeted by the Depression, the national Bahá'í community's funds ran dry. Work on the gallery story, the main story, and the nineteen steps encircling the whole structure had yet to begin. The estimated total cost of the remaining work was $350,000 (the equivalent of over $5,750,000 in 2015), a hefty sum for a national organization of fewer than three thousand members.

For the American Bahá'ís, few of whom were wealthy even before the economic collapse, completion of their national house of worship was not just a point of collective pride but a matter of spiritual devotion and community solidarity that they had sensed from the beginning would aid in the growth of their religion. Contributing money toward the temple was an expression of commitment to their faith and of love for 'Abdu'l-Bahá, who had approved the project and laid the building's cornerstone during his 1912 visit. They saw the temple, the first of its kind outside the Islamic heartland, as evidence not only of the faith's worldwide spread but of their new religious identity as American Bahá'ís; even the Augusta-area group, small and relatively far removed from the geographic center of the movement, had been contributing since 1911. From an organizational perspective, the project had provided the initial impulse for the formation of a national coordinating body, and the Bahá'ís saw it as tangible evidence that they could work together as a national movement and achieve practical results. Perhaps it was for these reasons that Shoghi Effendi repeatedly linked progress of the temple project with the growth of the community. In January 1936, for instance, he underlined the spiritual links among the development of the Bahá'í administrative system, progress on the temple, and the new thrust in teaching: "Now that the administrative organs of a firmly established Faith are vigorously and harmoniously functioning, and now that the Symbol of its invincible might is lending unprecedented impetus to its spread, an effort unexampled in its scope and sustained vitality is urgently required so that the moving spirit of its Founder may permeate and transform the lives of the countless multitudes that hunger for its teachings." For Shoghi Effendi and for the American Bahá'ís, then, building the house of worship was primarily a spiritual endeavor that had important consequences for other areas of endeavor as well.[6]

As daunting as the temple project was, the second objective of the plan—expanding the geographic reach of the community into virtually every territory of the Western Hemisphere—would prove to be even more difficult. Based on some three decades' experience of expansion efforts within the United States and Canada, Shoghi Effendi and the National Spiritual Assembly realized early on that establishing so many new local communities so far distant from the movement's American heartland would require both a major shift of the Bahá'í population and a more active engagement by the rank and file of the community. Surely the mixed results of the teaching efforts in South Carolina since 1910 figured in this analysis. As Leroy Ioas, at the time a member of both the National Spiritual Assembly and the National Teaching Committee, recalled, the movement's leaders knew that "the previous methods of extending the Faith into new areas by itinerant teachers, lecturers and limited follow-up"—in other words, the main approaches that Louis Gregory and others had employed in South Carolina—"were not sufficiently effective, but that the only method whereby lasting results could be achieved was through the settlement plan." During the course of the Seven Year Plan, individuals or families from the established local communities would need to leave their homes and take up residence as "pioneers" of the faith in each of the "virgin territories" of North and South America. As Margaret Klebs had done for years in the Augusta area, they would seek to integrate themselves into the life of their new localities through work, school, and other activities, come in contact with receptive individuals, and build new Bahá'í communities from the ground up. Ideally, each pioneer would find employment or be otherwise self-supporting, but many would require at least temporary monetary assistance from the community. Traveling teachers would continue to circulate, but they would focus on visiting areas where pioneers had settled, reinforcing local efforts by offering public lectures and generating press coverage—much as Stanwood Cobb's 1934 teaching campaign in Augusta had led to a rapid expansion of the community and election of a Local Spiritual Assembly. In contrast to the relative handful of believers who had acted as traveling teachers before, the magnitude of the goals meant that far larger numbers would need to be engaged in some form of teaching—settling in or traveling to new areas or strengthening the base of the movement in long-established localities—and in the necessary fundraising effort to finance both the teaching and temple work.[7]

An initial survey by the National Teaching Committee indicated that expansion in the South would figure prominently in the Seven Year Plan. Three decades after the faith's arrival in Baltimore, Washington, and Fairhope, the South accounted for nearly half of the plan's twenty-six virgin territories in North America. The relatively robust development of the Augusta-area community had been the exception rather than the rule in the region. In 1937, only six cities south of Washington—Nashville, Memphis, Tuskegee, Miami, and St. Augustine in addition to Augusta—had enough Bahá'ís to form a Local Spiritual Assembly, and several of these only barely. Of the sixteen southern states that 'Abdu'l-Bahá had addressed in the Tablets of the Divine Plan, seven contained only a few isolated Bahá'ís and five none at all.[8]

Aside from the logistical challenges of deploying pioneers and traveling teachers and building strong new communities in the region's twelve goal states, the plan heralded significant cultural and demographic change for the Bahá'ís, as a national movement that was still mostly white, northern, and urban sought to establish new local communities in the heartland of black America. While they were already well represented at the local level—at least in comparison to their proportion of the population in the northern and western states where the faith was already established—the concentrated push southward represented an opportunity to engage unprecedented numbers of African Americans. Even after the acceleration of migration surrounding World War I, by the 1930s more than three-fourths of African Americans still resided in the South, and they were a far more significant presence there than in any other region of the country. One in four southerners was black, compared to one in ten people in both the Northeast and the Midwest and only one in a hundred in the West. The three states of North Carolina, South Carolina, and Georgia, which together represented only 7 percent of the total national population, accounted for more than 20 percent of all African Americans. South Carolina alone, with barely more than 1 percent of all Americans, was home to more than 6 percent of the country's blacks. If Louis Gregory's assessment of black southerners' spiritual receptivity remained true, then prosecution of the plan seemed likely to increase the racial diversity of the national Bahá'í community, enabling it thereby to reflect more fully the faith's bedrock principle of the oneness of humanity.[9]

As the Bahá'í movement turned southward, it had important experiences to draw on. Since the turn of the century, local communities, including a handful in southern cities and towns, had been working to foster interracial fellowship within their own ranks. Through the Race Amity Conventions and similar local initiatives, the Bahá'ís had created public spaces to speak out against prejudice and segregation in concert with other organizations. And beginning with Louis Gregory's 1910 trip, he and other teachers had established and nurtured positive contacts with progressive individuals and groups, white and black, across the South. On the other hand, despite the movement's early record on race, few of its members were prepared for the challenges of building interracial local communities in the South. The same black demographic strength that made the region important to the development of the national Bahá'í movement had provoked white America's most energetic reactions: while anti-black discrimination and violence were nationwide phenomena, the South's codification and enforcement of racial separatism were more rigid, more pervasive, and more violent than anything most American Bahá'ís had so far been forced to face. During the 1930s, despite a growing chorus of protest from inside and outside the South, Jim Crow still held a firm grip across the region, and the forces of racial and religious orthodoxy often responded brutally to dissent. The southern teaching campaign would require the national Bahá'í community to confront some of the ugliest realities of American racism, and on a far larger scale than it had ever attempted. The same challenges that the early Washington and Augusta groups had faced would now be repeated simultaneously in multiple localities, over at least a seven-year period of sustained community-building that would directly involve a substantial portion of the movement's existing members.

New Footholds in South Carolina

By the time the Seven Year Plan began, although many early teaching successes and a substantial portion of the local believers had been in North Augusta, the national administration counted the entire Augusta-area community—including the half dozen or so members living on the South Carolina side of the Savannah River—as being in Georgia. For the purposes of the plan, then, the state of South Carolina was a "virgin territory" in need of settlement. Aside from the North Augustans, only a few resident South Carolinians had affiliated themselves with the faith since Louis Gregory's first visit in 1910. Widely scattered and isolated from the mainstream of the American movement, by the mid-1930s they had all evidently fallen out of contact with the community, lost interest, or died.

Not surprisingly, the Augusta-area community provided an initial base for the new effort to expand in South Carolina. In the early months of the plan, Christine Bidwell and Marie Kershaw from North Augusta visited nearby Aiken, where Margaret Klebs had first arrived a quarter century earlier, "to see about opening that town." They located a hotel where they could rent a room for speakers and found that the local newspaper would publicize meetings. About the same time, other Bahá'ís, mostly financially independent white women from outside the South, began spending winters in South Carolina. In 1936–1937, Amelie Bodmer and May Fisher traveled the state in a trailer, visiting "several cities" and making "good Bahai contacts." In December 1937, another pair, Emogene Hoagg and Agnes O'Neill, arrived in Charleston and spent the rest of the winter there. In 1938–1939, Louise Thompson from Maine took the place of Hoagg and O'Neill in Charleston and "followed up the interest which had been established" the year before. In February and March 1939, Charles Mason Remey from Washington, D.C., made a teaching trip to several localities in the state.[10]

In the fall of 1939 Emogene Hoagg returned to Charleston. She was one of the most prominent and respected early believers in the United States, having learned of the faith in 1898 from Phoebe Hearst in California and become an active traveling teacher and administrator in North America and Europe. After the passing of 'Abdu'l-Bahá, while she was living in Italy, Hoagg had been one of the believers whom Shoghi Effendi invited to Haifa to discuss an early election of the Universal House of Justice. A woman with no family commitments (her husband had died in 1918 and they had no children), during the Seven Year Plan she put herself at the disposal of the National Teaching Committee and traveled extensively to help fulfill pioneering goals in North America and the Caribbean. Late in 1939, after traveling through the Midwest, Hoagg suggested to the National Teaching Committee that she go to back to Charleston. The committee accepted her offer, sending $100 for train travel expenses, a stock of books for distribution to interested seekers, and a list of believers and "contacts" from previous teachers in South Carolina. Regarding the list, the committee's secretary, Charlotte Linfoot, wrote: "I am inclined to think that most of these contacts are pretty *cold* if not completely frozen by this time."[11]

One of the believers on the list was Clarence Westendorff, whom Louis Gregory had taught more than a decade before. The National Teaching Committee had corresponded with him over the years, and Linfoot suggested that Hoagg visit to see whether he would formally register as a member of the faith and participate in a study group. But years of isolation from the rest of the American Bahá'í community had evidently left Westendorff with little connection to an evolving movement. "Really it was a circus!" Hoagg exclaimed in a report of her visit:

> I said we had heard he had accepted the Baha'i Faith. He immediately said that he did not confine himself to any organization, nor would he sign a card; that a few people up "there" could make laws, but it was not necessary to follow them; that he loved Jesus and felt that he could teach people more easily through the Christian teachings. . . . He talks incessantly and to be able to say something I had to take hold of his arm and actually said, "Just wait a moment I want to say something." Then I explained that it was not a few "up North," but that we had a Guardian of the Faith etc. etc. This seemed to be something he had not heard about. . . . I invited him to a study class, and he said he did not have to study, as he received his knowledge direct.

Hoagg said that Westendorff's neighbors and family regarded him as "erratic," and he had a reputation for both kindness and dishonesty. His son, she wrote, "laughs at him because he talks so much." Hoagg recommended that the National Teaching Committee no longer consider him a Bahá'í: "That he accepts Baha'u'llah in a certain way, may be true, but that he has [no] conception of His real station, or knows anything about the Master or the Guardian, or the Administration, is also true."[12]

Other teaching activities seemed more promising. Hoagg's landlady, Orie Walpole, a Georgia native married into an old Charleston family, arranged for her to speak at a meeting of the King's Daughters, a white women's Christian service organization. The participants were "all Charlestonians," Hoagg noted with satisfaction. "They were so pleased that I am asked to speak again the second Tuesday of April." A positive contact with a Unitarian minister led to a meeting with his church's Women's Alliance. And she spoke to a gathering at the home of the city's black librarian. "Two people are much interested, and another is reading what she can get—sometimes from the Library." Despite the disappointment with Westendorff, she said that a year of teaching "may bring forth some real fruits" and result in a new community of believers. But Hoagg did not stay in Charleston. Requested by the Inter-America Committee to go to Havana, Cuba, she left South Carolina around the beginning of November 1940. Louise Thompson, who had spent the previous winter in Charleston, promptly returned with her sister, Emma Thompson, and the two moved into the apartment Hoagg had been renting. They continued teaching Walpole and her husband and tried to start a study group, apparently without success.[13]

Bahá'ís also moved to the capital of South Carolina, Columbia. Late in 1938, Maud Mickle, a single white woman who, like the Thompson sisters, had been living near Green Acre in Maine, brought her ill and invalid sister, Jennie Mickle, to spend the winter in the mild climate of Columbia. Accompanying them was another white believer, Alta Wheeler, a trained nurse who helped care for Jennie. In a pattern similar to Margaret Klebs's in Augusta, the three returned to Columbia each year at least until the mid-1940s, and they were able to the lay the foundations of a new local community. One of the first people they met was Louella Moore, a white woman from North Augusta who had learned of the faith there and kept in touch with the Augusta-area community after moving to Columbia. After studying a short time with Mickle and Wheeler, she was ready to become a Bahá'í. In early 1939, Moore wrote to the National Teaching Committee to request enrollment as a believer, likely the first person in the state to do so since the formalization of membership procedures earlier in the decade.[14]

In addition to their relationship with Moore and her family, Maud Mickle and Alta Wheeler reached out to Columbia's large African American population. It was an endeavor for which Mickle, at least, had some preparation. A decade earlier, Mickle and another white woman, Leonora Holsapple-Armstrong, had been among the first American pioneers in Latin America, settling in Salvador de Bahia, the capital city of Afro-Brazilian culture on that country's northeastern coast. The two had worked in health care in the city's vast slums and taught the faith to the people they met. After Mickle's Brazilian experience, reaching out to African Americans in Columbia probably came quite naturally. One black woman Mickle and Wheeler met was interested enough in the faith to ask her landlady whether they could come to the house to tell more. The landlady, Pearl Dixon, was the widow of an African Methodist Episcopal minister from the rural community of Killian northeast of Columbia. After her husband's death, Dixon had moved her family to town. In 1939 she lived in a house on Richland Street where she rented rooms to boarders and was a member of Sidney Park Colored Methodist Episcopal Church, where Louis Gregory had spoken some eighteen years before. Dixon approved of the Bahá'í meeting in her home and invited some of her own friends and family. Dixon and her daughter, Jessie Dixon Entzminger, were among the most interested of the listeners. Dixon embraced the faith immediately, but Entzminger was more hesitant. As she later recalled: "I had never heard tell of the Bahá'í Faith. It sounded like a funny name."[15]

At Dixon's invitation, Wheeler began leading a study group in the home, and after six months, Entzminger became a Bahá'í as well. At least a few members of Louella Moore's family also attended the class. In late 1940, Moore's adult daughter, Louise Moore Montgomery, was "interested but not confirmed" in the faith. She continued to study and worship with the Bahá'í community for nearly a decade before declaring her faith at Dixon's house. The tiny community also met at the house that the Mickle sisters and Wheeler rented. When Emma and Louise Thompson visited from Charleston in November 1940, they attended a Holy Day observance there "with Maud & Alta, Mrs. Moore (white) and the 2 colored believers." According to Louise Thompson, the white pioneers could have black visitors in their home because they did not share it with anyone else: "They are able to have this mixed meeting as they have a cottage or 5-room bungalow all to themselves and no one the wiser."[16]

Over the next few years, at least two African American traveling teachers visited Columbia to assist the small group. One was Zenobia Dorsey of Scranton, Pennsylvania. During her first visit, from November 1941 to January 1942, she gave a series of talks to the Waverly Friendship Club, a women's social and service organization in the middle-class black neighborhood surrounding Allen University and Benedict College; three of the club's members became Bahá'ís. Dorsey came back to Columbia in the spring of 1943, and she attracted three more people to the ongoing study class at Pearl Dixon's house. In the early spring of 1942, Louis Gregory made a stop in Columbia as part of a lecture tour of black schools and colleges in West Virginia, Virginia, and the Carolinas. He spoke at Benedict and Allen; at Booker T. Washington High School, the city's only high school for African Americans, located near the University of South Carolina campus in the working-class black neighborhood of Wheeler Hill; and to a meeting of the Palmetto Medical Association, the statewide professional organization of black physicians.[17]

As the Augusta-area community had done since its inception, the small group in Columbia used the local press, both black and white, to advertise its aims and activities. In the spring and fall of 1940, for example, the *Palmetto Leader*, a black newspaper, carried stories about the Bahá'í house of worship in Chicago under the titles "The Universal House of Worship" and "World's Most Beautiful Temple." One pointed out that the crystalline quartz for the exterior ornamentation was mined in Spartanburg County in the South Carolina Piedmont. In December 1940, the *Columbia Record*, a white paper, carried a similar item. In March 1942, the society section of the *State* reported a celebration of Bahá'í New Year at the home of Maud Mickle and Alta Wheeler that included visitors from Augusta and Charleston.[18]

The first pioneers to Greenville, in the Upstate, came from the Augusta-area community. In the spring of 1938, just days after returning from the National Convention in Chicago, William and Christine Bidwell moved from North Augusta to pursue a business opportunity in Greenville, the capital of the regional textile industry, located near Christine's family home of Pendleton in neighboring Anderson County. The couple took over operations at the Chick Springs Sanitarium, a health facility located six miles east of Greenville in the small community of Taylors. The sanitarium had been closed since the death of its founder five years previously, and the Bidwells went into partnership with a woman from Miami (where they had first encountered the Bahá'í Faith) to reopen the facility. William, a chiropractor and naturopathic physician who specialized in healing through diet, saw patients, and Christine oversaw the kitchen. They "hope[d] to interest friends in the teachings and soon have a study group," and Christine dreamed of the facility becoming a "Baha'i School for the South" like the ones that already existed in California, Maine, and Michigan. But the business venture was unsuccessful; by the onset of winter the Bidwells had paid out the partner and moved to downtown Greenville, where they were to remain for nearly two decades. Their new house on North Main Street had space for an office, and William Bidwell began to see patients there.[19]

It did not take long to make contacts for teaching. In early December 1938, William wrote a friend: "Last night I had three wonderful souls listening to the story of the Bab, Baha'u'llah and Abdul Baha until 11:30 and *were* they interested." Another "wonderful soul" was attracted to the new faith but seemed unable to leave her Baptist church. She said that "she was afraid to believe and afraid not to believe." In the spring of 1939, William Bidwell noted that one seeker, likely the same woman, was still visiting their house to investigate the faith. As a public schoolteacher, however, she was "working under a system where she cannot come out openly" as a Bahá'í. He counseled her "to go ahead and develop herself to the fullest extent" in her individual practice of the faith and assured her that "her opportunity would come" for public expression of her belief.[20]

Formulating a Regional Racial Policy

Like the other fledgling groups that emerged in the South during the Seven Year Plan, the Bahá'ís in Greenville, Columbia, and Charleston faced the challenge of spreading their faith and building functional interracial communities in the midst of an oppressive and segregated society. These local efforts can best be understood in the context of regional and national developments in the Bahá'í movement. In fact, amid the social and economic experimentation of the New Deal era other liberal and radical organizations in the South—Highlander Folk School, the Southern Conference on Human Welfare, the Communist Party, and labor unions, to name a few—were facing similar challenges. Like the Bahá'ís, these organizations were essentially opposed to segregation and disfranchisement, but circumstances compelled them to function within the constraints of a racial caste system that made substantive interracial contacts very difficult to achieve and maintain. In particular, they faced the dilemma of how to pursue a forthrightly interracial agenda while maintaining at least a modicum of white southern participation. During the campaign of the late 1930s and 1940s, the difficulties that Bahá'ís had earlier faced in such cities as Washington and Augusta were repeated, to varying degrees, in many localities at once. Many of the questions remained the same, even as specific local circumstances differed. How could the Bahá'ís implement their faith's cardinal teaching of the oneness of humanity in a society that was segregated by practice and by law? Since Bahá'u'lláh enjoined his followers to obey civil authorities, Bahá'ís in the South had little choice but to abide by segregation as far as local and state statutes mandated, but the principles of their faith also seemed to dictate that they seek spaces within the system—such as private homes as in the case of Columbia—where blacks and whites could meet together regularly for worship and other community activities.[21]

There were also questions of methodology. To whom should the pioneers and traveling teachers—most of whom were white and middle-class—initially address themselves in their new localities? Should they focus on liberal-minded whites, seeking conversions among the power-brokers of southern society who would then be able to afford black adherents some measure of protection? Should they first teach educated blacks, who over the years of efforts by traveling teachers like Louis Gregory had shown a great deal of interest in the faith, and approach the rest of the society through them? Or should they attempt to reach the black masses directly and risk white retaliation, as in the case of the short-lived meetings at the home of the North Augusta washerwoman? How much should the Bahá'ís—many of whom, at least in the early stages of the plan, would be from other parts of the country—challenge local conventions and push the limits of acceptable behavior? How could they teach their faith forthrightly to blacks without alienating most whites? On the other hand, if they coddled white prejudices, how could they avoid becoming just another Jim Crow church? If they brought blacks and whites together indiscriminately—especially in large numbers—

how could they avoid provoking social and economic reprisals, or violence, against themselves and their seekers? Perhaps most importantly given previous experience in the region, would enough white Bahá'ís be willing to risk discomfort and opposition to champion the issue?

A national policy for teaching in the South began to emerge late in 1936 as the National Spiritual Assembly prepared to visit the fledgling Bahá'í community of Nashville, part of a plan to conduct its regular meetings in different parts of the country (not just at the Bahá'í National Center in suburban Chicago) in order "to provide occasions for the holding of Regional Conferences with the friends, as well as public meetings for promoting the Faith." Two years previously, Louis Gregory had spent several months in Nashville, forming and nurturing a Bahá'í study group through contacts at Fisk University. Several black women had embraced the faith, augmenting what he described as a "tiny group of believers, six southern whites and one colored," that already existed in the city. The small community had elected Nashville's first Local Spiritual Assembly in April 1935, the same year the believers in the Augusta area elected theirs. A visit by the national body was likely to reinforce the Nashville group through an influx of experienced teachers and the holding of public meetings that could attract new seekers and generate press coverage. However, at least some members of the National Assembly—few of whom had any significant experience teaching in the South—apparently questioned the advisability of holding interracial public gatherings, because the body addressed a letter to Shoghi Effendi asking for his advice.[22]

Replying through his secretary, Shoghi Effendi heartily approved the Nashville visit, saying it would "greatly encourage the believers in that center," and he strongly endorsed the holding of interracial meetings: "The holding of public meetings in that city should be avoided only in case it would lead to grave and very serious results. Slight local criticisms and unpopularity should not act as a deterrent. The issue [of racial segregation] should be met squarely and courageously." Bolstered by Shoghi Effendi's advice, a member of the Regional Teaching Committee that served Tennessee arranged to hold several mixed gatherings, one at Fisk, two at an exclusive hotel, and two in private homes, during the National Assembly's visit in January 1937. Particularly noteworthy were the meetings at the Hermitage Hotel, the premier social venue in the city, where the management relaxed its strict segregation policy and admitted blacks at the Bahá'ís' request. As one black Nashville believer recalled, it was at least "a foot in the door" of segregation in a citadel of the city's white high society.[23]

In addition to his specific thoughts about the Nashville visit, Shoghi Effendi's letter also contained advice that appeared to suggest a general approach to teaching in the region. Likely based on his extensive correspondence with Louis Gregory and other experienced traveling teachers, his guidance became the basis for an explicit national policy for teaching in the South: "An effort should be made to attract at first the most cultured element among the colored, and through them establish contact with the white and the masses. Such individuals and groups, whether white or colored, who are relatively free from racial prejudice, should be approached, separately if necessary, and an endeavor should be made to bring them together eventually, not only on formal occasions and for specific purposes, but in intimate social gatherings, in private homes as well as in formally recognized Bahá'í centers." Shoghi Effendi's advice, intended to assist the Bahá'ís to establish viable interracial communities in the midst of pervasive segregation, seems to reflect a rather subtle analysis not only of the complex racial and class dynamics of the region but also of the needs and capacities of the national Bahá'í community as a whole and of the individual pioneers and traveling teachers who would be at the forefront of the effort. He suggested a pragmatic, long-range approach that would enable the Bahá'ís to establish the foundations of interracial local communities as quickly and effectively as possible while protecting them somewhat from suspicion, social ostracism, or violent reaction.[24]

Shoghi Effendi took the complete integration of the Bahá'í community itself, "in intimate social gatherings, in private homes as well as in formally recognized Bahá'í centers," as a given. But his comments indicate an acknowledgement that, depending on local conditions, blacks and whites might have to be approached separately in the initial stages of teaching. Even if local or state laws did not specifically prohibit interracial mingling in private homes or in Bahá'í-owned buildings, social pressure from neighbors, ministers, employers, and family members and the ever-present danger of white violence could make even interested individuals who were "relatively free from racial prejudice" wary of mixed gatherings. Identification with the new faith required a measure of courage—involving as it did a simultaneous rejection of both white male supremacy and traditional Protestantism. Yet it was precisely the individual spiritual commitment and strong group solidarity associated with religious community—factors that necessarily took time to cultivate—that would enable new believers to withstand the opposition that would inevitably come. By not insisting on interracial gatherings at the outset, Bahá'í teachers could nurture seekers of varying backgrounds and temperaments into full acceptance of essential Bahá'í teachings while perhaps postponing a head-on confrontation with the upholders of racial and religious orthodoxy.

Shoghi Effendi's advice also seems to have taken into account the class dynamics both of the region and of the national Bahá'í movement. By the mid-1930s, there was ample evidence that interracial cooperation in the southern working class tended to provoke brutal suppression, while that which was initiated by the "respectable" class of blacks and whites was often tolerated. As Louis Gregory's interactions with I. E. Lowery suggested, "the most cultured element among the colored" in a given locality could certainly contain its defenders of the status quo, but it was also likely to include individuals who would be sympathetic to the faith and willing to use their familiarity with local conditions to help the Bahá'ís gain an entrée into the community. "Through them," the teachers could "establish contact" with racially progressive individuals among the white leadership class and with receptive audiences among the "masses" of blacks and whites, perhaps avoiding dangerous missteps in the process. Moreover, the black middle class was probably the element of a given local population with whom the pioneers and traveling teachers—mostly well-educated, non-southern whites—could initially communicate most freely and effectively about the challenging message of the faith.

Based on what it considered a successful visit in Nashville, the National Spiritual Assembly sought Shoghi Effendi's approval of a policy for teaching in the South that distinguished, in effect, between what was expected of seekers and what of confirmed believers. A local community's internal functions—the Nineteen Day Feast and Holy Day observances, voting for and membership on the Local Spiritual Assembly, and social, educational, and devotional gatherings—had to be conducted on an integrated basis, but teaching activities such as firesides, study classes, and lectures held in public venues could be conducted separately for black and white seekers if local conditions seemed to require it. Shoghi Effendi wrote to approve the policy, but he underlined that it was a temporary, practical measure the goal of which was to reach "the two races in the South without the slightest discrimination." He reiterated that blacks and whites "should be ultimately brought together, and be urged to associate with the utmost unity and fellowship, and be given full and equal opportunity to participate in the conduct of the teaching as well as administrative activities of the Faith." As it launched the Seven Year Plan, the National Assembly shared the new policy—including the text of Shoghi Effendi's second letter—both with the delegates at the National Convention in April 1937 and in the June issue of *Bahá'í News*.[25]

The Advent of Divine Justice

In December 1938, less than two years into the Seven Year Plan, Shoghi Effendi wrote a major treatise that would shape the American Bahá'í community's engagement with issues of race, class, and gender for decades. The overall theme of the book-length letter, addressed to the Bahá'ís of the United States and Canada and subsequently published as *The Advent of Divine Justice*, was the spiritual prerequisites and practical means for successful completion of the Seven Year Plan, and a significant portion of it called attention to the movement's need to purge itself of every trace of racial prejudice. The letter gave a renewed impetus to interracial community-building in the South and had an immediate impact on the development of local Bahá'í communities in South Carolina and other southern states.

Set against the backdrop of a "world, torn with conflicting passions, and perilously disintegrating from within" and the consequent restrictions imposed on the Bahá'í communities in several countries, Shoghi Effendi's letter focused the attention of the North American believers on the two principal goals of the Seven Year Plan while significantly broadening their social and world-historical vision of the community's mission at home and across the globe. As far-reaching as their responsibilities were, however, the immediate sphere for their actions was close at hand. Essential to Shoghi Effendi's thesis was a sophisticated arraignment of certain aspects of American culture and a call for the Bahá'ís to admit and remedy their harmful effects on their own community. Namely, he argued that "an excessive and binding materialism" had fostered severe racial prejudice, widespread laxity in personal morality, and endemic political corruption within the American nation. The essential, ongoing task of the believers was to eliminate all such tendencies from the Bahá'í community, first so that they could successfully prosecute the Seven Year Plan and subsequent teaching campaigns, and eventually so that their movement could lead in the reformation of the nation itself.[26]

The lengthiest portion of Shoghi Effendi's critique was a frank discussion of the problem of lingering racial prejudice among the American Bahá'ís. Shoghi Effendi called it "the most vital and challenging issue confronting the Bahá'í community at the present stage of its evolution." Citing a series of unequivocal passages from the writings of Bahá'u'lláh and 'Abdu'l-Bahá and giving specific instructions to both white and black believers, he warned that not only the success of the Seven Year Plan but ultimately the destiny of the entire American nation depended on the extent to which the Bahá'í movement was able to build "an interracial fellowship completely purged from the curse of racial prejudice." He emphasized the need for all the Baháʼís, "in whichever state they reside, in whatever circles they move, whatever their age, traditions, tastes, and habits," to root out all traces of prejudice from their hearts. Moreover, he said, they should demonstrate freedom from racial prejudice consistently in their lives, "whether in the Baháʼí community or outside it, in public or in private, formally as well as informally, individually as well as in their official capacity" in the faith's administrative institutions. They should cultivate interracial fellowship "through the various and everyday opportunities, no matter how insignificant, that present themselves, whether in their homes, their business offices, their schools and colleges, their social parties and recreation grounds, their Baháʼí meetings, conferences, conventions, summer schools and Assemblies." In particular, he noted, it should be the "keynote" of the policy of the National Spiritual Assembly, which must "set the example" and "facilitate the application of such a vital principle" in the life of the entire national community. At all levels of Baháʼí governance, Shoghi Effendi stated that in cases of ties in elections or when the qualifications for appointed positions were otherwise equal, "priority should unhesitatingly be accorded the party representing the minority." Such a policy, he suggested, would both encourage those from underrepresented groups and demonstrate to the public the universality of the faith.[27]

Much as ʻAbduʼl-Bahá had done during his North American tour in 1912, Shoghi Effendi's letter made clear that for every believer and every institution, in every phase of life, interracial fellowship was part of the very definition of the Baháʼí Faith in the United States. In explicit terms, Shoghi Effendi renewed ʻAbduʼl-Bahá's insistence on complete social and political equality within the community and, as far as opportunities allowed, in the Baháʼís' normal social, economic, and educational activities with the society at large. They could permit no compromise with their country's pernicious racial ideology: "Casting away once and for all the fallacious doctrine of racial superiority, with all its attendant evils, confusion, and miseries, and welcoming and encouraging the intermixture of races, and tearing down the barriers that now divide them, they should endeavor, day and night, to fulfill their particular responsibilities in the common task which so urgently faces them." The implications for the southern campaign of the plan were clear: building interracial fellowship should be at the forefront of the Baháʼís' efforts, and the means they employed must harmonize with the ends they sought. Shoghi Effendi was asking the Baháʼís across the segregated South to openly demonstrate the faith's power to unite blacks and whites, from the level of village and neighborhood to that of the region and nation. No individual

Bahá'í was exempt, whatever his or her background, upbringing, or personal inclinations; no state, however strong its upholders of orthodoxy, could be considered too inhospitable for the faith to be established on a soundly interracial basis. And the National Spiritual Assembly had ultimate responsibility to ensure the project's success.[28]

Underlying Shoghi Effendi's critique of American society and his vision of the role of the Bahá'í movement within it was an assumption of the primacy of spiritual forces in social change. In the context of the New Deal era, it was an important reminder of essential Bahá'í beliefs. Indeed, during the 1930s a growing chorus of local, state, and regional organizations across the South—from the Communist Party, labor unions, and New Deal agencies to Southern Baptist student groups, women's associations, and the NAACP—were working across lines of race and class and calling for a new reconstruction of the region. While the Bahá'ís could welcome such developments and wholeheartedly support the broad goals of economic justice and political democracy, Shoghi Effendi wrote that they could not depend on other organizations for solutions. Rather, they would have to chart their own path and make a distinctive contribution to the cause of racial justice. In fact there were important differences, at the levels of both ideology and practical implementation, between the Bahá'í community and other advocates of reform in the South. Neither the Marxist-inspired economic determinism that influenced the work of many progressive civil rights and labor organizations nor the NAACP's efforts to achieve civil rights within and through the Democratic Party were completely compatible with Bahá'í beliefs and practices, which militated against the petty loyalties and manipulation inherent in political parties and class antagonism. Shoghi Effendi maintained that the overriding task of the American Bahá'í community was to broaden the foundations of the new system envisioned by Bahá'u'lláh, a system that represented, in the words of 'Abdu'l-Bahá, the "highest aims" of the peoples of the world—of whatever religion, nation, or political faction—for justice, freedom, and equality.[29]

In *The Advent of Divine Justice*, Shoghi Effendi placed the specific struggles of the American Bahá'ís to build an interracial community within the context of the world-shaping spiritual revolutions of the past as well as the spiritual mission their country was destined to carry out in the future. He noted that all the messengers of God, including the Báb and Bahá'u'lláh, had appeared amidst peoples who were "either fast declining, or had already touched the lowest depths of moral and spiritual degradation." Each one of them had given birth to a new community of faith distinguished by high morals and social cohesion, "and with it as a lever ha[d] lifted the entire human race to a higher and nobler plane of life and conduct." By the same principle, it was because of the evils that materialism had engendered within the United States—not its supposed political or economic strength—that Bahá'u'lláh and particularly 'Abdu'l-Bahá had specified it to be the "cradle" and the "standard-bearer" of the future global order. By raising up a spiritually vibrant new community "from the midst of a people immersed in a sea of materialism, a prey to one of the most virulent and long-standing forms of racial prejudice, and notorious for its political corruption, lawlessness and laxity in moral standards," Bahá'u'lláh would demonstrate his "almighty power" to a "heedless generation" and begin to prepare the nation to take its proper role in the world's spiritual regeneration. The problem, however, was that the Bahá'ís were "incapable as yet, in view of the restricted size of their community and the limited influence it [then wielded], of producing any marked effect on the great mass of their countrymen." Their overriding concern should be to "regenerate the inward life of their own community" along the lines Shoghi Effendi described: building and refining the institutions of their administrative system; reflecting more fully the faith's high standards of sexual morality, gender relations, and marriage and family life; and, most importantly, cultivating a distinctive interracial fellowship. Systematic and sustained attention to these essential matters, Shoghi Effendi assured, would not only conduce to success in the community's immediate objectives but would also, as it grew in size, resources, and spiritual vitality over many decades, enable "future generations" of American Bahá'ís to "assail the longstanding evils that have entrenched themselves in the life of their nation."[30]

Shoghi Effendi's letter had immediate and far-reaching effects on the American Bahá'ís. The National Spiritual Assembly took a more active leadership role in promoting interracial unity by a variety of means, including appointing a new Race Unity Committee and providing ample time at the 1939 National Convention for discussion of the letter. At that convention, described by one participant as "unified and more mature" than in the past, Louis Gregory was reelected to the National Spiritual Assembly after several years of it having gone without a black member; the Assembly subsequently elected Gregory its first recording secretary. The five-member Race Unity Committee included both Louis Gregory and Dorothy Beecher Baker, who also served as vice chair of the National Spiritual Assembly. A white Ohioan descended from the abolitionist Beecher family of New England, Baker was well respected among the Bahá'ís and had already emerged as a champion of racial justice within the community. Together, she and Gregory coordinated a renewed "southern college project" beginning in 1940 that sent black and white teachers to some 160 colleges in the region, lecturing "before chapels, assemblies, classrooms, and student clubs" on the oneness of humanity, presenting Bahá'í books to libraries, and distributing pamphlets to students and professors. As a result of Shoghi Effendi's letter and the National Assembly's strong endorsement, the 1940s witnessed a new wave of national and local efforts similar to the race amity activities of the 1920s and early 1930s, including a wide variety of conferences, courses, exhibits, and interracial dinners and social activities across the country. At the same time, the national movement made its first concerted efforts to teach the faith to Native Americans, Chinese Americans, and, significantly (given the extent of wartime prejudices), Japanese Americans.[31]

The prosecution of the plan, and particularly the southern campaign, provided ample opportunities to test and refine the interracial character of the American Bahá'í movement. The first major challenge to the National Spiritual Assembly's southern strategy and Shoghi Effendi's instructions in *The Advent of Divine Justice* came in Atlanta in 1940, when the racial conservatism of a group of white believers nearly succeeded in creating an all-white local community. The National Assembly's intervention in the crisis set a strong precedent for the subsequent development of the faith in the South, including nearby South Carolina. By the late 1930s, there was a small local community in Atlanta that included both black and white members. They all met together regularly for Nineteen Day Feasts and Holy Days and, according to the national policy, sometimes held separate meetings for white and black inquirers. Difficulties only arose late in 1939, when Orcella Rexford, a traveling health and nutrition lecturer who combined her professional engagements with teaching campaigns, visited Atlanta and attracted a new group of seekers—all of them white—to a study group led by Terah Smith, a local white believer and secretary of the Regional Teaching Committee. Five of the seekers became Bahá'ís. However, the new converts were apparently only dimly aware that the faith was an interracial movement and, indeed, that there were already black believers in the city. At Ridván 1940, when a Local Spiritual Assembly was elected for the first time, all the members were white; it is unclear whether the black Bahá'ís were even invited to participate in the election.[32]

One white couple from among the older group of Bahá'ís, Raymond and Estelle Lindsey, decided to press the issue of race in the community by initiating a series of integrated firesides in their home. They invited their black neighbors, as well as the black and white Bahá'ís, for dinner and discussion of the faith. Afterward, other white Baháʼís protested, and Terah Smith asked the Lindseys not to have any more integrated meetings. At the same time, the new Local Assembly took no action on the request of a black seeker, Essie Robinson, to be enrolled as a believer. By the fall of 1940, it was clear to the National Spiritual Assembly that the conservatism of the new white Baháʼís—and evidently at least one of the veteran teachers in the community as well—was compromising the integrity of the southern teaching policy in one of the region's leading cities.[33]

To remedy the situation, the National Assembly arranged to visit Atlanta in November 1940. Perhaps not coincidentally, it was Louis Gregory and Dorothy Baker who formed the National Assembly's advance team. Gregory was the first member to arrive. When he went to a meeting with the community that had been arranged for that evening, only a portion of the believers—those favorable to integration—showed up. The next night, when Dorothy Baker arrived and called a meeting with her and Gregory, everyone came. Baker took the lead in the discussion. "Every single individual," according to one account, "was given an opportunity to express himself." Yet Baker left no room for vacillation. Calling attention to the fact that Essie Robertson was waiting to be enrolled in the faith, she "made it clear that the Baha'i Community could never restrict anyone because of color." She insisted that interracial unity was a matter of spiritual principle and an article of their faith, and that there could be only one, integrated local community in Atlanta. Any white person, she said, who could not fully embrace the ideal and the practice of interracial fellowship was welcome to leave the faith. Additional gatherings held after the arrival of the other members of the National Assembly reinforced Baker's message. At the Biltmore Hotel, a prestigious venue that promoters dubbed "the South's Supreme Hotel," the audience for a major public meeting included a large number of blacks—a concession by the management at the Baháʼís' request. A subsequent regional teaching conference drew some thirty Baháʼís—black and white, pioneers and recent converts—from six southeastern states, including South Carolina, and their deliberations included means by which to reach the white, black, and Jewish populations.[34]

Altogether, the message to the Atlanta community was clear, and a few whites indeed "ceased attending Baha'i Assembly and Feast meetings." For the rest, however, the National Assembly's visit cemented the interracial character of the community. At the next meeting of the Local Assembly, Essie Robertson was enrolled as a believer, and her home quickly became a center of activity. The following Ridván, Robertson was elected to the Local

Assembly, and the body remained integrated for the rest of the decade. By the end of the 1940s, the community had built and occupied its first Bahá'í Center, located a block off Auburn Avenue in the heart of Atlanta's black business district—a modest two-story structure, but an important statement of the community's interracial commitment.[35]

Beyond Atlanta, the National Assembly's firm stance made clear to Bahá'ís across the South that the goal of its 1937 policy on teaching in the region was nothing less than fully integrated local communities. A letter from Shoghi Effendi (writing through his secretary), published subsequently in *Bahá'í News*, underlined the regional implications of the Atlanta incident and reinforced his insistence on black participation in local Bahá'í governance: "The Guardian is very pleased to learn of the success that has attended the sessions at Atlanta and the removal of the disagreement within the community of that city and the work achieved by the regional conference and the public meeting open to both races. A special effort, he feels, should now be made to lay a foundation of unity between the white and colored Bahá'ís and weld the groups [across the South] into communities capable of forming Assemblies representative of both races." The message was certainly not lost on William and Christine Bidwell, who came from Greenville for the events. Writing to Emogene Hoagg on the defeat of the segregationists at the "great meeting," William Bidwell reported with apparent satisfaction that "some of the Georgia cracker[s] could not *take* being in the same room with the colored brethren." In the far less cosmopolitan atmosphere of Greenville, however, building an interracial community was easier said than done.[36]

Activism and Suppression in Depression-Era Greenville

In December 1938, William Bidwell had written to a friend that a white Baptist seeker in Greenville was "afraid to believe and afraid not to believe" in the Bahá'í Faith. Indeed, the decade of the Great Depression had left people in the Greenville area with plenty to fear. In contrast to the situation in Atlanta and a few of the other fledgling communities in the South, the initial barrier to the growth of the faith in Greenville seems to have been less a lingering racial conservatism on the part of at least one of the pioneers than a local history of brutal suppression of racial and religious heterodoxy. By the time the Bidwells moved to Greenville in 1938, the city and its surrounding rural communities had been reeling from economic disaster, race and class antagonisms, and an upsurge in political violence for nearly two decades.[37]

In the South Carolina Piedmont, like other cotton-dependent areas in the

South, the Great Depression began not with the 1929 stock market crash but with the collapse of the agricultural economy nearly a full decade earlier. During the decade of the 1920s, as cotton prices plummeted and the boll weevil devastated crops, half of South Carolina's counties lost population. In just the eight months after the particularly disastrous cotton harvest of 1922, some fifty thousand blacks, mostly farm families from the Piedmont, left the state for good. In Greenville, the black population declined during the 1920s and 1930s to less than 40 percent as thousands sought opportunities in the cities of the North and West. The city's cotton mills became a magnet for hard-hit white farming families, but after 1929 the nationwide economic downturn meant that industrial employment was not safe, either.[38] For those blacks and whites who remained in Greenville, the gravity of the economic crisis and, after 1933, the work and relief programs of the New Deal began to alter traditional social and economic relationships. But by the time the Bidwells arrived, every effort for a decade to promote social and economic justice and interracial cooperation had ended in abject failure, either sabotaged by officials of the state's largest and most influential Christian denomination and their political friends or violently suppressed by the coordinated efforts of local police and the Ku Klux Klan.[39]

Protests by Greenville workers, particularly when blacks and whites attempted to cooperate, were violently suppressed. In 1929 and 1931, the Communist-led National Textile Workers Union (NTWU) organized strikes against the "stretch-out" (the use of fewer workers for increased production) in the area's cotton mills. In 1929, a female NTWU organizer was abducted and beaten by hooded men. In 1931, the NTWU organized an Unemployed Council made up of jobless whites and blacks, which staged a series of marches and made repeated appeals to the local Red Cross and the city council for relief. Klan members, often with police officers standing by, attended city council meetings to intimidate the workers' representatives, raided the organization's headquarters, broke up clandestine meetings in houses, and beat up black and white members. In 1936, when organizers for the Workers Alliance, a union of employees of the federally funded Works Progress Administration (WPA), came to Greenville, they set up separate black and white locals, but the two groups' leaders worked closely together and white members accompanied black members as the latter attempted to register to vote. In response, city police raided houses looking for Communist literature and arrested both black and white members.[40]

In 1938 and 1939, similar methods defeated an ambitious voting rights campaign launched by the Greenville branch of the NAACP. While black residents' grievances were many, the incident that sparked the campaign was the city council's rejection of a plan by the local housing authority to replace dilapidated houses in black neighborhoods with new low-cost construction. In response to the defeat, the NAACP launched a campaign to register 6,000 African American voters in time for municipal elections in September 1939. Approximately 250 African Americans succeeded in registering before violence and intimidation crushed the campaign. The Ku Klux Klan copied the names of registrants from local newspaper reports, beat up organizers and innocent bystanders during night rides in black neighborhoods in Greenville and smaller towns in the county, and denounced the campaign in the press as a Communist plot. Campaign leaders were fired from their jobs and some were jailed by police. Tensions ran high as armed black men patrolled their neighborhoods on the lookout for the Klan. One African American resident said that if the vigilantes had located any Klansmen, "there would have been a race riot in Greenville that would have made previous Southern race riots look like interracial good will meetings." Only 34 of the registered black voters cast ballots in the municipal election, while white voters, stirred by Klan propaganda, turned out in larger-than-normal numbers.[41]

Even members of the area's white elite risked retribution if their efforts on behalf of blacks passed from the realm of traditional paternalism into substantive advocacy and interracial cooperation. In 1936 Bennette Eugene Geer, a prominent textile executive and president of Furman University, a Baptist men's college in downtown Greenville, founded the Greenville County Council for Community Development, an agency designed to channel the spirit and resources of the New Deal into a wide range of community development projects. A cooperative venture among Furman, the city of Greenville, local schools and libraries, charitable organizations, and state and federal agencies, the council initiated projects in health, education, housing, recreation, and environmental stewardship among the area's residents, black and white. When the local NAACP launched its voting rights campaign in 1939, the council sought to distance itself. Nevertheless, in the eyes of many whites, the fact that the council had carried out the research on which the housing authority had based its application for federal slum-clearance funding meant that the organization had gone too far in its support of black demands. It also contributed to a growing perception among conservative Baptist leaders that Furman University was becoming a citadel of biblical modernism, social-gospel liberalism, and interracial mixing. As the controversy over slum clearance put the council in the middle of the area's divisive racial politics, Furman professors clashed with trustees and local Baptist ministers when a visiting speaker encouraged students to deemphasize study of doctrine and focus on applying the Christian faith to social conditions. (It mattered little that the speaker was a Baptist minister himself and the son of a former president of the university.) The trustees fired one professor over the matter, and Geer was forced to resign as president. He remained the head of the council, but, deprived of sponsorship by the university, the organization folded the next year. The suppression of the area's labor movement and NAACP branch and the demise of the Council for Community Development made it clear that Greenville, dubbed by its boosters as the progressive "Textile Capital of the South," was in reality a dangerous place for blacks *and* whites—together or separately, regardless of their class background—to challenge the rule of the city's business and political elite and their powerful allies in the Baptist ministry. In such an oppressive local climate, it is perhaps not surprising that the Bahá'í Faith was slow at first to gain converts in Greenville.[42]

Reinforcements, but Few Recruits

White supremacist reaction to the Greenville area's incipient labor and civil rights movements—in addition, perhaps, to recollections of the crackdown on Bahá'í teaching among working-class blacks in North Augusta—seems to have created a climate of fear that reinforced the conservative tendencies of some of the pioneers, strained relationships within the struggling young community, and slowed early expansion efforts. In 1939, two years after their arrival, the Bidwells remained the only Bahá'ís in Greenville, and the prospects of establishing a local community there by the end of the Seven Year Plan looked bleak. While the Bidwells worked to build their business and nurture a few seekers, it was a challenge to remain connected to the wider Bahá'í community. William Bidwell maintained that he had informed the National Spiritual Assembly of their move to Greenville in 1938. Yet when Shoghi Effendi cabled to the American Bahá'ís in January 1939 calling for "nine holy souls" to settle in the nine remaining virgin states and provinces in North America, South Carolina was still included in the list. The Bidwells wrote to the secretary of the National Teaching Committee asking to be put on the national mailing list of isolated believers, and they wrote directly to Shoghi Effendi to tell him they had moved to South Carolina. Shoghi Effendi informed the National Spiritual Assembly of the Bidwells' move, but not in time for them to be listed as pioneers in the body's annual report in April 1939. Horace Holley, the secretary of the National Assembly, wrote to the couple that month: "The members of the National Spiritual Assembly have been very pleased to receive a letter from Shoghi Effendi reporting that you have settled in South Carolina as Baha'i pioneers. Both the Teaching Committee and the N.S.A. will be more than happy to extend all possible cooperation in your important work." But William Bidwell still felt slighted. "Holley knew," he noted, "that I was at Chick Springs last year." If the national administration seemed remote and inefficient, the Augusta-area community was completely unhelpful. Bidwell complained to a friend: "The Augusta crowd asked that we keep our membership there but they have forgotten we are living and never mail us a news letter." Even their personal practice of the faith was adversely impacted by being outside a local community. "We do not know when the fast begins," Bidwell noted, "and I wrote today asking."[43]

By early 1940, the Bidwells felt isolated and dispirited, and their efforts to establish the Bahá'í Faith in Greenville had yielded few tangible results. To remedy the situation, the National Teaching Committee and its newly established branch, the Regional Teaching Committee for North Carolina, South Carolina, and Georgia, directed a succession of new pioneers and traveling teachers to Greenville. Most of the new arrivals were single or widowed white women from the established communities in the North and West; later, following the onset of war, some women whose husbands were away in military service were also able to move as pioneers. At least one of the new arrivals, Amelie Bodmer, had taught the faith in South Carolina before, at the beginning of the plan. By early 1941, there were six Bahá'ís residing in Greenville.[44]

In 1942, with the end of the Seven Year Plan less than two years away, Shoghi Effendi modified the expansion goal for North America from simply having "a nucleus of believers in every State and Province" to establishing at least one Local Spiritual Assembly in each territory. To accomplish the revised goal would require herculean efforts; experience around the country indicated that without steady growth in membership it was extraordinarily difficult to establish and maintain a Local Assembly. Even nearby Augusta, the oldest Bahá'í community in two states, was struggling. In 1940, Shoghi Effendi had reiterated a previous policy that all Local Spiritual Assembly jurisdictions should conform to civil boundaries. In the Augusta area, the immediate result was that there were enough Bahá'ís living in both Augusta and North Augusta for each city to form its own Local Assembly. Late the same year, however, when Louise Thompson visited for a meeting of the Regional Teaching Committee, she reported: "The N. & S. Augusta Assemblies are not very cooperative and need help." By early 1943, the number of believers in Augusta and North Augusta had each fallen below nine and both Local Assemblies were dissolved.[45]

The difficulties in the Augusta area underlined the magnitude of the goal of establishing a Local Spiritual Assembly in every state and province of the continent. As Leroy Ioas of the National Teaching Committee recalled, "What in the past had been a matter of sporadic effort now compelled primary and complete concentration." The Regional Teaching Committees led the effort by selecting a goal city in each virgin area and sending additional pioneers and visiting teachers. For South Carolina, the Regional Teaching Committee serving the Carolinas and Georgia selected Greenville as the goal city. It was in some ways a logical choice. Greenville had become the state's largest population center (just edging out Charleston and Columbia according to the 1940 census), and it was the only city in the state with permanent Bahá'í pioneers. However, in terms of the development of interracial community, it was probably the least favorable of South Carolina's three main urban areas. Greenville's black population was much smaller (less than a quarter of the total, compared to more than a third in Columbia and almost half in Charleston), and given the area's recent history of racial violence and massive black out-migration, its black community was generally less vibrant, less prosperous, and less stable than its counterparts in Columbia and Charleston. Moreover, in more than four years of permanent residence by the Bidwells, no one in Greenville had embraced the faith. In Columbia, by contrast, during essentially the same period, seasonal residence by Maud Mickle and Alta Wheeler and visits by two black traveling teachers had resulted in the enrollment of one white and five black new believers (along with Mickle and Wheeler, nearly enough to elect a Local Spiritual Assembly), the establishment of a regular study class and other activities with participation by several seekers, and use of the local media. Selection of Columbia as the goal city would surely have led to growth of the promising group there. It is easy to imagine a stronger, thoroughly interracial Columbia community, situated in the center of the state, eventually sending its own pioneers and traveling teachers to other localities, including Greenville and Charleston. Whether the Regional Committee was disinclined to concentrate resources on a budding community made up mostly of African Americans, or whether the Bidwells, who were members, unduly influenced the decision, Greenville would be the focus of the regional movement's efforts until the end of the plan.[46]

In 1942, following the selection of Greenville as a goal city, a new wave of pioneers began to arrive. Among them was Grace Wilder, a single young white woman from Los Angeles, who left for South Carolina right after a summer program at the Geyserville Bahá'í School in northern California.

Shortly after her arrival, Wilder met and befriended a young white woman named Virginia Ford, who soon became the first Bahá'í convert in the city. Virginia Allen Ford, age twenty-one, and her husband had both grown up in the cotton mill town of Williamston in neighboring Anderson County. With her husband serving overseas in the army, Ford was alone at home with their young daughter. Her study of the faith and involvement in community activities appear to have been haphazard at first. For some time after joining the religion, she did not even realize that Bahá'ís believed Bahá'u'lláh to be the return of Christ. She later recalled that it was difficult to attend Bahá'í meetings because some of the other members did not like children.[47]

In the fall of 1942, the Regional Teaching Committee held a "Teaching Conference" in Greenville, one of a series of similar efforts across the country to train more individuals as competent and confident teachers of the faith. Twenty Bahá'ís and sixteen seekers, including residents of the Carolinas and Georgia and two traveling teachers from outside the region, attended the weekend program. According to the Regional Committee's newsletter, an important feature of the conference was the "first inter-racial public meeting" on the Bahá'í Faith in South Carolina, an "outstanding precedent" for the state. Eva Lee Flack and Adrienne Ellis, single young African American women from California who were pioneers in Greensboro, the goal city for North Carolina, provided a "musical contribution" to the program. It is unclear in what kind of venue the conference was held or whether there were any other blacks in attendance.[48]

More pioneers, mostly white, came to Greenville in 1943: Adline Lohse and her young daughter came from Washington, D.C.; Luda Dabrowski from Larchmont, New York; Villa Vaughn from New York City; Virginia Camelon from Illinois; and Emogene Hoagg from Cuba. Few were able to stay permanently. Late in June, the Regional Teaching Committee organized another Teaching Conference in Greenville. Fifteen Bahá'ís, including a visiting teacher, Charles Mason Remey from Washington, D.C., and four seekers attended. The topics of study during the conference were "Prophecies Fulfilled," the "Dawnbreakers," and "Living the Bahá'í Life." Carolyn Glazener, a white Greenville woman who had been studying the religion with the Bidwells for some time, became a Bahá'í during the conference, only the second convert in four years. A South Carolina native married to a man from the North Carolina mountains, she owned and managed a secondhand store a block off South Main Street in the city's black business district.[49]

By the fall of 1943, three more pioneers had been added to the Greenville group. Viola Bower came from New York City, and Roy and Bernice Williams, also longtime New Yorkers, came from Rocky Mount, North Carolina, where they had recently settled. With the arrival of the Williamses, Greenville received its first black pioneers, and they seemed particularly well suited to attracting local African Americans to the faith. Roy Williams was already somewhat familiar with the area; more than twenty years earlier, during the course of an extended visit to the state, he and Louis Gregory had spoken on the faith "in many churches in Greenville and Anderson Count[ies]." Further, the Williamses' social and economic background made it likely that they could stay in Greenville indefinitely. Roy Williams was a master woodworker, and he opened a shop for fine furniture restoration where he catered to a mostly white clientele. Bernice Williams, a teacher, worked first at an elementary school and later at Sterling High School, the county's only high school for African Americans. While both were to some extent dependent on whites for their livelihood and may therefore have needed to remain circumspect about their radical religious and racial beliefs, each enjoyed a position of respect in a black community that was painfully short on professionals, and each had ample opportunity to serve and befriend large numbers of people in their new locality. In November 1943, the membership of the Greenville Baháʼí community having risen to more than nine, a Local Spiritual Assembly was elected for the first time. With the Williamses as members, it reflected the tiny community's tentatively interracial character.[50]

Racial Politics in Wartime

If the New Deal had strained traditional patterns of economic dependency and encouraged agricultural and industrial workers to press their concerns, mobilization for a new global war brought even more thoroughgoing change to South Carolina—trends that, continuing after the war, opened new opportunities for growth of the state's Baháʼí movement. For South Carolinians, World War II meant the end of the Great Depression, an acceleration of urbanization and industrialization, an unprecedented level of federal government involvement in daily life and livelihoods, and often a sense of broadened personal horizons and expectations. For African Americans in particular, the war provided a new impetus to activism, and the organization that led and embodied their struggle was a revived and expanded NAACP.

The chief architect of South Carolina's new NAACP was Levi Byrd, a poorly educated, self-employed, and amazingly energetic plumber in Cheraw, the seat of Chesterfield County in the upper Pee Dee. Between 1933 and 1939, he organized a largely underground branch of the NAACP in Cheraw, a town little different from those where the organization had folded in the face of repression in the 1920s. During the summer of the Greenville voting rights effort, Byrd began writing to the other remaining branches in South Carolina to urge the creation of a statewide conference of the association. In the fall of 1939, as Klan violence descended on blacks in Greenville, the branches there and in Charleston, Columbia, Florence, Georgetown, and Sumter sent representatives to an organizational meeting at Benedict College in Columbia. The new state conference immediately endorsed both the Greenville campaign and the national organization's call for an end to segregation and disfranchisement, and it began planning two statewide initiatives: a legal campaign to secure equal pay for black teachers and the creation of an alternative black political party to press for voting rights. While the twin initiatives represented only a partial struggle against segregation and disfranchisement—the salary equalization campaign did not contemplate the dismantling of the state's dual school system, and an all-black party was at best a stepping-stone to full and equitable political participation—both efforts were notable for their energy, for their tentative successes, and for the foundation they laid for continued activism in the postwar period.[51]

The state NAACP's campaign to equalize pay between black and white teachers began in 1943 with a class-action case representing black teachers in Charleston. Thurgood Marshall of the national organization's Legal Defense and Education Fund and Harold Boulware of the state conference's Committee on Legal Redress argued before Judge J. Waties Waring of the U.S. District Court for the Eastern District of South Carolina that a discrepancy in salary between black and white teachers violated the equal protection clause of the Fourteenth Amendment. Waring, scion of a prominent white Charleston family and an unlikely advocate of racial justice, upheld the plaintiffs' claims, and the Charleston school district submitted to a consent decree to phase in equal salaries. The state government attempted to subvert the ruling, but in 1945 Waring ruled in a second case that Richland County, too, had to equalize teachers' salaries.[52]

A simultaneous effort to secure voting rights focused on gaining access to the machinery of the state's Democratic Party, which leaders of the state conference believed was the key to realizing blacks' political potential. White Democratic leaders, however, fought energetically to exclude African Americans from the state's de facto single party. As Gov. Olin D. Johnston told a reporter in 1942, "The white people of this state have successfully run this government for generations, and . . . we intend to run it as we have in the past." Two years later he had a chance to put his promise into action. In early April

1944, when the U.S. Supreme Court ruled in a Texas case that party primary elections were an integral part of the electoral process and therefore could not exclude African Americans without violating the Fifteenth Amendment, South Carolina's white leaders immediately recognized the implications of the ruling. Johnston called the legislature into extraordinary session to insulate South Carolina's Democratic primary from attack. Over the course of six days, in an unprecedented feat of legislative efficiency, the General Assembly removed every reference to primary elections from the state code, passing instead 147 new laws designed to make them completely private affairs. If legal measures were not enough, Johnston assured the legislators, they would employ other "necessary methods" to retain white supremacy.[53]

On the opening day of the legislature's special session, the *Lighthouse and Informer* of Columbia, the unofficial newspaper of the statewide NAACP, announced the creation of the South Carolina Colored Democratic Party—a name quickly changed to the Progressive Democratic Party (PDP). At its first statewide convention, held on May 24, 1944, in the Masonic Temple in Columbia, Rev. James Hinton, president of the state conference of the NAACP, compared South Carolina's Jim Crow regime to Hitler's Germany, invoking black wartime service as a claim to full citizenship rights. "Black boys are dying on the battlefields," Hinton said, "and these South Carolina demagogues meet in extra sessions to further disfranchise what we are fighting for."[54] By the end of July, when PDP delegates appeared before the credentials subcommittee in Philadelphia to challenge the seating of South Carolina's all-white delegation at the Democratic National Convention, they claimed some forty-five thousand black members across the state. Supporters of the regular party were unmoved, smearing the PDP as the work of "Communists or Northern agitators," and the subcommittee ruled against the PDP on technicalities. At home, the party nominated Osceola McKaine, an activist from Sumter, to run against Gov. Olin Johnston for an open U.S. Senate seat. The first black South Carolinian to run for statewide office since Reconstruction, McKaine campaigned vigorously, lauding the progressive forces unleashed by the New Deal and the war. But those forces still had little sway at South Carolina polling places, where voter fraud—including intimidation by police and withholding ballots from black voters—marred the November elections.[55]

While the state's political elite fought to defend Jim Crow, other white South Carolinians, moved by the perversity of the Nazi regime's racial theories and the upheavals of wartime, began to criticize the system more openly than ever before. In July 1942, for example, a young assistant minister at

Columbia's Washington Street United Methodist Church voiced progressive racial views in a sermon entitled "This Conflict of Race," startling not only the church's congregation but an audience on local radio. In retaliation, the church's board of stewards voted overwhelmingly to bar him from preaching there again. In a letter to the editor of the *State* in 1944, a white soldier railed against the state's prohibition on servicemen voting by absentee ballot, a measure designed to prevent black soldiers from surreptitiously gaining the franchise. He laid the blame on racial paranoia: "It seems to me that the average [white] South Carolinian is so afraid that the negro will get ahead that he is willing to sacrifice his own rights just to make sure that the negro won't have any." Though hardly constituting a sea change in white public opinion, such incidents indicate that at least a few more white South Carolinians were awakening to the injustice of the state's racial system. During and after the war, Bahá'ís took advantage of the shift by teaching open-minded whites, seeking to influence public opinion, and pressing the claims of their own interracial community.[56]

Race in the Greenville Community

While the state NAACP confronted inequities in education and politics, a handful of Bahá'ís in Greenville continued their own no less difficult program of building an interracial faith community. Hampered by a local climate of fear, the practical constraints of segregation, and the conservative "traditions, tastes, and habits" of some of their own members, they often found themselves frustrated. But they did make some important progress during the war years. One measure of the community's attempt to foster interracial fellowship was its effort to establish a basic pattern of activities for both Bahá'ís and seekers. Black and white believers alike participated in the Nineteen Day Feast, the annual election of the Local Spiritual Assembly, and the Local Assembly's regular meetings, all of which were generally held in the homes of the Bahá'ís on a rotating basis. The whites had little trouble visiting the Williamses' home, an apartment in the back of Roy's furniture shop in a black neighborhood, but when the Williamses came to the Bidwells' house, for instance, they were careful to enter through the office door in the back so as not to arouse the suspicion of the Bidwells' white neighbors.[57]

Following the national policy of 1937, the Greenville Bahá'ís experimented with both separate and mixed gatherings in their outreach to the public. Beginning in 1944, they announced regular firesides in the local newspapers using language that would arouse a minimum of suspicion among white conservatives. Meetings intended primarily for white and black seekers were held at the Bidwell and Williams homes, respectively. A typical announcement in the "City News Briefs" section of the *Greenville News* read: "BAHA'IS TO MEET. 'Springtime in the World' will be the subject of Mrs. Adline Lohse's talk at the Greenville Baha'i meeting this afternoon at 3:30 o'clock at 800 North Main Street. Mrs. Wm. Bidwell will be the chairman for the afternoon. A Baha'i meeting for colored people will be held at 4:30 at 17 Madison Street." Despite the innocuous advertising, the meetings were often mixed in practice. The Bahá'ís also looked for public venues where they could hold integrated gatherings. In 1945, the community rented space in a downtown office building for use as a Bahá'í Center, but the cost likely being too much for the small group to bear, use of the room was short-lived. In 1947, Virginia Ford, pioneer Gertrude Gewertz, and traveling teacher Ali-Kuli Khan, a prominent Iranian-American Bahá'í and former diplomat, visited Mayor J. Kenneth Cass to discuss other options for holding interracial public meetings. Cass said that the only public space where blacks and whites could meet together was in the city council chambers, which he offered for use by the Bahá'ís. Ford recalled that after an initial mixed meeting at city hall, with Khan as the speaker and Mayor Cass in attendance, they used the chambers on an interracial basis "a number of times" without having to mention race at all in their advertising.[58]

While they were able to hold private and, eventually, public integrated activities, it appears that internal disagreements over racial policy prevented the Greenville Bahá'ís from making a concerted and sustained effort to teach their faith to local African Americans. While the economic position and social connections of the Williamses must have presented many opportunities to share the Bahá'í message, it appears likely that the attitudes of some of the white Bahá'ís may have dampened the enthusiasm of black inquirers, or even made the Williamses wary of inviting other blacks to investigate the religion. At least one influential pioneer was opposed to holding virtually any integrated meetings, even private ones among the Bahá'ís. Her opposition surely contributed to the community's relative caution in reaching out to blacks; moreover, disunity over racial policy may have carried over into other areas and prevented the tiny community from attracting many new members at all. The incident indicates the extent to which even one white believer could sabotage the National Spiritual Assembly's southern strategy in a nascent local community.

Late in 1943, a month before the reestablishment of Greenville's Local Spiritual Assembly, veteran pioneer and traveling teacher Emogene Hoagg

Figure 4.1. Greenville Bahá'ís and friends, Naw-Rúz (Bahá'í New Year), March 1944. L to r: William Bidwell, Thelma Bidwell, unknown, Grace Wilder, Emogene Hoagg, Adline Lohse, Luda Dabrowski, Christine Bidwell, unknown, Rachel Mothersill, Viola Bower. Lohse is holding a calligraphic rendering of the Greatest Name. Opposition from Hoagg, a prominent early American Bahá'í, tested the effectiveness of the national movement's policy for fostering interracial community in the South. Used with permission of the National Bahá'í Archives, United States.

expressed her views on race and teaching in a lengthy letter to Leroy Ioas, the chair of the National Teaching Committee. Hoagg argued that the Greenville Bahá'ís should follow the practice of the Bahá'ís in St. Augustine, Florida, who had apparently settled into a pattern of community activities that was only partly integrated. In St. Augustine, Hoagg wrote, the "white members go to the colored nineteen day Feasts [sic], but the colored never go to the other meetings." She argued for extreme caution in pressing Bahá'í racial views among Greenville's white population: "We simply cannot introduce the Cause here by breaking away from all their customs and inborn ideas. Shoghi Effendi knows this. The Cause suffers a setback in so doing, and the believers are classified as revolutionists."[59]

According to Hoagg's letter, several of the Greenville pioneers, especially Grace Wilder and Luda Dabrowski, were quite forceful in their contempt for southern white racism and defiance of Jim Crow. Hoagg indicated that indiscreet comments by Dabrowski and Wilder had aroused the scrutiny of the Federal Bureau of Investigation and brought accusations of Communism, already a common charge against any southern organization pursuing an interracial agenda: "Mrs. Glazener, the new Bahá'í here, has been told by the F.B.I. that they have been getting information regarding Grace Wilder from the time she left California. . . . One suspicion is that Grace is a communist. She constantly has criticized the people here saying: 'People must be changed here,' etc. This attitude is not received without comment, nor is it good judgment to criticize in this way." Hoagg accused another outsider, Ruth Moffett of Chicago, who had spoken at the teaching conference in the fall of 1942, of driving away prospective middle- and upper-class white converts and compounding the problem with federal law enforcement: "Here in Greenville where there were quite a number studying and interested, they were entirely upset by Mrs. Moffett['s] enthusiasm and bad judgment. . . . This is a serious difficulty to be met now as these people are actively opposed. One has gone so far as to report to the F.B.I. that we Baha'is hold 'secret meetings' here at 800 [N. Main St., the home of the Bidwells] every Tuesday evening. These 'meetings' are a class that we are having and are quite freely spoken of." Nor were white Bahá'ís the only culprits. According to Hoagg, Eva Flack McAllister, recently married young African American pioneer in Greensboro, was causing a stir in the small community there "by insisting there should be equality between colored and white in every way." The main problem with this approach, Hoagg continued, was that it "had prevented many of the better class" of whites in Greensboro "from investigating the teachings and caused no end of criticism." She asked that the National Teaching Committee not allow McAllister to come to Greenville as a traveling teacher, as "great confusion and trouble would follow" if McAllister and Dabrowski were allowed to join forces and insist upon "social equality."[60]

Hoagg's comments seem to echo those of some other white traveling teachers active in the South during the 1940s, and her invocation of the Guardianship (i.e., "Shoghi Effendi knows this.") to defend her own cautious approach indicates that at least some in the movement still had not come to terms with a national policy, suggested and approved by the head of the faith, that insisted on teaching both black and white southerners and on promoting complete social equality. Mabel Ives, another teacher active in the South, expressed views similar to Hoagg's in a 1941 letter to Shoghi Effendi. Ives shared impressions of her 1939 visit to Memphis, Tennessee, to help establish a Local Spiritual Assembly there. She said that strong racial prejudice in Memphis had hampered both teaching activities and efforts to build an interracial local community. Her view was that the faith should not be taught to blacks in large numbers until a sizeable group of whites became Bahá'ís, so that they could either change southern society or, through their numbers, offer protection to black Bahá'ís. Ives received the following reply on behalf of Shoghi Effendi in 1942:

> Regarding the whole manner of teaching the Faith in the South: The Guardian feels that, although the greatest consideration should be shown the feelings of white people in the South whom we are teaching, under no circumstances should we discriminate in their favor, consider them more valuable to the Cause than their Negro fellow-southerners, or single them out to be taught the Message first. . . . The Negro and white races should be offered, simultaneously, on a basis of equality, the Message of Bahá'u'lláh.
>
> This does not mean that we should go against the laws of the state, pursue a radical course which will stir up trouble, and cause misunderstanding. On the contrary, the Guardian feels that, where no other course is open, the two races should be taught separately until they are fully conscious of the implications of being a Bahá'í, and then be confirmed and admitted to voting membership. Once, however, this has happened, they cannot shun each other's company, and feel the Cause to be like other Faiths in the South, with separate white and black compartments.

Ives replied to Shoghi Effendi that she would follow his advice and forward copies of the letter to other teachers in the South, and in March 1943, pertinent excerpts of the letter were printed in *Bahá'í News*. One way or another, then, Emogene Hoagg certainly would have known of Shoghi Effendi's latest advice on the matter before she wrote to Leroy Ioas in October. It seems, however, to have had little effect on her attitude toward the situation in Greenville.[61]

The success of the Seven Year Plan in the South depended on the commitment of white Bahá'ís in particular to fully support a vigorous program of teaching both blacks and whites and to nurture an interracial community life. Further, Shoghi Effendi insisted that social and political equality of the races within the Bahá'í community was a prerequisite for the movement's growth and development. In Greenville, however, concern about how local whites and federal law enforcement perceived them prevented at least one of the white Bahá'ís from fully carrying out the policies of the national and international leadership of their religion; in such a small and fragile local community, even one white believer who was opposed to the policy could sabotage the rest of the group's worthwhile efforts. Because she was a respected senior member of the faith in the United States, Emogene Hoagg's strong views probably had an even larger effect on the community. Perhaps she, Glazener, and the Bidwells—all of whom were native to or had lived previously in the Greenville area—were more conscious of its recent history of racial violence and suppression than the others and were wise to counsel a cautious approach. However, at a moment when black activists were demonstrating increasing courage in their challenges to Jim Crow and a growing minority of whites seemed more open to change, it seems reasonable to believe that the Greenville community could have reached out more energetically to African Americans had it been more focused and unified. While it is difficult to draw firm conclusions without more in-depth studies of other local communities in the region, it appears that in areas where pioneers and traveling teachers were applying in full the national policy for the southern campaign—in Nashville, Atlanta, Greensboro, and Columbia, for example, which all faced obstacles similar to those in Greenville—a steady trickle of new black and white believers were indeed joining the faith, and confident and viable interracial communities were beginning to emerge.

Culmination

By early 1944, the exterior ornamentation of the Bahá'í house of worship in Chicago was complete, and in March, with the formation of three remaining Local Spiritual Assemblies in Canada, the faith's administrative system was represented in every state of the United States, every province of Canada, and every republic of Latin America. In April, Shoghi Effendi announced that the North American Bahá'ís had achieved "total victory" in their prosecution of the Seven Year Plan. In fact, the transformation of the community over seven years went beyond the plan's twin goals. The teaching effort had elicited broad participation by the rank and file of the movement. Nearly three hundred individuals—more than 10 percent of the North American community at the outset of the plan—had become pioneers at home or abroad, and more than three hundred others had served as members of Regional Teaching Committees within North America. During the last year of the plan alone, more than one hundred had served as domestic traveling teachers. The campaign also had results beyond the planting of new local communities: overall, Bahá'í membership in the United States and Canada had nearly doubled in seven years to approximately forty-eight hundred people, and these from a much broader diversity of social, economic, and racial backgrounds than before. As Shoghi Effendi had written in *The Advent of Divine Justice*, they were still far too few, at the national level or in any particular locality, to have more than a token effect on society, but the plan represented an important step forward in building real models of unity.[62]

Late in May, with war still raging in Europe and Asia, their accomplishments were on display as the National Spiritual Assembly hosted a special "All-America Convention" in Chicago to mark both the centenary of the faith's birth and the successful completion of the plan. Honorary delegates from Latin America and some sixteen hundred believers from the United States and Canada—fully one-third of the movement's members in North America—attended the proceedings, a remarkable achievement in itself given wartime travel restrictions. The week of devotional programs, artistic performances, consultations, and inspirational speeches concluded on May 25 with a banquet and formal program at the Stevens Hotel, the largest hotel in the city and among the largest in the world, broadcast live over a local radio station. One of the speakers, an American pioneer to Panama named Alfred Osborne, pointed to the diversity of the participants and hailed the convention as "the highest type of democracy." While Osborne was likely unaware of the formation of the Progressive Democratic Party in South Carolina the day before, those who had witnessed the labor and civil rights struggles there and across the South surely noted how his comments contrasted the Bahá'í administrative system with the assumptions and practices of mainstream politics:

> Every delegate, regardless of his education, social status, color or nationality, had the right and the privilege of contributing to the deliberations of the Convention. And each contribution was given consideration regardless of its source. Here was an assembly composed of delegates motivated not by sectional interests, not seeking the favors of their constituents, not previously instructed as to their voting, their attitudes or their decisions; not concerned with their own locality; but delegates working for the welfare of the whole world community.

The convention, he said, indicated "that human nature can change, that new social values can deliberately be created; that in fact, the new world is already in existence in the worldwide Bahá'í family."

For Louis Gregory, who was a member of the convention planning committee, the size and diversity of the gathering was evidence of the community's transformation in the more than three decades since his first encounter with it. Although he had long been one of the most tireless proponents of interracial fellowship, in his convention report Gregory took no credit himself. Instead he linked successful completion of the plan to the faith's early heroes in Iran and to his own mentors, the first generation of American Bahá'ís, "the Dawn-Breakers of the East and the Trail-Blazers of the West, whose deeds and traces laid an imperishable foundation for this triumph."[63]

In view of the long-term development of the Bahá'í Faith around the world, the presence at the centenary convention of black and white believers from the Deep South was almost as significant as that of the representatives from Latin America. For seven years, as blacks in South Carolina and other southern states agitated for political inclusion and most whites struggled to keep them disfranchised, small groups of Bahá'ís had been erecting local units of their own brand of interracial democracy. The American Bahá'í movement had struggled to establish footholds in a region whose ruling caste strenuously opposed anything resembling the faith's cardinal teaching of the oneness of humanity, and it had largely succeeded. As examples from South Carolina showed, a few white believers resisted and some local communities lagged behind others in their interracial character, but the aggregate result of seven years of effort was a closely connected network of black and white believers, with fledgling local institutions that included and represented both races, in towns from Virginia and the Carolinas to Oklahoma and Texas. To the South Carolina Bahá'ís attending the Chicago events, the title "All-America Convention" might as well have referred to their own participation as to that of their Latin fellow believers.

For Louella Moore, who had recently moved from Columbia to Charleston, where her husband was serving in the Army Air Force, the convention was an opportunity to expand her horizons beyond the tiny community of Bahá'ís in South Carolina and Georgia. She renewed old acquaintances and made new ones, sharing lodging with her Columbia friends Maude Mickle and Alta Wheeler and meeting other believers from across the country and across the Western Hemisphere. For the first time she saw in person the gleaming exterior of the house of worship, toward the construction of which she had made financial contributions. "Sure enjoyed seeing the Temple," she wrote to her husband in Charleston on a special centenary postcard featuring a picture of the completed structure. Among the special mementos she brought home were a booklet prepared by Shoghi Effendi, *A World Survey of the Bahá'í Faith, 1844–1944,* and a large photograph of all the convention

Figure 4.2. Participants in the All-America Convention on the steps of the Bahá'í temple, Wilmette, Illinois, May 1944. The largest gathering of Bahá'ís in the Western Hemisphere up to that time, it included representatives from new outposts of the faith in Latin America and the southern United States. *Highlighted, L to r:* Louis G. Gregory, South Carolina's native son, standing near other members of the National Spiritual Assembly; Louella Moore of Columbia; and (probably) Roy and Bernice Williams of Greenville. Louella Moore's copy, author's personal collection.

participants. The booklet outlined the religion's geographic spread and diversity of membership, including lists of countries and territories opened to the faith, cities and towns with Local Spiritual Assemblies, and languages in which Bahá'í literature had been published. The photograph, picturing some sixteen hundred believers of European, African, Amerindian, Asian, and Middle Eastern heritage standing proudly on the steps of their national temple, gave visible expression to the unity and diversity that the movement claimed as its essential strength. It was, to say the least, a religious image uncommon in white South Carolina—an indication of the potential of the faith to engender a new consciousness of multiracial fellowship and global citizenship among perhaps the unlikeliest of people.[64]

For Roy and Bernice Williams of Greenville, even an unexpected courtesy on the long train trip to Chicago seemed to demonstrate the spirit of

change at work in the Baháʼí community and in the world at large. When they proceeded from their sleeping car to the dining car, waiters escorted them to a separate, curtained section for blacks. Observing the scene from their table nearby, a young white couple whom the Williamses had never met asked to join them. The two couples effectively turned the segregated section into an integrated private dining room: they drew the curtains closed and "had a delightful time" sharing a meal together. In a certain sense, the incident mirrored the experience of the Baháʼís in the southern campaign of the Seven Year Plan. While their task was far from finished, they had attempted to build a new kind of community in the midst of, but not a part of, the Jim Crow order. In so doing, they had managed to turn normally segregated spaces across the region—from Greenville's city hall to a Chicago-bound dining car—into arenas for interracial spiritual fellowship.⁶⁵

Postwar Opportunities, Cold War Challenges, and the Second Seven Year Plan, 1944–1953

As the world began to recover from nearly seven years of horrific warfare, the Baháʼí movement in the South sought to grow in a region facing unprecedented social, economic, and political change. In South Carolina and other states, white veterans returned from service overseas ready to take limited steps to improve governance and education, while black veterans and their families contemplated far more thoroughgoing reforms. During the postwar decade, South Carolina's civil rights movement grew in size and confidence. For the first time since Reconstruction, white leaders took a public stand against anti-black violence, but they tolerated no real challenges to the Jim Crow order. For the state's Baháʼís, the period was essentially one of consolidation. In the context of a second Seven Year Plan announced by Shoghi Effendi, they built on previous expansion efforts in Greenville and Columbia, working to establish and maintain Local Spiritual Assemblies, using the mass media to address postwar concerns and attract public attention, and increasing the size and diversity of the community. An effective regional committee structure, which coordinated resources across three states, proved indispensable to the South Carolina community's progress. While their interracial activities made them continued targets of occasional intimidation and violence, by the end of the period the South Carolina Baháʼís had also achieved, in the form of a decision of the Greenville city council, the first official acknowledgement by the state of their distinctively interracial identity and practices.

Baháʼís in South Carolina believed that the growth of their own movement and the dramatic changes in society—apparent from the local level to the global—were closely related. In 1946, Shoghi Effendi predicted that the second century of the Bahá'í Faith would witness an acceleration of two distinct but interrelated processes. The first was a "tremendous deployment" and a "notable consolidation" of the Bahá'í administrative system around the world, and the second was the "first stirrings" of a new global political order in the wake of World War II, a stage referred to in Bahá'u'lláh's writings as the "Lesser Peace" that would presage humanity's future golden age. In the former process, the American Bahá'í movement, continuing to carry out its mandate for teaching in the Tablets of the Divine Plan, would largely set the pattern for other emerging national communities. In the latter, the government of the United States would be the principal driving force. Significantly, issues of race, power, and justice came to the fore as each process unfolded. Within the Bahá'í Faith, broadening and strengthening the interracial character of the community continued to be a central concern in plans for growth at every level, while for the federal government, the persistent denial of equality to African Americans—especially in the South—became a cause of increasing domestic instability and a serious embarrassment to its claim of leadership in the emerging international order. In South Carolina, the Bahá'í community was affected by both processes.[1]

South Carolina and Civil Rights in Postwar America

In South Carolina, the demographic, economic, and political shifts of the early Cold War years were dramatic. The mechanization and centralization of agriculture, begun during the New Deal, meant fewer opportunities for tenants, sharecroppers, and day laborers, black and white. Consequently, flight from the countryside to urban areas—or, in the case of rural blacks in particular, out of the state and region altogether—accelerated after World War II. Some rural hamlets disappeared entirely from loss of population. The state's wartime industrial boom continued virtually unabated with the emergence of a protracted new conflict between the United States and the Soviet Union. An extensive network of military facilities—including Fort Jackson in Columbia, the Navy Yard in Charleston, smaller installations in Beaufort, Greenville, Myrtle Beach, and Sumter, and the Atomic Energy Commission's massive bomb-making plant, the Savannah River Site south of Aiken and North Augusta—brought an influx of money and new residents. Private corporations in search of low-wage, non-union workers followed the defense contractors, and the textile, lumber and paper products, and tourism industries expanded significantly throughout the 1950s.[2]

Training and fighting around the globe during World War II had brought nearly two hundred thousand young South Carolinians, black and white, into contact with new people and new ideas. As in other states across the region, veterans returned to South Carolina expecting honest elections, responsible local government, and better economic opportunities. Thousands took advantage of the GI Bill of Rights to attend college or vocational schools or to secure loans to buy houses, businesses, and farms. Led by J. Strom Thurmond of Edgefield County, a former state senator and judge and a decorated war hero, a new generation of reform-minded young veterans took over the governorship and the General Assembly beginning in 1946. Thurmond and his legislative allies passed laws to modernize the state's ports, prisons, and schools, and voters approved constitutional amendments abolishing the poll tax and allowing divorce.[3]

For black veterans, the successful war against the Nazi regime and its allies brought expectations of the downfall of Jim Crow at home. During the mid-1940s, even white South Carolinians' responses to racial violence seemed to indicate the possibility of change. Two cases that received national attention illustrated the shift. In February 1946, Isaac Woodard, a uniformed black veteran on his way home to Winnsboro, was permanently disabled while in police custody in Batesburg, a town in Lexington County. Reaction around the country to Woodard's case was swift, and at the request of NAACP executive director Walter White, President Harry Truman ordered the Justice Department to investigate. After a trial in U.S. district court that was marred by improprieties, a jury of white South Carolinians deliberated less than thirty minutes and found the accused police officers not guilty. Less than four months later, in February 1947, state and local officials reacted quite differently to a second case of anti-black violence. When a white mob removed Willie Earle, a young black man charged with the murder of a white taxi driver in Greenville, from police custody in nearby Pickens and shot, beat, and stabbed him to death, Gov. J. Strom Thurmond ordered a vigorous prosecution of those responsible for Earle's death. In May, after a highly publicized trial that *Time* magazine called the "biggest lynching trial the South had ever known," a Greenville jury acquitted the defendants. But many prominent whites around the state—including the presiding judge, J. Robert Martin, who left the courtroom without thanking the jury—openly expressed their disgust. The white elite were certainly motivated in no small part by a concern for the effects of racial violence on the area's reputation as a progressive manufacturing center. However, the fact that local, state, and federal officials had worked so strenuously for justice in the case, that the mob's actions had been openly aired in court and in the national media, and that so many of the state's leaders expressed dismay at the trial's outcome indicate the degree to which more than a decade of depression and war had eroded South Carolina's racial status quo. At least with respect to extrajudicial violence, the shift would prove to be permanent: the lynching of Willie Earle was the last one recorded in the state.[4]

In Charleston, a sense of the possibilities for postwar interracial cooperation came during the winter of 1945–1946, when black and white women workers at a cigar plant, members of the Communist-affiliated Food, Tobacco, Agricultural, and Allied Workers Union (FTA), went out on strike for better pay and working conditions. Charleston police constantly harassed the strikers, and the *News and Courier* published the names of union leaders and meeting places. But the same winter, a "New South Lecture Series" sponsored by the union brought together an impressive cross-section of Charleston's population for consideration of a sweeping regional reform agenda. Held at black churches, the series featured several of the leading lights of the southern New Deal and attracted hundreds of listeners, including black and white industrial workers, small businesspeople, teachers, and ministers. One of the organizers pointed to the strike and the lectures as evidence that the New Deal, the struggles of the labor movement, and the recent war had created a "strong progressive element in the South, an element which is attempting to better labor conditions, to improve the educational and economic and social and political conditions of the poor whites and the Negro." Once white South Carolinians had been given a chance "to understand their economic and political plight," he believed, they would "make the right decision" about civil rights for blacks. In October 1946, scholar and activist W.E.B. Du Bois struck a similar note at the annual conference of the Southern Negro Youth Congress, a Communist-inspired organization, at the Township Auditorium in Columbia. Du Bois called for "mutual cooperation," "acquaintanceship," "friendship," and "social intermingling" among the South's black and white working people as the key to their own emancipation and that of oppressed peoples around the world.[5]

As South Carolina's left-leaning organizations promoted interracial cooperation, the state NAACP and its de facto political arm, the Progressive Democratic Party, continued their campaign to secure black participation in South Carolina's Democratic primary elections. When George Elmore, the secretary of the Richland County PDP, and other blacks were turned away from the polls during the August 1946 primaries, the state conference of the NAACP filed a class action suit in U.S. district court. On June 12, 1947, Judge J. Waties Waring, who had already sided with the NAACP in its teacher pay equalization campaign, found that the Democratic Party was effectively an agent of the state and had illegally excluded blacks from voting. Ignoring the General Assembly's 1944 attempt to make party primaries into private affairs, Waring wrote that it was time for South Carolina to "rejoin the Union" and to "adopt the American way of conducting elections." Party leaders attempted to circumvent Waring's ruling, but the following summer he issued an injunction that forced them to open the registration books to all. In August 1948, some thirty-five thousand blacks voted in South Carolina's Democratic primary. The NAACP's success translated into impressive growth for the organization. As the first executive secretary of the state conference, Eugene A. R. Montgomery, a young Marine Corps veteran from Orangeburg whose youngest son would become a Bahá'í decades later, traveled thousands of miles organizing new branches and recruiting new members. The number of branches increased from forty-nine in 1946 to eighty-four in 1951, and membership reached a peak of more than fourteen thousand in 1948. The association represented an even more broadly based movement than official records suggested: thousands of sharecroppers and tenants, vulnerable to eviction by their landlords, were involved in the work of the branches without placing their names on membership rolls or petitions.[6]

For South Carolina's white Democrats, events at the national level, combined with the successes of the NAACP at home, seemed to confirm a sense that their party was slipping from their control. During the New Deal, African Americans had become an important constituency in the national Democratic coalition. Their influence was evident in 1944, when labor and civil rights leaders blocked the nomination of South Carolina native James F. Byrnes, a leader of the conservative southern wing of the party, as Franklin Roosevelt's vice presidential running mate. In the months leading up to the 1948 elections, President Truman, seeking a full term of his own, proposed a civil rights agenda that included creating a permanent Fair Employment Practices Commission, ending poll taxes, and making lynching a federal crime. In advance of the party's 1948 national convention, Strom Thurmond led the defeat of the PDP's second attempt to unseat South Carolina's white regulars. During the convention, however, delegates adopted a strong civil rights plank, and southern delegates staged a walkout.[7]

Convening the next week in Birmingham, the defectors founded the States' Rights Democratic Party, known popularly as the "Dixiecrats," and nominated Thurmond for president. While he generally avoided overtly racist remarks on the campaign trail, Thurmond's position on the maintenance of Jim Crow was clear. "There's not enough troops in the Army," he told the Birmingham meeting, "to force the southern people to break down segregation and admit the Negro race into our theaters, into our swimming pools, into our schools and into our houses." Though they failed to take the presidency from Truman, the Dixiecrats took over the machinery of the party in Alabama, Louisiana, Mississippi, and South Carolina and carried those states in November—an impressive showing for a breakaway party. While Communist activists in Charleston and Columbia were probably correct in identifying a "progressive element" among white South Carolinians, the strength of the Dixiecrat revolt indicated that in the face of an increasingly insistent and well-organized black population, many whites would go to great lengths—even sacrificing traditional party loyalties that had seemed inviolate a few short years before—in order to maintain white supremacy.[8]

A "Respite" and a New Plan

For the Bahá'ís in South Carolina, even the intransigence of white conservatives could be seen as positive—a sign that the guardians of white supremacy felt themselves increasingly under threat. The upsurge of black protest in South Carolina and the political upset it provoked were among many events, at home and abroad, that seemed to bear out Shoghi Effendi's predictions of the consequences of World War II. The latest stage of the "most great convulsion envisaged by the Prophets from Isaiah to Bahá'u'lláh, cataclysmic in violence, planetary in range," the war, he had written, was an "essential pre-requisite to world unification" that would go far toward welding "the limbs of humanity into one single organism." Though devastating in its immediate impact, the conflagration would inevitably "release world-shaking, world-shaping forces" that would "throw down the barriers" dividing the human race. In particular, the entry of the United States into the war would provide the means for the country's "effective and decisive participation" in the "future reconstruction of human society."[9]

In the second half of the 1940s, significant barriers to global order that had withstood both World War I and the Great Depression indeed seemed to be rapidly falling away. Led by the United States—whose Congress had rejected ratification of the League of Nations treaty only a generation before—world leaders of widely divergent political philosophies created a new and more broadly based international peacekeeping organization, the United Nations. At the Nuremberg trials in Germany, leaders of a sovereign state were put on public trial before an international court for the first time and convicted of crimes against humanity. The French and British empires, which had not only survived but grown as a result of the previous war, began to totter in the face of newly invigorated independence movements in Africa and Asia. Even as the rift between the United States and the Soviet Union hobbled efforts to create a new international order, it was clear that the world's political ground had shifted dramatically. At the very least, the genocidal campaigns of the Nazi regime had discredited racism as a basis for public policy. Viewed in global perspective, Baháʼís in South Carolina and elsewhere could be certain that, despite the intransigence of the system's defenders, the demise of Jim Crow was only a matter of time.

In terms of the global mandate for teaching in the Tablets of the Divine Plan, the termination of the conflict would mean a new stage in the American Baháʼí movement's domestic and international campaign. During 1944–1945, the "first year of the second Baháʼí century," Shoghi Effendi enumerated the tasks that lay immediately ahead in preparation for a second multi-year effort: increasing the number of pioneers, both at home and in Latin America; fostering the development of new and existing Local Assemblies and groups; producing more literature in Spanish and Portuguese for the new Latin American communities; and using radio and special events, proclaiming the faith's teachings to "the masses of the population" of "all races and classes" as well as to "leaders of public thought" throughout the Americas. Consolidating the basis of the community in the Western Hemisphere and broadening its reach to the general public, he indicated, were an "indispensable prelude" to launching an even more ambitious teaching plan in Europe as soon as conditions there permitted.[10]

While the National Spiritual Assembly and its agencies pursued all the lines of action that Shoghi Effendi recommended, two areas held particular relevance for the development of the faith in South Carolina. In terms of public relations and use of the media, the national movement gained important experience that local communities built on in the postwar period. In conjunction with the founding conference of the United Nations in San Francisco, for example, the National Spiritual Assembly addressed a letter to President Truman, sponsored a symposium and banquet for members of the international diplomatic corps, and created a thirteen-week series of local radio broadcasts on the theme "Foundations of Universal Peace." During the rest of 1945, local communities in twenty-five states and six provinces—including Atlanta in the Southeast—sponsored additional radio broadcasts that reached an estimated audience of nine million people. For the rest of the decade, Baháʼís in South Carolina would pursue similar efforts, using print and broadcast media and public events to present the faith's teachings on timely issues.[11]

Another area in which Shoghi Effendi's instructions related closely to the situation in South Carolina was the strengthening of Local Spiritual Assemblies. While he had generally been quick to praise the accomplishments of the North American Bahá'ís during the Seven Year Plan, Shoghi Effendi's assessment of the grassroots of the community's administrative order was realistic. Since the beginning of the plan, the administrative foundation had broadened considerably, from 94 Local Spiritual Assemblies and Bahá'í groups in 30 states and provinces to 472 Local Assemblies and groups in 60 states, provinces, and territories—a fivefold increase in eight years. However, most of the new local communities were quite small, and many were made up more of home-front pioneers than of local converts. In communities that were large enough to elect a Local Spiritual Assembly, the basis for the nascent institution was often tenuous, as deaths, military transfers, and moves for other economic or family reasons could quickly reduce the number of believers below the minimum threshold of nine adults. Even where it was possible to maintain the Local Assembly, smallness of numbers meant that disharmony or personality conflict among only two or three believers could severely hamper the functioning and growth of the entire group. To attempt to address such issues, from 1942 to 1946 the National Spiritual Assembly appointed a Committee on Assembly Development. Made up entirely of members of the national body, the committee's initial members included Dorothy Baker and Louis Gregory, who served as secretary. In addition to conducting frequent correspondence with Local Assemblies, the members of the committee made personal visits to counsel communities in need of assistance.[12]

One such struggling Local Assembly was that of Greenville, South Carolina. First formed late in 1940 and soon dissolved because pioneers had been forced to leave, the body was reestablished in November 1943. Its new members—Christine Bidwell, William Bidwell, Viola Bower, Luda Dabrowski, Emogene Hoagg, Adline Lohse, Grace Wilder, Bernice Williams, and Roy Williams—and the body's officer structure reflected both the strengths and weaknesses of the young community. The only two resident believers not elected to the body were the two Greenville natives, Virginia Ford and Carolyn Glazener. Ford may not have known enough about the faith's administration yet to want to participate in the election, and Glazener, perhaps upset by her encounter with the FBI or pressure from her social circle, may well have been keeping her distance from the other Bahá'ís. Whatever the reasons, the only two local converts appear to have been absent from the fledgling community's administrative affairs. Except for the Bidwells, both native southerners, all the members of the Local Spiritual Assembly were transplants from the North and West. If not in terms of geographic origins, then at least in terms of race and gender the body was as diverse as possible given the community's small size. The only two men in the community, one white and one black, were both members. Of the remaining seven, six were white women and one was a black woman. The body's officers, elected by plurality vote of the members, were William Bidwell, chair; Luda Dabrowski, vice chair; Adline Lohse, secretary; and Christine Bidwell, treasurer. Thus, with a majority of seven from outside the region, the two native southerners on the Local Assembly had both been elected as officers. On the other hand, with a majority of seven women, one of the men had been elected chair. And neither of the two African Americans on the Local Assembly—both of them quite capable individuals—had been elected as an officer.[13]

Beyond its demographic shortcomings, the factors that limited the effectiveness of the Local Assembly had to do with differences of personality and approach. As Emogene Hoagg had revealed in her letter to Leroy Ioas just before the arrival of the Williamses, the Greenville Bahá'ís were severely divided in their understanding of how to teach the faith in a racially segregated city. Hoagg and, she had intimated, "four others of the group" preferred extreme caution in teaching African Americans, and she had accused Dabrowski and Wilder of "bad judgment" by practicing social equality. Such disagreements certainly continued after the Williamses arrived and the Local Assembly was reformed. Further complicating the situation was a conflict between William Bidwell and Roy Williams that seems to have had nothing to do with race. As one Bahá'í who worked closely with both men in later years recalled, the two loved each other like brothers—but they also fought like brothers. Williams accused Bidwell, the alternative healer, of mixing bizarre scientific theories with the pure teachings of the faith. Bidwell accused Williams, who had seen 'Abdu'l-Bahá in person in 1912 and received two tablets from him, of being too attached to him and not enough to Shoghi Effendi and the faith's evolving Administrative Order. The men argued frequently and sometimes avoided each other.[14]

By early 1944, the Greenville community was paralyzed. The chair of the Local Assembly, William Bidwell, was attempting to dictate when meetings would be held, and Roy Williams was refusing to attend and asking the National Teaching Committee to be sent to another goal city. Circumventing the normal process of consultation within the Local Assembly, Emogene Hoagg reported the matter directly to Horace Holley, the secretary of the National

Spiritual Assembly. By the fall, several pioneers—Bower, Lohse, Wilder, and Hoagg herself, who was back in Charleston—had left Greenville. Although at least one more pioneer was expected to arrive and one of the Greenville natives, Carolyn Glazener, was now "coming along fine" in deepening her understanding of the faith, disagreement over how to fill the vacancies on the Local Assembly—whether to hold an election immediately or wait for new pioneers sent by the National Teaching Committee—brought the work of the body to a standstill. Horace Holley, recognizing that the Greenville community was "going through a real ordeal," referred the matter to the national Committee for Assembly Development with the hope that it could send a representative to Greenville to "try and take hold of the situation." Louis Gregory, who often combined his regular teaching trips with visits to struggling communities on behalf of the committee, came to Greenville during a winter 1944–1945 tour through five southern states. He met with the communities in Columbia and in the Augusta area, and in Greenville he likely took the opportunity to counsel the members of the Local Assembly. The rifts remained unhealed, however, and the constant fluctuation of pioneers—departure of those unable to stay, followed by insufficient replacements—left the Greenville community unstable and sometimes unable to focus on growth.[15]

At Ridván 1946, after a "two-year respite" since the end of the previous plan, Shoghi Effendi called on the American Bahá'ís to launch a new Seven Year Plan, the second stage of their domestic and international teaching program. The new plan, like the first, would end with a major anniversary celebration. In this case, 1952–1953 marked the centenary of the period when Bahá'u'lláh, imprisoned in a subterranean dungeon in Tehran, received the first stirrings of his prophetic mission. In a cable to the 1946 National Convention, Shoghi Effendi outlined four main objectives that built on those of the previous plan and of the interim period. One was completion of the interior ornamentation of the national temple in Chicago, thus preparing it for public dedication by the end of the plan. Another goal—undoubtedly informed in part by the struggles in South Carolina and other states during the previous plan—related to expansion and consolidation of the community in the Americas, in particular through strengthening existing local communities, establishing new ones, and continuing a "bolder proclamation of the Faith to the masses" through the media. Another was the formation of a separate National Spiritual Assembly in Canada and two more, one for Mexico, Central America, and the Caribbean and one for South America, that would eventually devolve into separate national bodies for each country.[16]

Finally, the Bahá'í movement in the United States would extend its teaching campaign from the New World to the "war-torn, spiritually famished European continent." While the British Bahá'í community had been left intact and those in France and West Germany were able to quickly reconstitute themselves once the war was over, the widely scattered groups and individuals that had existed in the rest of the continent before the war were dead, dispersed, or, in the case of those in the Soviet Union and the countries its army occupied, too isolated and oppressed to undertake systematic teaching activities of their own. Shoghi Effendi called for the establishment of Local and National Spiritual Assemblies in ten countries where U.S. citizens could easily settle and where religion was not being officially suppressed by Communist regimes: Belgium, Denmark, Italy, Luxemburg, the Netherlands, Norway, Portugal, Spain, Sweden, and Switzerland. To coordinate the new effort, the National Spiritual Assembly formed a European Teaching Committee, which quickly began to dispatch pioneers to the "Ten Goal Countries." Drawing on the diverse national origins represented within the American community, the committee prioritized sending pioneers who were natives of the countries in which they were to serve.[17]

Before the end of the second Seven Year Plan, Shoghi Effendi initiated an additional phase of the faith's worldwide diffusion. In 1951 he called for a special two-year effort to establish the faith in selected territories in Africa. While the faith already had a long history in Egypt and Sudan, few Bahá'ís had established residence elsewhere in North Africa or in the vast portion of the continent south of the Sahara. With oppressive colonial regimes imposing serious travel restrictions, Shoghi Effendi asked the National Spiritual Assembly of the British Isles—whose citizens could most easily settle in the majority of the continent's territories—to lead the program. Twenty-five colonies would receive pioneers and traveling teachers, mostly from Britain but also from Egypt, India, Iran, and the United States. It was a prelude, Shoghi Effendi indicated, to future global campaigns that would involve the cooperation of all the world's National Spiritual Assemblies.[18]

The Second Seven Year Plan in South Carolina

In South Carolina, the fledgling local communities established during the previous plan were still too small and weak to offer much direct support for the American movement's new overseas campaign. But they did figure prominently in the domestic goals of the second Seven Year Plan. In June 1946, in a short cablegram and a lengthy inspirational letter, Shoghi Effendi elaborated on the new plan's domestic goals, reiterating that the number of localities where Baháʼís resided should continue to increase and that the "groups scattered throughout the length and breadth of the states and provinces of the United States and Canada" should grow enough to enable the formation of Local Spiritual Assemblies. In particular he recommended that the National Teaching Committee focus on the thirty localities with six or more members, helping them to "speedily attain Assembly status" and raise the number of such institutions in North America to 175 by the end of the second year of the plan. "Attainment of this immediate objective," he noted, would not only strengthen the administrative foundations of the movement at home but would also "challenge and galvanize" the believers at work in Latin America and Europe.[19]

At the end of the summer of 1946, a new Regional Teaching Committee of Georgia, South Carolina, and North Carolina announced "WHAT THE SEVEN YEAR PLAN MEANS TO OUR REGION" in its newsletter. First, the committee called for the establishment of a Local Assembly in Columbia, the only city in the three-state region with a group of at least six believers, by Riḍván 1947, noting that "three new Bahá'ís or three Baha'i settlers" would therefore be needed in Columbia "almost at once." Second, a Local Assembly was to be reestablished in North Augusta, where there was a group of five, by Riḍván 1948. Third, the new Local Assembly in Greenville needed the "full support and aid" of the regional community; two new pioneers for Greenville had already been identified. Fourth, the committee called for an immediate doubling of the region's contributions to the national fund—an indirect way of supporting the teaching work abroad—over the previous year. Finally, the committee said, each individual would have to "stand by on the home front," teaching the faith in his or her locality with a "renewed spirit of dedication."[20]

The expansion goals for Columbia, North Augusta, and Greenville proved to be quite interconnected in execution. Moreover, they were part of a concerted effort that also included localities in North Carolina and Georgia. While Regional Teaching Committees had been a feature of the previous plan, in the Carolinas and Georgia at least, the regional structure proved particularly effective during the second Seven Year Plan. As in previous years, traveling teachers from outside the state or region tended to cover multiple localities in a circuit, such that several communities in rapid succession often found themselves with more activity, more publicity, and more seekers than usual. During the 1940s and 1950s, however, as the Baháʼí population of the Carolinas and Georgia rose slowly, the Baháʼís from within the three states became increasingly capable of planning and executing their own teaching and deepening activities, and they traveled frequently to assist and encourage each other. In August 1946, for example, Roy and Bernice Williams of Greenville spent a long weekend in Greensboro, North Carolina, visiting "in some of the Baha'i homes," giving two talks at the city's Baháʼí Center, and sharing news of a recent teaching trip by Agnes Alexander, a prominent believer from Hawaii, to other cities in the region. The following November, when Marjorie McCormick, the secretary of the National Teaching Committee, visited the region from Illinois, five Baháʼís from Augusta and North Augusta came to Columbia to attend a public meeting there. During 1946 and 1947, Annie Romer, one of the new pioneers in Greenville, traveled each week to Columbia and occasionally to Augusta and North Augusta to assist with local activities. Meetings of the Regional Teaching Committee itself generally rotated among the three states, giving the members an opportunity to meet with local believers and seekers and assist with public events. Sometimes, pioneers moved from one city to another according to the priorities of the regional plan. For example, in October 1946, Josie Pinson, a pioneer who had settled in Charleston (which was not a goal city), relocated to Greenville, and in 1947 or 1948, Annie Romer moved from Greenville to Columbia to help establish the Local Assembly there.[21]

Columbia

For the small group of believers in Columbia, attention from the Regional Teaching Committee during the second Seven Year Plan led to an expanded membership, an improvement in local community life and teaching activities, and the formation of a Local Spiritual Assembly. While the Columbia group was affected by many of the same social and economic factors that had kept the Greenville community small—the transience of some of the Baháʼís (including those serving in the military) and the difficulties imposed by racial and religious orthodoxy—the believers in Columbia, beginning with Louis Gregory's early teaching trips and continuing with the efforts of pioneers Maude Mickle and Alta Wheeler over nearly a decade, had much more consistently worked to spread the faith among the area's substantial black population. Also in contrast to the community in Greenville, they appear to not have been subject to serious personality conflicts. Both factors seem to have combined to result in more growth and a more solid interracialism. Significantly, the Columbia community was not made up of a majority of white pioneers from outside the region but of local black converts, many of whom were already connected with each other through familial or social ties. There was also at least one family of native white South Carolinians. Louella Moore's husband, Edward, became a Bahá'í sometime during the 1940s. After the war they moved to the small town of Irmo in Lexington County, but they continued to participate in community activities in Columbia. Their grown daughter, Louise Montgomery, attended study classes and other gatherings long before she declared her faith, at a Nineteen Day Feast in the home of black believer Pearl Dixon, in late 1949.[22]

The community life and outreach efforts of the Columbia group indicated a continuing commitment to teaching both whites and blacks. Nineteen Day Feasts, Holy Day observances, and firesides were held not only in the homes of believers but also those of seekers. The center of Bahá'í community activities during the 1940s and early 1950s was Waverly, the relatively prosperous African American neighborhood surrounding the campuses of Benedict College and Allen University, where most of the black believers and seekers lived and where mixed groups could meet with minimal interference. In the summer of 1946, for example, Esther Sego came from Augusta and met with seven white and four black believers and one seeker at the home of one of the black Bahá'ís, Celia Glenn, a dressmaker and beauty shop owner, on Oak Street five blocks south of Allen. Another "meeting for our Negro non-Baha'i friends" took place at the home of Lutie McKim, who had been studying the faith for some years, on the Benedict campus where her husband was superintendent of buildings and grounds. McKim's sister-in-law from Baltimore attended, as did two Benedict students from West Africa, two white pioneers, and a black believer who was also a Benedict student.[23]

Several traveling teachers came to Columbia during the opening phase of the plan. The topics of their public lectures reflected the national community's continuing focus, built on its recent experience using the mass media, on addressing some of the broad social concerns in postwar America, including international affairs. The Columbia Bahá'ís arranged for coverage in local black and white newspapers, secured prominent public venues for the events, and had some success broadcasting the teachings of the faith on the radio. In November 1946, for example, Marjorie McCormick spoke to an audience of local believers and seekers and visiting Bahá'ís from Augusta at the Wade Hampton Hotel, a prominent landmark on Main Street across from the State House. The title of her lecture, "Security for a Failing World," was timely, and notices in the *State* and the *Columbia Record* emphasized McCormick's travels in Africa, Europe, and the Middle East. McCormick also spoke about the Bahá'í teachings for fifteen minutes over radio station WKIX and met

Figure 5.1. Louis Gregory with Bahá'ís and friends, Columbia, South Carolina, ca. 1940s. *L to r*: Celia Glenn, Lutie McKim, Alta Wheeler, Ethel Lowery, Louis G. Gregory, Eunice Long, Louella Moore, Jessie Entzminger, Mrs. Carroll. During the 1940s and 1950s, Columbia's small Bahá'í community was centered in the middle-class black neighborhood of Waverly. Courtesy of Columbia Bahá'í Archives, Columbia, S.C.

individually with seekers. In March 1947, Ruth Moffett of Chicago conducted a four-week teaching campaign in Columbia. She gave a series of lectures in private homes, on the campus of the University of South Carolina, and at the Wade Hampton Hotel on a range of topics that included "The Emerging New World Order" and "What Hope in the United Nations Charter?" Newspapers identified her, like McCormick, as a world traveler, noting that she had served as an accredited observer from Washington University in St. Louis at the founding conference of the United Nations. In December 1947, Dr. Glenn A. Shook, a professor of physics at Wheaton College in Massachusetts, visited several cities in the region. In Columbia, he spoke on "Science and Revelation" at the chamber of commerce building on Lady Street a block from the capitol. A favorable account in the *Columbia Record* noted: "In view of the world crisis, the speaker said that it was absolutely necessary that scientists and religionists work together and that people think more clearly as to values. . . . For many years the idea of a universal religion has been a vital element in Dr. Shook's research and writing and he quoted the Baha'i Faith as containing great truths for the establishment of world peace and unity."[24]

Despite the rather energetic teaching efforts of the Columbia community and assistance from outside, at Riḍván 1947 there were still not enough believers to form a Local Assembly. One of the believers, Celia Glenn, had passed away during the previous administrative year, and another, Wilhelmina Daniels, may have already moved to Union, South Carolina. While Ruth Moffett's teaching campaign, conducted just before Riḍván in March, "attracted four souls to the Faith, who wish[ed] to continue studying," it did not immediately result in any new members. The region's primary goal for the second Seven Year Plan was accomplished late, apparently in 1949, and only then by shifting several pioneers from Greenville to Columbia. By 1950, there were still just enough believers in the city to maintain the Local Assembly. In at least one respect, however, the Columbia community was far stronger than others in the state. Only three of the members—Alice Dudley, Eugenie Meyer, and Josie Pinson—were pioneers. The rest—Della Clark, Pearl Dixon, Henrietta Dukes, Jessie Entzminger, Eunice Grant Long, and Annie Mae Robinson—were black Columbians, several of whom had been associated with the faith for at least a decade. Interestingly, all the members of the state's most deeply rooted local community in 1950 were women.[25]

Greenville

The regional movement's efforts to strengthen the local community in Greenville during the second Seven Year Plan were less successful. There was a flurry of activity early on. In June 1946, Marjorie Ullrich, a Bahá'í from Oak Park, Illinois, visited the region with her two young daughters and a male youth. In Greenville, she spoke on "Outstanding Episodes from the Life of Baha'u'llah" at the home of the Williamses and on "God's Call to the Nations" at the home of the Bidwells, with ten seekers attending the latter meeting. A third meeting was held at the home of the Savages, "interested friends" of the Bidwells. Later that fall, William Bidwell began teaching a class on *The Dawn-Breakers,* also at the home of the Savages, with other seekers participating. In July, Agnes Baldwin Alexander of Honolulu, a scion of a prominent family of Protestant missionaries and pineapple planters who had been one of the first Bahá'ís in Hawaii, visited as part of a tour of the region, accompanied by Emma Lawrence, a pioneer in Charleston. Alexander secured an interview with the head of Greenville's powerful ministerial union and, with introductions from him, met with the editor of the *Greenville News* and the manager of local radio station WFBC. These contacts resulted in a story in the newspaper and, later in August, the local community's first radio broadcast, a program entitled "Pattern for Future Society." In November 1946, the visit of Marjorie McCormick, secretary of the National Teaching Committee, included a meeting with the members of the Local Assembly, an informal dinner fireside with twelve "interested friends," and an advertised public meeting on a "World Safe for Humanity" with another twelve seekers. The Regional Committee reported that "six new contacts were made" during McCormick's visit and that the study class was continuing. But the visits apparently did not result in the enrollment of any new believers.[26]

More teaching efforts followed in subsequent years. In December 1948, for example, the community reported holding weekly study classes and firesides and was planning to start a monthly public meeting. But pioneers continued to form most of the tiny community. After a lapse in 1945, there were enough resident Bahá'ís each Ridván to maintain the Local Spiritual Assembly for six years in a row, from 1946 to 1951. In 1947, native Greenvillian Virginia Ford left with her husband for military posts in Georgia and then Japan, and in 1952 the Local Assembly lapsed again. Lonely and dispirited, William and Christine Bidwell bought a farm outside the city limits in 1954. When Ford returned permanently to Greenville two years later, only four Bahá'ís remained.[27]

In the postwar years, as South Carolina's civil rights movement grew and began to register additional breaches in the Jim Crow system, the small groups of Bahá'ís around the state still had to be discreet about how they brought blacks and whites together for teaching, worship, and other community functions, in public and in private. Jessie Entzminger recalled an incident from the early years of the second Seven Year Plan in Columbia. She and her mother, Pearl Dixon, went to a Nineteen Day Feast at the home of Marie Kershaw Frain, who had moved to Columbia from North Augusta to take a job at the veterans' hospital near Fort Jackson. In an incident recalling the crackdown on teaching at the home of her black washerwoman in North Augusta more than a decade before, Frain's neighbors called the police, who came to the house and ordered the black Bahá'ís to leave. After that, Entzminger said, the Columbia community met only in the homes of blacks, where neighbors and police were less concerned about the presence of a few whites, or in rented halls. In Greenville, the Ku Klux Klan attacked Virginia Ford's house after black Bahá'ís visited. One witness to the event was a white child, Gail Fassy. She already knew Ford as the kind woman at the local bakery who gave her cookies when she went there with her parents to pay their rent, and her grandparents were Ford's neighbors. Fassy recalled: "Going to visit my grandparents on Maco Terrace and seeing a cross burning in the front yard of Virginia's house two doors away, and the windows of her house knocked out, I was very disturbed. I asked my grandmother why they were burning a cross there. She said, 'They have black people visiting there and the Ku Klux Klan doesn't like it.'" More than a decade later, when she embraced the faith in Ford's home as a young woman, it was with a clear understanding of the risks of being part of an interracial community.[28]

While their interracial activities made Bahá'ís around the state targets of intimidation and occasional violence, the Greenville group set an important precedent by securing an initial measure of legal protection. In early 1953, just before the end of the plan, Roy Williams appeared before the Greenville city council to ask for a formal acknowledgement of the local community's interracial character and protection for its activities. The council decided that interracial religious gatherings were not contrary to city ordinances and that "as a religious organization," the Bahá'í community "could not be interfered with in the process of its meetings because of the guarantee of freedom of worship." The decision by the city council did not end the Greenville community's difficulties, but it likely formed the basis for their efforts less than a decade later to secure formal legal recognition of the religion by state officials.[29]

Louis Gregory's Final Years

Notably absent from South Carolina during the second Seven Year Plan was the region's ablest and most experienced traveling teacher, Louis Gregory. After his trip through Georgia and the Carolinas in the winter of 1944–1945, Gregory had to curtail his teaching and administrative work as his own health and that of his wife, Louise, began to decline. In December 1948, after returning from a short plane trip to Kansas City for the funeral of a Bahá'í friend, Gregory suffered a stroke. Though he recovered quickly, thereafter he stayed close to the couple's home, a modest cottage near Green Acre in Maine. In addition to caring for Louise, he focused his attention on several writing projects, teaching classes at Green Acre, hosting firesides, and maintaining a voluminous correspondence. He also remained vitally interested in affairs inside and outside the Bahá'í community in South Carolina until the end of his life, seeking out ways to spread the teachings of the faith in his home state even from a distance.

In January 1949, barely a month after his stroke, Louis Gregory wrote to the postmaster at Darlington, South Carolina—apparently without revealing his own racial identity—to request information on the Dargan family, his white kinfolks in the area. The postmaster forwarded the letter to George E. Dargan, a local attorney and son of a four-term congressman, who wrote a lengthy reply to Gregory including birth, marriage, and death records from the family Bible. From the information that Dargan supplied, Gregory would have discovered that the two of them were second cousins—that is, their grandfathers had been brothers. Gregory wrote directly to Dargan, this time enclosing "papers" that apparently indicated either the nature of their familial relationship, the Bahá'í views on race, or both. "I think," Dargan averred in a curt second reply, "that the promotion of harmonious relations between the white and colored people of the South has been greatly retarded by political demagogues and agitators, both North and South."[30]

Surely on Dargan's list of "political demagogues and agitators" who were disrupting race relations in South Carolina were U.S. district court judge J. Waties Waring and his wife, Elizabeth Avery Waring, with whom Gregory corresponded in 1950. Waring's troubles had begun in 1945, when he had scandalized himself among Charleston's upper crust by divorcing his first wife, a well-to-do Charleston native, and marrying Elizabeth Avery Hoffman, a twice-divorced woman from Connecticut and an outspoken racial liberal. Rumors had flown that the couple entertained black guests in their home. In the wake of Waring's decisions equalizing teachers' salaries and striking down the white primary, their relationships with white Charleston had deteriorated further. The final break came in January 1950, when Elizabeth Waring spoke to a mixed gathering at the city's black YWCA. She exhorted African Americans to take and use the civil rights that were already rightfully theirs and castigated conservative southern whites as "a sick, confused and decadent people," "full of pride and complacency, introverted, morally weak and low." The comments were too much for the city's white elite to bear. "I walk from my house to the courthouse every morning," Waties Waring told a reporter from a national newspaper. "I pass many former friends, many of them men and women I grew up with. There is no friendly greeting, not even a sign of recognition. They look straight ahead or, if they see me in time, cross over to the other side of the street. About the only white people who speak to me are lawyers—and they do so only because they can't afford not to speak to the judge."[31]

Louis Gregory wrote to Judge Waring twice in 1950, once in the spring and once in the fall, apparently expressing encouragement and enclosing Bahá'í booklets both times. "Mrs. Waring and I deeply appreciate the literature you have sent us and your very kind message," Waring replied to Gregory's first letter. "We are indeed happy since we feel sure that we are on the right road, and communications like yours convince us that that is true." To Gregory's second letter he replied: "It is very heartening to receive letters from decent thinking people like yourself, and Mrs. Waring and I appreciate your kind words about us." Gregory forwarded the correspondence to the National Spiritual Assembly, apparently suggesting that the body address its own words of encouragement to the judge and to other whites who were taking a stand for racial justice. In March 1951, the National Assembly wrote to Waring to commend him for "the spiritual nature of [his] decisions concerning race," sending him three Bahá'í books that they hoped would "confirm [his] own convictions." Gregory lived just long enough to see Waring's most significant contribution to the civil rights movement, his May 1951 dissenting opinion in a landmark school desegregation case from rural Clarendon County, South Carolina, but not the couple's flight the following year from ostracism in Charleston to the safety of New York City.[32]

In late July 1951, Louis Gregory passed away suddenly at his home in Eliot. A cable from Shoghi Effendi a few days later attested to Gregory's decades of service to the faith, posthumously lifting him to the highest office (aside from the Guardianship itself) in the Bahá'í community and placing his contributions in global and historical context: "Profoundly deplore grievous loss of dearly beloved, noble-minded, golden-hearted Louis Gregory, pride and example to the Negro adherents of the Faith. Keenly feel loss of one so loved, admired and trusted by 'Abdu'l-Bahá. Deserves rank of first Hand of the Cause of his race. Rising Bahá'í generation in African continent will glory in his memory and emulate his example. Advise hold memorial gathering in Temple in token recognition of his unique position, outstanding services." The institution of the Hands of the Cause of God to which Shoghi Effendi referred had been created by Bahá'u'lláh. During his ministry, he had appointed four prominent Iranian Bahá'ís to assist in stimulating teaching and the development of communities in the Middle East. Later, 'Abdu'l-Bahá had continued to direct these four and referred to at least four more individuals, also Iranians, as Hands of the Cause after their deaths. In his will and testament, 'Abdu'l-Bahá outlined the responsibilities of the Hands and gave the Guardian the responsibility to appoint additional ones and direct their activities. For some thirty years, Shoghi Effendi did not take steps to develop the institution, concentrating instead on the establishment and development of local and national executive bodies, but he did continue 'Abdu'l-Bahá's practice of naming Hands of the Cause posthumously, conferring the title on ten men and women from a variety of national, ethnic, and religious backgrounds. A few months after Gregory's death, Shoghi Effendi began to appoint living Hands and assign them specific tasks. Those who, like Gregory, were appointed posthumously, however, had distinguished themselves in service to the faith largely through their own initiative.[33]

In addition to honoring Louis Gregory's spiritual station, Shoghi Effendi's cablegram also suggested a strong connection with the African continent. At first glance, such statements may seem curious. Gregory's practical links to Africa—his own racial heritage and his brief visit to Egypt during the course of his 1911 pilgrimage—were rather indirect. But Shoghi Effendi's assessment makes sense in light of the Bahá'í writings on interracial unity and long-range developments within the faith and in the world at large. In his talks and writings, 'Abdu'l-Bahá had repeatedly linked the achievement of interracial unity in the United States with the establishment of world peace. "When the racial elements of the American nation unite in actual fellowship and accord," he had told a mixed gathering in Washington during his 1912 visit, "the lights of the oneness of humanity will shine, the day of eternal glory and bliss will dawn, the spirit of God encompass, and the divine favors descend.... This is the sign of the Most Great Peace." Indicators of the connection between racial justice within the United States and around the world had already come in the wake of World War I with the development of an international Pan-African movement and after World War II with the acceleration of the civil rights movement in the United States and anticolonial movements in Africa. At both historical moments, activists and theorists had explicitly linked black people's struggles for justice on both sides of the Atlantic, and at both moments, initiatives of the worldwide Bahá'í community—the Race Amity Conventions in the first instance and the first systematic plan to establish the faith across the African continent in the second—had sought to apply the faith's teachings to emerging opportunities.[34]

In the context of these trends, clear to Shoghi Effendi or any other astute observer by the early 1950s, Louis Gregory's "unique position" in the development of a solidly interracial Bahá'í movement in the United States—and his intellectual and spiritual influence, indirect but no less significant, on the tenor and focus of African American aspirations during the early twentieth century—were enough to connect him to the future of independent Africa and to the nascent Bahá'í communities there. Louis Gregory did not live to see the complete dismantling of the Jim Crow regime, the political independence of the African colonies and their accession to the United Nations as equal members, or the influx of large numbers of people in Africa and the African Diaspora into the Bahá'í Faith—phenomena that he and the successive heads of the faith certainly saw as interrelated and that seemed to proceed with such rapidity during the quarter century after he died. But at the end of his life he was certain that such positive changes were both inevitable and imminent. In the concluding chapter of "Racial Unity," an unpublished manuscript he finished shortly before his passing, he wrote: "Light is everywhere breaking for the oppressed peoples of the earth. Deep shadows prove the intensity of the light. The interests of no groups or classes will be overlooked or forgotten.... Assuming that the victims of injustice will continue their struggle, no human might can long debar them from the long sought goal. Earth and air, fire and water, the stars in their courses, the high tide of destiny, and the Will of divine Providence are all arrayed against the forces of oppression." The "rising Baháʼí generation in [the] African continent"—fruits of the two-year Africa Campaign that had involved the settlement of black and white American pioneers, themselves the products of Louis Gregory's "outstanding services" in the creation of an interracial Baháʼí movement in the United States—would "glory in his memory and emulate his example," not only as one of the most distinguished teachers and administrators of the faith but also as a radical activist of African descent who had recognized in its program for the reconstruction of the world the "highest aims" of oppressed peoples for justice and peace.[35]

"Brilliant Victories"

By late 1951, as the second Seven Year Plan entered its final months, it was clear that the worldwide Baháʼí community had reached a new stage in its geographic diffusion and administrative consolidation. In a November 1951 cable, Shoghi Effendi called for the holding of four intercontinental conferences—in Kampala, Uganda; Chicago, Illinois; Stockholm, Sweden; and New Delhi, India—between February and October 1953. The conferences, he wrote, would serve a triple purpose in the history, identity, and growth of the faith. They would commemorate the "Great Jubilee," the centenary of the dawn of Baháʼu'lláh's prophetic mission in the Black Pit of Tehran. They would provide a "demonstration of Baháʼí solidarity of unprecedented scope and intensity," befitting the emerging stage in the religion's worldwide development. And they would enable the believers around the world to "adopt effectual measures" for the inauguration of a third Seven Year Plan set to run from 1956 to 1963. Unlike the first and second plans, which had been primarily the work of the community in the United States, the third Seven Year Plan would involve all the National Spiritual Assemblies and "embrace all the continents of the earth." Its ambitious goal would be the diffusion of the faith to all the remaining countries and territories of the globe, "the world establishment of the Cause of Bahá'u'lláh, as prophesied by 'Abdu'l-Bahá and envisioned by Daniel," in time for the celebration of the "Most Great Jubilee," the centenary of Bahá'u'lláh's formal assumption of the prophetic office in 1863 on the eve of his departure from Baghdad.[36]

In a cablegram of March 1952, a full year before the formal close of the then-ongoing effort, Shoghi Effendi lauded the "brilliant victories won in the course of the second Seven Year Plan." Indeed, progress had been made on several fronts. In the Americas, there was a wider base of Local Spiritual Assemblies, and the formation of three new National Spiritual Assemblies—that of Canada in 1948 and those of Central America and South America in 1951—meant that the faith's Administrative Order embraced the whole hemisphere. By April 1952, Shoghi Effendi could announce the completion of the interior ornamentation of the Chicago temple and the initiation of landscaping in preparation for the building's dedication for public worship. In Central and Western Europe, new Local Assemblies were functioning in each of the ten goal countries. The rapid growth of the faith in Italy moved Shoghi Effendi to call for the formation, at Riḍván 1953, of an additional National Spiritual Assembly, bringing to twelve the total number of such "pillars of the future House of Justice" worldwide. At the World Center of the faith in Haifa and 'Akká, a related step was the formation, in 1951, of the International Bahá'í Council, a secretariat that Shoghi Effendi called the "forerunner" of the Universal House of Justice. He charged the council primarily with establishing relations with the new state of Israel and assisting him with completion of the superstructure of the Shrine of the Báb on Mount Carmel, a project that was also scheduled for completion by the end of the upcoming plan.[37]

Even more stunning in Shoghi Effendi's estimation than the development of the faith in Latin America and Europe had been its initial growth in Africa, an aspect of the second Seven Year Plan not even contemplated at the outset. In April 1952, he enumerated the "first fruits" of the two-year Africa Campaign: the "settlement of Persian, American, British, Egyptian and Portuguese pioneers in Liberia, Northern Rhodesia, Angola, Libya, Spanish Morocco and Mozambique" and the inauguration of "teaching classes, public meetings and firesides" in each of those areas; "the enrollment of several native Africans" into the faith; the establishment of Local Spiritual Assemblies in Kampala, Uganda, and Dar-es-Salaam, Tanganyika; and the purchase of a Bahá'í Center in Kampala. The following January he announced to the worldwide community that in a little more than a year, more than two hundred

Africans from some sixteen ethnic groups had become Baháʼís in Kampala and the surrounding rural districts. He anticipated the early establishment in Africa of several regional-level National Spiritual Assemblies like those already functioning in Central and South America.[38]

Paralleling the development of the faith's local and national elected bodies, Shoghi Effendi formalized the institution of the Hands of the Cause of God. In December 1951 he took the "long inevitably deferred step" of appointing an initial contingent of twelve Hands—including Louis Gregory's longtime associates Dorothy Baker, Horace Holley, Leroy Ioas, and Charles Mason Remey—whom he assigned to serve at the World Center and in Asia, Europe, and the Americas. Three months later, in February 1952, he appointed an additional contingent of seven Hands, including residents of Africa and Australia, bringing the total number to nineteen. He assigned the Hands responsibility for "the propagation and preservation of the unity of the Faith of Baháʼuʼlláh" and noted that they were "destined" eventually to direct institutions "paralleling those revolving around the Universal House of Justice." Later in 1952, he brought into being the first such institution by asking the Hands of the Cause in each continent to appoint Auxiliary Boards whose members, acting "as their adjuncts or deputies," would systematically visit Baháʼí communities to assist them in carrying out the teaching plans.[39]

The second Seven Year Plan had been quite successful at the global scale, but within the United States its record was mixed. In particular, the imperatives of international pioneering and completion of the temple seem to have adversely impacted the other home-front goals. The initial drive to raise the number of Local Spiritual Assemblies, from 123 in 1945 to 175 in 1948, had been accomplished, but only with great difficulty. In February 1948, at the "eleventh hour," Shoghi Effendi had been "moved to plead . . . that the rank and file of the community, particularly the members in the long-established leading strongholds of the Faith—New York, Chicago, Los Angeles, San Francisco, Washington—issue forth" from their homes to settle in the goal cities. The 175 Local Assemblies were formed on schedule less than three months later, but by the end of 1951, the number had fallen again, often as members of those bodies left the country as pioneers to Latin America, Europe, and Africa. In November 1951, Shoghi Effendi expressed his disappointment that the "constant broadening and the steady reinforcement of this internal administrative structure" had been "allowed to fall into abeyance" and been "eclipsed" by the community's successful deployment of international pioneers. When the plan ended in the spring of 1953, there were organized groups in some six hundred localities across the country, nearly double the total from 1945. But there were only 171 Local Assemblies, an increase of less than 50 during the same period and four short of the goal. In the same message of November 1951, Shoghi Effendi also lamented the "accumulating deficit" in the national fund. Skyrocketing construction costs in the postwar economic boom had increased the budget for the interior ornamentation and landscaping of the house of worship, prompting Shoghi Effendi to order drastic cost-saving measures during 1949 and 1950, including suspension of publications, public relations efforts, and programs at the three summer school campuses in California, Maine, and Michigan. In part to compensate for the school closings, the National Spiritual Assembly had initiated the "Bahá'í Institute," a decentralized program of study conferences held around the country for the "self-education" of communities "by mutual participation."[40]

In South Carolina, the plan had achieved similarly mixed results. On the one hand, the difficulty in forming and maintaining Local Spiritual Assemblies in South Carolina's goal cities had contributed directly to the shortfall in that national goal. On the other, the Bahá'í movement was more widespread, more diverse, and more confident in 1953 than it had been at the end of the previous plan. In terms of the geographic spread of the faith, new communities were functioning far from the environs of Augusta. In addition to those in North Augusta and Aiken County, there were organized groups of believers in Columbia and Greenville with their own community activities and efforts at expansion and consolidation. The only major shortcoming in this regard was Charleston, long the state's largest and most important city, where, despite its being the scene of relatively vibrant black and interracial activism and of the first mention of the faith in South Carolina, a succession of relatively short-term pioneers since the late 1930s had been unable to raise a Bahá'í community. Elsewhere, the faith was even making some tentative forays into rural and small-town South Carolina. In the late 1940s, a transplant from the Atlanta community had resided in Bennettsville in the Pee Dee, and during the early 1950s there were individual believers living in Allendale, Orangeburg, and Walterboro in the Lowcountry and in Clemson and Union in the Upstate.[41]

The size and diversity of the South Carolina community had grown in tandem with geographic expansion. By the end of the plan there were more than thirty Bahá'ís in the state, and perhaps dozens of other South Carolinians participated in local worship, study, and social activities without having joined the faith. To be sure, those associated with the Bahá'í Faith in South Carolina still formed an insignificant portion of the state's population, but their qualitative accomplishments during the plan should not be underestimated. While pioneers had been instrumental in the establishment of the religion around the state, some two-thirds of the believers in 1953 were natives or longtime residents who had encountered the faith locally. The community included both black and white members in rough proportion to the racial composition of the state as a whole, and they ranged in occupational and social background from black domestic workers in Columbia to white textile mill families in Greenville to well-to-do scions of the antebellum elite in North Augusta. Beyond the circle of individual believers' family members, neighbors, and coworkers, there was significant experience in several localities in contacting local government officials and leaders of thought, as well as in using radio, newspapers, and public meetings to bring the history and tenets of the faith to the attention of a wider audience. The state's Bahá'í movement was still quite small, but it was certainly more deeply rooted and more broadly based in 1953 than it had been in 1944.

While their efforts to establish grassroots units of the faith's administrative system were only partially successful, some elements of the system worked well. In stark contrast to the situation when Alonzo Twine had embraced the faith in Charleston in 1910, administrative agencies in 1953 effectively connected the Bahá'ís in South Carolina to each other and to a wider religious community at the regional, national, and international levels. During the course of the first and second Seven Year Plans, Local Spiritual Assemblies had been established in North Augusta, Greenville, and Columbia, although, as in other states, maintaining the necessary numbers had been a constant challenge. By Ridván 1953, even the new Columbia body had lapsed as pioneers departed for new posts in the United States or abroad—Alice Dudley to Washington, D.C.; Eugenie Meyer to Switzerland; Josie Pinson to Union, South Carolina; and Annie Romer to New Orleans—contributing to the shortfall in the national goal for new Local Assembly formation. Especially important given the struggle to build an administrative base at the local level, however, a strong regional committee—an improvement over the first Seven Year Plan—gave the movement coherence, fostered a sense of shared mission and identity across state boundaries, and channeled human and financial resources to various localities relatively efficiently. In 1950, for example, a member of the Regional Teaching Committee from North Augusta conducted the first of the National Spiritual Assembly's "Bahá'í Institute" programs, a course on the Covenant, for the Aiken County and Columbia communities, and a visiting teacher from New York did the same for Greenville. Regardless of whether a group was large enough to have a

Local Spiritual Assembly, regional and national newsletters kept each individual informed of news and events close to home and around the world. And every believer could participate in the process of electing the National Spiritual Assembly. In 1944, when Shoghi Effendi instructed that delegates to the National Convention be apportioned by state and not just by localities with Local Assemblies, the believers in South Carolina began gathering each fall to elect their delegate. Together with Local Assembly elections, the state convention formed an arena of religious governance that, despite its limited size, united South Carolinians across lines of race, class, and gender in ways that most other organizations in the state, religious or secular, could barely imagine. Small and limited in resources as it was, still tenuous in both its legal and administrative foundations, and generally either dismissed or persecuted by those few who were even aware of its existence, during two successive plans of systematic growth an indigenous Bahá'í movement that was both coherent and distinctively diverse had established itself in South Carolina.[42]

The Ten Year Plan and the Fall of Jim Crow, 1950–1965

In April 1963, when sixteen-year-old Richard Abercrombie arrived in London, England, for the Baháʼí World Congress, it was the first time he had made more than a short car trip from his home in Greenville, South Carolina. Indeed, much had changed in his life since he had first heard of the Baháʼí Faith less than two years before. In the scriptures of his new religion he had found answers to spiritual questions that the ministers at his family's Baptist church were unwilling or unable to answer. His circle of friends had widened. There was the white family who had defied segregation to befriend him and other youths and introduce them to the faith, and the feisty black woman from California—a sister of former boxing heavyweight champion Joe Louis, she was always quick to point out—who had visited Greenville and converted his father through her exposition of Biblical prophecy. The whole family had become Baháʼís, and at least ten of his school friends had followed suit. Then there was the traveling. He had gone to Augusta, Georgia, the closest city with a local Baháʼí administrative body, to be formally enrolled as a member of the faith. And several times already he had been to St. Helena Island at the southern tip of South Carolina, where black and white Baháʼís from several southeastern states gathered twice a year for a week of study and fellowship at the historic campus of Penn Center, founded as a school for freedpeople after the Civil War and more recently used as a retreat center by Martin Luther King Jr. and his colleagues in the Southern Christian Leadership Conference.[1]

Now Abercrombie was making the biggest trip of his life, to the Baháʼí World Congress in London. Seven thousand Baháʼís from seventy countries were gathering to celebrate the successful completion of a ten-year worldwide expansion program and the establishment, on the centenary of

Bahá'u'lláh's public announcement of his prophetic mission, of the Universal House of Justice called for in his writings. When Abercrombie entered Royal Albert Hall, the premier convention venue in London, on the first day of the Congress, the sight of the participants stunned him. People from every corner of the globe, many of them in the traditional dress of their culture, met and greeted each other as brothers and sisters. The African participants particularly impressed Abercrombie, an African American teenager coming of age amid the civil rights movement. He noticed the great variety of languages, clothing styles, and physical features among them, from the tall and slender Ethiopians to the Pygmies from the rain forests of the Congo. He had grown up thinking of Africa as one big country, but now, among the African Bahá'ís he met, he saw for the first time a glimpse of the continent's diversity.[2]

For Abercrombie and the other participants, the five days of the World Congress provided a foretaste of the peaceful global civilization that was both the central theme and the goal of their religion—an emerging phenomenon that was at once worldwide and grand in scope and intensely local and personal in the lives of its protagonists. One speaker at the gathering, an indigenous man from the highlands of Bolivia, said: "I am not a literate man, and I am very happy to be here to see my brothers from all over the world. . . . We want unity and love for the whole world." Another, speaking of how he would describe the Congress on his return to his native Philippines, said: "When I go back to the villages I can tell them that I saw the garden of God!" Richard Abercrombie had a similar reaction. He recalled: "Seeing all these people from different ethnic and religious backgrounds, the beauty of these diverse people coming together for one purpose, I knew it could happen all over the world. It wasn't just in Greenville, South Carolina; this was a *world* community." "I already knew that," he added, "but at the World Congress I saw it."[3]

Richard Abercrombie's presence at the London Congress testified to the development during the late 1950s and early 1960s of a South Carolina Bahá'í movement with a larger, more diverse, and more youthful membership than before, a stronger institutional and legal basis, and an orientation that sought increasingly to influence the course of social change in the state. In some ways, the fortunes of the Bahá'í Faith in South Carolina mirrored those of the civil rights movement. During much of the 1950s, in the context of a new campaign by political leaders and citizens' groups to dismantle the NAACP, the interracialism of the Bahá'ís seemed more dangerous than usual, and the statewide community could do little more than hold itself together. During the early 1960s, however, as the civil rights movement began to register more gains and the state's political and business elite attempted to ease the transition to desegregation, the legal, social, and economic risks of identifying with an interracial movement—to both blacks and whites—began to soften somewhat. In this environment, the Bahá'ís became bolder in their public outreach and more open about the interracial character of their community, and more South Carolinians seemed inclined to associate with or become members of the faith. By the middle of the 1960s, with the framework of the worldwide Bahá'í administrative system completed and the Jim Crow regime collapsing, South Carolina's Bahá'í movement—strengthened by a stream of new members from a variety of backgrounds and new local communities in the rural Black Belt—began to prepare for more substantial growth.

Briggs, *Brown*, and "Massive Resistance" in South Carolina

In the evening of his life, Louis Gregory had predicted intensification both of the African American civil rights movement and of opposition to it. "Deep shadows," he had observed, "prove the intensity of the light." In South Carolina during the 1950s, events seemed to bear out Gregory's statement. In the first half of the decade, the state's NAACP led a concerted attack on segregation in public schools that culminated with the U.S. Supreme Court's *Brown v. Board* decision in 1954. In response, conservative whites mounted a new effort to defend segregation and to destroy the NAACP and its supporters, forcing South Carolina's civil rights movement into temporary retreat during the second half of the decade. The fresh campaign of suppression also helped stifle the growth of the Bahá'í community, at least until a new group of pioneers arrived in 1956 and 1957. In particular, the segregationists' association of interracialism with Communism—an old charge that took on new currency as Cold War fears intensified—made for an unusually difficult few years.[4]

In the late 1940s and early 1950s, the revived and expanded NAACP that had emerged in South Carolina following World War II accelerated its campaign to challenge the legal foundations of the state's Jim Crow order. In the summer of 1947, NAACP member and African Methodist Episcopal Church minister Rev. J. A. De Laine began organizing black families in Summerton, a small town in Clarendon County, to press for improvements in the local school system. In May 1950, rebuffed at every turn by local officials and suffering economic reprisals and intimidation, the parents filed suit in U.S. district court to force Clarendon County School District 22 to provide equal educational facilities. When the case, *Briggs v. Elliott*, came before Judge J. Waties Waring—the same judge whose earlier decisions on teacher pay and the white primary had made him a pariah in white Charleston—he instructed the plaintiffs' attorneys to refile it as a direct challenge to the state constitution's provision for segregated schools and, by extension, the "separate but equal" doctrine itself. On May 28, 1951, less than two months before Louis Gregory's death, a three-judge panel consisting of Waring and two inveterate segregationists ruled two to one against the plaintiffs, ordering the schools in District 22 to be equalized, not desegregated. In Waring's dissent, however, he ridiculed the very logic of racialism and called for an immediate end to segregation. It was a landmark opinion, the first of its kind in the country by a federal judge. The plaintiffs' attorneys, Thurgood Marshall and Harold Boulware of the national and state NAACP legal teams, respectively, immediately began preparing an appeal to the U.S. Supreme Court.[5]

For most white South Carolinians, the *Briggs* case was a call to arms, energizing defenders of segregation in state government. Even before the decision came down, the General Assembly had begun a massive school equalization program in an effort to forestall desegregation. The brainchild of Gov. James F. Byrnes, who had served prominently in all three branches of the federal government before returning to South Carolina and winning the governorship, the plan used proceeds from a new sales tax and a large bond issue to bring black schools up to par with white schools. Shortly after taking office, Byrnes had told legislators that they should provide equal school facilities for blacks because it was the right thing to do. But with cases already underway in Clarendon County and in a number of other states, his appeal was a cold political calculation. "If any person wants an additional reason," he had pointedly added, "I say it is wise." Over the next four years the state poured money into school construction, replacing hundreds of antiquated one- and two-room buildings with state-of-the-art new facilities, mostly to serve black children. But other measures indicated that the equalization campaign's true purpose was to defend segregation, not moderate it. The same year it approved the school overhaul, the General Assembly put a referendum to the voters to delete the constitutional requirement for any public school system at all and passed a law withholding funding from any school to which a student was transferred by court order. Then, when *Briggs v. Elliott* and similar cases from three other states and the District of Columbia made their way to the U.S. Supreme Court, Gov. Byrnes used public and private means to influence the outcome, hiring one of the country's best appellate lawyers to defend the state and lobbying both his former colleagues on the court and

President Dwight D. Eisenhower. Despite Byrnes's efforts, on May 17, 1954, a unanimous court reversed its more than half-century-old verdict in *Plessy v. Ferguson*, overturning segregation in public education and, by implication, all other aspects of public life. Although known by the title of the headline case, *Brown v. Board of Education of Topeka, Kansas*, the decision's most moving language derived largely from J. Waties Waring's dissent in *Briggs v. Elliott*. "In the field of public education," the court announced, "the doctrine of 'separate but equal' has no place. Separate educational facilities are inherently unequal."[6]

Reaction among South Carolina whites, both inside and outside of government, was swift and intense. As they had after World War I, the state's senior politicians set the tone. While white leaders had associated integration with Communism as early as the aftermath of World War I, such arguments gained new currency in the context of the Cold War. In the U.S. Senate, former governor J. Strom Thurmond wrote the first draft of the "Southern Manifesto," a document signed by a majority of southern congressional delegations that called for "massive resistance" to the Supreme Court's decision. His colleague in the Senate, former governor Olin D. Johnston, was a close associate of James Eastland of Mississippi, one of the chamber's most vituperative segregationists and chair of its Internal Security Subcommittee, which investigated alleged Communist activities in the United States. In the House of Representatives, W.J.B. Dorn of South Carolina's Second District warned his colleagues about a Kremlin plot to divide America over race and thereby bring about a Communist revolution. At home, a statewide group of white business, political, and religious leaders published a statement calling for maintenance of separate schools at all costs and asking the state government to "interpose" itself between the federal courts and local school districts. The editor of the *Greenville News* called the *Brown* decision "an insult to the intelligence of White people," while Bob Jones Sr., the head of Greenville's fundamentalist Bob Jones University, said that racial intermingling was contrary to the will of God and that every effort to create "one world and one race outside the body of Christ has been of the devil."[7]

Jones's comments in particular heralded the emergence after the *Brown* decision of a new grassroots movement in which popular anti-Communist, anti-secular, and anti–civil rights sentiments coalesced and took on institutional form. Its spearhead was a network of White Citizens' Councils, formed in Mississippi and spreading across the Deep South in the second half of the 1950s. Claiming to represent the "respectable" majority of whites, South Carolina's Citizens' Councils worked closely but informally with the Federal

Bureau of Investigation, the State Law Enforcement Division (SLED), local and state political bosses, conservative newspapers, ministers of various denominations, and professional anti-Communist activists. Like their counterparts in other southern states, defenders of segregation in South Carolina smeared any individual or organization who questioned Jim Crow, leftist or not, as advocating atheism, Communism, and miscegenation. By the summer of 1956, the Citizens' Councils counted some forty thousand members in South Carolina, with the most active support in Midlands and Lowcountry counties with large black populations—not coincidentally, the same areas that had voted overwhelmingly for Strom Thurmond's Dixiecrat ticket in 1948. While the Citizens' Councils publicly disavowed violence, their energetic campaign emboldened the Ku Klux Klan around the state.[8]

Employing propaganda, economic pressure, intimidation, and violence, segregationist organizers and vigilantes attacked civil rights activists and virtually anyone, black or white, who favored compliance with the Supreme Court's ruling. In Clarendon County, the plaintiffs in the *Briggs* case faced a new round of reprisals, including denial of credit, firing from jobs, threats of physical violence, and arson. When black parents in Orangeburg petitioned the local school board for an immediate end to segregation in accordance with *Brown*, the Citizens' Council turned white economic power against the petitioners and the local NAACP, and SLED investigated the "subversive activities" of State College students and faculty members. Dissent was even silenced in the state's white universities and press, where those who cautiously voiced acceptance of the Supreme Court's decision faced intimidation and firing.[9]

The Citizens' Councils and the Klan and their allies in state government worked together in a campaign to dismantle the NAACP. In 1956, during a legislative session that one white journalist dubbed the "Segregation Session," the General Assembly passed a resolution requesting that the U.S. Justice Department investigate the state NAACP as a "subversive organization" and a law barring members of the organization from employment in local, county, or state government. In 1957, Gov. George Bell Timmerman (formerly one of the judges who had ruled against the plaintiffs in *Briggs v. Elliott*) and Attorney General T. C. Callison backed the firing of members of the Allen University and Benedict College faculties for alleged Communist ties. In 1958, the General Assembly created a Committee to Investigate Communist Activities. Together, the measures cowed the faculty and staff of black schools and colleges, the backbone of the NAACP support in localities across the state. At the same time, informal tactics targeted the leaders of the NAACP state conference. In 1957, conference secretary Modjeska M. Simkins was ousted from her role after the *Charleston News and Courier* smeared her for alleged Communist sympathies. The following year, conference president James Hinton, having suffered an attack on his house and behind-the-scenes pressure from powerful whites, resigned. The official and unofficial campaigns had their intended effect: between 1955 and 1957 the number of NAACP branches in the state fell from eighty-four to thirty-one, and membership from more than eight thousand to just over two thousand. At a time when the organization should otherwise have been capitalizing on its legal victories to mobilize a broader attack on segregation and disfranchisement, it was instead forced to contract and grew largely silent.[10]

The World Crusade

In South Carolina, with the civil rights movement in retreat and the white masses mobilized to oppose any attempt at integration, the state's Baháʼís sought simply to hold their ground. From a global perspective, however, the situation of the Baháʼí community looked quite different. As early as October 1952, when the Holy Year commemorating the centenary of the first stirrings of Baháʼu'lláh's mission began, the results of the second Seven Year Plan up to that point had convinced Shoghi Effendi to move quickly to start the next stage in the faith's worldwide propagation. Instead of a third Seven Year Plan, which he had earlier suggested would begin in 1956 after a "brief respite of three years," he decided that the world's twelve National Spiritual Assemblies should immediately launch a new Ten Year Plan, starting at the international conferences that were already scheduled for 1953 in Kampala, Chicago, Stockholm, and New Delhi. In a cable sent at the start of the Holy Year, Shoghi Effendi announced a "fate-laden, soul-stirring, decade-long, world-embracing Spiritual Crusade" to establish the faith and build its administrative institutions in "all [the] remaining Sovereign States [and] Principal Dependencies . . . scattered over the surface of the entire planet." He called the Baháʼís around the world essentially to leap over what otherwise might have been several stages of the religion's development "to achieve in a single decade feats eclipsing in totality the achievements which in the course of the eleven preceding decades illuminated the annals of Baháʼí pioneering."[11]

The specific goals of the ten-year endeavor included developing the institutions at the World Center of the faith in Israel, strengthening the foundations of the community in all the countries where it already existed, and opening "the remaining chief virgin territories on the planet" through the settlement of new pioneers. The specific tasks involved staggered the imagination of the Bahá'ís. Some 250 territories around the world would require pioneers. The number of National Spiritual Assemblies would be more than quadrupled, and national headquarters, publishing trusts, temple sites, and other properties would be acquired. Bahá'í literature would be translated and published in an additional ninety-one languages. Two new houses of worship would be built, one in Tehran, Iran, and the other in Frankfurt, West Germany. At the World Center, major projects would include improvements to the Shrine of Bahá'u'lláh and construction of the International Bahá'í Archives, the first of a series of administrative buildings Shoghi Effendi envisioned for the slope of Mount Carmel.[12]

The lion's share of the work went to the Bahá'ís of the United States, the "envied custodians" of 'Abdu'l-Bahá's Tablets of the Divine Plan. In his message to the National Convention in 1953—part of more than a week of activities associated with the Intercontinental Conference in Chicago and the dedication of the national temple for public worship—Shoghi Effendi assigned the American community a series of twenty-four tasks, including sending pioneers to fifty-two territories in Africa, the Americas, Asia, and Europe, assisting with the establishment and legal incorporation of new National Spiritual Assemblies and the purchase of properties in dozens of countries, and arranging for the translation of Bahá'í literature into twenty minority languages. Within the United States, the goals were less exotic, perhaps, but no less daunting: to complete the landscaping around the temple, establish a publishing trust, initiate the community's first systematic teaching among Native Americans, continue and expand the public relations campaign through the press and radio, and nearly double the number of Local Spiritual Assemblies, from 171 to 300. The plan's culmination would come at Ridván 1963, the centenary of Bahá'u'lláh's declaration of his prophetic mission to the followers of the Báb in Baghdad. During the twelve-day festival, the members of all the National Spiritual Assemblies then in existence would constitute an International Convention in Haifa to elect the first Universal House of Justice, and Bahá'ís from throughout the world would gather in Baghdad for a World Congress to celebrate the centenary, the completion of the Ten Year Plan, and the establishment of the crowning unit of the faith's Administrative Order.[13]

For some thirty Bahá'ís in South Carolina, the prospect of the Ten Year Plan must have seemed daunting. They had built a religious community that represented much of the state's diversity and established components of the faith's basic administrative framework, but the gains so far had required herculean efforts and had been difficult to sustain. During the previous two plans, the international goals of the faith had sometimes even seemed to compromise local development as capable pioneers were diverted elsewhere. Now the outlook seemed even dimmer. Unlike the last two plans, which had occurred amidst a general expansion of civil rights activism in South Carolina, the new one would have to be carried out in the midst of a conservative backlash against interracialism.

The Crusade, the Cold War, and Race in America

During the Ten Year Plan, Shoghi Effendi continued his effort to explain contemporary trends and the immediate tasks of the American Bahá'í community in the context of Bahá'u'lláh's vision for the future of humanity. In particular, he linked the black freedom struggle in the United States and the work of the plan with a global shift in the balance of power between subject peoples and their oppressors. As it tore down barriers to the unification of humanity, he predicted that this massive shift would create unprecedented opportunities for the growth and development of the faith in the United States and around the world. From the outset of the plan, he reminded the American community of the continuing critical importance of broadening and strengthening their interracial fellowship.

Shoghi Effendi set an unmistakable tone of urgency by sending a special messenger to the Intercontinental Conference in Chicago, the occasion for the formal launching of the plan in the Western Hemisphere. In May 1953, when Dorothy Baker, a member of the National Spiritual Assembly, Hand of the Cause of God, and longtime associate of Louis Gregory as a champion of interracialism, addressed the Chicago gathering, she was fresh from a pilgrimage to the Bahá'í World Center and participation in the first of the four Intercontinental Conferences, in Uganda. Addressing some twenty-three hundred believers from across North and South America, Baker recounted the emphatic instructions she had received from Shoghi Effendi: that the "most important teaching work on American shores today" was to bring the faith to peoples of African and Amerindian descent. In particular, he had said "one driving thing over and over—that if we did not meet the challenging requirement of raising to a vast number the believers of the Negro race, disasters would result." Urging those in attendance to commit to the task, Baker used the example of 'Alí Nakhjavání from Iran and Philip Hainsworth from Great Britain, young pioneers to Uganda who had recently helped establish the faith in the villages around Kampala:

They lived with the Teso people; they ate the food of the Teso people; they slept on straw mats or leaves, or whatever it is that you sleep on among the Teso people. The rain falls on your head and salamanders drop in your tea, if there is tea. And they stayed! And they did not say, "Conditions do not warrant it because these people eat herbs and things that would just kill us." They stayed! Is there an 'Alí Nakhjavání, then, in America? At the present, no. I mean, up to the present. Is there a Philip Hainsworth? Up to the present, no.

Baker reported Shoghi Effendi's comments about the plan's relationship to the coming revolutionary changes in race relations worldwide:

> Now the dark-skinned people, he said, would have an upsurge that is both spiritual and social. The spiritual upsurge will rapidly bring them great gifts because this is an act of God and it was so intended. And all the world's prejudiced forces will not hold it back one hair's breadth. The Bahá'ís will glorify it and understand it. The social repercussions of race suppressions around the world will increase at the same time, and frightened, the world's forces will see that the dark skinned peoples are really rising to the top—a cream that has latent gifts only to be brought out by Divine bounties. Where do the Bahá'ís stand in this? Again and again he pointed out that the Bahá'ís must be in the vanguard of finding them and giving them the base. For the social repercussions will at times become dreadful, if we do not, and we shall be judged by God.

She concluded with another plea, directed primarily at those from the United States:

> I thought that I was rather a fanatic on the race question, at least a strong liberal, but I sat judged by my Guardian, and I knew it. My sights were lifted immeasurably and I saw the vistas of these social repercussions, coming because of our spiritual negligence through the years, and I saw the Indian tribes dotted around this continent unredeemed, waiting—waiting for an 'Alí Nakhjavání. Are the African friends going to have to come and awaken us for the dark skinned races in our midst? . . .
>
> God grant that we may raise up our heroes who will dedicate their lives to the Indians, to the great dark skinned races, to the Eskimos, to the Negro peoples so brilliant, so promising in our national life. Which one will be our 'Alí Nakhjavání?[14]

In July 1953, only three months after the inauguration of the plan, Shoghi Effendi wrote a lengthy letter to the American community in which he elaborated on the relationship between the "upsurge" to which Baker had referred and the worldwide development of the Bahá'í Faith. The plan, he predicted, must "awaken the select and gather the spiritually hungry amongst the peoples of the world"; "create an awareness" of the religion among the cultural, intellectual, and political elites of every country; carry it "to regions so remote, so backward, so inhospitable that neither the light of Christianity or Islam has, after the revolution of centuries, as yet penetrated"; and complete the "structural basis" of its global Administrative Order that would eventually "assemble beneath its sheltering shadow peoples of every race, tongue, creed, color and nation." In Shoghi Effendi's vision, the plan opened the way for new stages in the faith's worldwide development extending decades or centuries into the future. Delineating those stages, he wrote that the enlistment of "fresh recruits" around the globe in the "slowly yet steadily advancing army of the Lord of Hosts" would presage a period of rapid growth to which Bahá'u'lláh and 'Abdu'l-Bahá had both referred in their writings: "the entry by troops of peoples of divers nations and races into the Bahá'í world." The phenomenon of entry by troops, in turn, would be a "prelude" to more momentous world events, "possibly catastrophic in nature," that would bring "a mass conversion of these same nations and races" to the Bahá'í Faith—a phenomenon of world-historical proportions that would "suddenly revolutionize the fortunes of the Faith, derange the equilibrium of the world, and reinforce a thousandfold the numerical strength as well as the material power and the spiritual authority of the Faith of Bahá'u'lláh."[15]

As in previous plans, Shoghi Effendi connected the teaching efforts of the American Bahá'ís to their own spiritual welfare and to the immediate destiny of their country. In July 1954, barely a year into the Ten Year Plan and just two months after the Supreme Court's announcement of the *Brown* decision, Shoghi Effendi addressed another major letter, entitled "American Bahá'ís in the Time of World Peril," to the believers in the United States. Echoing themes he had raised since the early years of his ministry, and especially in *The Advent of Divine Justice* in 1938, Shoghi Effendi insisted that the United States was passing through a serious moral, spiritual, and political crisis, "which to a superficial observer [was] liable to be dangerously underestimated."[16]

The root of the crisis, he asserted, was "crass materialism." Implicitly pointing out the hollowness of postwar culture, Shoghi Effendi described materialism as an approach to life that placed "excessive and ever-increasing emphasis on material well-being, forgetful of those things of the spirit on which alone a sure and stable foundation can be laid for human society." The phenomenon, he noted, was not uniquely American. Without referring directly to the country's visceral anti-Communism, he wrote that materialism was an "evil" which "all those within the capitalist system" shared with their "sworn enemies" in the Communist countries and that was rapidly infecting the rest of the world like a cancer in the wake of World War II. Bahá'u'lláh, he reminded his readers, had clearly denounced materialism in his writings and predicted its consequences, comparing it to a "devouring flame" that would precipitate "dire ordeals and world-shaking crises that must necessarily involve the burning of cities and the spread of terror and consternation in the hearts of men." Indeed, the most recent war had been only the latest stage in the "global havoc" that a wayward humanity seemed destined to suffer. Shoghi Effendi pointed to the nuclear arms race, the burden of continued military spending, and the recent victory of the Communists in the Chinese civil war as factors that had "contributed . . . to the deterioration of a situation which, if not remedied, is bound to involve the American nation in a catastrophe of undreamed-of dimensions and of untold consequences."[17]

The Ten Year Plan unfolded during a period of deepening crisis for the United States abroad and at home. As the plan began, the Korean War was drawing to a close and the anti-Communist campaign of Joseph McCarthy in the U.S. Senate was at its height. The decade following the armistice in Korea was the darkest in the Cold War rivalry with the Soviet Union. The phenomena of political assassinations, overt and covert military interventions, and proxy warfare among clients of the rival superpowers became commonplace on all continents, evidenced by U.S.-sponsored coups in Iran and Guatemala in 1953 and 1954, respectively, the deepening conflict in Vietnam after the failure of the 1954 Geneva Accords, and the Suez Crisis and the Hungarian Revolution in 1956. The nuclear arms race quickened as new technologies put the possibility of unprecedented destruction within the grasp of the superpowers and several of their allies. Following the Soviets' launching of *Sputnik*, the world's first artificial satellite, in 1957, the arms race moved into space. Toward the end of the plan, in October 1962, the world came closer to nuclear annihilation than ever before when the United States and the Soviet Union faced off over the positioning of Soviet nuclear missiles in Cuba.

Within the United States, a "culture of conformity" took hold of the postwar generation. Bolstered by the mass media—including the new phenomenon of television—and by federal government policy, the trend was characterized by unprecedented prosperity and an explosion of consumer goods, the increasing suburbanization of the population, a resurgence of religious practice in general and of evangelical Protestantism in particular, and political conservatism. At the same time, social commentators and political leaders pointed to an increase in juvenile delinquency and the rise of iconoclastic movements in art, literature, and music—epitomized by the raging of the Beat poets and the unabashed sexuality of rock and roll—as evidence that the culture of conformity was leaving many Americans, particularly the young, profoundly discontented. Most significantly, an increasingly broad-based and assertive civil rights movement—and the widespread opposition and violence that it provoked—mocked postwar perceptions of prosperity and stability and compromised the U.S. government's efforts to secure the Cold War allegiance of black and brown peoples in Africa, Asia, and Latin America.[18]

In the context of the Cold War, Shoghi Effendi argued that persistent racial problems posed a threat to the security and integrity of the nation. Unlike southern ideologues, however, who blamed black activists and Communist infiltrators for upsetting the country's race relations, Shoghi Effendi placed the onus of change squarely on the shoulders of the masses of white Americans and their government officials. In his view, the twin keys to averting even more severe racial violence—which the Soviet Union would surely seek to exploit—were a fundamental shift in the social consciousness of white America accompanied by decisive structural change. The "governed and governors alike" had neglected the "supreme, the inescapable and urgent duty" of "remedying, while there is yet time, through a revolutionary change in the concept and attitude of the average white American toward his Negro fellow citizen, a situation which, if allowed to drift, will, in the words of 'Abdu'l-Bahá, cause the streets of American cities to run with blood."[19]

The difficulties that threatened the United States from inside and out, including the challenge of establishing racial justice, were to Shoghi Effendi part of the divine plan for the unification of the human race. By dealing successfully with such tests, the country would "find itself purged of its anachronistic conceptions, and prepared to play a preponderating role, as foretold by 'Abdu'l-Bahá, in the hoisting of the standard of the Lesser Peace, in the unification of mankind, and in the establishment of a world federal government on this planet." These "fiery tribulations" would not only "firmly weld the American nation to its sister nations in both hemispheres" but would also cleanse it of the "accumulated dross which ingrained racial prejudice, rampant materialism, widespread ungodliness and moral laxity have combined, in the course of successive generations, to produce."[20]

The implications for the prosecution of the Ten Year Plan were serious. The American Bahá'í movement could not expect, Shoghi Effendi said, "at this critical juncture in the fortunes of a struggling, perilously situated, spiritually moribund nation, to either escape the trials with which this nation is confronted, nor claim to be wholly immune from the evils that stain its character." The spiritual "primacy" with which 'Abdu'l-Bahá had invested the American community by the Tablets of the Divine Plan could "lose its vital power and driving force" through the "neglect and apathy" of the believers. In contrast to the sad state of the nation of which they formed a part, the American Bahá'ís must remain focused, consecrate themselves to "every single objective" of the plan, and make sacrifices for its completion.[21]

In the first year of the plan, the formidable international goals assigned to the American community elicited an immediate and overwhelming response. One hundred fifty-seven believers left the country as pioneers, including five members of the National Spiritual Assembly who resigned their posts and were replaced in a by-election. By the end of the second year, another 125 would settle abroad. However, as in the second Seven Year Plan, the multiplication of Local Spiritual Assemblies within the United States was receiving less attention. Shoghi Effendi advised that the international pioneering effort must be "increased, doubled, nay trebled" at home, "particularly in the goal cities, where hitherto the work has stagnated." Noting the concentration of believers in the leading urban centers, "where, owing to the tempo and the distractions of city life, the progress of the Faith has been retarded," he called for the New York and Chicago communities to lead a "veritable exodus" to the goal cities. "Indeed," he added emphatically, "so grave are the exigencies of the present hour, and so critical the political position of the country, that were a bare fifteen adult Bahá'ís to be left in each of these cities, over which unsuspected dangers are hanging, it would still be regarded as adequate" to maintain their Local Spiritual Assemblies—among the oldest and strongest in the country.[22]

The response of the American Bahá'ís to Shoghi Effendi's appeal was slow. Two years later, in a letter dated July 1956, he again called them to the "revitalization" of their own national community and the "broadening and consolidation of its foundations." He wrote that a "far greater proportion of the avowed supporters of the Faith" must arise to teach an "infinitely greater number" of new believers, increase the number of new localities through an unprecedented flow of home-front pioneers, and accelerate the formation of Local Spiritual Assemblies "while safeguarding those already in existence." Barely a year later, he repeated his call that the American movement be "spiritually reinvigorated, administratively expanded, and materially replenished." "The flame of devotion," he wrote, " . . . must, in whatever way possible, be fanned and continually fed throughout the entire area of the Union, in every state from the Atlantic to the Pacific seaboards, in every locality where Bahá'ís reside, in every heart throbbing with the love of Bahá'u'lláh." Repeating the message of his previous letters and of Dorothy Baker's address at the outset of the plan, he wrote that the same spirit that had sent so many pioneers around the world must be "recaptured" at home in order to combat the "militant racialism, political corruption, unbridled capitalism, wide-spread lawlessness and gross immorality" that were proliferating "with ominous swiftness" throughout their country."[23]

The lukewarm response of the community to the home-front goals and the rising tide of white opposition to the *Brown* decision prompted Shoghi Effendi to scrap the earlier national policy regarding teaching in the South. A spate of letters in 1957 directed the Bahá'ís to focus on teaching African Americans, particularly in the southern states. Shoghi Effendi implied that while the previous policy's provision for teaching black and white seekers separately had been just in principle, the complacency of white Bahá'ís had rendered it ineffectual. The proof, he wrote through his secretary, was the fact that too few people of either race had joined the faith:

> The attitude toward teaching the Faith in the southern states of the United States must be entirely changed. For years, in the hope of attracting the white people, in order to "go easy" with them and not offend their sensibilities, a compromise has been made in the teaching work throughout the South. The results have been practically nil. The white people have not responded, worth mentioning, to the Faith, and the colored people have been hurt and also have not responded.

If most southern whites, embracing a militant racial conservatism, proved unresponsive to the Bahá'í message, the believers should focus instead on teaching blacks: "He feels it is time that the Bahá'ís stopped worrying entirely about the white element in a community, and that they should concentrate on showing the negro element that this is a Faith which produces full equality and which loves and wants minorities." In the face of white retrenchment, Shoghi Effendi renewed his call to practice complete social equality, with all its possible ramifications, regardless of local conditions: "The [white] Bahá'ís should welcome the Negroes to their homes, make every effort to teach them, associate with them, even marry them if they want to. We must remember that 'Abdu'l-Bahá Himself united in Bahá'í marriage a colored and a white believer. He could do no more."[24]

Shoghi Effendi's encouragement of social equality stood in stark contrast to the mood of white America. Interracial marriage remained illegal in twenty-four of the forty-eight states, and since the *Brown* decision, the Citizens' Councils and their allies had consistently equated school desegregation with interracial sex. The arguments of white parents, clergymen, Citizens' Councils, and politicians across the South mixed contemporary anti-Communism with a traditional regional rhetoric that involved defense of Protestant orthodoxy, defiance of unjust federal government authority, and protection of the sexual purity of white girls from black predators. In the words of one Citizens' Council report, "the malignant powers of mongrelization, communism, and atheism" were conspiring to destroy the United States through school desegregation. "Racial intermarriage," it warned, "has already begun in the North and unless stopped will spread to the South." In September 1957, when South Carolina Gov. George Bell Timmerman learned that President Eisenhower was preparing to send soldiers of the 101st Airborne Division to protect nine black students who had enrolled in Central High School in Little Rock, Arkansas, he told a local reporter that if the President was directing white parents "to mix the children of Arkansas against their will, he is attempting to set himself up as a dictator and this action may be taken as further evidence of an effort to Communize America."[25]

Shoghi Effendi took the Little Rock crisis as a reason for more boldness. In one letter, published in the November 1957 issue of *Bahá'í News*, Shoghi Effendi urged the American Bahá'ís, particularly in the South, not to be surpassed by other organizations:

> They should be courageous in their racial stand, particularly as so many non-Bahá'ís and non-Bahá'í organizations are showing marked courage at this time, when the decisions of the Supreme Court are being so hotly contested in the South. The friends must remember that the cardinal principle of their Faith is the Oneness of Mankind. This places an obligation on them far surpassing the obligation which Christian charity and brotherly love places upon the Christians. They should demonstrate this spirit of oneness constantly and courageously in the South.

He expected the Bahá'ís to put their faith's "cardinal principle" into practice not only by supporting the necessary structural changes in society but also by practicing social equality in their own community and personal relations and focusing their teaching efforts on African Americans. He acknowledged that such a course might well result in the emergence of local Bahá'í communities that were mostly or completely black, an outcome he explicitly welcomed. He wrote that the faith should be representative of the local population: "In a great many places in the South, the majority of the population is still Negro. This should be reflected in the Bahá'í Community, fearlessly."[26]

Shoghi Effendi's encouragement of all-black local communities added another challenge for a movement that was already having trouble meeting its domestic expansion goals. By referring to places in the South "where the majority of the population is still Negro," he was implicitly directing the settlement of more pioneers in the towns and farms of the southern Black Belt, the broad arc from Virginia to Texas with high African American population. Disproportionately afflicted by acute poverty and rural exodus, the Black Belt counties were generally areas where opportunities for outsiders were limited and where Citizens' Councils were most powerful. In South Carolina, where the black population as a whole had fallen under 50 percent during the decade of the 1920s, nearly half of the state's counties, mostly in rural areas in the Midlands and the Lowcountry, still had black majorities. These did not include the four urban counties—Aiken, Charleston, Greenville, and Richland—where most Bahá'í activity had been concentrated for the previous forty years. To apply Shoghi Effendi's advice in South Carolina would mean a level of systematic exertion and focused redistribution of the Bahá'í population not unlike the efforts to establish footholds across the region during the previous two plans—with perhaps a greater degree of cultural adjustment than before as believers from urban areas shifted their attention to the world of the countryside.[27]

Revitalization in Greenville

In South Carolina, the "revitalization" of the American home front that Shoghi Effendi had called for began during the second half of the Ten Year Plan, with the arrival of an energetic new group of pioneers and traveling teachers, a renewal of growth in some of the existing communities and the establishment of new ones, and the emergence of more native South Carolinians as capable teachers and administrators of the faith. In Greenville, the change began in 1956, when Richard and Joy Benson, a young white couple from Michigan, moved to town. Joy Benson was from a Bahá'í family. Her father, born a Muslim in Iran, embraced the faith after immigrating to the United States, along with her mother, a white American. She had recently graduated from medical school at the University of Michigan, and her husband, of Christian background and investigating the Baháʼí Faith, had just graduated from law school there. Joy had attended the Intercontinental Conference in Chicago in 1953 and had been moved by Dorothy Baker's appeal for Baháʼís to dedicate themselves to teaching among African Americans, and when the time came to apply for her medical residency, she looked at programs in South Carolina. Richard already had some experience in the state, having served in the navy in Charleston. They visited with Baháʼís in Greenville, Columbia, Charleston, and North Augusta before she decided to apply at Greenville General Hospital.[28]

In 1956, when the Bensons moved to Greenville, only a few Baháʼís—Roy and Bernice Williams, white pioneers Grace von der Heydt and Martha Fettig, Carolyn Glazener, and Virginia Ford, who had recently returned with her family from an overseas military post—remained in the city. Glazener was estranged from the community, and Roy and Bernice Williams moved to neighboring Anderson County shortly after the Bensons arrived. Early in 1957, Richard Benson became a Baháʼí, making a functional group of five. Around the same time, additional pioneers and new local converts augmented the Greenville community. Pearl Easterbrook and Zoe Meyer, retired schoolteachers from Illinois who were teaching in the South, arrived. Cleo Lindsey, a white Baháʼí from Atlanta who, with her son and daughter-in-law, had taken a stand for integration of the community in the 1940s, and Thelma Allison, a black Atlanta Baháʼí who had been taught the faith by Louis Gregory in Nashville, came as well. One of the pioneers befriended a local white woman, Dorothy Thomas Buchanan, a married mother of one, and her mother, Dorothy L. Thomas, both of whom became Baháʼís. Joy Benson's parents, John and Junie Faily, came to Greenville to live with them. And Thelma Allison's grown son, Bill, joined his mother there. The Local Spiritual Assembly was reestablished at Ridván 1957, but, as in previous plans, the departure of several pioneers meant that it was often a struggle to keep nine people to maintain the Local Assembly. Virginia Ford recalled that "every year from January to March there would be a search for believers to hold the LSA."[29]

From virtually the moment they arrived in Greenville, Richard and Joy Benson faced ostracism and intimidation for their unorthodox racial and religious views. Their first confrontation with the city's white elite came when Richard interviewed at the prestigious Haynsworth law firm, where Clement Furman Haynsworth Jr., whose great-grandfather had founded Furman University, was senior partner. The interview went well and Richard was given an appointment time to return and sign a contract. Before leaving, however, he asked to use the office telephone to call his wife at the home where the couple was staying. The receptionist said she would dial and asked for the name. When he replied that they were staying with Grace von der Heydt, it became apparent that everyone in the office knew the Bensons' host as a Baháʼí and a proponent of racial equality. When Richard returned to sign his contract, he waited for two hours while no one in the office spoke to him. He left only to find that every law firm he applied to in town turned him down. The next year, President Eisenhower nominated Haynsworth to the federal bench.[30]

Richard Benson, on the other hand, struggled to practice law on his own in a city where he had been blacklisted; to make ends meet he worked part-time in real estate. With a down payment from Joy's parents, the couple bought a large house on Overbrook Circle in a fashionable neighborhood near downtown. While the city council had already acknowledged the Baháʼís' right to hold interracial meetings, that fact did not stop individual whites and the city's police force from targeting the community. As soon as they began hosting integrated Baháʼí gatherings, the Bensons began to receive threatening phone calls. Rumors circulated among their neighbors that Joy Benson was an Indian princess, that the NAACP had bought their house for them, and that the couple was running a gambling ring. Neighbors yelled vulgar remarks at the Bensons and their black guests. The children of one family chased the Benson children out of their yard. Another neighbor was P. Bradley Murrah, an attorney and state senator who had defended his cousin in the Willie Earle lynching trial in 1947. Murrah organized a petition to the General Assembly alleging that the Bensons were Communists and illicit race-mixers. The police frequently staked out the house during Baháʼí meetings, shining lights on the front door as visitors departed and recording license plate numbers of the cars outside, and more than once Richard Benson went to the police station to explain that the Baháʼís were not Communists.[31]

While Richard Benson struggled to support a growing family in a hostile environment, his mother-in-law, Junie Faily, began making connections with black Greenvillians. She decided to attend a black church to get to know people, and one of the teenage girls she met began babysitting the Benson children from time to time. In 1960, the Bensons hosted a birthday party for her, attended by a few Baháʼís and ten to fifteen black youth, all students at Sterling High School. Before the party started, one of the guests, William Tucker, a white Baháʼí from Asheville, North Carolina, gave a short talk about the faith.

Richard Abercrombie, one of the young people in attendance, was not impressed with the party or the talk. Mixing socially with white people was strange enough, but the thought that a southern white man had anything worthwhile to tell black people about religion was ridiculous. When a school friend invited him to a fireside a few months later, he decided not to attend. But the night of the meeting, while in the middle of the dress rehearsal for a school play, he felt a strong compulsion to go. He ran to where the meeting was being held, the home of the Shumates, another black family Junie Failey had befriended, nearby on Anderson Road. The speaker was Eulalia Barrow Bobo, an African American woman from California and a sister of Joe Louis Barrow, the former world heavyweight boxing champion. Raised a Baptist in Alabama and Detroit, Bobo had become a Bahá'í in 1954 as a result of a mystical vision, and now she had come south to teach the faith among African Americans. When Abercrombie arrived, she had already begun her presentation on the Bahá'í concept of religious history—the progressive revelation of God's will to humanity by a succession of divine messengers including Abraham, Krishna, Moses, Buddha, Jesus, Muhammad, and, most recently, the Báb and Bahá'u'lláh. Abercrombie was intrigued. When he asked questions about Biblical prophecies, Bobo's answers were unlike anything the pastor at his Baptist church had ever said. Abercrombie recalled: "I was dying to ask questions about things that had bothered me, like the return of Christ, His returning in the clouds, and the dead rising from the grave. I couldn't accept what I had previously been taught." While Bobo was speaking Abercrombie remembered that he had promised to return to the dress rehearsal. "I ran back to school," he recalled, "and found that everyone had left, including the janitor. I turned around and ran all the way back to the Shumates' to have further discussion with Eulalia. She explained about the clouds of doubt and materialism and about the spiritually dead being born again." When he went home that night, he told his parents what he had heard about the Bahá'í Faith and said he "knew it was the truth."[32]

Charles and Lillie Abercrombie, staunch Baptists, wanted to investigate the strange-sounding religion that seemed to be winning over their son. Lillie Abercrombie recalled: "Ricky kept going to Bahá'í meetings, would come home and tell us what had transpired, and we would be up until 3 a.m. talking about it. Ricky just changed when he heard about the Faith, so I had to find out just what it was." Richard invited Joy Benson and Eulalia Bobo to the house. "I could talk to Joy," Lillie Abercrombie recalled. "She was a mild mannered, loving person, but Eulalia was too much for me. Charles couldn't talk to Joy; he would just chew her up. But he couldn't chew Eulalia up. She was too tough.[33]

Charles Abercrombie, a building contractor and church deacon, admitted, "Jacob wrestled with an angel all night long, [but] I wrestled with something worse than that, Eulalia Bobo." After about three weeks of late-night discussions in which Bobo explained the claims of the Báb and Bahá'u'lláh based on the Bible, Charles became a Bahá'í. Soon, like Richard Benson, he began to suffer economic reprisals for his association with the faith. Charles recalled: "We had an advertisement in the newspaper that a Bahá'í meeting would be held here [at the Abercrombies' home]. When that happened, the contracts I had to build houses were just cut off. People said that they had someone else who could do it cheaper." The Abercrombies took Charles's unemployment as a chance to travel to teach the faith. They visited a son in college in Tennessee and drove from there to Detroit where Lillie's mother lived. They arranged for a fireside at her mother's home, but the local speaker they had called did not come. Charles recalled: "Two young Bahá'ís there said that they couldn't handle a crowd of that size, so I said to Lillie, 'We can handle it.'" They gave the presentation, and Lillie's mother, niece, and nephew became Bahá'ís. Within the year, most of the rest of the family, including all their children and two of Charles's brothers, had embraced the faith. It was the first time in South Carolina that a whole extended family had become Bahá'ís.[34]

Back in Greenville, Charles Abercrombie made income from a piece of farmland outside of town, and his building contracts slowly returned. The local police monitored Bahá'í meetings at the Abercrombies' home, a large house on Rebecca Street in the Nicholtown neighborhood. "The police kept close watch and harassed the youngsters," recalled Lillie Abercrombie. "They wanted to know what we were drinking and what we were selling. After about a year, things began to change for the better. Instead of harassing our young people, the police started protecting [them]. Ricky would talk to bus drivers and taxi drivers and give them literature. Ricky invited the officers to come into our meetings, but no one did." She added: "Of course we had both the whites and the blacks down on us. Because the blacks thought we were bringing trouble into their neighborhood, they didn't like us either."[35]

Despite opposition from blacks and whites, the community continued to grow. Several more young African Americans, mostly school friends of the Abercrombie children who were attending a Bible study class conducted by the Bahá'ís, became believers in 1961 and 1962. At least one of the new Bahá'ís was from a mill village background. Luther B. Silver was a white Spartanburg County native who, along with thousands of other white rural folk, had abandoned farming in the 1920s and moved to Greenville in search of work in the textile industry. His whole family had worked at Dunean Mill, one of the string of textile factories that encircled the city. In September 1962, at the age of seventy-three, he addressed a letter to the members of West Greenville Baptist Church to resign his membership. Since meeting Baháʼís late the previous year, he wrote, he had been "very forcibly impressed with the teachings and practice of this Faith and decided to join in with them and help promote [it]." Later, other members of Silver's family became Baháʼís. Almost overnight, the decades-long problem of having enough believers to maintain the Local Spiritual Assembly seemed solved. In 1962, there were even enough outside the city limits to form the first Local Assembly of Greenville County. By 1963, there were some thirty adult Baháʼís in the Greenville area, and at least a dozen more youth and children.[36]

Reentering the Pee Dee

In late 1956, Jordan and Annette Young, new Baháʼís and recent graduates of Palmer College of Chiropractic in Davenport, Iowa, consulted with their Baháʼí friends at the school about where they could move both to start a successful practice and to help meet the goals of the Ten Year Plan. They learned that there were not many chiropractors in South Carolina, and not many Baháʼís, either. In January 1957, they arrived in the town of Florence, the economic and cultural center of the Pee Dee region of eastern South Carolina. While believers had previously resided in Charleston and several smaller Lowcountry localities, the Youngs' move began the first significant penetration of the Baháʼí Faith into the state's rural Black Belt.

Jordan Young came from a family of Polish and English Jews in Springfield, Massachusetts. Inquisitive about religion from a young age, by the time he shipped off for the Korean War, Young had concluded that there was one God, that there should be only one religion, and that all the clergy of the different faiths "should stop begging money off of poor people and get jobs." He first heard of the Baháʼí Faith from a black fellow soldier in a troop carrier on the Pacific Ocean, when both were slumped over the rails suffering from seasickness. After his return to the United States and his decision to enter Palmer, he seriously investigated the religion. Eventually he brought his girlfriend to a fireside at the home of a Baháʼí who was on the college's administrative staff. Annette McNeely, raised a Baptist in Thomaston in west-central Georgia, was just finishing her studies at Palmer. That night, the first words of the speaker, Ruth Moffett of Chicago, to the assembled guests were: "The sound of my voice is Gabriel's trumpet to you." As Moffett proceeded to use Bible verses to demonstrate that Bahá'u'lláh was the return of Christ, she had McNeely's undivided attention. But neither Young nor McNeely embraced the faith right away. When they were first married in a civil ceremony, he was Jewish and she was Baptist. In order to keep peace in his family she agreed to convert to Judaism, but by the time she had completed the conversion process he had already become a Bahá'í. In October 1956, a few months after their Jewish wedding ceremony, Annette McNeely Young became a Bahá'í as well. The following January, they arrived in Florence with their three-month-old son.[37]

When the Youngs opened their Florence office in March 1957, they hoped to defy racial segregation by having both black and white patients use the building's only entrance. Instead, they found that only white patients came. In order to attract any black patients at all, they had to cut another door in the back and install one of the ubiquitous symbols of Jim Crow, a "colored entrance in rear" sign. Inside, however, they maintained only one waiting room, used the two treatment rooms interchangeably for black and white patients, and, even more importantly, demonstrated uncommon courtesy to their black patients. In an effort to make quality health care more widely available in an impoverished region, they decided that rather than charging a set fee, they would put a box on the wall with a sign asking people to pay what their conscience dictated. Their practice quickly went from dozens of patients to hundreds, both white and black. One man charged black motel workers a dollar to drive them from Myrtle Beach, a town sixty miles away in Horry County, to Florence for treatment. Jordan Young recalled using humor to diffuse tense situations in an integrated practice. A flustered white patient once pulled him aside and whispered, "Dr. Young, there's n_____s in the waiting room!" Young replied, "You're a Christian, right? Then you should know there's only one God, one salvation, one baptism, one heaven—and one waiting room!"[38]

When the Youngs gradually began to invite some of their patients to their home to learn about the Bahá'í Faith, blacks expressed reluctance to visit their home for fear of negative consequences—not for themselves, they said, but for their hosts. The office was a safer gathering place, so they hosted evening meetings there with a steady trickle of listeners over the next few years. Several of the Youngs' black patients from Florence and Myrtle Beach, as well as their white receptionist and her husband, became Bahá'ís. In 1961, another white couple who had discovered the faith at Palmer College moved to Lake

Figure 6.1. Eight members of the first Local Spiritual Assembly, Florence, South Carolina, 1961. *L to r, back*: David Jurney, Mattie Bacote, Paul Bacote. *Middle:* Almetta Player, Fannie Williams. *Front:* Unknown, Otis Williams, Robert Bacote. Otis Williams holds a calligraphic rendering of the Greatest Name. The Local Spiritual Assemblies of Florence, in the Pee Dee, and of Frogmore, on St. Helena Island, represented a major step in establishing the Bahá'í Faith in South Carolina's Black Belt. Courtesy of Florence Bahá'í Archives, Florence, S.C.

City, a black-majority market town in the southern part of Florence County. Lee Grimsley had grown up in a rural area north of Florence, and his wife, Genelle, was from nearby Georgetown County. In April 1962, there were enough Bahá'ís in the area to form a Local Spiritual Assembly in Florence County. Of the nine members, six were white and three were black, and five were recent local converts. The next year, there were ten adult Bahá'ís in the city of Florence, nine in unincorporated Florence County, and four in Horry County. Of the twenty-three, seventeen were working-class African Americans. When a Local Spiritual Assembly was first elected in the city of Florence in 1961, eight of its nine members were local African Americans; when the body was reestablished in 1964, all of them were. Together, the experience in the Florence and Greenville areas seemed to indicate that a focus on teaching the faith among African Americans could bring the results that Shoghi Effendi had hoped for—not only new black believers but white ones as well; a revival of older communities and the establishment of new ones; and growth both in both urban settings and in smaller towns and rural areas.[39]

Seasonal Schools and the Frogmore Community

During the Ten Year Plan, a new element of Bahá'í community life connected members of the faith in South Carolina more closely to a vigorous regional movement. During the 1930s and 1940s at the National Spiritual Assembly's retreat centers in California, Maine, and Michigan, "summer schools," usually lasting a long weekend or longer, had emerged as programs to deepen participants' knowledge of the faith and train them to be more confident and competent teachers. As membership grew during the 1950s, regional summer schools held in rented facilities were established across the country. In some areas, winter schools were added. During the second year of the Ten Year Plan, Bahá'ís in the southeastern states inaugurated a regional summer school at Blue Ridge Assembly near Asheville, North Carolina. By the 1950s, the YMCA facility that had figured prominently in the formation of the Interracial Commission a generation before was virtually unique in the Carolinas for offering overnight accommodations for interracial groups. For a regional movement most of whose members lived in localities with only a handful of believers, summer schools became important gathering places that provided opportunities for social interaction and group identity formation on a larger scale. At the 1955 summer school, for example, more than one hundred Bahá'ís and seekers attended, of whom at least thirteen were African Americans. In violation of regional racial etiquette, blacks and whites shared not only study sessions but dormitory, dining, and recreational spaces—including the swimming pool and the rocking chairs on the grand front porch of Robert E. Lee Hall. Paul Haney, the chair of the National Spiritual Assembly and a recently appointed Hand of the Cause of God, was the conference's special guest; other presentations covered such topics as youth in the faith, international pioneering, and teaching racial minorities.[40]

By the end of the decade the administrators of Blue Ridge were complaining that the Bahá'í programs included "too many" blacks, so in 1960 the southeastern summer school moved to Penn Center, a former school near Beaufort, South Carolina, with a long record of interracialism. Located in the unincorporated community of Frogmore on St. Helena Island at the southern tip of the state, Penn Center held an important place in the area's history. Founded as a school for newly freed slaves in 1862, it was the oldest surviving institution of the "Port Royal Experiment," the precursor to Reconstruction carried out on the Union-occupied Sea Islands during the Civil War. It had closed as a school in 1948 but reopened shortly thereafter as Penn Community Services Center, a social and economic development

agency serving the area's Gullah-speaking population. Located as it was on an isolated, black-majority island, Penn Center was even farther from the gaze of the white public than Blue Ridge and an ideal facility for a racially diverse Bahá'í community. Also in 1960, increased demand led to the addition of an annual winter school during the Christmas holiday. With two gatherings of believers and seekers each year from 1960 to 1965, Penn Center became an important rallying point for the growing Bahá'í movement in the Southeast, a place where a new generation of young believers in particular formed lifelong friendships and solidified their identity as Bahá'ís.[41]

The new location coincided with other changes in the regional movement. Beginning around 1960, new members of the Area Teaching Committee of the South Atlantic States (the successor of the Regional Teaching

Figure 6.2. Some of the participants in the Southeastern Bahá'í Summer School, Penn Center, St. Helena Island, South Carolina, July 1961. Penn Center, a black-run institution on a remote Sea Island, was among only a few places in the region during the early 1960s that would host the Bahá'ís' racially integrated seasonal conferences. Courtesy of Joy F. Benson.

Committee, serving Florida, Georgia, and South Carolina), including Richard and Joy Benson and Martha Fettig of Greenville and Lee and Genelle Grimlsey of Lake City, brought renewed energy to the teaching work in the area. Among the most visible results was an increase in the rate of membership growth. In the 1959–1960 administrative year, seven adults and youth became Bahá'ís in the entire three-state region. The next year, the number more than doubled to fifteen. In 1961–1962, the number tripled to thirty-six adults and nine youth. There were other, qualitative shifts as well. The committee actively encouraged teaching among African Americans and youth, conducting a survey of local communities' outreach efforts to blacks and holding several conferences each year just for young people. In Greenville and Columbia, Bahá'ís began weekly spiritual education classes for children, including not only their own but those of friends and neighbors. As more African Americans and young people became involved in Baháʼí activities, music took on added importance in the community's collective life. Several believers composed original words and melodies or set prayers and passages from the Baháʼí writings to music. According to the Area Teaching Committee, the new emphasis on music "had a great effect on reaching many hearts and providing great inspiration in many meetings." They added: "In Georgia and South Carolina, there is scarcely a meeting now without the singing of truly appropriate songs."[42]

An unexpected result of the relocation of the summer and winter schools to Penn Center was the emergence of a local Baháʼí community on St. Helena Island. After their first use of the facility, members of the Area Teaching Committee sensed a receptivity to the Baháʼí message among the island's inhabitants and adopted it as an "extension teaching project." During the 1961–1962 winter school session, they arranged for Eulalia Barrow Bobo to speak "from the pulpit of a local Baptist church on Emancipation Day, Jan. 1, 1962." The result was a "wide distribution of literature among the islanders and firesides in the home of one of the Frogmore residents." Among the four people who embraced the faith during the winter school was Viola Chapman, an island native who had worked as the dean of women at Hampton Institute in Virginia. She was likely the first native Gullah-speaker to become a Baháʼí in South Carolina since Alonzo Twine in 1910. Reporting to the National Spiritual Assembly at Ridván 1962, the committee expected more declarations of faith in the area and went so far as to suggest that "the spark of mass enrollment in the South may well be ignited in this locality." In fact, several more islanders became Baháʼís during 1962, and a longtime white North Augusta believer, Claire Glover Michaels, arrived as a pioneer. At Ridván 1963, there were enough Baháʼís to form a Local Spiritual Assembly. When a ninth islander became a Baháʼí, Michaels, who was terminally ill with cancer, stepped down from the body and returned to North Augusta. At Ridván 1964, St. Helena Island, like Florence, had a Local Assembly made up entirely of African Americans.[43]

Civil Rights Movement at High Tide

As Shoghi Effendi had anticipated, the ten years of the World Crusade witnessed an unprecedented "upsurge" of people of African descent in South Carolina and across the South. During the late 1950s, faced with increasing pressure from inside and outside the state, South Carolina's white leadership initially closed ranks to oppose black demands. In the early 1960s, however, as challenges at home mounted and violence rocked other states in the region—and as the glare of national press coverage and intervention by various agencies of the federal government brought unwelcome attention—they moved to desegregate key institutions with a minimum of chaos and economic upset, attempting all the while to maintain a veneer of order and dignity. It took until the beginning of the 1970s for the public school system—the largest public institution in South Carolina's white supremacist order—to be completely desegregated. But by the middle of the 1960s, the grassroots movement in the state and region had achieved, in the form of landmark federal legislation and a host of ad hoc local agreements, the formal dissolution of the Jim Crow regime. It was a social transformation that would have profound implications for the Bahá'í community of South Carolina.

While white reaction to the *Brown* decision in the mid-1950s temporarily quieted most black protest in South Carolina, it did not take long for activists to begin to regroup, rebuild their organizational structures, and consider new strategies—much as the state's Bahá'ís began to do at about the same time. Between 1957 and 1959, James T. McCain, president of the Sumter County branch of the NAACP, organized nine South Carolina chapters of the Congress of Racial Equality (CORE), a Chicago-based organization inspired by Mohandas K. Gandhi's program of nonviolent direct action in India. Working closely together, CORE and the NAACP (whose local members and leadership frequently overlapped) orchestrated a new wave of direct-action protest in South Carolina. The first such demonstration came in response to an incident in early 1959 in which a black passenger was forcibly removed from the white waiting room of the Greenville airport. On Emancipation Day, January 1, 1960, following an unsuccessful lawsuit in federal court, some 250 protesters marched from Springfield Baptist Church in Greenville to the airport. Representatives of the NAACP and CORE presented a petition to the airport authority calling for an end to the "stigma, the inconvenience, and the stupidity of racial segregation." By the time an appeals court ordered the desegregation of the airport a year later, direct action protest had swept communities across the state and region.[44]

In February 1960, just a few weeks after the Greenville march, college students in Greensboro, North Carolina, staged a sit-in protest to demand equal treatment in downtown department stores. Inspired by the Greensboro example, CORE quickly organized students from Friendship Junior

College for a sit-in campaign in downtown Rock Hill, South Carolina. In March, students from State College staged sit-ins in the Kress Department Store in Orangeburg, prompting local police to attack with water hoses and tear gas and arrest four hundred students. The next day, the *New York Times* carried a front-page story of the violence in Orangeburg, including a picture of the wet and battered protesters held in a makeshift outdoor stockade. Young people across the state were galvanized. During the next few weeks, high school and college students staged similar demonstrations in Charleston, Columbia, Denmark, Greenville, Manning, Spartanburg, and Sumter. In Greenville, students from Sterling High School staged "study-ins" at the main library and "skate-ins" at a whites-only skating rink, resulting in several arrests and lawsuits to overturn segregation in the city. By year's end, some seventy thousand black students—and a few white allies—had staged similar demonstrations in every southern state.[45]

In the spring of 1961, as the sit-in movement continued across the region, CORE's national office planned a two-week "Freedom Ride" through the South, designed to test a 1960 U.S. Supreme Court ruling that had ordered the desegregation of interstate travel. Two interracial groups of riders left Washington, D.C., with plans to stop at bus stations in Virginia, the Carolinas, Georgia, Alabama, and Mississippi on their way to New Orleans. The first violence of the ride came in Rock Hill, South Carolina, where tensions were already high because of the sit-in movement, when a white mob attacked a group of riders in the bus station. South of Rock Hill in Winnsboro, a black-majority town with a powerful Citizens' Council, two riders, one black and one white, were arrested at the bus station lunch counter and narrowly escaped being lynched. For the state's white politicians, the Freedom Riders' short trip across the state amounted to little less than a foreign invasion. In the U.S. Senate, Strom Thurmond denounced the riders as "outside agitators" who were part of a Communist conspiracy to subvert the "southern way of life," and Olin Johnston issued a public letter to his constituents insisting that the riders were Communists who should not be "allowed to prey upon the religious, racial and social differences of our people." When one of the riders, a student at Morris College who had joined the group as it passed through Sumter, returned home, he was abducted by white men, taken to a clearing in the woods, stripped, and threatened with castration as the letters "KKK" were carved into his chest and legs. He asked the U.S. Justice Department to investigate, but Governor Ernest F. Hollings publicly dismissed the allegations as "a hoax."[46]

While prominent political leaders resorted to familiar conspiracy theories, other white leaders sought a more pragmatic approach to the sit-ins and the Freedom Rides. In July 1961 at the annual Watermelon Festival in Hampton, a county-seat town near Beaufort, Greenville construction magnate Charles Daniel urged whites to embrace desegregation—or at least influence the course it would take. "The desegregation issue," he said, "cannot continue to be hidden behind the door. This situation cannot be settled at the lunch counter and bus station levels. We must handle this ourselves, more realistically than heretofore; or it will be forced upon us in the harshest way. Either we act on our own terms, or we forfeit the right to act." In the words of one Greenville textile executive, Daniel "gave the blessing of the establishment to desegregation." His "Watermelon Speech" signaled a new willingness on the part of the state's business elite—motivated in no small part by economic self-interest—to allow desegregation with a minimum of disruption. The following year, white business, civic, and religious leaders in Greenville and Columbia each formed an interracial committee to quietly negotiate an end to segregation in their respective business districts, but progress there and in other localities was slow.[47]

By the spring and summer of 1963, pressure to desegregate South Carolina's downtowns was mounting, both from inside and outside the state. On May 2 and 3, the nation watched on television as police in Birmingham, Alabama, unloosed dogs and fire hoses on demonstrators, including hundreds of schoolchildren. On June 5, the South Carolina conference of the NAACP announced that eight cities—Charleston, Columbia, Florence, Greenville, Orangeburg, Rock Hill, Spartanburg, and Sumter—would be targets of massive protests. A few days later President John F. Kennedy, spurred by the violence in Birmingham and fearing that it would spread, announced that he would send to Congress a major civil rights bill to outlaw segregation and discrimination in public facilities, education, employment, voting, and government agencies. Powerful segregationists in Congress blocked the bill in committee, and in August a quarter of a million people representing a broad coalition of civil rights, labor, and religious groups marched on the National Mall in Washington to call for its passage. In November, during a trip meant to shore up support for the Democratic Party among white southerners, Kennedy was shot to death in Dallas.[48]

Against the backdrop of dramatic events across the region, the downtown desegregation campaign in South Carolina proceeded, albeit with varying degrees of success based on the responses of local whites. In Florence, Greenville, Rock Hill, and Spartanburg, even the threat of demonstrations was enough for business and political leaders to reach desegregation agreements, and several smaller cities acted to end discriminatory practices even though they had not been on the NAACP's list. In Columbia, white leaders came to the table only after demonstrations began, and in Charleston, city officials did not respond until protests descended into violence. In Orangeburg, local whites were intransigent, and the situation remained tense and unresolved. By July 1964, when President Lyndon B. Johnson signed the Civil Rights Act—the only adequate memorial, he had told Congress, to his slain predecessor—most cities and towns in South Carolina had at least taken initial steps to end segregation in their business districts, and several had formally repealed their segregation ordinances.[49]

The campaign to desegregate South Carolina's downtowns coincided with another in higher education. Here, too, white officials and business leaders were concerned above all with avoiding violence that would embarrass the state and drive away investors. In the fall of 1962, when the University of Mississippi campus erupted in deadly violence over the admission of its first black student, Governor Hollings and other white leaders determined that the same thing would not happen in South Carolina. When black Charlestonian Harvey Gantt applied for admission to Clemson College, Hollings, who had been elected as a segregationist, worked publicly and privately to prepare for a smooth enrollment. On January 9, 1963, as Gantt's case came before the U.S. Fourth Circuit Court of Appeals, the outgoing governor made his farewell address to the state legislature. "As we meet," Hollings said, "South Carolina is running out of courts. If and when every legal remedy has been exhausted, this General Assembly must make clear South Carolina's choice, a government of laws rather than a government of men. . . . This should be done with dignity. It must be done with law and order." A few days later, the court ruled to admit Gantt, and he enrolled without incident. The following fall, the University of South Carolina admitted its first black students since Reconstruction. By May 1965, all of the state's white public colleges and half of its white private colleges had admitted black students or agreed to do so.

While white leaders acquiesced in the desegregation of business districts and colleges and universities, the state's public school system was another matter. Nearly a decade after the U.S. Supreme Court's *Brown* ruling, South Carolina's public primary and secondary schools remained largely segregated. In response to federal court orders in 1963, the Charleston and Greenville school districts created desegregation plans that allowed for a relative handful of black students—mostly from privileged backgrounds—to attend formerly all-white schools. A Richland County plan was somewhat more successful, resulting in the enrollment of some 1,250 black students in formerly all-white schools by 1966. But complete dismantling of the state's dual school system did not take place until the 1970–1971 academic year.[50]

In 1965, a second piece of federal legislation dramatically altered South Carolina's political landscape. While the Civil Rights Act included a provision intended to prohibit discrimination in voter registration, it did not eliminate the use of poll taxes, intimidation, and violence against black prospective voters, and civil rights organizations across the South pushed for new a new, stronger voting rights law. In March 1965, days after "Bloody Sunday," when police attacked voting-rights marchers in Selma, Alabama, with billy clubs, cattle prods, and tear gas, President Johnson presented a voting rights bill to Congress. Arguing that racism was a national problem, not just a regional one, Johnson's speech to the body signaled the strongest public support by the federal government for the rights of African Americans since Reconstruction. "Even if we pass this bill," Johnson said, "the battle will not be over. What happened in Selma is part of a far larger movement which reaches into every section and state of America. It is the effort of American Negroes to secure for themselves the full blessings of American life. Their cause must be our cause, too, because it is not just Negroes but really it is all of us who must overcome the crippling legacy of bigotry and injustice." In August, Johnson signed into law the Voting Rights Act of 1965, and the effect in South Carolina was immediate. With federal marshals stationed in several parts of the state, CORE registered thirty-seven thousand new black voters in twenty-four counties. In 1968, twelve blacks were among South Carolina's delegation to the Democratic National Convention in Chicago, and in stark contrast to the days of the PDP in the 1940s, theirs was the only delegation from the Deep South to not have its credentials challenged because of racial discrimination. By the end of the decade, black registered voters made up more than a quarter of South Carolina's electorate.[51]

The civil rights legislation of 1964 and 1965 meant that, as a political and social system endorsed by the federal government, the Jim Crow system was no more. The first serious attempt by the federal government in nearly a century to make good on the Reconstruction-era promise of an interracial republic, they represented a major reconception of American citizenship and nationhood. From the point of view of the Baháʼís, one of the greatest structural barriers to the realization of the oneness of humanity in their country (and to their own ability to grow and function freely as an interracial movement) had fallen. While many southern whites resisted the implications of the laws and implementation often came slowly, especially in the all-important field of public education, a number of factors—the participation of whites from across the country in the southern civil rights movement, the nationwide media coverage that thrust the claims of African Americans (and the often violent opposition they faced from their white fellow citizens) into the public spotlight, the energetic and very public support of a white southern president and the decisive majorities each bill received in Congress, and the broad public support for the measures throughout most of the country—indicated that some measure of the "revolutionary change in the concept and attitude of the average white American toward his Negro fellow citizen" that Shoghi Effendi had called for was taking place.

Civil Rights and the Greenville Bahá'í Community

As the Bahá'í community in Greenville grew during the turbulent years of the early 1960s, its members took steps to secure legal protection for their activities, project a more openly interracial public image, and lend support to local civil rights initiatives. The legal measures, undertaken in response to goals of the Ten Year Plan, gave the community more security than it had ever enjoyed. Richard Benson approached Rex L. Carter, a fellow attorney in Greenville and the speaker of the South Carolina House of Representatives, about securing state recognition for the Bahá'í marriage ceremony. Carter wrote to the state's attorney general, Daniel McLeod, who issued an opinion in April 1961 that the officers of a Local Spiritual Assembly were empowered to perform marriages in accordance with state law. Citing the bylaws of the Greenville Local Assembly and case law from South Carolina and other states, the opinion stated that the relevant section of the state code, though specifically providing only for "ministers of the Gospel or accepted Jewish Rabbis" to perform marriages, extended in principle "to any person authorized by a religious faith to conduct a marriage ceremony in accordance with the tenets of such faith." "It is the opinion of this office," McLeod wrote, "that those persons authorized by the Baha'i Faith to perform marriage ceremonies are 'ministers of the Gospel' within the meaning of the marriage statutes of South Carolina and such persons may validly perform marriages in this State." Following the attorney general's opinion regarding Bahá'í marriages, the Local Assembly of Greenville filed incorporation papers. In September 1962, the body secured legal entity as "The Spiritual Assembly of the Bahá'ís of Greenville, South Carolina, Inc." Taken together, both legal actions would have important long-term effects, inside and outside the Bahá'í community.[52]

Although the city council of Greenville had publicly pledged to not interfere with the Bahá'í community's interracial activities nearly a decade earlier, securing incorporation and the right to perform marriages in 1961 and 1962 gave the Bahá'í movement in South Carolina specific legal protections for the first time—and a new measure of dignity and respectability. By granting legal entity to a lay religious council from outside the Christian and Jewish traditions and by conferring on its officers the same power to solemnize marriages as that formerly held only by ministers and rabbis, the state had significantly broadened its definition of acceptable religion, a precedent that would benefit other religious minorities in South Carolina following passage of the Immigration and Nationality Act of 1965. Moreover, because they touched on the important issues of the occupation and use of public spaces, management of the significant life passages of marriage and death, and interracial association, both decisions strengthened Bahá'í identity and community solidarity in South Carolina. The main practical effect of incorporation—a step that many Local Spiritual Assemblies would take in subsequent years—was to enable Bahá'í institutions to acquire property, such as cemeteries and local centers, on behalf of the community. In subsequent years, not only would such properties be sites for carrying out important community functions, but they would add to its legitimacy in the eyes of its own members and those of its neighbors. Because the Local Assembly of Greenville included black members, incorporation also implied a measure of legal recognition for the faith's interracial character that went beyond the city council's earlier ruling. In addition to legitimizing the community's role in attending to the personal affairs of its own members, recognition of the Bahá'í marriage ceremony also solidified the South Carolina movement's interracial character. After the U.S. Supreme Court invalidated the remaining state anti-miscegenation laws in 1967, decades' worth of work to dismantle the color line reached a logical conclusion when the community's first interracial couple—a local Gullah man and a white woman home-front pioneer from Michigan, both widowed—settled on St. Helena Island and began to raise their blended family. It was the first of scores of interracial marriages in the South Carolina Bahá'í community.[53]

Encouraged alike by their religion's national and international leaders and by the serious blows that a surging civil rights campaign was dealing to the Jim Crow regime both locally and nationally, a larger, more diverse, and more legally secure Bahá'í community in Greenville became more confident in upholding social equality in its public and private activities, more creative in its outreach efforts, and more vocal in its support for the mainstream civil rights movement. During the late 1950s and early 1960s, the Baháʼís hosted interracial picnics, study groups, and Holy Day services that regularly included their non-Baháʼí friends, classmates, coworkers, and family members. They organized programs for Human Rights Day and United Nations Day—uncommon occurrences in a city many of whose conservative Protestant religious leaders were openly hostile toward internationalism—and the speakers included not only local and visiting Baháʼís but local attorneys, civil rights workers, teachers, and students. In December 1958, for example, they observed Human Rights Day at the Phillis Wheatley Center, a black community center in Nicholtown near Charles and Lillie Abercrombie's house. On the program were Matthew J. Perry of Spartanburg, the new head of the state NAACP's legal committee, and Laura Townes, a local white Quaker and sister-in-law of Charles Townes, the Greenville native who invented the laser. The 1964 observance took place at the Citizens & Southern National Bank on Camperdown Way, with Robert Anderson, a Sterling High School graduate who had helped integrate the University of South Carolina the previous semester, and Hattie Smith, one of Bernice Williams's fellow teachers at Sterling, as speakers.[54]

In September 1964, the community hosted a "Spiritual Singing Convention" at Greenville Memorial Auditorium, the city's premier concert venue. Thirty-five area musical groups, mostly affiliated with African American churches, participated, and the speakers included attorney Matthew Perry, Asheville Baháʼí William Tucker, and Rev. James Bevel of Atlanta, a prominent leader of the Southern Christian Leadership Conference. Printed advertisements for the event named John Bolt Culbertson, a prominent local white lawyer with ties to both civil rights and labor organizations, as its sponsor. For a local community that only a few years before had been cowed nearly out of existence, it was a major event that publicly allied the Baháʼí Faith with the civil rights movement and its spiritual and institutional basis in the black church.[55]

The community took additional steps to inform an overwhelmingly Protestant local population about the relationship between the Baháʼí Faith and Christianity. In addition to regular notices of its activities in local newspapers, the community frequently placed large advertisements about the origins and purposes of the faith. Among them were such bold headlines as "BAHA'U'LLAH, The Promised One of All Ages," "5,000,000 Baha'is Believe BAHA'U'LLAH Is Christ's Return," "Why Should I Become a Baha'i?" and "Do You Know in What Day You Are Living?" Each included explanatory text, attractive graphics, and local contact information. In advance of the 1964 Human Rights Day program, Luther Silver addressed a letter to the editor of the *Greenville News* that called for the United States to uphold the provisions of the Universal Declaration of Human Rights and promote a spirit of "brotherhood and human dignity" at home and abroad. "No nation, great or small," wrote the elderly former mill worker, "can for long keep from becoming entangled in this web of international association which the hand of Divine Providence is weaving." In contrast to popular conservative Protestant thought, which frequently linked international cooperation with Communism and the rise of the Antichrist, Silver argued that the world's increasing interconnectedness was part of God's plan for humanity.[56]

During 1963 and 1964, the community took a stand for the desegregation of public facilities when Greenville officials moved to permanently close the city's public swimming pools. In April 1963, ruling in a case argued by NAACP attorney Matthew Perry on behalf of African Americans denied access to two state parks, federal judge J. Robert Martin gave the state sixty days to desegregate its entire park system. In order to block the decision, Attorney General Daniel McLeod and the General Assembly's segregation committee recommended closing the parks, and the Greenville city council, fearing the implications of the ruling for city parks, closed its swimming pool for whites in Cleveland Park and for blacks in Green Forest Park. City officials publicly insisted that the closings were for only maintenance, but when the Greenville Zoo requested permission to house six sea lions at the Cleveland Park facility, it became clear that the city had no intention of operating swimming pools if they had to be on an integrated basis. Greenville Bahá'ís joined the public outcry against the pool closings, citing the need for more recreation facilities for area youth, not fewer, and recommending that city officials reopen the pools and at least try integration for a year. During one public hearing at the city hall, Bernice Williams, whose position as a public schoolteacher had previously made it hard for her to participate in overt Bahá'í or civil rights activism, excoriated aldermen for their dishonesty: "We all know why the pools were not opened this year, and it is a shame that for this reason we must sacrifice wholesome pleasures for our children for the sake of a few sea lions."[57]

In addition to Robert Anderson at the University of South Carolina, another Sterling High School graduate who associated with the Greenville Bahá'í community became intimately involved in desegregating the state's institutions of higher education. In 1965, Joseph Vaughn became the first black resident undergraduate student at Furman University, the Baptist-affiliated

institution that had long been a bastion of racial and religious conservatism in Greenville. At Sterling, Vaughn had been a respected student leader with a "cosmopolitan outlook that left fellow students with the impression that he had studied abroad," thanks in large part to his French teacher, Bernice Williams. Early in 1964, Furman's president and dean of students, both proponents of desegregation, recruited Vaughn and encouraged the board of trustees to allow his enrollment, but when the South Carolina Baptist Convention

Figure 6.3. Greenville Bahá'ís and friends, Phillis Wheatley Community Center, April 1964. By the mid-1960s, a focus on teaching African Americans in Greenville had yielded South Carolina's largest and most active local Bahá'í community—and, as Shoghi Effendi had predicted, more success in attracting whites to the faith, too. Courtesy of Joy F. Benson.

met in November, it narrowly reversed the university's new policy. At an emergency meeting, the board of trustees—made up entirely of Baptists appointed by the convention—defied its parent body by reaffirming its earlier decision to desegregate. In February 1965, Vaughn and three black graduate students were admitted to Furman, becoming the first African Americans to attend a private institution of higher education in South Carolina. The following year, Vaughn became a Bahá'í.[58]

"Upsurge"

During the period of the Ten Year Plan, the process that Shoghi Effendi had termed the social and political "upsurge" of the dark-skinned peoples became everywhere apparent, perhaps most dramatically in the rapid course of decolonization in Africa and Southeast Asia and in the black freedom movement in the United States. During the same period, the Bahá'í Faith went far toward vindicating its claim to be a world religion, embodying a measure of the spiritual upsurge that Shoghi Effendi had also predicted. However, Shoghi Effendi himself did not live to see the fruit of his life's work. On November 4, 1957, at the mid-point of the World Crusade he had conceived and directed, he died unexpectedly from complications of influenza while on a trip to London. He had named no successor to the Guardianship, but in the months before his death he had taken several measures that would prove critical to the completion of the plan and the formation of the Universal House of Justice. In June 1957, he had added to the role of the Hands of the Cause of God the "obligation to watch over and insure protection to the Bahá'í world community." In an October message, he had appointed a third contingent of eight Hands (including a native Ugandan of the Teso people) and had designated them as the "Chief Stewards of Bahá'u'lláh's embryonic World Commonwealth." In the same message, he had also called for the holding of five intercontinental conferences in 1958 to deliberate on the completion of the plan, appointing a Hand as his personal representative to each. Based on Shoghi Effendi's instructions, the Hands of the Cause assumed temporary collective leadership of the faith after his death, guiding the worldwide community toward completion of the Ten Year Plan and making preparations for the formation of the Universal House of Justice. The five intercontinental conferences he had called for became venues for the believers not only to rededicate themselves to the work of the plan but also to come to terms with the death of their leader.[59]

Despite what could have been a devastating leadership crisis, the Bahá'ís met or surpassed virtually all the goals of the Ten Year Plan. In some countries, persecution by religious authorities or the state severely constrained the functioning of Bahá'í communities, but difficulties in one area seemed to be more than made up for with growth elsewhere. In the wake of a 1953 coup in Iran, for example, Shia clerics and military leaders instigated a new wave of persecution of the world's largest Bahá'í population, resulting in the destruction of the national Bahá'í headquarters, desecration of Bahá'í cemeteries and holy sites, and the rape, murder, or dismissal from employment of individual believers and families across the country. The orgy of violence scuttled plans for the planned erection of a house of worship in Tehran, but in order to "compensate for the disabilities" of the Iranian community, Shoghi Effendi called for three such structures—in Kampala, Uganda; Sydney, Australia; and Frankfurt, West Germany—to be built instead. The completion of continental temples in Africa and the Pacific region, in particular, reflected new demographic realities. During the decade of the plan, a long-term shift in worldwide Bahá'í membership had begun that would soon tip the scales away from Iran and North America and toward the Global South, away from major urban areas and toward small towns and villages. A tally of the plan's results indicated the extent of the community's growth. The number of countries, territories, and major islands opened to the faith more than doubled during the plan to 259, and members of hundreds of indigenous groups across the Americas, Africa, Asia, and the islands of the Indian and Pacific Oceans became Bahá'ís. Scores of new Local Spiritual Assemblies and forty-four new National Spiritual Assemblies were formed. Many of these institutions were able to acquire legal incorporation, national and local headquarters, investment properties, cemeteries, sites for future temples, recognition of Bahá'í marriages and Holy Days, publishing facilities, and literature in appropriate languages—surpassing most of the associated numerical goals of the plan.[60]

Beyond the completion of specific goals, a development that would have far-reaching importance—both for the worldwide community in general and for the Bahá'ís of South Carolina in particular—was a marked acceleration during the plan of the process of entry by troops. Following the initial experiments in Uganda that Dorothy Baker had recounted to build support for the plan in 1953, teaching projects aimed at bringing the faith to rural areas spread to countries around the world. The most impressive results occurred in Africa and Asia, in countries large and small, with a wide range of political and economic circumstances. In the former Belgian Congo, for example, which gained independence and descended into civil war during the plan, some twenty thousand people became Bahá'ís. In South Korea, two thousand people did in the last four months of the plan alone. In India, where the faith had largely been confined to urban areas, village teaching began in 1961 with a conference in the central state of Madhya Pradesh. Campaigns during the rest of the plan raised the number of believers in the country a hundredfold, from 850 to 87,000, and the number of Local Assemblies more than tenfold, from 58 to 675. Even in tiny Mauritius off the East African coast, the faith expanded from a lone pioneer in 1953 to a network of 19 groups and 16 Local

Spiritual Assemblies ten years later. Similar changes were also apparent in the Americas. By the end of the plan, most of the Baháʼís in Latin America were from rural and indigenous communities, and in Canada, natives representing eleven tribes made up a quarter of the Baháʼí population.[61]

In the United States as well, new growth was occurring in several areas. Members of thirty-five Native American tribes—including the Cherokee, Choctaw, and Creek in the Southeast—became Baháʼís during the plan. In South Carolina and Georgia in particular, African Americans in cities, small towns, and rural areas showed signs of high receptivity to the faith. Across the country, the community was growing at its fastest rate since the 1890s. By 1963, membership was more than ten thousand, with some twelve hundred new enrollments in each of the previous few years. About a third of the new believers were young people ages fifteen to twenty, and various activities for children and youth, including Baháʼí associations on college and university campuses, became widespread. After lagging during the first half of the plan, its administrative goals had been surpassed after Shoghi Effendi's death. At Ridván 1963, there were 331 Local Spiritual Assemblies in the United States, of which 111 were incorporated—well above the goals of 300 and 100, respectively. Even in sparsely populated Alaska, the growth of the community had prompted Shoghi Effendi to call for the establishment of a separate National Spiritual Assembly for the territory in 1957, the first time such a body had been created in a political subdivision of a country.[62]

In South Carolina, the faith had grown both quantitatively and qualitatively. In ten years the state's Baháʼí community had more than doubled in size, to nearly eighty adults and probably as many children and youth. They resided in seventeen localities, from cities to hamlets. At the end of the plan there were four Local Spiritual Assemblies, in Greenville, Greenville County, Florence County, and St. Helena Island, and one of these had achieved incorporation as well as secured statewide recognition for the Baháʼí marriage ceremony. Renewed efforts to teach the faith to African Americans, including the working class and the middle class, young and old, rural and urban dwellers, had met with initial success in several localities. At the end of the plan, African Americans accounted for at least half of the statewide community, surpassing their proportion of the population at large. And they had begun to bring aspects of their rich cultural and religious heritage—for example, congregational singing and embracing the faith as kinship networks rather than as individuals—with them into the Baháʼí movement. The statewide community reached the end of the plan still numerically quite small in relation to the state's population but with a more vibrant interracial fellowship than ever and stronger legal, administrative, and cultural bases for further growth.[63]

Altogether, the experience in the state during the Ten Year Plan appeared to vindicate Louis Gregory's assessment, made decades earlier, of the spiritual receptivity of African Americans, as well as Shoghi Effendi's more recent insistence on bringing the faith to them in larger numbers. Lillie Abercrombie recalled that William Bidwell, observing the revitalization of the Greenville Bahá'í community that began during the late 1950s, recognized the wisdom in Shoghi Effendi's analysis. Bidwell admitted that his priority all along had been reaching the white population: "The whites were the ones doing bad things and the ones who needed to be taught. So that's what I tried to do, but with little result. Now, as I look back . . . I wish I had tried to teach more blacks. If I had, maybe things would have been different." Perhaps the most important lesson of the decade in South Carolina was that when the community made outreach to African Americans the priority, open-minded whites would be attracted to the faith in larger numbers as well. Given the growth that was apparent across the United States and around the world, by the end of the plan the Bahá'ís in South Carolina were beginning to conceive of themselves as part of an international, interracial mass movement in the making.[64]

Even the election of the Universal House of Justice, the crowning achievement of the Ten Year Plan, seemed to affirm more than half a century of interracial community-building in the South and link the Bahá'ís in South Carolina more closely with their co-religionists around the world. On April 21, 1963, the one hundredth anniversary of Bahá'u'lláh's arrival in the Garden of Ridván in Baghdad, at an International Convention held in 'Abdu'l-Bahá's house in Haifa, the ballots of the members of fifty-six National Spiritual Assemblies, representing the choice of a cross-section of the human race who had voted in local and national conventions the previous year, brought the Universal House of Justice into being. Conducted in a spiritual atmosphere free of nominations or campaigning, it was likely the first global democratic election. A week later more than six thousand believers, new and old, including an interracial delegation from South Carolina, assembled for the Bahá'í World Congress in London, considerable political instability and opposition to the faith in Iraq having made Baghdad an impractical venue. The South Carolinians, including Richard Abercrombie of Greenville, were astonished at the human diversity represented at the Congress, a living testimony to the worldwide community's success in the Ten Year Plan. And when the nine members of the Universal House of Justice were presented to the gathering, they could not help but notice that one of them was a southerner of African descent. Born in 1918 in Washington, D.C., to mixed-race Virginia migrants who had become Bahá'ís some six years before, Amoz Everett Gibson had grown up in the integrated children's classes and Nineteen Day Feasts that Louis Gregory and others had worked so hard to create. A World War II veteran, public schoolteacher with a master's degree, and home-front pioneer on the Navajo Reservation, Gibson had also been, until the election the previous week in Haifa, one of two black members of the National Spiritual Assembly.[65]

With his roots in the early Washington community, the template and staging-ground for the faith's development in the South, Amoz Gibson's election to the Universal House of Justice was a testimony to the struggles and accomplishments of southern Bahá'ís over the previous half-century. Before the civil rights movement reached its apogee in the mid-1960s, black and white Bahá'ís in South Carolina and other southern states had managed to establish and nurture a new religious culture in which the unity and equality of the diverse members of the human race were not only cherished goals but the normative practice of the community. They had contributed to the building of a new global religious polity, working together in their faith's unique governance system as both voters and candidates, as members of Local Spiritual Assemblies, as delegates to the National Convention, and as members of the National Spiritual Assembly. Now, one of their fellows, a black man from the region's mother community, had been elected to the faith's highest office. Well before decisive federal action removed the legal basis for the Jim Crow order, the Bahá'ís of South Carolina, a microcosm of their state's population, had essentially dismantled the color line within their own ranks, contributing decisively to the development of a new model of community, identity, and polity that was at once local and global in scope.

Coda

Toward a Bahá'í Mass Movement, 1963–1968

More than any other religious group in the state, by the middle of the 1960s the Bahá'ís of South Carolina embodied the vision of the "beloved community" that Martin Luther King Jr. had articulated as the civil rights movement's ultimate goal: a spiritualized polity, rooted in Christian millennial expectation and characterized by justice, love, and the "total interrelatedness" of all people. Notwithstanding the leap forward that the Ten Year Plan represented globally, however, the Bahá'ís' small numbers in South Carolina and elsewhere severely limited their ability to promote the wholesale social transformation anticipated in their sacred scriptures and for which enlightened leaders of thought like King were increasingly calling. Some six months after its formation, the Universal House of Justice wrote pointedly that in order for the worldwide Bahá'í community to "extend its influence into all strata of society," it must "grow rapidly in size." Referring to the achievements of the previous decade, the body wrote that the "foundation of the Kingdom has been securely laid, the framework has been raised," making further expansion both possible and necessary. The next task facing the worldwide community, it wrote, was to "gather the peoples and kindreds of the world into the ark which the Hand of God has built." Announcing a Nine Year Plan (1964–1973), the first in a series that would continue Shoghi Effendi's pattern of global teaching plans, it called for "a huge expansion of the Cause of God" marked by consolidation of the gains of the previous decade, the continued dispersal of pioneers to new territories, and a "vast increase in the number of Bahá'ís" around the world. Early on, the House of Justice encouraged all National Spiritual Assemblies to experiment with the methods that had successfully introduced the faith to the "masses of mankind" in rural areas of several countries during the previous plan. It also outlined a campaign designed to bring the faith to the attention of the world's political and religious leaders, set for 1967 and 1968 to coincide with the centenary of Bahá'u'lláh's initial proclamation of his mission to the monarchs and ecclesiastics of his own time.[1]

In Greenville, South Carolina's largest local Bahá'í community, the opening years of the Nine Year Plan saw continued measured growth, both in new members and seekers and in public activities in support of civil rights. These trends continued even after Richard and Joy Benson and their children, who had been central actors over the course of almost a decade in the revitalization of the Greenville community, left for Guam as international pioneers in late 1966. In South Carolina as a whole, however, there was little discernible growth.[2]

"Dark Heart"

In the second half of the 1960s, as formal racial barriers faded across the South and cultural and political upheavals rocked the country, imperatives within the Bahá'í community met heightened social and spiritual concerns in American society at large. In October 1967, in a message to six intercontinental conferences called to commemorate the centenary and to generate commitments to fulfill the goals of the Nine Year Plan, the Universal House of Justice indicated that a "hundred-year respite" since the beginning of Bahá'u'lláh's proclamation had come to an end. Its political and religious leaders having largely rejected Bahá'u'lláh's counsels, humanity was now entering "the dark heart of this age of transition," a long period of increasing social disintegration along the route to the global order that he had envisioned. But the House of Justice did not counsel despair. Amidst the deepening gloom, it wrote, the Bahá'ís would find new opportunities to extend the influence of the faith: "Sustained by our love for each other and given power through the Administrative Order . . . the Army of Light can achieve such victories as will astonish posterity."[3]

World events during the following year certainly seemed to bear out the prediction of increasing chaos. In Nigeria, Africa's most populous state, secessionist warfare in the southeast resulted in a widely publicized humanitarian crisis. In Tokyo and several European capitals, massive demonstrations against the war in Vietnam ended in violent confrontations with police. In France, student protests led to a general strike that paralyzed the country and nearly toppled the government, while in Czechoslovakia, Soviet troops invaded to overthrow a new liberalizing regime. On the eve of the opening of the Olympic Games in Mexico City, soldiers killed more than five hundred students demonstrating for greater democracy.[4]

The United States was hardly immune from social and political upheaval. In January 1968, Viet Cong guerillas launched the Tet offensive, a massive assault against the South Vietnamese government and its U.S. allies that belied American civilian and military leaders' confident public assertions that their forces were close to winning. Support for the war effort among the public and in the mass media plummeted, and the Democratic Party—the dominant force in American politics for a generation—began to splinter. Two anti-war senators mounted challenges to the sitting president, Lyndon Johnson, for the party's nomination, and in a televised address on the last day of March, Johnson stunned the country by announcing that he would not seek a second full term in the election that fall. Four days later, Rev. Martin Luther King Jr. was shot and killed on the balcony of a motel in Memphis, where he had come to assist a strike of black sanitation workers. News of the assassination spread quickly across the country, and black residents in some 125 cities took to the streets to pour out their grief and anger. The rioting, the worst in a wave of ghetto uprisings that had begun in the summer of 1964, seemed to confirm what King himself had come to fear: in the face of white intransigence and black impatience with the slow pace of change, there might be nothing civil rights leaders could do but let violence "take its course."[5]

Indeed, King's assassination and the riots that followed heralded a season of unprecedented violence and political upheaval. At the end of April, New York police forcefully removed black and white student radicals who were occupying buildings at Columbia University, leading to demonstrations that shut down the university. In June, a Palestinian nationalist assassinated Sen. Robert F. Kennedy, younger brother of the slain president and front-runner in the Democratic primaries. In August, Chicago police used tear gas and nightsticks against anti-war activists, counterculture radicals, and journalists outside the Democratic National Convention, while inside the hall, a deeply divided party nominated Vice President Hubert Humphrey, a close associate of Johnson, as its presidential candidate. In the fall general election campaign, former Alabama governor and third-party candidate George Wallace set the tone by calling for "law and order," an appeal to many whites' resentment of Johnson's domestic policy initiatives and four years of campus protests and urban uprisings. Wallace and former vice president Richard M. Nixon, the Republican candidate, won most of the South, signaling an end to white southerners' traditional loyalty to the Democratic Party. In one of the closest elections in American political history, Nixon emerged as the victor without receiving a majority of the vote.

In early February, deadly violence came home to South Carolina when state highway patrolmen opened fire on a crowd at State College in Orangeburg, the first shooting of unarmed student demonstrators on an American university campus. Nearly four years after the passage of the Civil Rights Act of 1964, the young people—all local high school and college students—had been protesting the continued segregation of Orangeburg's only bowling alley. The culmination of three nights of tension between students and police, the shooting left three students dead and more than thirty injured, the majority shot from the side or rear as they dove for cover from the advancing highway patrolmen. At a press conference the morning after the shooting, Gov. Robert McNair, who had been elected as a racial moderate, expressed primary concern not for the dead and injured but for South Carolina's public image, blaming the violence on "black power advocates." Based on reports by the state police, McNair believed that the protests in Orangeburg had been part of the national Black Power movement and pinned the blame on Cleveland Sellers, a young South Carolina native and veteran civil rights worker who had come to the State College campus to develop "Black Awareness" among students. Later, nine highway patrolmen were acquitted of civil rights violations in connection with the shootings, and Sellers, who had come to campus that night to attempt to quiet the students, was convicted of rioting and sentenced to a year in prison. The violence at Orangeburg and the miscarriage of justice that followed it left many black South Carolinians shaken and bitter. Rev. I. DeQuincey Newman, field secretary for the South Carolina NAACP, lamented that "despite all that might be considered progress in terms of interracial cooperation, beneath the surface South Carolina is just about in the same boat as Alabama and Mississippi." Annette Reynolds, a State College student who had grown up in a middle-class home in Darlington, recalled the event as a traumatic first encounter with the ugliness of racism. On the night of the shootings, she was walking from the library with two friends when they saw the crowd of students. One friend, Samuel Hammond, went to investigate and was killed in the ensuing gunfire. Like many other students, Reynolds fled the campus the day after the shootings. She refused to return out of fear for her safety, opting instead to enroll as the first black student at Limestone College in Gaffney. She became a Bahá'í a few years later.[6]

Toward a Bahá'í Mass Movement

Against a backdrop of increasing turmoil at home and abroad, Bahá'í teaching and community development in South Carolina accelerated. In 1966, when the National Spiritual Assembly appointed a new statewide teaching committee, called the State Goals Committee, there were seventy-six voting-age Bahá'ís in nineteen localities around South Carolina, almost the same as at the end of the Ten Year Plan three years earlier. That fall, the annual state convention was a small affair, held in the banquet room of a Columbia restaurant. Only twenty-two people voted in person, selecting two white South Carolina natives as the convention officers and a black South Carolina native, Charles Abercrombie of Greenville, as their delegate to the 1967 Bahá'í National Convention. But there were indications of a new vibrancy in several quarters. In Greenville, the Local Spiritual Assembly reported a population of nineteen adults and nine youth, with a full calendar of activities open to the public, four marriages, a doubling of contributions to the local fund, and four enrollments during the previous year. In the Pee Dee region, Jordan Young's black and white patients arranged for him to speak about "Bahá'u'lláh of Persia" to large audiences in local churches, and Bahá'ís and their friends in Florence, Dillon, and Lake City gathered frequently to observe the Nineteen Day Feast and Holy Days. More than a half-century after Louis Gregory's first visit to his hometown as a Bahá'í, a local community was finally emerging in Charleston with the settlement of new pioneers—including a white Charleston expatriate who had become a Bahá'í in the navy—and the enrollment of local residents.[7]

With regular community activities in the Augusta, Beaufort, Charleston, Columbia, Florence, and Greenville areas as a solid basis for expansion, an increasing pool of energetic teachers willing to travel within the state, and occasional visits by teachers from outside, there was a steady stream of enrollments during 1967 and 1968. Virtually every issue of the State Goals Committee's newsletter welcomed new believers. They included individuals in the established urban communities, in nearby small towns, and, in the midst of an escalating conflict in Vietnam, on military bases: Charleston, Charleston Air Force Base, Columbia, Clemson, Darlington, Florence, Fort Jackson, Greenville, Hanahan, Myrtle Beach Air Force Base, Pendleton, St. Stephen, and St. Helena Island. In the Columbia area, growth during the summer and fall of 1968 was robust enough that a new Local Spiritual Assembly for Richland County and a Bahá'í student association at Benedict College were formed the following year.[8]

Also during 1968, home-front pioneers settled in Rock Hill and Winnsboro, bringing the faith to two towns that had been stops on the first Freedom Ride seven years earlier. In June, a white family originally from the Midwest, Charles and Helen Thomas and their children, relocated from Laurinburg, North Carolina, to Rock Hill. They quickly began teaching acquaintances made through his chiropractic office and her sewing business. At about the same time, three families also from the Midwest—two black and one white—settled in Winnsboro, part of a regional plan to establish the faith in small towns in several southern states. They secured employment or started businesses, enrolled their children in the segregated local schools, and began to teach their neighbors and host interracial gatherings in each other's homes. One of the new Winnsboro pioneers was Elizabeth Allison Martin, formerly of Adrian, Michigan, whose family had learned of the faith from Louis Gregory in Nashville and whose mother and brother had helped establish the Local Spiritual Assembly of Greenville. Another was Lacey Crawford of Chicago, a professional photographer who had become a Bahá'í after shooting a major story on the faith for *Ebony* magazine. By 1968, the number of adult Bahá'ís in the state, including new believers and home-front pioneers, had nearly doubled to 132. The 1968 state convention, held at Columbia's Masonic Temple, was three times as large as the one two years earlier, with 49 voting adults and some 20 children and youth in attendance.[9]

While the South Carolina community was growing in numbers, the State Goals Committee also encouraged active engagement in public relations. In late March 1968, only six weeks after the shootings in Orangeburg, a delegation of Columbia Bahá'ís presented a new volume entitled *The Proclamation of Bahá'u'lláh*, comprising passages from his letters to the kings and rulers of the world, to Gov. Robert McNair as part of the campaign called for by the Universal House of Justice. Immediately after Martin Luther King's assassination in early April, the committee sent a telegram of sympathy to his widow, Coretta Scott King, assuring her of the prayers of the South Carolina Bahá'ís "for the spiritual progress of humanity." Later that month, Horace Brown, a member of the committee and the lone believer in Spartanburg, mounted a local proclamation effort that involved some five hundred mailed announcements, press coverage, and a favorable meeting with the mayor. In the fall, the committee organized the presentation of a booklet about the ghetto uprisings, prepared by the National Spiritual Assembly and entitled *Why Our Cities Burn*, to state-level government officials and encouraged individuals to share it with friends and business associates.[10]

The growth in South Carolina was part of a nationwide trend. Between 1963 and 1968, the Baháʼí population of the United States grew by around 60 percent, from eleven thousand to nearly eighteen thousand. Most of the new believers were teenagers and young adults, and college campuses became centers of Baháʼí activity. In 1967, a national task force proposed concerted action to teach the faith to blacks, including sending youth and young adults "to live and teach in [black] neighborhoods and towns until a breakthrough occurs." In June 1968, a national youth conference held at the temple in Chicago adopted a five-year youth program, subsidiary to the Nine Year Plan, that called for deploying 500 young pioneers at home and abroad, including 350 in the southern states. Meeting less than three weeks after Robert Kennedy's assassination, the conference attendees focused their deliberations on how to bring the Baháʼí teachings to the younger generations more effectively than before. In November, buoyed by their own successes as well as by national developments, the Baháʼís who assembled at the South Carolina state convention adopted a new expansion goal for the rest of the Nine Year Plan: to form three new Local Spiritual Assemblies per year in the state during 1969, 1970, and 1971 and four per year during 1972 and 1973. Given the South Carolina community's record of slow growth over several decades, such a vision must have seemed audacious. However, neither the Baháʼís in South Carolina nor the national leaders of their religion had any idea of the magnitude of the changes that would come in the wake of Jim Crow's demise. At the end of the Nine Year Plan in 1973, the goals of the 1968 state convention—if anyone remembered them at all—would have appeared as an artifact from another era. For beginning in 1969, Baháʼís in the Deep South, led by the South Carolina community, launched an energetic new teaching program that resulted in growth that was unprecedented for the faith anywhere in the Western world. The expansion they wrought would permanently alter the identity, structure, and aspirations of the Baháʼí movement in the United States, cementing the place of the South Carolina Baháʼí community in the sweeping social transformations of the twentieth century.[11]

Notes

Abbreviations

ABA	Augusta Baháʾí Archives, Augusta, Ga.
ARC	Avery Research Center for African American History and Culture, College of Charleston, S.C.
CBA	Columbia Baháʾí Archives, Columbia, S.C.
EBA	Eliot Baháʾí Archives, Eliot, Maine
FY	Elmer Kenneally, "Fifty Years of the Baháʾí Faith in Greenville, S.C., 1939–1989," TS, Greenville Baháʾí Archives, Greenville, S.C.
HBC	Esther Sego, "History of the Bahaʾi Cause in Augusta, Ga.," TS, Augusta Baháʾí Archives, Augusta, Ga.
H-KFP	Hannen-Knobloch Family Papers, National Baháʾí Archives of the United States, Wilmette, Ill.
HEHP	H. Emogene Hoagg Papers, National Baháʾí Archives of the United States, Wilmette, Ill.
NBA	National Baháʾí Archives of the United States, Wilmette, Ill.
SCDAH	South Carolina Department of Archives and History, Columbia, S.C.
SR	Louis G. Gregory, "Some Recollections of the Early Days of the Bahai Faith in Washington, D.C.," TS, Louis G. Gregory Papers, National Baháʾí Archives of the United States, Wilmette, Ill.
SW	*Star of the West*
TMW	Gayle Morrison, *To Move the World: Louis G. Gregory and the Advancement of Racial Unity in America* (Wilmette, Ill.: Baháʾí Publishing Trust, 1982).
USBC	United States Bureau of the Census. Census of Population and Housing.

Preface

1. Among general introductions to Baháʼí history, theology, and community, two of the best are Hatcher and Martin, *Baháʼí Faith*, and Peter Smith, *Introduction*. For South Carolina Baháʼí population data and comparison with other religious bodies, see Brisley interview; Kristina Lee Knaus, "One Region, Many Faiths," *State* (Columbia, S.C.), September 5, 2003; and Reid Wilson, "The Second-Largest Religion in Each State," *Washington Post* website, GovBeat, June 4, 2014, accessed November 9, 2014, http://www.washingtonpost.com/blogs/govbeat/wp/2014/06/04/the-second-largest-religion-in-each-state/. The maps in Wilson's blog post come from *2010 U.S. Religion Census: Religious Congregations & Membership Study*, published by the Association of Statisticians of American Religious Bodies (www.asarb.org) and distributed by the Association of Religion Data Archives (www.thearda.com).

2. So far the most comprehensive treatment of South Carolina's religious history is Lippy, ed., *Religion in South Carolina*, based on a 1991 conference at Lutheran Theological Seminary in Columbia. While most of the essays deal more or less with issues of race, the volume offers scant treatment of Afro-Carolinian Christianity and of the roles of religion in the state's long civil rights movement.

3. Kahn, "Encounter of Two Myths," 235, 262–65; Stockman, "U.S. Baháʼí Community Membership," 27. With growth of the Baháʼí population elsewhere during the last quarter of the twentieth century, South Carolina's portion of the total fell. In the early twenty-first, however, it remained the state with the second-largest Baháʼí population (after California) and the only one in which the Baháʼí Faith was the second-largest religious body. (*2010 U.S. Religion Census*, accessed through the Association of Religion Data Archives)

4. *American Baháʼí*, special edition, October 1970, 1–3.

5. "Carolina Story," *American Baháʼí*, February 1971, 4; Bennett, "Baháʼí: A Way of Life for Millions" and booklet of the same name in author's possession.

6. Universal House of Justice, *Messages, 1968–1973*, 65; *American Baháʼí*, May 1971, 4–5; Hampson, "Growth and Spread," 281.

7. "Operation 'Gabriel,'" *American Baháʼí*, January 1972, 3; Hampson, "Growth and Spread," 344–50. For an overview and analysis of larger-scale growth of the Baháʼí Faith around the world in the second half of the twentieth century, see Universal House of Justice, *Century of Light*, chapter 9.

8. Gustav Niebuhr, "Hemingway Journal: A Little Bit of a Change From Old-Time Religion," *New York Times*, March 31, 2000 (for Radio Baháʼí); Stephanie Harvin, "The Ripple Effect: Influencing the Tide of History," *Charleston (S.C.) Post and Courier*, February 2, 2003 (for the museum). Prominent South Carolinians to embrace the Baháʼí Faith included influential jazz trumpeter and Cheraw native John Birks "Dizzy" Gillespie (1917–1993); physicist Dr. Ronald E. McNair (1950–1986), a Lake City native who was the second African American in space;

and award-winning Columbia television journalist and humanitarian Susan Audé (b. 1952). Likenesses of both Gillespie and McNair appear in the African American Monument on the grounds of the South Carolina State House, dedicated in 2001, and Audé was awarded the Order of the Palmetto, the state's highest civilian honor, in 2006. Gillespie became a Baháʾí in Los Angeles in 1968 and was well known for mentioning the faith (and his hometown) in appearances worldwide. In 1976 he was invited to play for the South Carolina General Assembly in the state house, and in 1985 he and his band were the headline guests for the inauguration of WLGI Radio Baháʾí near Hemingway. McNair and other members of his family participated in Baháʾí activities for children and youth in Lake City, and he maintained his Baháʾí affiliation until his death in the space shuttle *Challenger* disaster. Audé withdrew from the faith in 2010.

9. The basic elements of the new global strategy for the growth and development of the Baháʾí Faith are outlined in Universal House of Justice, *Four Year Plan* and *Five Year Plan*.

Introduction

1. Du Bois, *Souls of Black Folk*, 9. On Du Bois's approach to the relationship between religion and society, essential reading is Blum, *American Prophet*, and Kahn, *Divine Discontent*, both of which attempt to correct the long-held notion that Du Bois was an atheist or agnostic. On the Protestant origins of Jim Crow, see another important work by Blum, *Reforging the White Republic*.

2. Du Bois, "Men of the Month"; Du Bois, "Fourth Annual Conference." For the arrival and early spread of the Baháʾí Faith in the United States, see Stockman, *Baháʾí Faith in America*: vol. 1, *Origins*, and vol. 2, *Early Expansion*. The extent and significance of the long and sometimes rocky relationship between Du Bois (and his first wife, Nina Gomer Du Bois) and the Baháʾí Faith has yet to be acknowledged, much less adequately explored, in the field of American religious history. Two initial contributions are Buck, "Case of W.E.B. Du Bois," and Mount, "Troubled Modernity."

3. Baháʾuʾlláh, *Tablets*, 167.

4. Baháʾuʾlláh, *Tablets*, 87. According to the World Religion Database, the Baháʾí Faith was the fastest-growing major religion between 1910 and 2010, with an estimated total of more than seven million adherents worldwide in 2010. (Johnson and Grim, *World's Religions in Figures*, 59)

5. Du Bois to Ruth R. Shipley, March 23, 1953, in Aptheker, ed., *Correspondence of W.E.B. Du Bois*, 345. Although the composition of the Universal House of Justice, the supreme governing council of the Baháʾí Faith, is an imperfect indicator of the diversity of the worldwide community, it is interesting to note that of the ten Americans who have been members, three have been black, including one Jamai-

can immigrant. There was an African American member of the body in each of its first fifty years (until 2013, when, coincidentally, the first native-born African, a Zambian, was elected).

6. Smith, *Introduction*, 82–83. Among the best-known works by historians in the Middle Eastern Studies vein are Amanat, *Resurrection and Renewal*, and Cole, *Modernity and the Millennium*. Notable recent exceptions to this trend are three works by sociologists: McMullen, *The Bahá'í*, which focuses on the Bahá'í communities of greater Atlanta, Georgia, and Saeidi, *Logos and Civilization* and *Gate of the Heart*.

7. While his field of inquiry was certainly larger than the United States, one notable exception is the eminent British historian Arnold Toynbee, a pioneer in the field of world history. In his massive twelve-volume *Study of History*, an assessment of the rise and fall of all the world's recorded civilizations, Toynbee predicts that the next stage in human social evolution is the birth of a universal religion that will foster the emergence of a universal state on a planetary scale. Based on his model, he identifies the Bahá'í Faith and the Ahmadiyya sect of Islam as the only two possible candidates for that role. (Toynbee, *Study of History*, vol. 5, 174–76; vol. 7, 417–18, 771; vol. 8, 117) Elsewhere he seems more impressed with the Bahá'í Faith than the Ahmadiyya. See, for example, Toynbee, *Christianity among the Religions*, 104.

8. TMW; Stockman, "Bahá'í Faith and American Protestantism," *Bahá'í Faith in America*: vol. 1, *Origins*, and vol. 2, *Early Expansion*, and *'Abdu'l-Bahá in America*. Also invaluable to the study of Bahá'í history in North America are several volumes in the Studies in Bábí and Bahá'í History series (1982–) by Kalimát Press, an independent Bahá'í publisher in Los Angeles. Works on moments of interracial cooperation in the post–Civil War South that I have found particularly insightful include Kelley, *Hammer and Hoe*; Letwin, *Challenge of Interracial Unionism*; and Sullivan, *Days of Hope*. Among those that place religion at the center of their analysis (of black activism, interracial cooperation, or both), some of the most important include Chappell, *Stone of Hope*; Hahn, *Nation under Our Feet*; Harvey, *Freedom's Coming*; Higginbotham, *Righteous Discontent*; and K'Meyer, *Interracialism and Christian Community*.

9. For a concise statement of the Protestant hegemony theory, see, for example, Reed, *Enduring South*, 57–59. In addition to those by Chappelle, Higginbotham, Harvey, and K'Meyer noted above, important works on religious diversity and dissent in the post–Civil War South include Conser and Payne, eds., *Southern Crossroads*; Norman and Armentrout, eds., *Religion in the Contemporary South*; Schweiger and Mathews, eds., *Religion in the American South*; and Stricklin, *Genealogy of Dissent*.

10. On early Pentecostalism, see Cox, *Fire from Heaven*; MacRobert, *Black Roots and White Racism of Early Pentecostalism*; and Wacker, *Heaven Below*.

11. For an analysis of the Bahá'í principle of the equality of the sexes and a histori-

cal overview of the roles of women in the Bahá'í community, see Khan and Khan, *Advancement of Women*.

12. McDonough, "Men and Women of Good Will"; Letwin, *Challenge of Interracial Unionism*; Kelley, *Hammer and Hoe*.

13. K'Meyer, *Interracialism and Christian Community*.

14. Louis G. Gregory, "A Gift to Race Enlightenment," *World Order* 2, no. 1 (April 1936): 36–39, quoted in TMW, 28–29.

15. Hahn, *Nation under Our Feet*, 47; Blum, *Reforging the White Republic*, 3–4.

16. Bahá'u'lláh, *Gleanings*, 96; *Tabernacle of Unity*, sec. 2.5.

17. As long-lived, broadly based, and consequential as it was, South Carolina's phase of the civil rights movement remains marginalized in the traditional "Montgomery to Memphis" version of the national civil rights narrative. Among specialists, who have done much to broaden that story over the past few decades, South Carolina has recently begun to command greater attention (and as the notes testify, this book is deeply indebted to them). To date, however, there has been no monograph treatment of the South Carolina movement across the entire Jim Crow era. The closest thing to it, Newby's *Black Carolinians* (1973), remains invaluable but is more than a generation out of date.

18. Fairclough, *Race and Democracy*, xl–xlii.

Chapter 1. First Contacts, 1898–1916

1. *Washington Bee*, November 18, 1905, and December 11, 1909.

2. SR, 1; "Republican Meeting," *Washington Bee*, April 23, 1904; "The Southern White Man," *Washington Bee*, August 27, 1904; "The Civil Rights Law," *Washington Bee*, January 1, 1904; "No Negro Wanted," *Washington Bee*, September 3, 1907. James A. Cobb was one of Booker T. Washington's allies in the national capital; likely as a result of the latter's recommendations, he was appointed assistant U.S. attorney and judge of the District of Columbia Municipal Court. Correspondence between Cobb and Washington and his aides was extensive. For evidence of Washington's influence in securing appointments for Cobb, see Booker T. Washington to Theodore Roosevelt, September 19, 1907, *Washington Papers*, vol. 9, *1906–8*, ed. Harlan and Smock, 337–38; and Washington to Joseph Patrick Tumulty, August 4, 1914, *Washington Papers*, vol. 13, *1914–15*, ed. Harlan and Smock, 108.

3. SR, 1–2.

4. SR, 2; USBC, *Twelfth Census, 1900*; USBC, *Fourteenth Census, 1920*; USBC, *Fifteenth Census, 1930*. On Getsinger, one of the best-informed of the early American Bahá'ís, see Metelmann, *Lua Getsinger*, and Stockman, *Origins*. For accounts of Kheiralla's career and of his unsuccessful attempt to usurp authority from 'Abdu'l-Bahá, see Smith, "American Bahá'í Community," in *Studies in Bábí and Bahá'í History*, vol. 1, ed. Momen, 85–99; and Stockman, *Origins*. While Nellie Gray has been

hard to positively identify in the historical record, circumstantial evidence suggests that she and Mildred York were cousins. Louis Gregory indicates that his second Bahá'í meeting was at their home. In 1910, Mildred York lived at home with her mother, Carrie York, two sisters, and two nieces. In 1900, another young woman, Jennie Gray, listed as an adopted daughter, lived in the home. In the 1920 census, Jennie Gray is listed as a boarder, in 1930, as a cousin. Like Carrie York, Jennie Gray's parents were from North Carolina. Nellie Gray could easily have been another Gray cousin who lived with the Yorks for some time. In Washington in 1900, there was a Nellie Gray living with her mother, Mary Gray, a washerwoman born in North Carolina, and three younger sisters; she would have been twenty years old at the time of the meeting Louis Gregory attended.

5. SR, 2. The best scholarly biographies of the twin founders of the Bahá'í Faith are Balyuzi, *The Báb* and *Bahá'u'lláh: King of Glory*. For more recent comprehensive analyses of their major writings, see Saeidi, *Gate of the Heart* and *Logos and Civilization*. Major works of Bahá'u'lláh addressed to Christian audiences include the Most Holy Tablet, likely written for a Bahá'í of Syrian Christian background, and letters sent to Pope Pius IX, Queen Victoria, Emperor Napoleon III, and Czar Alexander II. See Bahá'u'lláh, *Tablets*, 7–17, and *Summons*, 54–96. For an early association of the Plain of Sharon with a future messianic figure, see Isaiah 35:1–2. The best scholarly biography of 'Abdu'l-Bahá is Balyuzi, *'Abdu'l-Bahá*.

6. Gregory, *Heavenly Vista*.

7. SR, 2–3. Personal devotional practices in the Bahá'í Faith include an annual period of fasting and daily obligatory prayer, scripture reading, and meditation. Bahá'u'lláh, the Báb, and 'Abdu'l-Bahá revealed hundreds of prayers for individual and collective worship. For a representative sample, see *Bahá'í Prayers*.

8. Gregory, *Heavenly Vista*. The notion of the Kingdom of God on earth is both a persistent concern in American Protestantism and an organizing principle of the Bahá'í Faith. The classic treatment is Neibuhr, *Kingdom of God in America*. More recent works include Boyer, *When Time Shall Be No More*, and Moorhead, *World without End*. In terms of Protestant typologies, Bahá'í thought contains elements of both pre- and postmillennialism (that is, whether Christ returns to himself inaugurate God's Kingdom on earth, or the efforts of Christians to spread the Gospel and improve the world prepare the Kingdom for his eventual coming), but it differs radically from Christian orthodoxy by placing the return of Christ in the past. In the Bahá'í conception, the realization of the Kingdom will result from the operation of spiritual forces released by the return of Christ (the appearance of the Báb and Bahá'u'lláh) on the Bahá'í community, the world's political and religious leaders, and the masses of humanity over a historical period of at least one thousand years. For American Protestants who became Bahá'ís, then, a powerful motif of their religious heritage took on new, immedi-

ate, and revolutionary meaning. For Bahá'u'lláh's interpretation of the biblical and Qur'anic terms "heaven" and "earth," see Bahá'u'lláh, *Kitáb-i-Íqán*, esp. ¶ 51.

9. Thornton Chase, *In Galilee* (Los Angeles: Kalimát Press, 1985; first published 1908), 71, quoted in Smith, "American Bahá'í Community," 102. Bahá'u'lláh appointed 'Abdu'l-Bahá as "Center of the Covenant" (*Markaz-i míthaq-i iláhí*) in passages in the Súriy-i-Ghusn ("Tablet of the Branch"), the Kitáb-i-Aqdas ("Most Holy Book"), and the Kitáb-i-Ahd ("Book of the Covenant"). See Bahá'u'lláh, *Kitáb-i-Aqdas*, ¶ 121, 174; *Tablets*, 217–23; and quoted in Shoghi Effendi, *World Order of Bahá'u'lláh*, 135. In this context, the "Covenant" refers to the system of institutional relationships by which Bahá'u'lláh protected his religion from schism after his passing. For a historical overview of the Covenant, see Taherzadeh, *Covenant of Bahá'u'lláh*.

10. Gregory, *Heavenly Vista*; SR, 1. For the practice of writing "supplications" to 'Abdu'l-Bahá, see Smith, "American Bahá'í Community," 105.

11. Charlotte E. Brittingham Dixon, "How I Became a Believer and Was Given the Bahai Revelation by and through Visions," TS, Charlotte E. Brittingham Dixon Recollections, NBA, quoted in Stockman, *Origins*, 118; Stockman, *Origins*, 130. For scholarly treatment of William Miller and his followers, see, for example, Rowe, *God's Strange Work*. Bahá'í authors have argued that Miller's interpretation of the time prophecies of the Bible correctly identified the date of the Báb's declaration of his mission in May 1844 but that the Millerites, adhering to a literal approach to the concept of "return," missed his appearance. The classic popular Bahá'í treatment of such prophecies is Sears, *Thief in the Night*.

12. Mírzá Abu'l-Fazl's important introductory work, *Bahá'í Proofs*, was written and published during his stay in Washington. For a discussion of the work and of the impact of Mírzá Abu'l-Fazl's American sojourn, see Stockman, *Early Expansion*, 81–87. For Washington's early role in publishing and communication in the American Bahá'í movement, see Stockman, *Early Expansion*, 220. The Bahá'í calendar consists of nineteen months of nineteen days each, plus four intercalary days (five in leap years). Bahá'u'lláh enjoined his followers "to offer a feast, once in every month, though only water be served; for God hath purposed to bind hearts together, albeit through both earthly and heavenly means." (*Kitáb-i-Aqdas*, ¶ 57) This provision is the origin of the Bahá'í institution of the Nineteen Day Feast. For its establishment in the United States, see Stockman, *Early Expansion*, 137.

13. Stockman, *Early Expansion*, 137, 224.

14. Bahá'u'lláh, *Hidden Words*, Arabic no. 68; USBC, *Twelfth Census, 1900*; USBC, *Thirteenth Census, 1910* (both for York family); *Branson's Raleigh City Directory, 1891*, 209; USBC, *Twelfth Census, 1900*; USBC, *Fourteenth Census, 1920* (all for Pope); Pauline Hannen to Mirza Ahmad Sohrab, May 1909, Ahmad Sohrab Papers, NBA, quoted in Buck, *Alain Locke*, 38; Stockman, *Early Expansion*, 224–26. Pocahontas Pope received a tablet from 'Abdu'l-Bahá in which he praised her for

arising to teach the faith, encouraged her to work for the "edification of the people," and, in a startling inversion of prevailing American racial imagery, compared her to the pupil of the eye that, while dark, was the "source of light." (Taylor, ed., *Pupil of the Eye*, 12–13)

15. Moses, "Lost World of the New Negro," 65, 67–72; Green, *Secret City*, 136, 154, 162. For additional treatment of black culture and politics in post-Reconstruction Washington, see Moore, *Leading the Race*; Moses, *Alexander Crummell*; and Moss, *American Negro Academy*.

16. Green, *Secret City*, 155–60, 163 (for the quote), 164–66.

17. Pauline Hannen to Mirza Ahmad Sohrab, May 1909; Jos. H. Hannen, *Bahai News* 1, no. 1 (March 21, 1910): 18–19; and Joseph H. Hannen, "Washington, D.C.," *Bahai News* 1, no. 3 (April 28, 1910): 19, both quoted in TMW, 33.

18. "Bethel Literary," *Washington Bee*, April 9, 1910; "Bethel Literary," *Washington Bee*, November 20, 1909; SR, 5.

19. 'Abdu'l-Bahá to Louis Gregory, translated November 17, 1909, Tablets of 'Abdu'l-Bahá, NBA, quoted in TMW, 7.

20. *Bahai News* 1, no. 1 (March 21, 1910): 18–19, quoted in TMW, 33.

21. "News Notes," *Bahai News* 1, no. 18 (February 7, 1911): 9; HBC, 2.

22. USBC, *Ninth Census, 1870*; USBC, *Fourteenth Census, 1920*; Jenkins, *Seizing the New Day*, 160–61. Ebenezer George was born in Camden, Kershaw District, South Carolina, and Mary Elizabeth George in Darlington. The family resided in Darlington as late as 1870.

23. TMW, 11–16.

24. Fraser, *Charleston!*, 160–61, 304–5, 309, 351; Edgar, *South Carolina*, 425–27; Fraser, *Charleston!*, 160–61, 309.

25. Edgar, *South Carolina*, 412, 448; Newby, *Black Carolinians*, 160–61; Fraser, *Charleston!*, 336; Doyle, *New Men, New Cities, New South*, 160, 310.

26. Morrison, "Louis George Gregory"; TMW, 11.

27. TMW, 13–14; National Park Service, Civil War Soldiers and Sailors Database, "George Gregory"; USBC, *Thirteenth Census, 1910*; TMW, 16–17; Morrison, "Louis George Gregory"; TMW, 11; *Afro-American Citizen* (Charleston, S.C.), January 17, 1900. For an excellent treatment of military service as a critical school of political education for freedmen, see Hahn, *Nation under Our Feet*, 89–102. On Avery Institute, a key institution in black Charleston from the 1860s to the 1950s, see Drago, *Initiative, Paternalism, and Race Relations*.

28. Louis G. Gregory to Joseph A. Hannen, November 9 and 12, 1910, H-KFP.

29. *Walsh's 1910 Charleston City Directory*, 642; Louis G. Gregory to Joseph A. Hannen, November 12, 1910, H-KFP; "Attorney Gregory South (From the Charleston Messenger)," *Washington Bee*, November 26, 1910. The biblical passage Gregory was referring to is Matthew 24:29–31. For the likely source of his interpretation, see Bahá'u'lláh, *Kitáb-i-Íqán*, ¶ 24, 74–83. Of the sixty-one attorneys or law firms in the

1910 Charleston city directory, only five—J. B. Edwards, John A. Gaillard, Edward T. Smith, Daniel B. Summers, and Alonzo E. Twine—were listed as "colored." Another black attorney, Thaddeus St. Mark Sasportas, lived in nearby Summerville in Dorchester County but handled cases in Charleston. (Burke and Hine, "South Carolina State College Law School," in Burke and Gergel, eds., *Matthew J. Perry*, 22)

30. USBC, *Twelfth Census, 1900*; National Park Service, Civil War Soldiers and Sailors Database, "Charles Twine"; USBC, *Thirteenth Census, 1910*; Tindall, *South Carolina Negroes*, 137–40; "Catalogue of the Teachers and Pupils of Avery Normal Institute, Charleston, S.C.," June 1899, Avery School Memorabilia Collection, ARC.

31. "He Had Wrong Religion," *Washington Bee*, November 25, 1911; "Afro-American Cullings," *Savannah (Ga.) Tribune*, February 10, 1912; Oldfield, "African American Bar," in Underwood and Burke, eds., *At Freedom's Door*, 129; Burke and Hine, "South Carolina State College Law School," in Burke and Gergel, eds., *Matthew J. Perry*, 22; *Walsh's 1910 Charleston City Directory*, 118–19; *State* (Columbia, S.C.), July 22, 1910 and August 6, 1910; I. E. Lowery, "Rev. I. E. Lowery's Column," *Southern Indicator* (Columbia, S.C.), February 19, 1921; Alonzo E. Twine to James R. Logan, August 12, 1898, James R. Logan Scrapbooks, ARC; "Resolutions Adopted by the Aurorean Coterie of Charleston, S.C.," February 6, 1907, Logan Scrapbooks, ARC; miscellaneous musical programs, Logan Scrapbooks, ARC; USBC, *Thirteenth Census, 1910*. Begun in 1797 and completed in 1809, the building housing Old Bethel United Methodist Church is the third-oldest surviving church structure in Charleston. Originally home to a biracial congregation, the building was moved in 1852 and again in 1880 to accommodate a growing rift between black and white members. ("Old Bethel United Methodist Church," National Register Properties in South Carolina, SCDAH website, accessed November 10, 2014, http://www.nationalregister.sc.gov/charleston/S10817710089/index.htm)

32. SR, 3. Several of Booker T. Washington's deputies in Washington, D.C., accused another man, Ralph Waldo Taylor, a journalist and auditor of the Department of the Navy, of being the "Sage of the Potomac." (Charles William Anderson to Booker T. Washington, September 26, 1913, *Washington Papers*, vol. 12, *1912–1914*, ed. Harlan and Smock, 297–99) Tyler vigorously denied the charge and said he had proof that Roscoe Conkling Bruce was the "Sage." (Ralph Waldo Tyler to Emmett Jay Scott, March 1, 1914, *Washington Papers*, vol. 12, *1912–1914*, ed. Harlan and Smock, 462–64)

33. "Public Men and Things," *Washington Bee*, January 7, 1911; "Public Men and Things," *Washington Bee*, June 24, 1911.

34. "Bahai Revelation," *Washington Bee*, November 11, 1911.

35. "He Had Wrong Religion," *Washington Bee*, November 25, 1911; "Afro-American Cullings," *Savannah (Ga.) Tribune*, February 10, 1912.

36. McCandless, *Moonlight, Magnolias, and Madness*, 179; "Alonzo Twine," South Carolina State Hospital Commitment Files, SCDAH. Twine may have been singing

a Christmas carol, "Chime on, Shine on," by George Frederick Root (1820–1895), a popular New England composer. The hymn includes the refrains, "Shine on, shine on, O Star!" and "Shine on! shine on! bright star of his love!" (Wendte, *Heart and Voice*, 246)

37. Edgar, *South Carolina*, 289; McCandless, *Moonlight, Magnolias, and Madness*, 283–84, 294–96; Record of Deaths 1893–1979, South Carolina State Hospital Records, SCDAH. On pellagra, see McCandless, *Moonlight, Magnolias, and Madness*, 284.

38. McCandless, *Moonlight, Magnolias, and Madness*, 284; Thompson, *Of Shattered Minds*, ed. Roof, 51; McCandless, *Moonlight, Magnolias, and Madness*, 274–75, 283, 287. In Alonzo Twine's case, the notes of his initial examination are copied verbatim from the commitment papers into the hospital's record book with no additional observations. There are notes of one or two subsequent examinations for almost every white male patient, but not a single black male during the years Twine was confined appears to have had a subsequent examination. (Personal History Book for Males, South Carolina State Hospital Records, SCDAH)

39. McCandless, *Moonlight, Magnolias, and Madness*, especially chapter 7; Newby, *Black Carolinians*, 67–79.

40. Lowery, I. E., "Rev. I. E. Lowery's Column," *Southern Indicator* (Columbia, S.C.), February 19, 1921.

41. Hampson, "Growth and Spread," 248; Thornton Chase to A. M. Bryant (copy), May 16, 1905, Thornton Chase Papers, NBA, quoted in Stockman, *Early Expansion*, 230. In 1906, Baháʼí groups in more than twenty localities reported to the USBC that they regularly rented public halls for activities, implying the existence at least of a community fund and a treasurer, if not also of a secretary and a librarian. (Stockman, *Early Expansion*, 230–31) On the early administrative development of the American Baháʼí community, see Stockman, *Early Expansion*, especially part 1. For the ordination of the House of Justice, see Baháʼu'lláh, *Kitáb-i-Aqdas*, ¶ 30.

42. Chase to Bryant, quoted in Stockman, *Early Expansion*, 230; Herrmann, "Baháʼí Faith in Kansas," in *Community Histories*, ed. Hollinger, 70–76, 79–80; Stockman, *Origins*, 105–9; Herrmann, "Baháʼí Faith in Kansas," in Hollinger, ed., *Community Histories*, 77–78; Chase to Bryant, quoted in Stockman, *Early Expansion*, 230.

43. Ayers, *Promise of the New South*, 24; Gregory, *Southern Diaspora*, 12–13. For a biography of True, see Rutstein, *Corinne True*. Diggett's obituary, written by her daughter, states that "she taught from Coast to Coast and from the Gulf to the Great Lakes" and that she personally served 'Abdu'l-Bahá on his visit to Chicago in 1912. (SW 10, no. 19 [March 2, 1920]: 346) She is likely the same person as Julia E. Diggett, who was elected to the Chicago Baháʼí "Women's Assembly" in 1909. (Stockman, *Early Expansion*, 322) For references to Coles, see Stockman, *Early Expansion*, 222; TMW, 42; and an obituary, SW 22, no. 4 (July 1931): 117.

44. Stockman, *Early Expansion*, 346; Clark, "Baháʼís of Baltimore," in Hollinger,

ed., *Community Histories*, 112–14; USBC, *Twelfth Census, 1900*; 'Abdu'l-Bahá, *Tablets*, vol. 2, 444. 'Abdu'l-Bahá's tablet seems to imply that Harry Doty was already a Bahá'í.

45. Stockman, *Early Expansion*, 346; "History," Austin, Tex., Bahá'í website, accessed November 15, 2014, http://www.austinbahai.org/?view=history; Stockman, *Origins*, 86–88, 93–94; Stockman, *Early Expansion*, 96–99; SR, 2; SW 3, no. 5 (June 5, 1912): 2; SW 3, no. 4 (May 17, 1912): 32; SW 3, no. 19 (March 2, 1919): 224–25; Stockman, *Early Expansion*, 132–33. For a history of the Fairhope colony, see Gaston, *Man and Mission*.

46. Stockman, *Early Expansion*, 74, 231, 310–14. The institution of the Mashriqu'l-Adhkár was ordained by Bahá'u'lláh in the Kitáb-i-Aqdas: "O people of the world! Build ye houses of worship throughout all the lands in the name of Him Who is the Lord of all religions. Make them as perfect as possible in the world of being, and adorn them with that which befitteth them, not with images and effigies. Then, with radiance and joy, celebrate therein the praise of your Lord, the Most Compassionate. Verily, by His remembrance the eye is cheered and the heart is filled with light." (*Kitáb-i-Aqdas*, ¶ 31) Bahá'u'lláh and 'Abdu'l-Bahá specified the nature and scope of the institution, to be built in the heart of every city, town, and village: a nine-sided central edifice dedicated to individual and collective worship, surrounded by beautiful gardens and agencies of social, scientific, and educational service for the entire community. The temple initiative and its transformative impact on the American Bahá'í community have been well documented. See Whitfield, *Dawning-Place*; Armstrong-Ingram, *Music, Devotions, and Mashriqu'l-Adhkár*, especially chapters 5 and 6; and Stockman, *Early Expansion*, chapters 20, 22, and 23. The world's first such temple, completed in 1908 in Ashgabat, Turkmenistan, was appropriated by the Soviet government in 1928 and demolished in 1963. The Wilmette temple was dedicated in 1953 and placed on the National Register of Historic Places in 1978. In 2014 there were additional temples serving continental areas in Australia, Germany, India, Panama, Uganda, and Western Samoa; a final continental temple under construction in Chile; and plans to build the first two national temples in the Democratic Republic of the Congo and Papua New Guinea and the first five local ones in Cambodia, Colombia, India, Kenya, and Vanuatu.

47. SR, 6; "News Notes," *Bahá'í News* (Chicago) 1, no. 18 (February 7, 1911): 9; SR, 6.

48. Gregory's administrative duties were wide-ranging. He served for two years (1912 and 1918) on the Executive Board of the Bahai Temple Unity and for fourteen years (1922–1924, 1927–1932, and 1939–1946) on its successor institution, the National Spiritual Assembly of the Bahá'ís of the United States and Canada. He was elected recording secretary of the National Spiritual Assembly and helped write its bylaws and was appointed to the National Teaching Committee and the Racial Amity Committee. He was also a frequent secretary, speaker, and reporter at the

annual national convention. In 1951, in recognition of his long record of service and teaching, Shoghi Effendi posthumously appointed him a "Hand of the Cause of God," one of the special deputies of the Guardianship.

49. See TMW, chapter 5.

50. There are several published firsthand accounts of 'Abdu'l-Bahá's tour of North America: Zaraqání, *Mahmúd's Diary*, ed. Sobhani and Macias; Thompson, *Juliet Thompson's Diary*, ed. Gail; and Parsons, *'Abdu'l-Bahá in America*, ed. Hollinger. For a compilation of 'Abdu'l-Bahá's public addresses during the trip, see 'Abdu'l-Bahá, *Promulgation of Universal Peace*, comp. MacNutt. The most complete scholarly analyses are Stockman, *'Abdu'l-Bahá in America*, and Ward, *239 Days*.

51. See McMullen, *The Baháʼí*, 159; Du Bois, "Fourth Annual Conference," 80.

52. 'Abdu'l-Bahá, *Promulgation of Universal Peace*, 57; Ober, "Louis G. Gregory," in *Baháʼí World*, vol. 12, *1950–1954*, comp. National Spiritual Assembly, 668. For southern newspaper coverage, see "Coming To Convert Us," *Greensboro (N.C.) Daily News*, December 24, 1911; "Abdul Baha on Religious Unity," *Washington Bee*, April 27, 1912; "A Persian Teacher," *Savannah (Ga.) Tribune*, May 11, 1912; "Head of New Religion of Peace Picturesque Figure Lake Mohonk," *Augusta (Ga.) Chronicle*, May 22, 1912; "Religious News and Views," *Charlotte (N.C.) Observer*, July 14, 1912.

53. SR, 6; Pascoe, *What Comes Naturally*, 63, 163–80.

54. TMW, chapter 7; Louise Gregory to Agnes Parsons, December 21, 1914, Agnes S. Parsons Papers, NBA, quoted in TMW, 173; SR, 4–5. For an account of the anti-segregation campaign by black federal employees, see Patler, *Jim Crow and the Wilson Administration*.

55. 'Abdu'l-Bahá to Edna Belmont, received May 1, 1914, Agnes S. Parsons Papers, NBA, quoted in TMW, 75–76.

56. SR, 6; TMW, 83–84.

57. Stockman, *Early Expansion*, 224, 226, 355–58.

Chapter 2. The Divine Plan, the Great War, and Progressive-Era Racial Politics, 1914–1921

1. USBC, Census of 1916, quoted in Smith, "American Baháʼí Community," 117. For a fuller discussion of 'Abdu'l-Bahá's encouragement of teaching, see Smith, "American Baháʼí Community," 127–31.

2. Esslemont, *Baháʼu'lláh and the New Era*, 243–44; Masson, "The Bahai Movement—Is It the Coming Universal Religion," *Helena (Mont.) Daily Independent*, February 2, 1919, quoted in SW 10, no. 3 (April 28, 1919): 33; *'Abdu'l-Bahá in Canada* (Forest, Ont.: National Spiritual Assembly of the Baháʼís of Canada, 1962), 51, quoted in Universal House of Justice, *Century of Light*, 28; SW 5, no. 1 (March 21, 1914): 8.

3. Smith, "American Baháʼí Community," 132. For a discussion of Louis and Lou-

isa Gregory's financial arrangements, see TMW, 91–95. For an account of 'Abdu'l-Bahá and the Bahá'í holy places during World War I and a Bahá'í interpretation of the biblical battle of Armageddon, see Maude and Maude, *Servant, General, and Armageddon*.

4. SW 7, no. 10 (September 8, 1916): 89.

5. SW 7, no. 10 (September 8, 1916): 90. The sixteen states referred to by 'Abdu'l-Bahá are identical to the "Census South," the southern region as defined by the USBC.

6. SW 7, no. 17 (January 19, 1917): 170; SW 7, no. 16 (December 31, 1916): 159, 170. In Islamic tradition, the Qur'án contains ninety-nine names of God, while the "Greatest Name" of God remained hidden. The Báb and Bahá'u'lláh wrote that the Greatest Name was *bahá'*, usually translated as "glory" or "splendor," the root of the prophetic title Bahá'u'lláh ("Glory of God") and of the proper name of the religion, the Bahá'í ("glorious") Faith. See Momen, *Islam and the Bahá'í Faith*, 242. In the United States, Ibrahim Kheiralla's early presentation of the faith in a series of thirteen lessons culminated in disclosing to believers the Greatest Name of God, that is, the identity of Bahá'u'lláh, a practice apparently echoed as late as 1916 in Gregory's talk in Memphis. See Stockman, *Origins*, 8–12.

7. The classic treatment of the social and political consequences of industrialization in South Carolina is Carlton, *Mill and Town*.

8. Edgar, *South Carolina*, 413–16.

9. The classic treatment of nineteenth- and early twentieth-century American racist ideology is Fredrickson, *Black Image in the White Mind*. For a useful overview of the concept of social equality and its relation to racial violence in the early twentieth century, see Litwack, *Trouble in Mind*, 206–16.

10. For a treatment of Tillman and his political movement, see Kantrowitz, *Ben Tillman*. On the violence in Phoenix, Lake City, and Georgetown, see Edgar, *South Carolina*, 448; Newby, *Black Carolinians*, 54–55; Gleijeses, "African Americans and the War against Spain," in Hine and Jenkins, eds., *Question of Manhood*, 320–45; and Rogers, *Georgetown County*, 481–84.

11. Newby, *Black Carolinians*, 36–48; Huff, *Greenville*, 264–65.

12. Newby, *Black Carolinians*, 60, 70, 73; *Crisis* 3 (December 1911): 61, quoted in Litwack, *Trouble in Mind*, 296; Congressional Record, 59th Cong., 2d sess., 440–44, quoted in Whitfield, *Death in the Delta*, 4; Newby, *Black Carolinians*, 64–65.

13. Hudson, *Entangled by White Supremacy*, 39.

14. *State*, September 16, 1906, quoted in Newby, *Black Carolinians*, 179; *State*, April 3, 1905, quoted in Newby, *Black Carolinians*, 179; *State*, September 27, 1906, quoted in Newby, *Black Carolinians*, 176–77; *State*, April 18, 1899, quoted in Moore, *Columbia and Richland County*, 373; *Charleston (S.C.) News and Courier*, December 18, 1904, quoted in Newby, *Black Carolinians*, 150–51.

15. Edgar, *South Carolina*, 469; Newby, *Black Carolinians*, 93.

16. Nash, "The Lynching of Anthony Crawford," quoted in Litwack, *Trouble in*

Mind, 309. This summary of the events surrounding Crawford's lynching is based on Litwack, *Trouble in Mind*, 309–12, and Lau, *Democracy Rising*, 15–16.

17. *Abbeville (S.C.) Scimitar*, February 15, 1917; Richard Carroll to W. W. Ball, November 9, 1916, W. W. Ball Papers, Duke University Libraries, both quoted in Litwack, *Trouble in Mind*, 311.

18. W. W. Ball, Diary 3, 1916–1918, entry for June 3, 1917, W. W. Ball Papers, Duke University Libraries, quoted in Litwack, *Trouble in Mind*, 206.

19. Moore, *Columbia and Richland County*, 377; *State*, March 14, 1918, quoted in Moore, *Columbia and Richland County*, 378; Lau, *Democracy Rising*, 40; Newby, *Black Carolinians*, 193; *Charleston (S.C.) News and Courier*, April 5, 1917, and May 9, 1917, quoted in Hemmingway, "Prelude to Change," 220; *Greenville (S.C.) Daily News*, October 2, 9, and 22, 1918, quoted in Hemmingway, "Prelude to Change," 220.

20. Hamer, "Seeds of Change," in Hamer, ed., *Forward Together*, 26–27; SW 9, no. 19 (March 2, 1919): 225–28.

21. *Charleston (S.C.) News and Courier*, December 31, 1916; Lau, *Democracy Rising*, 20–26, 34–37; "Catalogue of the Teachers and Pupils of Avery Normal Institute, Charleston, S.C.," June 1899, Avery School Memorabilia Collection, ARC; Drago, *Initiative, Paternalism, and Race Relations*, 253; Lau, *Democracy Rising*, 30–31, 40–44.

22. Lau, *Democracy Rising*, 47–48; Hemmingway, "Prelude to Change," 221; Newby, *Black Carolinians*, 188–89; Hemmingway, "Prelude to Change," 222.

23. Egerton, *Speak Now against the Day*, 47; Lau, *Democracy Rising*, 50–51.

24. Congressional Record, 66th Cong., 1st sess., 4302–5, quoted in Lau, *Democracy Rising*, 56–57.

25. *Charleston (S.C.) News and Courier*, January 21, 1921; Congressional Record, 67th Cong., 2d sess., 544, quoted in Tindall, *Emergence of the New South*, 170; Lau, *Democracy Rising*, 53–58.

26. Tindall, *Emergence of the New South*, 179. For an overview of the work of the Interracial Commission, see McDonough, "Men and Women of Good Will." For treatment of the Division of Women's Work and its successor organization, the Association of Southern Women for the Prevention of Lynching (ASWPL), see Hall, *Revolt against Chivalry*.

27. Woofter, *The Basis of Interracial Adjustment*, 240, quoted in Tindall, *Emergence of the New South*, 181; *An Appeal to the Christian People of the South Adopted by Church Leaders' Conference, Blue Ridge, North Carolina, August 18–21, 1920* (n.p., n.d.), quoted in Tindall, *Emergence of the New South*, 181.

28. Louis G. Gregory to Joseph A. Hannen, April 4, 1919, H-KFP; SW 10, no. 17 (January 19, 1920): 307–8.

29. SW 10, no. 17 (January 19, 1920): 309; SW 10, no. 4 (May 17, 1919): 55.

30. SW 10, no. 6 (June 24, 1919): 100–102.

31. SW 10, no. 5 (June 5, 1919): 88–89; *Teaching Bulletin* 1 (November 19, 1919): 1, National Teaching Committee Records, NBA.

32. *Teaching Bulletin* 2 (July 19, 1920): 7–8, National Teaching Committee Records, NBA; Evelyn Hardin, "Roy Williams: Teacher in Word and Deed," *Baha'i Bulletin* (South Carolina) 5, no. 4 (Summer 1974): 3; Roy Williams to Joseph A. Hannen, November 10, 1919, H-KFP; HBC, 1; *Bulletin "A" Issued by the Teaching Committee* (Teaching Bulletin), January 1921, 12, National Teaching Committee Records, NBA; *Bulletin No. 10 Issued by the Teaching Committee of Nineteen* (Teaching Bulletin), March 15, 1921, 9, National Teaching Committee Records, NBA.

33. Executive Board of Bahai Temple Unity, Minutes, September 11, 1919, Bahá'í Temple Unity Records, NBA, quoted in TMW, 131; Louis Gregory to Harlan Ober, September 9, 1919, Harlan F. Ober Papers, NBA, quoted in TMW, 132.

34. Bahai Temple Unity, "Proceedings of the Annual Meeting, 1922," 308–9, Bahá'í Temple Unity Records, NBA, quoted in TMW, 136–37.

35. Louis Gregory to Agnes Parsons, December 16, 1920, Agnes S. Parsons Papers, NBA, quoted in TMW, 137–38.

36. TMW, 138–41; "Great Inter-Racial Convention," *Washington Bee*, May 14, 1921; "Races for Amity," *Washington Bee*, May 21, 1921; "Convention for Amity to Be Held," *Savannah (Ga.) Tribune*, May 21, 1921; "Great Convention for Amity between the Colored and White," *Washington Bee*, May 28, 1921; "Negro Propaganda Hear[d]," May 24, 1921, *Macon (Ga.) Telegraph*; "Speakers Plead for Amity," *Savannah (Ga.) Tribune*, June 4, 1921.

37. TMW, 142, 144–52, 178–93; Hollinger, "Introduction," in Hollinger, ed., *Community Histories*, xxvii–xxviii. The survey in question, the "Bahá'í Historical Record Cards" collected in 1935 and 1936, may well have undercounted African American Bahá'ís. The fullest discussion of the survey is found in TMW, 203–9.

38. SW 13, no. 11 (February 1923): 305.

39. Hudson, *Entangled by White Supremacy*, 133, 142; *Teaching Bulletin* 10 (March 15, 1921): 9, National Teaching Committee Records, NBA; SW 13, no. 11 (February 1923): 305; Tindall, *Emergence of the New South*, 182–83. For Morse's influence on one white student who went on to become a liberal activist, see Randolph, "James McBride Dabbs," in Fraser and Moore, eds., *From the Old South to the New*, 255.

40. For a brief treatment of Mitchell's personal and professional life, see Carlton's introduction to the most important work of his son, Broadus Mitchell, who became a noted sociologist. (Mitchell, *Rise of Cotton Mills*, x–xvii) For an account of Mitchell's clash with Blease, see Hollis, "Samuel Chiles Mitchell," 20–37.

41. SW 20, no. 1 (April 1929): 9.

42. I. E. Lowery, "Rev. I. E. Lowery's Column," *Southern Indicator* (Columbia, S.C.), February 19, 1921. Lowery states that the column is a reprint of an editorial in the *Watchman and Defender*, a black newspaper located in Timmonsville in western Florence County and edited by Rev. H. C. Asbury. Lowery was a contributing

editor of the *Watchman and Defender* as well as its Columbia agent. Copies from January and February 1921 have not survived.

43. Lowery, *Life on the Old Plantation*, 15–28; *Palmetto Leader* (Columbia, S.C.), January 4, 1930; *Washington Bee*, April 3, 1909. Lowery's obituary in the *Leader* notes he reported for the *Daily Record*, the *State*, and the *Palmetto Leader* in Columbia. He was also an editor of the *Watchman and Defender* in Timmonsville and wrote for the *Southern Indicator* in Columbia. For a brief account of black Methodist denominations in the post–Civil War South, see Montgomery, *Under Their Own Vine and Fig Tree*, 71–73.

44. Lowery, *Life on the Old Plantation*, 11, 133–34, 136–37, 173–76.

45. *Savannah (Ga.) Tribune*, April 14, 1917; SCDAH, "Sidney Park Christian Methodist Episcopal Church," National Register Properties in South Carolina website, accessed November 15, 2014, http://www.nationalregister.sc.gov/richland/S10817740112/index.htm; Lowery, "Column," February 19, 1921.

46. Lowery, "Column," February 19, 1921. For Nicodemus, see John 3:1–21.

47. Louis G. Gregory, "A Brief Answer to Questions on the Fulfillment of Some Bible Prophecies Concerning This Day," probably distributed with *Teaching Bulletin*, June 19, 1922, 1, National Teaching Committee Records, NBA; John 5:39; Rev. 22:2; Gregory, "Brief Answer," 2–3. During his public addresses in the West in 1911–1912, 'Abdu'l-Bahá often explained some of the social and spiritual teachings of Bahá'u'lláh. Following his visit, American Bahá'ís compiled the teachings he mentioned as "twelve universal principles" and reprinted them widely. See, for example, "Twelve Basic Bahai Principles," SW 11, no. 1 (March 21, 1920): 4–5, and Louise R. Waite, "The Bahai Revelation," SW 12, no. 1 (March 21, 1921): 9–13. For a brief discussion of the impact of the principles on the Bahá'ís' teaching, see Smith, "American Bahá'í Community," 127–28.

48. Lowery, "Column," February 19, 1921.

49. Compare, for example, Bahá'u'lláh's tablet to Pope Pius IX, *Summons*, 1.105–10, 1.123, with Jesus's lengthy sermon on the "scribes and Pharisees," Matthew 23:1–39.

50. Lowery, "Column," February 19, 1921.

Chapter 3. Building a Bahá'í Community in Augusta and North Augusta, 1911–1939

1. Haney, "Margaret Klebs," in *Bahá'í World*, vol. 8, *1938–1940*, comp. National Spiritual Assembly, 670–71; "Illness Fatal to Miss Klebs," *Augusta (Ga.) Chronicle*, January 11, 1939; "Professor Edwin Klebs," *British Medical Journal* 2, no. 2760 (November 22, 1913): 1413–14; Baumgartner, "Arnold Carl Klebs, 1870–1943," *Bulletin of the History of Medicine* 14 (July 1943): 201–16; Passenger and Crew Lists of Vessels Arriving at New York, New York, 1897–1957, Records of the Immigration and Natu-

ralization Service, National Archives, Washington, D.C., accessed through www.ancestry.com; USBC, *Fourteenth Census, 1920*. Klebs and her other family members joined a wave of migrants from Germany to the United States that peaked at 1.3 million in the 1880s. Most of the migrants were rural dwellers and industrial workers displaced by Germany's rapid economic transformation, but some were members of the middle and upper classes who were dissatisfied with the regime's militarism and authoritarianism. Perhaps this helps explain the migration of Klebs and her relatives. See Nugent, *Crossings*, 66–69.

2. Southern Educational Association, *Journal of Proceedings and Addresses*, 279. For a history of Green Acre, see Atkinson et al., *Green Acre on the Piscataqua*.

3. Winckler, "Sarah Jane Farmer 1847–1916," unpublished reference material in the Green Acre Archives, 5, quoted in Atkinson et al., *Green Acre*, 29; Haney, "Margaret Klebs," in *Bahá'í World*, vol. 8, *1938–1940*, comp. National Spiritual Assembly, 671; Atkinson et al., *Green Acre*, 47; Wargha (Margaret) Klebs to a commemorative gathering at Green Acre, August 12, 1935, EBA. The record of financial contributions to the Bahá'í temple fund seems to place Klebs in North Augusta by 1911 or very early 1912. At the annual convention of the Bahai Temple Unity in April 1912, the Executive Board's financial secretary reported that during the previous administrative year (April 1911–April 1912), a contribution to the temple fund had been received from North Augusta, South Carolina. Klebs is the only Bahá'í known to have been associated with the Augusta area around that time. ("Record of the Fourth Annual Convention of Bahai Temple Unity," SW 3, no. 5 [June 5, 1912]: 5)

4. "Musical at Hampton Terrace," *Augusta (Ga.) Chronicle*, March 3, 1912, 9. Daisy Jackson, one of Klebs's first Bahá'í students in the Augusta area, recalled that Klebs met with 'Abdu'l-Bahá in Washington and that he directed her to move south. They may have met in Washington as well as at Green Acre. (Daisy Jackson Moore, handwritten note to "George," n.d., ABA.)

5. A Bahá'í who resided elsewhere at the time later recalled that Louis Gregory had visited the Augusta area in 1907, specifying that he spoke at Paine College and at "the Lucy Laney School," or Haines Normal and Industrial Institute. As Gregory was only discovering the Bahá'í Faith in 1907, she was probably referring to his 1910 tour. However, no other evidence of such a visit has come to light. (HBC, 2)

6. For treatments of Shultz, Hamburg, and industrialization in the Augusta area, see Cashin, *Story of Augusta*, 71–73; and Downey, *Planting a Capitalist South*, chapters 3 and 6.

7. For an account of the Hamburg incident and its impact on the election, see Holt, *Black over White*, chapter 8. After Hamburg, armed confrontations followed in Charleston and Beaufort Counties and at Ellenton, another small settlement in Aiken County less than twenty miles from Hamburg. After the Ellenton incident, white paramilitaries executed some thirty to fifty black men, including a state legislator. (Edgar, *South Carolina*, 403.)

8. *Augusta (Ga.) Chronicle*, June 24, 1894, quoted in Donaldson, "Standing on a Volcano," in Cashin and Askew, eds., *Paternalism in a Southern City*, 148; Donaldson, "Standing on a Volcano," 148–49, 158–61. For details of the forced labor system in South Carolina and Georgia after the Civil War, see Newby, *Black Carolinians*, 67–79, 129; and Dittmer, *Black Georgia in the Progressive Era*, 72–89.

9. The classic treatment of Watson's career is Woodward, *Tom Watson*.

10. McDaniel, *North Augusta*, 19; USBC, *Seventh Census, 1850*; USBC, *Eighth Census, 1860*; USBC, *Tenth Census, 1880*; McDaniel, *North Augusta*, 9–11, 19–23.

11. McDaniel, *North Augusta*, 9–11, 19–23, 47, 60–61.

12. McDaniel, *North Augusta*, 51.

13. *Augusta (Ga.) Chronicle*, March 6, 1912, 5; *Augusta (Ga.) Chronicle*, May 4, 1913, 9; *Augusta City Directory, 1901*, 219 (for Bracey); USBC, *Fourteenth Census, 1920* (for Irvin); McDaniel, *North Augusta*, 23; USBC, *Tenth Census, 1880* (both for Jackson); HBC, 1; USBC, *Fifteenth Census, 1930* (both for Moore); HBC, 1; USBC, *Fourteenth Census, 1920* (both for Hulse).

14. HBC, 1; Joseph H. Hannen to Margaret Klebs, March 11, 1916, March 28, 1916, and May 12, 1917, H-KFP; *Augusta (Ga.) Chronicle*, March 8, 1914, B2 (all for Hannen's trip); HBC, 1; Smedley, *Martha Schofield*, 271 (both for Landes).

15. "Tablet for Augusta, Georgia," 'Abdu'l-Bahá to Joseph Hannen, April 18, 1914, ABA. Hannen's letter to 'Abdu'l-Bahá has not been located. (Universal House of Justice, Department of the Secretariat, e-mail to the author, August 10, 2009)

16. USBC, *Thirteenth Census, 1910*; USBC, *Twelfth Census, 1900* (both for Talbots); *Official Railway List*, 5; *Handbook of South Carolina*, 455 (both for Verdery); USBC, *Fifteenth Census, 1930*; *Augusta (Ga.) Chronicle*, December 24, 1916, and January 7, 1917 (all for Tinsley); Margaret Klebs to Joseph Hannen, answered April 8, 1918, H-KFP (for Moore); Margaret Klebs to Alfred Lunt, February 26, 1920, Alfred E. Lunt Papers, NBA; Passport Applications, General Records of the Department of State, National Archives, Washington, D.C., accessed through www.ancestry.com (both for Irvin); HBC, 1; McDaniel, *North Augusta*, 93–94; USBC, *Fourteenth Census, 1920* (for Jackson and Bracey); HBC, 1; USBC, *Fourteenth Census, 1920*; USBC, *Fifteenth Census, 1930*; *Polk's Augusta City Directory, 1937*, 598 (for Sego); SW 10, no. 18 (February 7, 1920): 331; SW 11, no. 11 (September 27, 1920): 174 (for delegates).

17. HBC, 1; *Augusta (Ga.) Chronicle*, March 31, 1919, 3; Garis, *Martha Root*, 128; USBC, *Fifteenth Census, 1930*; HBC, 1–2.

18. *Augusta (Ga.) Chronicle*, January 16, 1917, June 12, 1915, and April 28, 1917.

19. "Seventeenth Annual Convention [1925]," TS, National Convention Files, Office of the Secretary Records, NBA, 63.

20. SW 12, no. 15 (December 12, 1921): 245. "Abhá (Most Glorious) Kingdom," in Bahá'í terminology, usually denotes the afterlife.

21. SW 12, no. 16 (December 31, 1921): 254; SW 12, no. 19 (March 2, 1922): 303; SW 12, no. 17 (January 19, 1922): 258.

22. Bahá'u'lláh, *Tablets*, 26–27; 'Abdu'l-Bahá, *Promulgation of Universal Peace*, 455; Rabbani, *Priceless Pearl*, 42–43. For detailed treatment of the Bahá'í Covenant, including the appointment of Shoghi Effendi as Guardian and the fate of the rest of 'Abdu'l-Bahá's family, see Taherzadeh, *Covenant of Bahá'u'lláh* and *Child of the Covenant*.

23. 'Abdu'l-Bahá, *Will and Testament*, 11, 14. On the hereditary principle in the Bahá'í Faith, see, for example, Bahá'u'lláh, *Kitáb-i-Aqdas*, ¶ 42, 121, 174; and *Tablets*, 221–22. While Shoghi Rabbani used his family name in interactions with the public, within the Bahá'í community he was always referred to by his first name and the Turkish title "Effendi," equivalent to the English "sir" or "mister." His wife, Rúhíyyih Rabbani (an American-Canadian née Mary Maxwell), was known within the community as Amatu'l-Bahá Rúhíyyih Khánum ("Madam Rúhíyyih, the Maidservant of Bahá").

24. SW 12, no. 18 (February 7, 1922): 273; SW 13, no. 1 (March 21, 1922): 17.

25. SW 13, no. 1 (March 21, 1922): 25; SR, 6; TMW, 114–16; Rabbani, *Priceless Pearl*, 50–51.

26. 'Abdu'l-Bahá, *Will and Testament*, 14; Rabbani, *Priceless Pearl*, 55–56, 247.

27. Rabbani, *Priceless Pearl*, 56; 'Abdu'l-Bahá, *Tablets*, vols. 1, 6.

28. SW 13, no. 4 (May 17, 1922): 68, 80, 92; Shoghi Effendi, *Bahá'í Administration*, 28–29; SW 13, no. 4 (May 17, 1922): 84, 87.

29. SW 13, no. 4 (May 17, 1922): 87.

30. For a discussion of the constitutive principles of the Bahá'í administration and their application, see Abizadeh, "Democratic Elections without Campaigns?"

31. The preceding summary is based on Loni Bramson's history of the relationship between Shoghi Effendi and the American community in the development of the Bahá'í administrative system. See Bramson-Lerche, "Administrative Order," in *Studies in Bábí and Bahá'í History*, vol. 1, Momen, ed., 254–300; and Bramson, "Plans of Unified Action," in Smith, ed., *Bahá'ís in the West*, 154–97.

32. Shoghi Effendi, *World Order of Bahá'u'lláh*, 98; Shoghi Effendi, *Bahá'í Administration*, 42; Shoghi Effendi, *God Passes By*, 324; Shoghi Effendi, *Bahá'í Administration*, 63, 111; Shoghi Effendi, *God Passes By*, 324; Shoghi Effendi, *Bahá'í Administration*, 63.

33. SW 14, no. 2 (May 1923): 48. During the ministry of Shoghi Effendi, the term "center" was used in two senses in the Bahá'í community, referring on the one hand (as here) to an organized group of believers and on the other (usually capitalized) to a room or building dedicated to the group's community functions.

34. Bramson, "Plans of Unified Action," in Smith, ed., *Bahá'ís in the West*, 161; National Teaching Committee, 1935 Annual Report, quoted in Dahl, "Three Teaching Methods," 3.

35. Margaret Klebs and Louise Talbott to Joseph Hannen, answered March 20,

1917, H-KFP; National Teaching Committee, "Teaching the Bahá'í Faith," 1936, quoted in Dahl, "Three Teaching Methods," 4.

36. National Teaching Committee, "Teaching the Bahá'í Faith," 1936, quoted in Dahl, "Three Teaching Methods," 5; Dahl, "Three Teaching Methods," 4–5.

37. Dahl, "Three Teaching Methods," 4–10.

38. TMW, 191, 242–43; "News of the Cause," *Bahai News Letter* 4 (April 1925): 4.

39. "News of the Cause," *Bahai News Letter* 4 (April 1925): 4; *Walsh's 1925-1926 Charleston City Directory*, 505; USBC, *Fourteenth Census, 1920*; "Seventeenth Annual Convention [1925]," TS, National Convention Files, Office of the Secretary Records, NBA, 61–62.

40. "George Gregory," South Carolina Death Records, SCDAH; George Gregory to Louis G. Gregory, January 20, 1914, Louis G. Gregory Papers, NBA; "Teaching Work of Mr. Gregory," *Baha'i News Letter* 38 (February 1930): 8; Gregory, South Carolina Death Records, SCDAH (for Mickey); "Annual Committee Reports, 1930–31: Teaching," *Baha'i News* 51 (April 1931): 4.

41. *Bahá'í World*, vol. 7, *1936-1938*, comp. National Spiritual Assembly, 664; "The Heart of Dixie: Teaching Amity in the South," *Baha'i News* 58 (January 1932): 2–3; USBC, *Fifteenth Census, 1930*; "Chauncey Northern," World War I Selective Service System Draft Registration Cards, 1917–1918, National Archives and Records Administration, Washington, D.C.; USBC, *Fourteenth Census, 1920*; *Portsmouth (N.H.) Herald*, August 21, 1930, and September 17, 1930.

42. "The Heart of Dixie: Teaching Amity in the South," *Baha'i News* 58 (January 1932): 2–3; *Gamecock* (University of South Carolina, Columbia), November 5, 1931; Memorial resolution for Josiah Morse, 1946, Samuel M. Derrick Papers, South Caroliniana Library, University of South Carolina, Columbia.

43. Newby, *Black Carolinians*, 260–64; "The Heart of Dixie: Teaching Amity in the South," *Baha'i News* 58 (January 1932): 2–3.

44. *Augusta (Ga.) Chronicle*, January 31, 1926, November 8, 1927, November 13, 1927, and May 29, 1928 (for Klebs); *Augusta (Ga.) Chronicle*, June 21, 1928, April 27, 1930, and June 4, 1934 (for Sego); van den Hoonaard, "Siegfried Schopflocher"; HBC, 2; *Augusta (Ga.) Chronicle*, April 22, 1933 (all for Schopflocher).

45. "Stanwood Cobb," in *Bahá'í World*, vol. 18, *1979-1983*, comp. Universal House of Justice, 814–17; Leroy Ioas to Margaret Klebs, February 6, 1934, Leroy Ioas Papers, NBA; HBC, 2; "Stanwood Cobb, Eminent Baha'i Lecturer to Speak Here Tuesday," *Augusta (Ga.) Chronicle*, March 25, 1934.

46. Frain, "Baha'i History of Augusta, Georgia," TS, ABA, 1; HBC, 2; *Polk's Augusta City Directory, 1938*, 878–79; W. T. Bidwell, "Memories," TS, HEHP, NBA, 1; USBC, *Twelfth Census, 1900*; USBC, *Fifteenth Census, 1930*; *Polk's Augusta City Directory, 1937*, 33.

47. USBC, *Fourteenth Census, 1920*; USBC, *Fifteenth Census, 1930*; *Polk's Augusta City Directory, 1937*, 549; List of Aliens, *SS Stockholm* sailing from Gothen-

burg, Sweden, January 10, 1920, and List of U.S. Citizens, *SS Kosciuszko* sailing from Copenhagen, October 8, 1930, both in Passenger and Crew Lists of Vessels Arriving at New York, 1897–1957, microfilm, Records of the Immigration and Naturalization Service, National Archives and Records Administration, Washington, D.C.

48. USBC, *Fifteenth Census, 1930* (for Wallace); USBC, *Fourteenth Census, 1920*; *Polk's Augusta City Directory, 1937*, 191 (both for Fletchers); USBC, *Fifteenth Census, 1930*; *Polk's Augusta City Directory, 1937*, 263 (both for Hoffman); *Polk's Augusta City Directory, 1937*, 214 (for Glover); USBC, *Fourteenth Census, 1920*; USBC, *Fifteenth Census, 1930*; *Polk's Augusta City Directory, 1937*, 51 (all for Barton).

49. Frain, "Baha'i History of Augusta, Georgia," TS, ABA, 1; *Augusta (Ga.) Chronicle*, May 27, 1934, October 8, 1934, November 26, 1934, April 1, 1935, and September 16, 1935. The local Spiritual Assemblies of Atlanta, Georgia, and Greenville, South Carolina, were not elected until almost the end of the decade.

50. Minutes of the Local Spiritual Assembly of Eliot, Maine, September 30, 1934, and "Baha'u'llah Group," newspaper clipping, n.d., both in EBA; W. T. Bidwell, "Memories," TS, HEHP, NBA, 1; *Augusta (Ga.) Chronicle*, April 1, 1935, and April 2, 1935; National Spiritual Assembly of the Bahá'ís of the United States and Canada to the Spiritual Assembly of the Bahá'ís of Eliot, Maine, June 25, 1935, and August 16, 1935, and Esther B. Sego to Louise Thompson, August 15, 1935, all in EBA; *Augusta (Ga.) Chronicle*, December 2, 1936, and November 18, 1936; Minutes of the Local Spiritual Assembly of Eliot, Maine, June 1, 5, and 6 and July 5, 1938, EBA; *Augusta (Ga.) Chronicle*, January 11 and 12, 1939; Daisy Jackson Moore, handwritten note to "George," n.d., ABA.

51. Frain, "Baha'i History of Augusta, Georgia," TS, ABA, 1.

52. Zia M. Bagdadi, Passport Applications, January 2, 1906–March 31, 1925, microfilm, General Records of the Department of State, National Archives and Records Administration, Washington, D.C.; *Augusta (Ga.) Chronicle*, August 21, 1936; Zeenat Bagdadi, Passport Applications, January 2, 1906–March 31, 1925, microfilm, General Records of the Department of State, record group 59, National Archives and Records Administration, Washington, D.C.; HBC, 2; Frain, "Baha'i History of Augusta, Georgia," TS, ABA, 1–2.

53. HBC, 2 (for Hoffman); *Polk's Augusta City Directory, 1937*, 345 (for Lynch); *Polk's Augusta City Directory, 1937*, 471; *Augusta (Ga.) Chronicle*, December 17, 1933 (both for Sample); USBC, *Fourteenth Census, 1920*; USBC, *Fifteenth Census, 1930*; *Polk's Augusta City Directory, 1937*, 195 (all for Frain); USBC, *Fifteenth Census, 1930*; *Polk's Augusta City Directory, 1937*, 301, 596 (both for Johnson and Wise); *Polk's Augusta City Directory, 1937*, 112 (for Cartledge); USBC, *Fourteenth Census, 1920*; USBC, *Fifteenth Census, 1930*; *Polk's Augusta City Directory, 1937*, 442 (all for Radford).

54. Frain, "Baha'i History of Augusta, Georgia," TS, ABA, 2; USBC, *Fourteenth*

Census, 1920; USBC, *Fifteenth Census, 1930*; *Polk's Augusta City Directory, 1937*, 478 (all for Scott); *Polk's Augusta City Directory, 1937*, 539 (for Toombs).

55. *Bahá'í World*, vol. 8, *1938–1940*, comp. National Spiritual Assembly, 683. Toombs was listed in the 1937 and 1938 Augusta city directories but not in the 1940 edition.

56. Perry, "Robert S. Abbott and the *Chicago Defender*: A Door to the Masses," *Michigan Chronicle*, October 10, 1995, accessed November 16, 2014, http://www.uga.edu/bahai/News/101095.html; Frain, "Baha'i History of Augusta, Georgia," TS, ABA, 1–2; Caldwell, *History of the American Negro*, 90–92; Frain, "Baha'i History of Augusta, Georgia," TS, ABA, 2.

57. Quoted in HBC, 2. After his death, Bagdadi's wife and daughter soon left for Palestine, and Marie Kershaw moved her home and professional office to the Bahá'í Center in order to maintain it. (HBC, 2; Frain, "Baha'i History of Augusta, Georgia," TS, ABA, 3; *Polk's Augusta City Directory, 1937*, 318)

Chapter 4. The Great Depression, the Second World War, and the First Seven Year Plan, 1935–1945

1. Shoghi Effendi, *Messages to America*, 4, 6–7.
2. Shoghi Effendi, *Messages to America*, 7.
3. Shoghi Effendi, *Messages to America*, 6–7; Shoghi Effendi, *World Order*, 30.
4. Busey, "Uniting the Americas," in *Bahá'í World*, vol. 9, *1940–1944*, comp. National Spiritual Assembly, 187; Ioas, "Teaching in North America," in *Bahá'í World*, vol. 9, *1940–1944*, comp. National Spiritual Assembly, 215–16; Shoghi Effendi, *Messages to America*, 7; TMW, 250–51.
5. Shoghi Effendi, *Messages to America*, 8.
6. Shoghi Effendi, *Messages to America*, 5–6.
7. Ioas, "Teaching in North America," in *Bahá'í World*, vol. 9, *1940–1944*, comp. National Spiritual Assembly, 200–202; Dahl, "Three Teaching Methods," 3–4.
8. National Teaching Committee, "Annual Report, May 1937–April 1938," National Teaching Committee Records, NBA.
9. Gibson and Jung, *Historical Census Statistics on Population Totals by Race*, appendix A-10.
10. Christine Bidwell to Alma Knobloch, 1936, H-KFP; National Teaching Committee, "Annual Report, May 1937–April 1938," National Teaching Committee Records, NBA; National Spiritual Assembly, *Annual Reports, 1938–1939*, 10, 12.
11. Cooper, "Henrietta Emogene Martin Hoagg, 1869–1945," *Bahá'í World*, vol. 10, *1944–1946*, comp. National Spiritual Assembly, 520–26; Rabbani, *Priceless Pearl*, 55–56, 247; Charlotte Linfoot to Emogene Hoagg, January 5, 1940, HEHP.
12. Emogene Hoagg to Charlotte Linfoot, March 22, 1940, HEHP.
13. USBC, *Fifteenth Census, 1930*; Horace Holley to Emogene Hoagg, October

28, 1940, HEHP; Philip Marangella to Emogene Hoagg, November 8, 1940, HEHP; Louise Thompson to Emogene Hoagg, November 28, 1940, HEHP.

14. Entzminger and Montgomery interview; Christine Bidwell to Alma Knobloch, January 27, 1937, H-KFP; National Teaching Committee to Louella Moore, April 17, 1939, private collection of Richard and Doris Morris.

15. Holsapple, "Some Experiences among the Poor in Brazil," SW 18 (April 1927): 220–22; Jackie Yasin, personal conversation with author, 2008; *Hill's Columbia City Directory, 1939,* 575; Entzminger and Montgomery interview.

16. Louise Thompson to Emogene Hoagg, November 28, 1940, HEHP; Entzminger and Montgomery interview; *Baha'i Regional Bulletin* (Regional Teaching Bulletin) 1 (October–December 1949): 3; Thompson to Hoagg, November 28, 1940, HEHP.

17. "News of the Bahá'í Friends of N. C., S. C. and So. Ga.," December 1941, CBA; National Spiritual Assembly, *Annual Reports, 1941–1942,* 32; *Regional Teaching Bulletin* 9 (April 1, 1943): 2; National Spiritual Assembly, *Annual Reports, 1942–1943,* 28.

18. "The Universal House of Worship," *Palmetto Leader* (Columbia, S.C.), March 6, 1940; "Traveling Around America," *Palmetto Leader* (Columbia, S.C.), November 30, 1940; "House of Worship Model Here," *Columbia (S.C.) Record,* December 20, 1940; "Baha'i Community Observes New Year," *State* (Columbia, S.C.), March 24, 1942, all clippings, private collection of Richard and Doris Morris.

19. Christine Bidwell to Alma Knobloch, May 11, 1938, H-KFP.

20. W. T. Bidwell to Alma Knobloch, December 11, 1938, H-KFP; W. T. Bidwell to Alma Knobloch, Monday 24th [early 1939], H-KFP.

21. TMW, 258.

22. "Meetings of the N.S.A.," *Bahá'í News* 103 (October 1936): 2; Louis G. Gregory to Edith M. Chapman, Edith M. Chapman Papers, NBA, quoted in TMW, 243; Martin interview. Martin's mother was one of the women who became Bahá'ís during Gregory's visit, and her father, an administrator at Fisk, embraced the faith later. The family lived on the Fisk campus. Martin became a pioneer in Winnsboro, S.C., in 1968 and subsequently served several terms as an Auxiliary Board member.

23. "Letters from the Guardian," *Bahá'í News* 103 (October 1936): 1; "Public Meetings in Nashville," *Bahá'í News* 105 (February 1937): 2; Albert James, memories of Louis Gregory tape, recorded January 4, 1981, NBA, quoted in TMW, 259.

24. "Letters from the Guardian," *Bahá'í News* 103 (October 1936): 1.

25. "Letters from the Guardian (to the National Spiritual Assembly)," *Bahá'í News* 108 (June 1937): 1–2; "Twenty-Ninth Annual Convention," *Bahá'í News* 108 (June 1937): 3.

26. Shoghi Effendi, *Advent of Divine Justice,* 3–5, 19.

27. Shoghi Effendi, *Advent of Divine Justice,* 33–34, 35–37, 41. Shoghi Effendi's policy was introduced more than twenty years before the Kennedy administration

ordered federal agencies and contractors to take "affirmative action" to ensure equitable treatment of racial minorities in employment.

28. Shoghi Effendi, *Advent of Divine Justice*, 40.

29. Shoghi Effendi, *Advent of Divine Justice*, 40; 'Abdu'l-Bahá, *Selections*, 227.27–30. For explorations of the relationship between the Bahá'í Faith and contemporary economic systems, see Eyford, ed., *Bahá'í Faith and Marxism*, and Rassekh, "Bahá'í Faith and the Market Economy." For an excellent treatment of the philosophical underpinnings of the "New World Order" in the writings of Bahá'u'lláh, see Saeidi, *Logos and Civilization*. For an explanation of the Bahá'í approach to politics, see Schaefer, Gollmer, and Towfigh, *Making the Crooked Straight*.

30. Shoghi Effendi, *Advent of Divine Justice*, 17–20, 22, 41.

31. TMW, 271–72; Baker, "The Bahá'í Faith in the Colleges," in *Bahá'í World*, vol. 9, *1940–1944*, comp. National Spiritual Assembly, 773–74; TMW, 276.

32. TMW, 83–84, 103, 191; McMullen, *The Bahá'í*, 158–60.

33. The situation is summarized in McMullen, *The Bahá'í*, 161–62.

34. Spiritual Assembly of the Bahá'ís of Atlanta, Georgia, Inc., "Early Bahá'í History of Atlanta, Georgia," TS, NBA, 24–25, quoted in TMW, 282; National Park Service, "Atlanta Biltmore Hotel and Biltmore Apartments."

35. Spiritual Assembly of the Bahá'ís of Atlanta, Georgia, Inc., "Early Bahá'í History of Atlanta, Georgia," TS, NBA, 24–25, quoted in TMW, 282–83; McMullen, *The Bahá'í*, 162–65. The building was still in use as a Bahá'í Center in 2015.

36. Shoghi Effendi, "Excerpts from Letter from the Guardian," *Bahá'í News* 145 (June 1941): 3, quoted in TMW, 284; William Bidwell to Emogene Hoagg, letter fragment, November 1940, HEHP.

37. W. T. Bidwell to Alma Knobloch, Monday 24th [early 1939], H-KFP.

38. Edgar, *South Carolina*, 485; Drake, "Negro in Greenville," 2.

39. Edgar, *South Carolina*, 510, 513.

40. Huff, *Greenville*, 302–5; Hoffman, "Genesis of the Modern Movement for Equal Rights," 362.

41. Drake, "Negro in Greenville," 178–79, 205–7; Huff, *Greenville*, 356–58.

42. Huff, *Greenville*, 363–64; Reid, "Greenville County Council for Community Development," in *Proceedings and Papers*, vol. 6, ed. Sanders, 78–88. For a good discussion of activism and violence in late-1930s Greenville, see Lau, *Democracy Rising*, chapter 3.

43. Shoghi Effendi, *Messages to America*, 16; W. T. Bidwell to Alma Knobloch, Monday 24th [early 1939], H-KFP; W. T. Bidwell to Alma Knobloch, March 6, 1939, H-KFP.

44. National Spiritual Assembly, *Annual Reports, 1940–1941*, 19.

45. Letter written on behalf of Shoghi Effendi, *Bahá'í News* 102 (August 1936): 2; *Bahá'í News* 132 (January 1940): 4; National Spiritual Assembly, *Annual Reports, 1940–1941*, 19; Louise Thompson to Emogene Hoagg, November 28, 1940, HEHP;

"Assembly Roll," North Augusta, S.C., 1941–1942, Local Spiritual Assembly Records, NBA; National Spiritual Assembly, *Annual Reports, 1942–1943*, 22.

46. Ioas, "Teaching in North America," in *Bahá'í World*, vol. 9, *1940–1944*, comp. National Spiritual Assembly, 207; USBC, *Sixteenth Census, 1940*.

47. Grace M. Wilder to John and Louise Bosch, September 20, 1942, John and Louise Bosch Papers, NBA; USBC, *Fifteenth Census, 1930*; *Hill's Greenville City Directory, 1945*, 189; Ford interview. Ford deduced that that Bahá'u'lláh was the return of Christ from her individual study after becoming a Bahá'í. Ali-Kuli Khan, a prominent Washington Bahá'í, confirmed her conclusion during his 1945 visit to Greenville.

48. *Regional Teaching Bulletin* 5 (December 1, 1942): 1.

49. Adline Lohse to Alma Knobloch, June 17, 1943, H-KFP; *Regional Teaching Bulletin* 11 (June 1, 1943): 1; National Spiritual Assembly, *Annual Reports, 1943–1944*, 38 (for Lohse, Dabrowski, Vaughn, Camelon, Hoagg, and teaching conference); Adline Lohse to Alma Knobloch, June 17, 1943, H-KFP; National Spiritual Assembly, *Annual Reports, 1943–1944*, 38; Emogene Hoagg to Leroy Ioas, October 4, 1943, HEHP (all for Glazener's conversion); *Hill's Greenville City Directory, 1941*, 161, 292; USBC, *Twelfth Census, 1900*; Huff, *Greenville*, 355 (all for Glazener's personal details). Lohse's letter says that one of the Bidwells' contacts was ready to become a Bahá'í, the Annual Report states that one person was "confirmed" as a believer at the summer conference, and Hoagg's letter refers to Glazener as "the new Bahá'í here."

50. Hardin, "Roy Williams: Teacher in Word and Deed," *Baha'i Bulletin* (South Carolina) 5, no. 4 (Summer 1974): 3; *Hill's Greenville (Greenville Co., S.C.) Directory, 1948*, 764; *Baha'i News Bulletin* (Regional Teaching Bulletin) 38 (October 1946): 3; Drake, "Negro in Greenville," 43; "Assembly Roll," Greenville, S.C., 1943–1944, Local Spiritual Assembly Records, NBA.

51. Lau, *Democracy Rising*, 117, 119.

52. Lau, *Democracy Rising*, 129–30.

53. AP clipping (1943), Papers of the NAACP, II-B, 209, quoted in Sullivan, *Days of Hope*, 158; Edgar, *South Carolina*, 516; Lau, *Democracy Rising*, 134–35.

54. Lau, *Democracy Rising*, 140.

55. Sullivan, *Days of Hope*, 170, 189–91.

56. Edgar, *South Carolina*, 513, 516.

57. FY, 4.

58. *Greenville (S.C.) News*, March 26, 1944, 12; *Baha'i Bulletin* (Regional Teaching Bulletin) 31 (November 1945): 2; FY, 5

59. Emogene Hoagg to Leroy Ioas, October 4, 1943, HEHP.

60. Emogene Hoagg to Leroy Ioas, October 4, 1943, HEHP. Locally and regionally, white supremacist activists and law enforcement agencies frequently equated any type of interracial organization with Communist attempts to overthrow south-

ern civilization. While such rhetoric became more widespread in the context of the Cold War, it was employed in South Carolina as early as World War I. For a recent study of the post–World War II southern red scare, see Woods, *Black Struggle, Red Scare*. For the impact of red baiting on a secular interracial organization, see Reed, *Simple Decency and Common Sense*, especially chapter 3.

61. Dahl, "Three Teaching Methods," 1–15; *Bahá'í News* 161 (March 1943): 2; Dahl, "Three Teaching Methods," 8.

62. Holley, "The Growth of the American Bahá'í Community to 1944," in *Bahá'í World*, vol. 10, *1944–1946*, comp. National Spiritual Assembly, 16; Ioas, "Teaching in North America," in *Bahá'í World*, vol. 9, *1940–1944*, comp. National Spiritual Assembly, 213; Stockman, "United States of America"; Shoghi Effendi, *Messages to America*, 69.

63. "Bahá'í Anniversary Banquet, Hotel Stevens, Chicago, May 25, 1944," in *Bahá'í World*, vol. 10, *1944–1946*, comp. National Spiritual Assembly, photographs between 172–73; "Bahá'í Centenary Banquet Radio Program," in *Bahá'í World*, vol. 10, *1944–1946*, comp. National Spiritual Assembly, 175–76; Louis G. Gregory, "The Historic Thirty-Sixth Convention," *Bahá'í News* 170 (September 1944): 1, quoted in TMW, 300.

64. Louella Moore to Edward Moore, postcard, May 24, 1944, in author's possession; Shoghi Effendi, *World Survey*; 1944 National Convention photograph, in author's possession.

65. Hardin, "Roy Williams: Teacher in Word and Deed," *Baha'i Bulletin* (South Carolina) 5, no. 4 (Summer 1974): 3. At the dawn of the Jim Crow era, blacks organized to oppose attempts to segregate passenger trains and streetcars. Robin Kelley has argued that trains, streetcars, and later buses, remained important public "theaters" of spontaneous resistance by black working-class people until the end of the period. See Kelley, "'We Are Not What We Seem.'"

Chapter 5. Postwar Opportunities, Cold War Challenges, and the Second Seven Year Plan, 1944–1953

1. Shoghi Effendi, *Messages to America*, 97.
2. Edgar, *South Carolina*, 530–35.
3. Edgar, *South Carolina*, 516–18.
4. *Crisis* 53, no. 9 (September 1946): 276; Egerton, *Speak Now against the Day*, 363 (both for Woodard); "South Carolina: Trial by Jury," *Time*, May 26, 1947; Egerton, *Speak Now against the Day*, 373; O'Neill, "Memory, History, and the Desegregation of Greenville," in Moore and Burton, eds., *Toward the Meeting of the Waters*, 288 (all for Earle).
5. Karl Korstad, "Introduction to 'New South,'" quoted in Korstad, "Could History Repeat Itself?" in Moore and Burton, eds., *Toward the Meeting of the Waters*, 254; Du Bois, quoted in Lau, *Democracy Rising*, 169.

6. Lau, *Democracy Rising*, 175–78 (for Waring); Edgar, *South Carolina*, 519–20 (for 1948 primary); Lau, *Democracy Rising*, 183–86 (for NAACP growth). Montgomery's youngest son from his second marriage, Bennett Montgomery, became a member of the Baháʾí Faith in the 1990s while living in Boston. The younger Montgomery and his wife, also a Baháʾí, were friends of the author in Columbia, South Carolina.

7. Egerton, *Speak Now against the Day*, 495–96.

8. Quoted in Bass and Thompson, *Strom*, 117; Edgar, *South Carolina*, 521.

9. Shoghi Effendi, *Messages to America*, 42, 45, 46, 53, 54.

10. "Current Baháʾí Activities," in *Baháʾí World*, vol. 10, *1944–1946*, comp. National Spiritual Assembly, 18–30, 67–68; Shoghi Effendi, *Messages to America*, 73.

11. "Current Baháʾí Activities," in *Baháʾí World*, vol. 10, *1944–1946*, comp. National Spiritual Assembly, 90–92.

12. "Current Baháʾí Activities," in *Baháʾí World*, vol. 10, *1944–1946*, comp. National Spiritual Assembly, 76; TMW, 297.

13. "Assembly Roll," Greenville, S.C., 1943–1944, Local Spiritual Assembly Records, NBA.

14. Hoagg to Ioas, October 4, 1943; Melvin Abercrombie, personal conversation with author, 2003.

15. Horace Holley to Emogene Hoagg, April 7, 1944, HEHP; Christine Bidwell to Emogene Hoagg, October 23, 1944, HEHP; TMW, 297.

16. Shoghi Effendi, *Messages to America*, 88, 99.

17. Shoghi Effendi, *Messages to America*, 88–89; Rabbani, *Priceless Pearl*, 403; Holley, "International Survey of Current Baháʾí Activities in the East and West," in *Baháʾí World*, vol. 11, *1946–1950*, comp. National Spiritual Assembly, 50.

18. Shoghi Effendi, *Unfolding Destiny*, 256–57; Hassall, "Africa"; "International Survey of Current Baháʾí Activities," *Baháʾí World*, vol. 12, *1950–1954*, comp. National Spiritual Assembly, 52–53.

19. Shoghi Effendi, *Messages to America*, 90, 93.

20. *Baha'i News Bulletin* (Regional Teaching Bulletin) 37 (August–September 1946): 1.

21. *Baha'i News Bulletin* (Regional Teaching Bulletin) 38 (October 1946): 2 (for the Williamses); *Baha'i News Bulletin* (Regional Teaching Bulletin) 39 (November 1946): 3–4 (for McCormick); National Spiritual Assembly, *Annual Reports, 1946–1947*, 48 (for Romer); *Baha'i News Bulletin* (Regional Teaching Bulletin) 42 (March 1947): 2 (for Committee); National Spiritual Assembly, *Annual Reports, 1946–1947*, 48; *Baha'i News Bulletin* (Regional Teaching Bulletin) 39 (November 1946): 3 (both for Pinson); *Baha'i Regional Bulletin* (Regional Teaching Bulletin) 1 (October–December 1949): 2 (for Romer).

22. *Baha'i Regional Bulletin* (Regional Teaching Bulletin) 1 (October–December 1949): 3.

23. *Baha'i News Bulletin* (Regional Teaching Bulletin) 36 (July 1946): 4; *Hill's Columbia City Directory, 1942,* 528; "Columbia Baha'i Group—Publicity Report," n.d., CBA; *Hill's Columbia City Directory, 1942,* 568.

24. *Columbia (S.C.) Record,* October 30 and November 1, 1946, clippings, private collection of Richard and Doris Morris; *Baha'i News Bulletin* (Regional Teaching Bulletin) 39 (November 1946): 4; *Columbia (S.C.) Record,* March 8, 1947; *Gamecock* (University of South Carolina, Columbia), March 11, 1947; *State* (Columbia, S.C.), March 23, 1947; *Columbia (S.C.) Record,* January 1, 1948, all clippings, private collection of Richard and Doris Morris.

25. National Spiritual Assembly, *Annual Reports, 1946–1947,* 48; South Carolina State Voting List, 1950, CBA. Records from 1947–1948 are incomplete, but a Local Spiritual Assembly was clearly in existence by 1949. William Bidwell stated that the Columbia Assembly was formed by "splitting" the one in Greenville. (*Regional Baha'i Bulletin for North and South Carolina* [Regional Teaching Bulletin] 1 [October–December 1949]: 3; W. T. Bidwell, "Memories," TS, HEHP, 1)

26. *Baha'i News Bulletin* (Regional Teaching Bulletin) 36 (July 1946): 3 (for Ullrich); *Baha'i News Bulletin* (Regional Teaching Bulletin) 38 (October 1946): 3 (for the Bidwell class); *Baha'i News Bulletin* (Regional Teaching Bulletin) 36 (July 1946): 3; *Baha'i News Bulletin* (Regional Teaching Bulletin) 37 (August–September 1946): 2 (both for Alexander); *Baha'i News Bulletin* (Regional Teaching Bulletin) 39 (November 1946): 3 (for McCormick).

27. *Regional Bulletin* (Regional Teaching Bulletin), December 1948, 3; letter to author, April 22, 1995, NBA; FY, 7.

28. Entzminger and Montgomery interview; FY, 14–15.

29. "Greenville, S.C. Group Wins Right to Hold Non-Segregated Meetings," *Bahá'í News* 266 (April 1953): 8.

30. George E. Dargan to Louis G. Gregory, February 26, 1949, Louis G. Gregory Papers, NBA. Dargan's father was George William Dargan (1841–1898), a former Confederate soldier, attorney, and Redeemer politician. He served as state representative (1877–1880), solicitor of the Fourth Judicial Circuit of South Carolina (1880–1883), and U.S. representative from the Sixth District of South Carolina (1883–1891). (Snowden and Cutler, eds., *History of South Carolina*)

31. "South Carolina: Marching Through Charleston," *Time,* January 30, 1950, accessed November 16, 2014, http://www.time.com/time/magazine/article/0,9171,856480,00.html; "'Disowned' by Dixie," *Christian Science Monitor,* January 10, 1951, clipping, Louis G. Gregory Papers, NBA.

32. J. Waties Waring to Louis G. Gregory, April 26, 1950, Louis G. Gregory Papers, NBA; J. Waties Waring to Louis G. Gregory, November 20, 1950, Louis G. Gregory Papers, NBA; National Spiritual Assembly of the Bahá'ís of the United States to Louis G. Gregory, March 26, 1951, Louis G. Gregory Papers, NBA; Na-

tional Spiritual Assembly of the Baháʾís of the United States to Judge Waties Waring, March 26, 1951, Louis G. Gregory Papers, NBA.

33. "Messages from the Guardian," *Baháʾí News* 247 (September 1951): 1; Braun et al., "Hands of the Cause of God."

34. ʿAbduʾl-Bahá, *Promulgation of Universal Peace*, 57.

35. Gregory, "Racial Unity," chapter 28, TS, Louis G. Gregory Papers, NBA; ʿAbduʾl-Bahá, *Selections*, 227.27–30.

36. Shoghi Effendi, *Messages, 1950–1957*, 16–17. The biblical reference is to Daniel 12:12.

37. Shoghi Effendi, *Messages, 1950–1957*, 7, 23, 25, 28.

38. Shoghi Effendi, *Messages, 1950–1957*, 26; Shoghi Effendi, *Unfolding Destiny*, 290; Shoghi Effendi, *Messages, 1950–1957*, 21.

39. Shoghi Effendi, *Messages, 1950–1957*, 19–20.

40. Holley, "Current Baháʾí Activities," *Baháʾí World*, vol. 11, *1946–1950*, comp. National Spiritual Assembly, 38; Shoghi Effendi, *Citadel of Faith*, 45, 102; Holley "International Survey of Current Baháʾí Activities," in *Baháʾí World*, vol. 10, *1944–1946*, comp. National Spiritual Assembly, 77; "Baháʾí Directory, 1953–1954," in *Baháʾí World*, vol. 12, *1950–1954*, comp. National Spiritual Assembly, 721–43; Shoghi Effendi, *Citadel of Faith*, 102; McDaniel and Haney, "Interior Ornamentation of the Baháʾí House of Worship," in *Baháʾí World*, vol. 12, *1950–1954*, comp. National Spiritual Assembly, 536; "Landscape Plan of the Baháʾí House of Worship by Hilbert Dahl," in *Baháʾí World*, vol. 12, *1950–1954*, comp. National Spiritual Assembly, 540; Rabbani, *Priceless Pearl*, 405–6; Holley, "Current Baháʾí Activities," in *Baháʾí World*, vol. 11, *1946–1950*, comp. National Spiritual Assembly, 44–45.

41. *Bahaʾi News Bulletin* (Regional Teaching Bulletin) 36 (July 1946): 3; South Carolina State Voting List, 1950, CBA; "Baháʾí Directory, 1953–1954," in *Baháʾí World*, vol. 12, *1950–1954*, comp. National Spiritual Assembly, 734.

42. "Baháʾí Directory, 1953–1954," in *Baháʾí World*, vol. 12, *1950–1954*, comp. National Spiritual Assembly, 734 (for Columbia group status); Dudley, "Unfinished Journey," TS, in author's possession (for Dudley); South Carolina State Voting List, 1963, private collection of Richard and Doris Morris (for Pinson); *Bahaʾi Regional Bulletin* (Regional Teaching Bulletin) 1 (October–December 1949): 3; "In Memoriam," in *Baháʾí World*, vol. 14, *1963–1968*, comp. Universal House of Justice, 375–77 (both for Romer); Eugenie Meyer to Mr. and Mrs. Edward Moore, postcards, November 20, 1960, and December 2, 1962, private collection of Richard and Doris Morris (for Meyer).

Chapter 6. The Ten Year Plan and the Fall of Jim Crow, 1950–1965

1. J. Richard Abercrombie interview. For King's relationship with Penn, see Power, *I Will Not Be Silent*.

2. J. Richard Abercrombie interview.

3. *Bahá'í World*, vol. 14, 1963–1968, comp. Universal House of Justice, 72; J. Richard Abercrombie interview.

4. Gregory, "Racial Unity," chapter 28, TS, Louis G. Gregory Papers, NBA.

5. Quoted in Kluger, *Simple Justice*, 366; Southern, "Beyond Jim Crow Liberalism," 219–20. This account of the Clarendon County case is based on Kluger, *Simple Justice*, and Hornsby, *Stepping Stone to the Supreme Court*.

6. Dobrasko, "Upholding 'Separate but Equal,'" 5–11, 35; Edgar, *South Carolina*, 523; Dobrasko, "Upholding 'Separate but Equal,'" 23–29; Edgar, *South Carolina*, 522; Kluger, *Simple Justice*, 782.

7. Edgar, *South Carolina*, 524; *Greenville (S.C.) News*, May 18, 1954, June 2, 1955, March 5, 1956, and September 18, 1960, quoted in Huff, *Greenville*, 401–2.

8. Woods, *Black Struggle, Red Scare*, 4–7, 36–38, 113–16; Edgar, *South Carolina*, 525.

9. Woods, *Black Struggle, Red Scare*, 36–38, 113–16; Edgar, *South Carolina*, 525; White, "White Citizens' Councils of Orangeburg County," in Moore and Burton, eds., *Toward the Meeting of the Waters*, 261–73; Edgar, *South Carolina*, 527.

10. Woods, *Black Struggle, Red Scare*, 67, 71, 113–14; Lau, *Democracy Rising*, 210–11.

11. Shoghi Effendi, *Messages to America*, 88; Shoghi Effendi, *Messages, 1950–1957*, 40.

12. Shoghi Effendi, *Messages, 1950–1957*, 42.

13. Shoghi Effendi, *Citadel of Faith*, 107–9, 120; Shoghi Effendi, *Messages, 1950–1957*, 42.

14. Dorothy Baker, address recorded at All-America Conference, Chicago, May 3–6, 1953, quoted in TMW, 292–93; Dorothy Baker, address at All-America Conference, quoted in Gilstrap, *From Copper to Gold*, 410–11.

15. Shoghi Effendi, *Citadel of Faith*, 114, 117. For earlier references to entry by troops, see Bahá'u'lláh, *Summons*, 1.270, and 'Abdu'l-Bahá, *Tablets*, vol. 3, 681. The phrase is apparently borrowed from "The Help," the short final sura of the Qur'án: "In the Name of God, the Compassionate, the Merciful! When the Help of God and the victory arrive, and thou seest men entering the religion of God by troops; then utter the praise of thy Lord, implore His pardon; for He loveth to turn in mercy." (Qur'án, trans. J. M. Rodwell, 110:1–3)

16. Shoghi Effendi, *Citadel of Faith*, 124.

17. Shoghi Effendi, *Citadel of Faith*, 124–26.

18. On links between the civil rights movement and the Cold War, see Dudziak, *Cold War Civil Rights*, and Borstelmann, *Cold War and the Color Line*.

19. Shoghi Effendi, *Citadel of Faith*, 126.

20. Shoghi Effendi, *Citadel of Faith*, 126–27.

21. Shoghi Effendi, *Citadel of Faith*, 127.

22. "International Survey of Current Bahá'í Activities," in *Bahá'í World*, vol.

13, *1954–1963*, comp. Universal House of Justice, 270; Shoghi Effendi, *Citadel of Faith*, 128.

23. Shoghi Effendi, *Citadel of Faith*, 147–48, 154.

24. Shoghi Effendi (through his secretary) to Bahá'í Inter-Racial Teaching Committee, Dorothy Frey, chair, May 27, 1957, Letters of Shoghi Effendi, NBA, quoted in TMW, 294.

25. Robert Patterson, annual report to the Mississippi Association of Citizens' Councils, 1956, quoted in Diamond, *Roads to Dominion*, 73; *State* (Columbia, S.C.), September 24, 1957, quoted in Lander, *History of South Carolina*, 205.

26. Shoghi Effendi (through his secretary), *Bahá'í News* 321 (November 1957), insert, quoted in Taylor, ed., *Pupil of the Eye*, 158.

27. Edgar, *South Carolina*, 526.

28. Benson interview.

29. *Hill's Greenville City Directory, 1950–1951*, 98; Benson interview; FY, 7–8.

30. In 1957, Clement F. Haynsworth Jr. (1912–1989), a Democrat who had supported Eisenhower in 1956, was appointed to the U.S. Circuit Court of Appeals for the Fourth Circuit, where he served for thirty-two years. In 1969, President Nixon nominated Haynsworth to the U.S. Supreme Court. The nomination was defeated by a coalition of labor and civil rights groups who pointed to his history of rulings unfavorable to their interests. ("Judge Clement Haynsworth," *Time*, August 29, 1969, accessed November 16, 2014, http://www.time.com/time/magazine/article/0,9171,901281,00.html; Alfonso A. Narvaez, "Clement Haynsworth Dies at 77; Lost Struggle for High Court Seat," *New York Times*, November 23, 1989, accessed November 16, 2014, http://www.nytimes.com/1989/11/23/obituaries/clement-haynsworth-dies-at-77-lost-struggle-for-high-court-seat.html?pagewanted=1). In 2009, the website of Haynsworth's firm, Haynsworth Sinkler Boyd, noted that the firm employed 4 African American attorneys out of a total of approximately 140, but by 2014 those statistics had been removed. ("Diversity," Haynsworth Sinkler Boyd website, accessed November 16, 2014, http://www.hsblawfirm.com/profile.php?AboutusID=8)

31. Benson interview; FY, 9.

32. Etter-Lewis, "Radiant Lights: African-American Women and the Advancement of the Bahá'í Faith in the U.S.," in Etter-Lewis and Thomas, eds., *Lights of the Spirit*, 55–56; FY, 9.

33. FY, 11.

34. FY, 11; Abercrombie interview.

35. FY, 12.

36. South Carolina State Voting List, 1963, private collection of Richard and Doris Morris.

37. Young interview.

38. Young interview.

39. Young interview (for Florence-area and Myrtle Beach–area teaching); USBC, *Fifteenth Census, 1930* (for the Grimsleys); "Baháʼí Directory 1962–1963," in *Baháʼí World*, vol. 13, *1954–1963*, comp. Universal House of Justice, 1040 (for the Florence County Assembly); South Carolina State Voting List, 1963, private collection of Richard and Doris Morris (for Baháʼís of Florence and Horry Counties); Photograph of first Local Spiritual Assembly of Florence, 1961, Florence Baháʼí Archives, Florence, S.C.; Young interview (both for Florence Assembly).

40. Group photograph and "3rd Blue Ridge Conference" brochure, private collection of Richard and Doris Morris.

41. Yvonne R. Harrop, personal conversation with author, June 2014; National Spiritual Assembly, *Annual Reports, 1961–1962*, 14. For a history of Penn Center, see Burton and Cross, *Penn Center*.

42. National Spiritual Assembly, *Annual Reports, 1959–1960*, 14; National Spiritual Assembly, *Annual Reports, 1961–1962*, 13; National Spiritual Assembly, *Annual Reports, 1962–1963*, 13 (all for committee membership); National Spiritual Assembly, *Annual Reports, 1959–1960*, 15; National Spiritual Assembly, *Annual Reports, 1961–1962*, 14 (both for enrollment statistics); National Spiritual Assembly, *Annual Reports, 1961–1962*, 13–14; National Spiritual Assembly, *Annual Reports, 1962–1963*, 13 (both for involvement of blacks and youth); National Spiritual Assembly, *Annual Reports, 1962–1963*, 13; Entzminger and Montgomery interview (both for children's classes); National Spiritual Assembly, *Annual Reports, 1962–1963*, 14 (for music).

43. National Spiritual Assembly, *Annual Reports, 1961–1962*, 14 (for the committee, Chapman, and the "spark of mass enrollment"); "Baháʼí Directory 1962–1963," in *Baháʼí World*, vol. 13, *1954–1963*, comp. Universal House of Justice, 1040 (for the St. Helena Assembly formation); *Area Teaching Committee Bulletin* 4 (June 1963): 2; South Carolina State Voting List, 1963, private collection of Richard and Doris Morris (both for Michaels and St. Helena Assembly members).

44. Lau, *Democracy Rising*, 217–18; O'Neill, "Memory, History, and the Desegregation of Greenville," in Moore and Burton, eds., *Toward the Meeting of the Waters*, 289.

45. Edgar, *South Carolina*, 536–37; Lau, *Democracy Rising*, 217 (both for Rock Hill and Orangeburg); Edgar, *South Carolina*, 536; Baker, "Schooling and White Supremacy," in Moore and Burton, eds., *Toward the Meeting of the Waters*, 309 (both for other cities); O'Neill, "Memory, History, and the Desegregation of Greenville," 289–90 (for Greenville); Lau, *Democracy Rising*, 217 (for the regional statistic).

46. Arsenault, "Five Days in May," in Moore and Burton, eds., *Toward the Meeting of the Waters*, 201–4, 209–14, 216–18.

47. O'Neill, "Memory, History, and the Desegregation of Greenville," 290–91.

48. Edgar, *South Carolina*, 540.

49. Huff, *Greenville*, 404; Edgar, *South Carolina*, 540.

50. Edgar, *South Carolina*, 538–39; Baker, "Schooling and White Supremacy," 309–10; Moore, *Columbia and Richland County*, 427.

51. Lyndon B. Johnson, Special Message to Congress, March 15, 1965, LBJ Presidential Library website, updated June 6, 2007, accessed November 16, 2014, http://www.lbjlib.utexas.edu/johnson/archives.hom/speeches.hom/650315.asp.; Edgar, *South Carolina*, 541; Kovacik and Winberry, *South Carolina: A Geography*, 154.

52. David R. McLeod to Rex L. Carter, facsimile of letter, in *Bahá'í World*, vol. 13, *1954–1963*, comp. Universal House of Justice, 692; "Certificate of Incorporation of the Spiritual Assembly of the Bahá'ís of Greenville, South Carolina, U.S.A.," facsimile of original, in *Bahá'í World*, vol. 13, *1954–1963*, comp. Universal House of Justice, 654; Benson interview.

53. Bryant, *"I'm Black and I'm Proud,"* 1; Karen Blair, "Lines Were Clearly Drawn for Woman Growing Up in Biracial Family," *Herald* (Rock Hill, S.C.), July 20, 2003.

54. Miscellaneous programs, invitations, flyers, and photographs, private collection of Joy F. Benson; *Greenville (S.C.) Piedmont*, December 11 and 13, 1958, clippings, private collection of Joy F. Benson; *Greenville (S.C.) Piedmont*, December 11, 1964, clipping, private collection of Joy F. Benson; Lesesne, *University of South Carolina*, 143–50. In 1976, Matthew Perry was appointed to the U.S. military court of appeals in Washington, D.C., and in 1979 he was appointed to the U.S. district court for the District of South Carolina, becoming the state's first black federal judge. A new federal courthouse in Columbia was named for him in 2000. See Burke and Gergel, eds., *Matthew J. Perry*.

55. Miscellaneous programs, invitations, flyers, and photographs, private collection of Joy F. Benson.

56. Miscellaneous newspaper clippings, private collection of Joy F. Benson; "Letters to the Editor," *Greenville (S.C.) News*, December 6, 1964, clipping, private collection of Joy F. Benson.

57. Moore, "Civil Rights Advocate," in Burke and Gergel, eds., *Matthew J. Perry*, 161–62; "Aldermen Hear Opposition to Greenville's 'Pool Zoo,'" *Greenville (S.C.) Piedmont*, October 17, 1963; "Council Faces Pool Question," *Greenville (S.C.) News*, August 10, 1964, 4, both clippings, private collection of Joy F. Benson.

58. David Shi, "Joe Vaughn Fought His Own Crusade," *Greenville (S.C.) News*, February 10, 2002, clipping, Joe Vaughn folder, Furmaniana Collection, Special Collections and Archives, James B. Duke Library, Furman University; Reid, *Furman University*, 199; Joe Vaughn, "Why I Am a Baha'i, Not a Christian," *Paladin* (Furman University, Greenville, S.C.), February 10, 1967, clipping, private collection of Joy F. Benson; "Feast of Ridvan," April 20, 1966, private collection of Joy F. Benson.

59. For a documentary account of the interregnum under the Hands of the Cause, see Rabbani, ed., *Ministry of the Custodians*.

60. Hofman, "Five Intercontinental Conferences, 1958," in *Bahá'í World*, vol. 13, *1954–1963*, comp. Universal House of Justice, 331–32; "Completion of the Bahá'í World Crusade, 1953–1963," *Bahá'í World*, vol. 13, *1954–1963*, comp. Universal House of Justice, 459–69.

61. "Completion of the Bahá'í World Crusade, 1953–1963," *Bahá'í World*, vol. 13, *1954–1963*, comp. Universal House of Justice, 459–69.

62. "Completion of the Bahá'í World Crusade, 1953–1963," *Bahá'í World*, vol. 13, *1954–1963*, comp. Universal House of Justice, 467 (for Native Americans); Stockman, "United States of America," 6 (for enrollment statistics); "Bahá'í Youth Activities, April 1954–April 1963," in *Bahá'í World*, vol. 13, *1954–1963*, comp. Universal House of Justice, 768–75 (for youth); "Current Bahá'í Activities," in *Bahá'í World*, vol. 13, *1954–1963*, comp. Universal House of Justice, 270–72 (for Local and National Assemblies).

63. South Carolina State Voting List, 1963, private collection of Richard and Doris Morris.

64. Abercrombie interview.

65. USBC, *Fourteenth Census, 1920*; Gibson, "Amoz Everett Gibson, 1918–1982," in *Bahá'í World*, vol. 18, *1979–1983*, comp. Universal House of Justice, 665–69.

Coda: Toward a Bahá'í Mass Movement, 1963–1968

1. King, *Why We Can't Wait*, 128; Universal House of Justice, *Messages, 1963–1986*, comp. Marks, 2.10, 6.5, 6.10, 14.4, 18.1. For treatments of the "beloved community," see Smith and Zepp, *Search for the Beloved Community*, esp. chapter 6, and Cone, *Martin and Malcolm and America*, esp. chapter 8.

2. "Good Afternoon," *Greenville (S.C.) Piedmont*, September or October 1966, clipping, private collection of Joy F. Benson.

3. Universal House of Justice, *Messages, 1963–1986*, comp. Marks, 4, 46.3.

4. A fine overview of events during 1968, inside and outside of the United States, and analysis of that year as a watershed, is Isserman and Kazin, *America Divided*, chapter 12.

5. Quoted in Garrow, *Bearing the Cross*, 612.

6. Bass and Nelson, *Orangeburg Massacre*, 137; Magdalene Bahia Laursen, "The War of Racism," undergraduate research paper, Francis Marion University, 2008, copy in author's possession. Released early from prison for good behavior, Sellers went on to complete graduate degrees at Harvard and the University of North Carolina at Greensboro, eventually becoming director of the African American Studies Program at the University of South Carolina and, in 2008, the president of historically black Vorhees College in his hometown of Denmark, South Carolina. Despite the trauma and grief she experienced, Reynolds went on to spend virtually her entire career as a home economics instructor with the Orangeburg County extension service. While the state has never conducted an official investigation of the event that became known as the Orangeburg Massacre, Gov. Mark Sanford issued an official apology in 2003.

7. "Preliminary letter to South Carolina State Goals Committee Newsletter,"

September 1966, copy in author's possession (for membership); *South Carolina Baha'i Faith State Goals Committee Newsletter* 1, no. 3 (November 1966) (for the convention); "Feast of Ridvan," April 20, 1966, private collection of Joy F. Benson (for Greenville); Young interview (for churches); Kahn, "Encounter of Two Myths," 244 (for Charleston). For Pee Dee–area meetings, see, for example, *South Carolina Baha'i Faith State Goals Committee Newsletter* 1, no. 3 (November 1966); *South Carolina Baha'i Bulletin*, October 1967. Jordan Young adopted the locution "Bahá'u'lláh of Persia," uncommon in the American Bahá'í community, for his talks in churches as an equivalent to "Jesus of Nazareth," a title used frequently among Protestants in reference to the historical Jesus.

8. *South Carolina Baha'i Bulletin*, June 1967, October 1967, November–December 1967, and January 1968; *South Carolina Baha'i Faith State Goals Committee Newsletter* 3, no. 1 (April 1968); *South Carolina Baha'i Faith State Goals Committee Newsletter* 3, no. 3 (June-July 1968); *South Carolina Bahái Faith State Goals Committee Newsletter* 3, no. 4 (August-September 1968); *South Carolina Baha'i Faith State Goals Committee Newsletter* 3, no. 5 (November 1968) (all for enrollments); *National Bahá'í Review* 19 (July 1969): 9; "By-Laws: Bahá'í Association of Benedict," CBA, Columbia, S.C. (both for Columbia).

9. *South Carolina Baha'i Faith State Goals Committee Newsletter* 3, no. 3 (June-July 1968) (for the Thomases); Jack McCants to Elizabeth Martin, May 18, 2006, copy in possession of the author; Martin interview; Bennett, "Bahá'í: A Way of Life for Millions" and booklet of the same name in author's possession (all for Winnsboro); Hampson, "Diffusion and Growth," 239 (for membership); *South Carolina Baha'i Faith State Goals Committee Newsletter* 3, no. 5 (November 1968) (for the convention). The *Ebony* article, written by a well-known journalist and author and published under a cover story on the death of Nat King Cole, likely brought the Bahá'í Faith to the attention of large numbers of African Americans. After its publication, the Bahá'ís received permission to reprint the article as a stand-alone booklet. The "*Ebony* reprint" was a standard teaching tool in South Carolina and other Deep South states during the 1970s.

10. *South Carolina Baha'i Faith State Goals Committee Newsletter* 3, no. 1 (April 1968); *South Carolina Baha'i Faith State Goals Committee Newsletter* 3, no. 4 (August–September 1968).

11. Hollinger, "Introduction," in Hollinger, ed. *Community Histories*, xxx; Hampson, "Diffusion and Growth," 232–33 (both for growth trends); Glenford Mitchell, Sarah Pereira, and Eugene Byrd, "The Most Challenging Issue: Teaching Negroes—A Task Force Paper," 1967, copy in author's possession; Hampson, "Diffusion and Growth," 236–37; *South Carolina Baha'i Faith State Goals Committee Newsletter* 3, no. 5 (November 1968).

Bibliography

Primary Sources

'Abdu'l-Bahá. *The Promulgation of Universal Peace: Talks Delivered by 'Abdu'l-Bahá during His Visit to the United States and Canada in 1912*. Compiled by Howard MacNutt. 2nd ed. Wilmette, Ill.: Bahá'í Publishing Trust, 2007. First published 1921.
———. *Selections from the Writings of 'Abdu'l-Bahá*. Wilmette, Ill.: Bahá'í Publishing Trust, 1997.
———. *Tablets of Abdul-Baha Abbas*. Vol. 1. Chicago: Bahá'í Publishing Society, 1909.
———. *Tablets of Abdul-Baha Abbas*. Vol. 2. Chicago: Bahá'í Publishing Society, 1915.
———. *Tablets of Abdul-Baha Abbas*. Vol. 3. New York: Bahá'í Publishing Committee, 1916.
———. *The Will and Testament of 'Abdu'l-Bahá*. Wilmette, Ill.: Bahá'í Publishing Trust, 1990.
Abercrombie, J. Richard. Interview by author, December 7, 2003, Greenville, S.C.
Abercrombie, Lillie. Interview by Frances Worthington, October 2003, Greenville, S.C. TS in author's possession.
Aptheker, Herbert, ed. *The Correspondence of W.E.B. Du Bois*. Vol. 3, *Selections, 1944–1963*. Amherst: University of Massachusetts Press, 1978.
Association of Statisticians of American Religious Bodies. *2010 U.S. Religion Census: Religious Congregations & Membership Study*. Accessed through the Association of Religion Data Archives website. Accessed November 10, 2014. http://www.thearda.com/rcms2010/.
Avery School Memorabilia Collection. Avery Research Center for African American History and Culture, College of Charleston, S.C.
Bahá'í Publishing Trust. *Bahá'í Prayers: A Selection of Prayers Revealed by Bahá'u'lláh, the Báb, and 'Abdu'l-Bahá*. Wilmette, Ill.: Bahá'í Publishing Trust, 2002.
Bahá'u'lláh. *Gleanings from the Writings of Bahá'u'lláh*. Translated by Shoghi Effendi. 1st pocket-sized ed. Wilmette, Ill.: Bahá'í Publishing Trust, 1983.
———. *The Hidden Words*. Translated by Shoghi Effendi. Wilmette, Ill.: Bahá'í Publishing Trust, 1985.

———. *The Kitáb-i-Aqdas: The Most Holy Book*. 1st pocket-sized ed. Wilmette, Ill.: Bahá'í Publishing Trust, 1993.

———. *The Kitáb-i-Íqán: The Book of Certitude*. Translated by Shoghi Effendi. New ed. Wilmette, Ill.: Bahá'í Publishing Trust, 2003.

———. *The Summons of the Lord of Hosts*. Haifa, Israel: Bahá'í World Centre, 2002.

———. *The Tabernacle of Unity*. Haifa, Israel: Bahá'í World Centre, 2006.

———. *Tablets of Bahá'u'lláh Revealed after the Kitáb-i-Aqdas*. Translated by Habib Taherzadeh. 1st pocket-sized ed. Wilmette, Ill.: Bahá'í Publishing Trust, 1988.

Bennett, Lerone, Jr. "Bahá'í: A Way of Life for Millions." *Ebony* 20, no. 6 (April 1965): 48–56.

Benson, Joy F. Interview by author, October 19, 2004, Columbia, S.C.

Bosch, John, and Louise Bosch. Papers. National Bahá'í Archives of the United States, Wilmette, Ill.

Brisley, Steve. Interview by author, December 20, 2001.

Derrick, Samuel M. Papers. South Caroliniana Library, University of South Carolina, Columbia.

Du Bois, W.E.B. "The Fourth Annual Conference of the National Association for the Advancement of Colored People." *Crisis* 4, no. 2 (June 1912): 80.

———. "Men of the Month." *Crisis* 4, no. 1 (May 1912): 14–16.

———. *The Souls of Black Folk*. With new introduction. New York: Dover Publications, 1994.

Entzminger, Jessie Dixon, and Louise Moore Montgomery. Interview by Doris Morris, n.d. [ca. 1980s], Columbia, S.C. Audio cassette, Columbia Bahá'í Archives, Columbia, S.C.

Esslemont, J. E. *Bahá'u'lláh and the New Era*. 5th rev. ed. Wilmette, Ill.: Bahá'í Publishing Trust, 1980.

Ford, Virginia. Interview by Elmer Kenneally, 1989, Greenville, S.C. Audio cassette, Greenville Bahá'í Archives, Greenville, S.C., and notes by Frances Worthington in author's possession.

Frain, Marie. "Baha'i History of Augusta, Georgia." TS, Augusta Bahá'í Archives, Augusta, Ga.

Furmaniana Collection. Special Collections and Archives. James B. Duke Library, Furman University, Greenville, S.C.

Gibson, Campbell, and Kay Jung. *Historical Census Statistics on Population Totals by Race, 1790 to 1990, and by Hispanic Origin, 1970 to 1990, for the United States, Regions, Divisions, and States*. Working Paper Series 56. Washington, D.C.: Population Division, United States Bureau of the Census, 2002. Last modified January 2, 2013. Accessed November 16, 2014. http://www.census.gov/population/www/documentation/twps0056/twps0056.html.

Gregory, Louis G. *A Heavenly Vista: The Pilgrimage of Louis G. Gregory*. Ferndale, MI: Alpha Services, 1997. First published 1911. Available online at http://bahai-library.com/file.php?file=gregory_heavenly_vista.

———. Papers. National Bahá'í Archives of the United States, Wilmette, Ill.

———. "Some Recollections of the Early Days of the Bahai Faith in Washington, D.C." TS, Louis G. Gregory Papers, National Baháʼí Archives of the United States, Wilmette, Ill.

Hannen-Knobloch Family Papers. National Baháʼí Archives of the United States, Wilmette, Ill.

Harlan, Louis R., and Raymond W. Smock, eds. *The Booker T. Washington Papers*. Vol. 9, *1906–8*. Urbana: University of Illinois Press, 1980.

———. *The Booker T. Washington Papers*. Vol. 12, *1912–1914*. Urbana: University of Illinois Press, 1982.

———. *The Booker T. Washington Papers*. Vol. 13, *1914–15*. Urbana: University of Illinois Press, 1984.

Hill Directory Co. *Hill's Columbia (Richland County, S.C.) City Directory*. Vol. 10, *1939*. Richmond, Va.: Hill Directory Co., 1939.

———. *Hill's Columbia (Richland County, S.C.) City Directory*. Vol. 13, *1942*. Richmond, Va.: Hill Directory Co., 1942.

———. *Hill's Greenville (Greenville Co., S.C.) City Directory, 1941*. Richmond, Va.: Hill Directory Co., 1941.

———. *Hill's Greenville (Greenville Co., S.C.) City Directory, 1945*. Richmond, Va.: Hill Directory Co., 1945.

———. *Hill's Greenville (Greenville Co., S.C.) Directory, 1948*. Richmond, Va.: Hill Directory Co., 1948.

———. *Hill's Greenville (Greenville County, S.C.) Directory, 1950–1951*. Richmond, Va.: Hill Directory Co., 1951.

Hoagg, H. Emogene. Papers. National Baháʼí Archives of the United States, Wilmette, Ill.

Ioas, Leroy. Papers. National Baháʼí Archives of the United States, Wilmette, Ill.

Kenneally, Elmer. "Fifty Years of the Baháʼí Faith in Greenville, SC, 1939–1989." TS, Greenville Baháʼí Archives, Greenville, S.C.

King, Martin Luther, Jr. *Why We Can't Wait*. New York: Harper & Row, 1963.

Levi Branson. *Branson's Directory of the Businesses and Citizens of Raleigh, also Farmers and Land-owners of Wake County, 1891*. Raleigh, N.C.: Levi Branson, 1891.

Local Spiritual Assembly Records. National Baháʼí Archives of the United States, Wilmette, Ill.

Logan, James R. Scrapbooks. Avery Research Center for African American History and Culture, College of Charleston, S.C.

Lowery, I. E. *Life on the Old Plantation in Ante-Bellum Days, or A Story Based on Facts, with Brief Sketches of the Author by the Late Rev. J. Wofford White of the South Carolina Conference, Methodist Episcopal Church and An Appendix*. Columbia: The State Co. Printing, 1911.

Lunt, Alfred E. Papers. National Baháʼí Archives of the United States, Wilmette, Ill.

Maloney Publishing Co. *Augusta City Directory, 1901*. Atlanta: Maloney Publishing Co., 1901.

Martin, Elizabeth. Interview by author, April 5, 2003, Columbia, S.C.

National Park Service. Civil War Soldiers and Sailors Database. Accessed November 10, 2014. http://www.civilwar.nps.gov/cwss/soldiers.cfm.

National Spiritual Assembly of the Bahá'ís of the United States. *Annual Bahá'í Reports Presented to the Bahá'ís of the United States for the Year 1959-1960*. Wilmette, Ill.: Bahá'í Publishing Trust, 1960.

———. *Annual Bahá'í Reports Presented to the Bahá'ís of the United States for the Year 1961-1962*. Wilmette, Ill.: Bahá'í Publishing Trust, 1962.

———. *Annual Bahá'í Reports Presented to the Bahá'ís of the United States for the Year 1962-1963*. Wilmette, Ill.: Bahá'í Publishing Trust, 1963.

National Spiritual Assembly of the Bahá'ís of the United States and Canada. *Annual Bahá'í Reports Presented to the Bahá'ís of the United States and Canada for the Year 1938-1939*. New York: Bahá'í Publishing Committee, 1939.

———. *Annual Bahá'í Reports Presented to the Bahá'ís of the United States and Canada for the Year 1940-1941*. Wilmette, Ill.: Bahá'í Publishing Committee, 1941.

———. *Annual Bahá'í Reports Presented to the Bahá'ís of the United States and Canada for the Year 1941-1942*. Wilmette, Ill.: Bahá'í Publishing Committee, 1942.

———. *Annual Bahá'í Reports Presented to the Bahá'ís of the United States and Canada for the Year 1942-1943*. Wilmette, Ill.: Bahá'í Publishing Committee, 1943.

———. *Annual Bahá'í Reports Presented to the Bahá'ís of the United States and Canada for the Year 1943-1944*. Wilmette, Ill.: Bahá'í Publishing Committee, 1944.

———. *Annual Bahá'í Reports Presented to the Bahá'ís of the United States and Canada for the Year 1946-1947*. Wilmette, Ill.: Bahá'í Publishing Committee, 1947.

National Spiritual Assembly of the Bahá'ís of the United States and Canada, comp. *The Bahá'í World: A Biennial International Record*. Vol. 7, 1936-1938. Wilmette, Ill.: Bahá'í Publishing Trust, 1980. First published 1939.

———. *The Bahá'í World: A Biennial International Record*. Vol. 8, 1938-1940. Wilmette, Ill.: Bahá'í Publishing Trust, 1980. First published 1942.

———. *The Bahá'í World: A Biennial International Record*. Vol. 9, 1940-1944. Wilmette, Ill.: Bahá'í Publishing Trust, 1981. First published 1945.

———. *The Bahá'í World: A Biennial International Record*. Vol. 10, 1944-1946. Wilmette, Ill.: Bahá'í Publishing Trust, 1981. First published 1949.

———. *The Bahá'í World: A Biennial International Record*. Vol. 11, 1946-1950. Wilmette, Ill.: Bahá'í Publishing Trust, 1981. First published 1950.

———. *The Bahá'í World: A Biennial International Record*. Vol. 12, 1950-1954. Wilmette, Ill.: Bahá'í Publishing Trust, 1981. First published 1956.

National Teaching Committee Records. National Bahá'í Archives of the United States, Wilmette, Ill.

Office of the Secretary Records. National Bahá'í Archives of the United States, Wilmette, Ill.

Parsons, Agnes. *'Abdu'l-Bahá in America: Agnes Parsons' Diary*. Edited by Richard Hollinger. Los Angeles: Kalimát Press, 1996.

Passport Applications. General Records of the Department of State. National Archives and Records Administration, Washington, D.C. Accessed through http://www.ancestry.com.

Rabbani, Rúhíyyih. *The Priceless Pearl.* 2nd ed. Oakham, England: Bahá'í Publishing, 2000.

Railway Purchasing Agent Co. *Official Railway List: A Directory.* Chicago: Railway Purchasing Agent Co., 1884.

Records of the Immigration and Naturalization Service. National Archives and Records Administration, Washington, D.C. Accessed through http://www.ancestry.com.

R. L. Polk. *Polk's Augusta (Richmond County, Georgia) City Directory, 1937.* Richmond, Va.: R. L. Polk, 1937.

———. *Polk's Augusta (Richmond County, Georgia) City Directory, 1938.* Richmond, Va.: R. L. Polk, 1938.

Sego, Esther. "History of the Baha'i Cause in Augusta, Ga." TS, Augusta Bahá'í Archives, Augusta, Ga.

Shoghi Effendi. *The Advent of Divine Justice.* 1st pocket-sized ed. Wilmette, Ill.: Bahá'í Publishing Trust, 1990.

———. *Bahá'í Administration: Selected Messages, 1922–1932.* 6th ed. Wilmette, Ill.: Bahá'í Publishing Trust, 1995.

———. *Citadel of Faith: Messages to America, 1947–1957.* Wilmette, Ill.: Bahá'í Publishing Trust, 1997.

———. *God Passes By.* Wilmette, Ill.: Bahá'í Publishing Trust, 1974.

———. *Messages to America: Selected Letters and Cablegrams Addressed to the Bahá'ís of North America, 1932–1946.* Wilmette, Ill.: Bahá'í Publishing Committee, 1947.

———. *Messages to the Bahá'í World, 1950–1957.* Wilmette, Ill.: Bahá'í Publishing Trust, 1971.

———. *The Unfolding Destiny of the British Bahá'í Community: Messages from the Guardian of the Bahá'í Faith to the Bahá'ís of the British Isles.* Oakham, England: Bahá'í Publishing, 1981.

———. *The World Order of Bahá'u'lláh: Selected Letters.* 1st pocket-sized ed. Wilmette, Ill.: Bahá'í Publishing Trust, 1991.

———. *A World Survey of the Bahá'í Faith, 1844–1944.* Wilmette, Ill.: Bahá'í Publishing Committee, 1944.

South Carolina Death Records. South Carolina Department of Archives and History, Columbia.

South Carolina Department of Agriculture, Commerce, and Immigration. *Handbook of South Carolina: Resources, Institutions and Industries of the State.* Columbia: South Carolina Department of Agriculture, Commerce, and Immigration, 1908.

South Carolina State Hospital Commitment Files. South Carolina Department of Archives and History, Columbia.

South Carolina State Hospital Records. South Carolina Department of Archives and History, Columbia.

Southern Educational Association. *Journal of Proceedings and Addresses of the Eleventh Annual Meeting Held at Columbia, S.C., December 26–29, 1901*. N.p.: Southern Education Association, 1902.

Southern Printing & Publishing Co. *Walsh's 1925–1926 Charleston, South Carolina, City Directory*. Charleston: Southern Printing & Publishing Co., 1925.

Taylor, Bonnie J., ed. *The Pupil of the Eye: African Americans in the World Order of Bahá'u'lláh*. Riviera Beach, Fla.: Palabra Publications, 1998.

Thompson, James Lawrence. *Of Shattered Minds*. Edited by Anita Warick Roof. Columbia: South Carolina Department of Mental Health, 1989.

Thompson, Juliet. *Juliet Thompson's Diary*. With a preface by Marzieh Gail. Los Angeles: Kalimát Press, 1995.

United States Bureau of the Census. *Seventh Census of the United States, 1850*. National Archives and Records Administration, Washington, D.C. Accessed through http://www.ancestry.com.

———. *Eighth Census of the United States, 1860*. National Archives and Records Administration, Washington, D.C. Accessed through http://www.ancestry.com.

———. *Tenth Census of the United States, 1880*. National Archives and Records Administration, Washington, D.C. Accessed through http://www.ancestry.com.

———. *Twelfth Census of the United States, 1900*. National Archives and Records Administration, Washington, D.C. Accessed through http://www.ancestry.com.

———. *Thirteenth Census of the United States, 1910*. National Archives and Records Administration, Washington, D.C. Accessed through http://www.ancestry.com.

———. *Fourteenth Census of the United States, 1920*. National Archives and Records Administration, Washington, D.C. Accessed through http://www.ancestry.com.

———. *Fifteenth Census of the United States, 1930*. National Archives and Records Administration, Washington, D.C. Accessed through http://www.ancestry.com.

———. *Sixteenth Census of the United States, 1940*. National Archives and Records Administration, Washington, D.C. Accessed November 16, 2014. http://www2.census.gov/prod2/decennial/documents/33973538v2p6ch4.pdf.

Universal House of Justice. *Century of Light*. Haifa, Israel: Bahá'í World Centre, 2001.

———. *The Five Year Plan, 2001–2006: Messages of the Universal House of Justice*. 2nd ed. Riviera Beach, Fla.: Palabra Publications, 2003.

———. *The Four Year Plan: Messages of the Universal House of Justice*. Riviera Beach, Fla.: Palabra Publications, 1996.

———. *Messages from the Universal House of Justice, 1963–1986: The Third Epoch of the Formative Age*. Compiled by Geoffry W. Marks. Wilmette, Ill.: Bahá'í Publishing Trust, 1996.

———. *Messages from the Universal House of Justice 1968–1973*. Wilmette, Ill.: Bahá'í Publishing Trust, 1976.

Universal House of Justice, comp. *The Bahá'í World: An International Record*. Vol. 13, 1954–1963. Haifa, Israel: Universal House of Justice, 1970.

———. *The Bahá'í World: An International Record*. Vol. 14, 1963–1968. Haifa, Israel: Universal House of Justice, 1974.

———. *The Bahá'í World: An International Record.* Vol. 18, 1979–1983. Haifa, Israel: Bahá'í World Centre, 1986.

Walsh Directory Co., Inc. *Walsh's 1910 Charleston, South Carolina, City Directory.* Charleston: Walsh Directory Co., Inc., 1910.

Wendte, Charles W. *Heart and Voice: A Collection of Songs and Services for the Sunday School and the Home.* Boston: George H. Ellis Co., 1909.

World War I Selective Service System Draft Registration Cards. National Archives and Records Administration, Washington, D.C. Accessed through http://www.ancestry.com.

Young, Jordan, and Annette Young. Interview with author, September 25, 2003, Easley, S.C.

Zaraqání, Mahmúd. *Mahmúd's Diary: The Story of Mírzá Mahmúd-i-Zaraqání Chronicling 'Abdu'l-Bahá's Journey in America.* Translated by Mohi Sobhani and Shirley Macias. Oxford: George Ronald, 1997.

Secondary Sources

Abizadeh, Arash. "Democratic Elections without Campaigns? Normative Foundations of National Bahá'í Elections." *World Order* 37, no. 1 (2005): 7–49.

Amanat, Abbas. *Resurrection and Renewal: The Making of the Babi Movement in Iran, 1844–1850.* Ithaca, N.Y.: Cornell University Press, 1989.

Armstrong-Ingram, R. Jackson. *Music, Devotions, and Mashriqu'l-Adhkár.* Los Angeles: Kalimát Press, 1987.

Arsenault, Raymond. "Five Days in May: Freedom Riding in the Carolinas." In *Toward the Meeting of the Waters*, edited by Winfred B. Moore Jr. and Orville Vernon Burton, 201–21. Columbia: University of South Carolina Press, 2008.

Atkinson, Anne Gordon, Rosanne Adams-Jenkins, Robert Atkinson, Richard Grover, Diane Iverson, Robert H. Stockman, and Burton W. F. Trafton Jr. *Green Acre on the Piscataqua.* Eliot, Maine: Green Acre Bahá'í School Council, 1991.

Ayers, Edward L. *The Promise of the New South.* New York: Oxford University Press, 1992.

Baker, R. Scott. "Schooling and White Supremacy: The African American Struggle for Educational Equality and Access in South Carolina, 1945–1970." In *Toward the Meeting of the Waters*, edited by Winfred B. Moore Jr. and Orville Vernon Burton, 300–315. Columbia: University of South Carolina Press, 2008.

Balyuzi, H. M. *'Abdu'l-Bahá: The Centre of the Covenant of Bahá'u'lláh.* Oxford: George Ronald, 1971.

———. *The Báb.* New ed. Oxford: George Ronald, 1973.

———. *Bahá'u'lláh: King of Glory.* Oxford: George Ronald, 1980.

Bass, Jack, and Jack Nelson. *The Orangeburg Massacre.* 2nd ed. Macon, Ga.: Mercer University Press, 1996.

Bass, Jack, and Marilyn W. Thompson. *Strom: The Complicated Personal and Political Life of Strom Thurmond.* New York: PublicAffairs, 2005.

Blum, Edward J. *Reforging the White Republic: Race, Religion, and American Nationalism, 1865–1898*. Baton Rouge: Louisiana State University Press, 2005.

———. *W.E.B. Du Bois: American Prophet*. Philadelphia: University of Pennsylvania Press, 2007.

Borstelmann, Thomas. *The Cold War and the Color Line: American Race Relations in the Global Arena*. Cambridge, Mass.: Harvard University Press, 2001.

Boyer, Paul. *When Time Shall Be No More: Prophecy Belief in Modern American Culture*. Cambridge, Mass.: Harvard University Press, 1992.

Bramson, Loni. "The Plans of Unified Action: A Survey." In *Bahá'ís in the West*, edited by Peter Smith, 154–97. Los Angeles: Kalimát Press, 2004.

Bramson-Lerche, Loni. "Some Aspects of the Development of the Bahá'í Administrative Order in America, 1922–1936." In *Studies in Bábí and Bahá'í History*. Vol. 1, edited by Moojan Momen, 254–300. Los Angeles: Kalimát Press, 1982.

Braun, Eunice, and the Editors. "Hands of the Cause of God." Bahá'í Encyclopedia Project website, accessed November 17, 2014, http://www.bahai-encyclopedia-project.org/index.php?option=com_content&view=article&id=64:hands-of-the-cause-of-god&catid=36:administrationinstitutions.

Bryant, Lynn Markovich. *"I'm Black and I'm Proud," wished the white girl.: The Autobiography of Lynn Markovich Bryant*. Lincoln, Neb.: iUniverse, 2002.

Buck, Christopher. *Alain Locke: Faith and Philosophy*. Los Angeles: Kalimát Press, 2005.

———. "The Interracial 'Baha'i Movement' and the Black Intelligentsia: The Case of W.E.B. Du Bois." *Journal of Religious History* 36, no. 4 (December 2012): 542–62.

Burke, W. Lewis, and Belinda F. Gergel, eds. *Matthew J. Perry: The Man, His Times, and His Legacy*. Columbia: University of South Carolina Press, 2004.

Burke, W. Lewis, and William C. Hine. "The South Carolina State College Law School: Its Roots, Creation, and Legacy." In *Matthew J. Perry: The Man, His Times, and His Legacy*, edited by W. Lewis Burke and Belinda F. Gergel, 17–60. Columbia: University of South Carolina Press, 2004.

Burton, Orville Vernon, and Wilbur Cross. *Penn Center: A History Preserved*. Athens: University of Georgia Press, 2014.

Caldwell, A. B. *History of the American Negro, Georgia Edition*. Vol. 2. Atlanta: A. B. Caldwell, 1920.

Carlton, David. *Mill and Town in South Carolina, 1880–1920*. Baton Rouge: Louisiana State University Press, 1982.

Cashin, Edward J. *The Story of Augusta*. Augusta, Ga.: Richmond County Board of Education, 1980.

Chappell, David L. *A Stone of Hope: Prophetic Religion and the Death of Jim Crow*. Chapel Hill: University of North Carolina Press, 2004.

Clark, Deb. "The Bahá'ís of Baltimore, 1898–1990." In *Community Histories*, edited by Richard Hollinger, 111–50. Los Angeles: Kalimát Press, 1992.

Cole, Juan. *Modernity and the Millennium: The Genesis of the Bahai Faith in the Nineteenth-Century Middle East*. New York: Columbia University Press, 1998.

Cone, James H. *Martin and Malcolm and America: A Dream or a Nightmare.* Maryknoll, N.Y.: Orbis Books, 1991.

Conser, Walter H., Jr., and Rodger M. Payne, eds. *Southern Crossroads: Perspectives on Religion and Culture.* Lexington: University Press of Kentucky, 2008.

Cox, Harvey. *Fire from Heaven: The Rise of Pentecostal Spirituality and the Reshaping of Religion in the Twenty-first Century.* Cambridge, Mass.: Da Capo Press, 2001.

Dahl, Roger. "Three Teaching Methods Used during North America's First Seven Year Plan." *Journal of Bahá'í Studies* 5, no. 3 (1993), 1–16.

Diamond, Sara. *Roads to Dominion: Right Wing Movements and Political Power in the United States.* New York: Guilford Press, 1995.

Dittmer, John. *Black Georgia in the Progressive Era, 1900–1920.* Urbana: University of Illinois Press, 1977.

Dobrasko, Rebekah. "Upholding 'Separate but Equal': South Carolina's School Equalization Program, 1951–1955." MA thesis, University of South Carolina, 2005.

Donaldson, Bobby J. "Standing on a Volcano: The Leadership of William Jefferson White." In *Paternalism in a Southern City: Race, Religion, and Gender in Augusta, Georgia,* edited by Edward J. Cashin and Glenn T. Askew, 135–76. Athens: University of Georgia Press, 2001.

Downey, Tom. *Planting a Capitalist South: Masters, Merchants, and Manufacturers in the Southern Interior, 1790–1860.* Baton Rouge: Louisiana State University Press, 2006.

Doyle, Don H. *New Men, New Cities, New South: Atlanta, Nashville, Charleston, Mobile, 1860–1910.* Chapel Hill: University of North Carolina Press, 1990.

Drago, Edmund L. *Initiative, Paternalism, and Race Relations: Charleston's Avery Normal Institute.* Athens: University of Georgia Press, 1990.

Drake, Joseph Turpin. "The Negro in Greenville, South Carolina." MA thesis, University of North Carolina, Chapel Hill, 1940.

Dudziak, Mary L. *Cold War Civil Rights: Race and the Image of American Democracy.* Princeton: Princeton University Press, 2000.

Edgar, Walter. *South Carolina: A History.* Columbia: University of South Carolina Press, 1996.

Egerton, John. *Speak Now against the Day: The Generation before the Civil Rights Movement in the South.* Chapel Hill: University of North Carolina Press, 1994.

Etter-Lewis, Gwendolyn, and Richard Thomas, eds. *Lights of the Spirit: Historical Portraits of Black Bahá'ís in North America, 1898–2000.* Wilmette, Ill.: Bahá'í Publishing, 2006.

Eyford, Glen, ed. *The Bahá'í Faith and Marxism: Proceedings of a Conference Held January 1986.* Ottawa, Ont.: Bahá'í Studies Publications, 1987.

Fairclough, Adam. *Race and Democracy: The Civil Rights Struggle in Louisiana, 1915–1972.* Athens: University of Georgia Press, 1995.

Fraser, Walter J. *Charleston! Charleston! The History of a Southern City.* Columbia: University of South Carolina Press, 1989.

Fredrickson, George M. *The Black Image in the White Mind: The Debate on Afro-*

American Character and Destiny, 1817–1914. With a new introduction. Middletown, Conn.: Wesleyan University Press, 1987.

Garis, M. R. *Martha Root: Lioness at the Threshold*. Wilmette, Ill.: Bahá'í Publishing Trust, 1983.

Garrow, David J. *Bearing the Cross: Martin Luther King, Jr., and the Southern Christian Leadership Conference*. New York: HarperCollins, 2004.

Gaston, Paul M. *Man and Mission: E. B. Gaston and the Origins of the Fairhope Single Tax Colony*. Montgomery, Ala.: Black Belt Press, 1993.

Gilstrap, Dorothy Freeman. *From Copper to Gold: The Life of Dorothy Baker*. Wilmette, Ill.: Bahá'í Publishing Trust, 1999.

Gleijeses, Piero. "African Americans and the War against Spain." In *A Question of Manhood: A Reader in U.S. Black Men's History and Masculinity*, edited by Darlene Clark Hine and Earnestine Jenkins, 320–45. Indianapolis: Indiana University Press, 1999.

Green, Constance McLaughlin. *The Secret City: A History of Race Relations in the Nation's Capital*. Princeton, N.J.: Princeton University Press, 1967.

Gregory, James N. *The Southern Diaspora: How the Great Migrations of Black and White Southerners Transformed America*. Chapel Hill: University of North Carolina Press, 2005.

Gulpaygání, Abu'l-Fadl. *The Bahá'í Proofs; And, a Short Sketch of the History and Lives of the Leaders of This Religion*. Facsimile of the first edition. Wilmette, Ill.: Bahá'í Publishing Trust, 2002. First published 1902.

Hahn, Steven. *A Nation under Our Feet: Black Political Struggles in the Rural South from Slavery to the Great Migration*. Cambridge, Mass.: Harvard University Press, 2003.

Hall, Jacquelyn Dowd. *Revolt against Chivalry: Jessie Daniel Ames and the Women's Campaign against Lynching*. Revised edition. New York: Columbia University Press, 1993.

Hamer, Fritz P. "Seeds of Change: World War I, South Carolina, Impact and Contributions." In *Forward Together: South Carolinians in the Great War*, edited by Fritz P. Hamer, 13–52. Charleston, S.C.: History Press, 2007.

Hampson, Arthur. "The Growth and Spread of the Baha'i Faith." PhD diss., University of Hawaii, 1980.

Harvey, Paul. *Freedom's Coming: Religious Culture and the Shaping of the South from the Civil War through the Civil Rights Era*. Chapel Hill: University of North Carolina Press, 2005.

Hassall, Graham. "Bahá'í Country Notes: Africa." Bahá'í Library website. Accessed January 25, 2015. http://bahai-library.com/hassall_notes_africa.

Hatcher, William S., and J. Douglas Martin. *The Bahá'í Faith: The Emerging Global Religion*. Revised edition. Wilmette, Ill.: Bahá'í Publishing Trust, 2003.

Hemmingway, Theodore. "Prelude to Change: Black Carolinians in the War Years, 1914–1920." *Journal of Negro History* 65, no. 3 (Summer 1980): 212–27.

Herrmann, Duane L. "The Bahá'í Faith in Kansas." In *Community Histories*, edited by Richard Hollinger, 67–108. Los Angeles: Kalimát Press, 1992.

Higginbotham, Evelyn Brooks. *Righteous Discontent: The Women's Movement in the Black Baptist Church, 1880–1920*. Cambridge, Mass.: Harvard University Press, 1993.

Hoffman, Edwin D. "The Genesis of the Modern Movement for Equal Rights in South Carolina, 1930–1939." *Journal of Negro History* 44, no. 4 (October 1959): 346–69.

Hollinger, Richard. "Introduction: Bahá'í Communities in the West, 1897–1992." In *Community Histories*, edited by Richard Hollinger, vii–xlix. Los Angeles: Kalimát Press, 1992.

Hollinger, Richard, ed. *Community Histories*. Los Angeles: Kalimát Press, 1992.

Hollis, Daniel W. "Samuel Chiles Mitchell, Social Reformer in Blease's South Carolina." *South Carolina Historical Magazine* 70, no. 1 (January 1969): 20–37.

Holt, Thomas. *Black over White: Negro Political Leadership in South Carolina during Reconstruction*. Chicago: University of Illinois Press, 1979.

Hornsby, Benjamin F. *Stepping Stone to the Supreme Court: Clarendon County, South Carolina*. Columbia: South Carolina Department of Archives and History, 1992.

Hudson, Janet. *Entangled by White Supremacy: Reform in World War I–era South Carolina*. Lexington: University Press of Kentucky, 2009.

Huff, Archie Vernon, Jr. *Greenville: The History of the City and County in the South Carolina Piedmont*. Columbia: University of South Carolina Press, 1995.

Isserman, Maurice, and Michael Kazin. *America Divided: The Civil War of the 1960s*. 2nd ed. Oxford: Oxford University Press, 2004.

Jenkins, Wilbert L. *Seizing the New Day: African Americans in Post–Civil War Charleston*. Bloomington: University of Indiana Press, 1998.

Johnson, Todd, and Brian J. Grim. *The World's Religions in Figures: An Introduction to International Religious Demography*. West Sussex, UK: Wiley-Blackwell, 2013.

Kahn, Jonathon. *Divine Discontent: The Religious Imagination of W.E.B. Du Bois*. New York: Oxford University Press, 2009.

Kahn, Sandra Santolucito. "Encounter of Two Myths: Bahá'í and Christian in the Rural American South—A Study in Transmythicization." PhD diss., University of California, Santa Barbara, 1977.

Kantrowitz, Stephen. *Ben Tillman and the Reconstruction of White Supremacy*. Chapel Hill: University of North Carolina Press, 2000.

Kelley, Robin D. G. *Hammer and Hoe: Alabama Communists during the Great Depression*. Chapel Hill: University of North Carolina Press, 1990.

———. "'We Are Not What We Seem': Rethinking Black Working Class Opposition in the Jim Crow South." *Journal of American History* 80, no. 1 (June 1993): 75–112.

Khan, Janet A., and Peter J. Khan. *Advancement of Women: A Bahá'í Perspective*. Wilmette, Ill.: Bahá'í Publishing Trust, 1998.

Kluger, Richard. *Simple Justice*. New York: Random House, 1977.

K'Meyer, Tracy. *Interracialism and Christian Community in the Postwar South: The Story of Koinonia Farm*. Charlottesville: University of Virginia Press, 1997.

Korstad, Robert R. "Could History Repeat Itself? The Prospects for a Second Reconstruction in Post–World War II South Carolina." In *Toward the Meeting of the Waters*, edited by Winfred B. Moore Jr. and Orville Vernon Burton, 252–60. Columbia: University of South Carolina Press, 2008.

Kovacik, Charles F., and John J. Winberry. *South Carolina: A Geography*. Boulder: Westview Press, 1987.

Lander, Ernest McPherson, Jr. *A History of South Carolina, 1865–1960*. Chapel Hill: University of North Carolina Press, 1960.

Lau, Peter F. *Democracy Rising: South Carolina and the Fight for Black Equality since 1865*. Lexington: University Press of Kentucky, 2006.

Lesesne, Henry H. *A History of the University of South Carolina, 1940–2000*. Columbia: University of South Carolina Press, 2002.

Letwin, Daniel. *The Challenge of Interracial Unionism: Alabama Coal Miners, 1878–1921*. Chapel Hill: University of North Carolina Press, 1998.

Lippy, Charles H., ed. *Religion in South Carolina*. Columbia: University of South Carolina Press, 1993.

Litwack, Leon. *Trouble in Mind: Black Southerners in the Age of Jim Crow*. New York: Vintage Books, 1998.

MacRobert, Iain. *The Black Roots and White Racism of Early Pentecostalism*. New York: St. Martin's Press, 1988.

Maude, Roderick, and Derwent Maude. *The Servant, the General, and Armageddon*. Oxford: George Ronald, 1998.

McCandless, Peter. *Moonlight, Magnolias, and Madness: Insanity in South Carolina from the Colonial Period to the Progressive Era*. Chapel Hill: University of North Carolina Press, 1996.

McDaniel, Jeanne M. *North Augusta: James U. Jackson's Dream*. Charleston, S.C.: Arcadia Publishing, 2006.

McDonough, Julia Anne. "Men and Women of Good Will: A History of the Commission on Interracial Cooperation and the Southern Regional Council, 1919–1954." PhD diss., University of Virginia, 1993.

McMullen, Michael. *The Bahá'í: The Religious Construction of a Global Identity*. New Brunswick, N.J.: Rutgers University Press, 2000.

Metelmann, Velda Piff. *Lua Getsinger: Herald of the Covenant*. Oxford: George Ronald, 1997.

Mitchell, Broadus. *The Rise of Cotton Mills in the South*. With a new introduction by David Carlton. Columbia: University of South Carolina Press, 2001. First published 1921.

Momen, Moojan. *Islam and the Bahá'í Faith: An Introduction to the Bahá'í Faith for Muslims*. Oxford: George Ronald, 2000.

Montgomery, William E. *Under Their Own Vine and Fig Tree: The African-American*

Church in the South, 1865–1900. Baton Rouge: Louisiana State University Press, 1993.

Moore, Jacqueline M. *Leading the Race: The Transformation of the Black Elite in the Nation's Capital, 1880–1920*. Charlottesville: University Press of Virginia, 1999.

Moore, John Hammond. *Columbia and Richland County: A South Carolina Community, 1740–1990*. Columbia: University of South Carolina Press, 1993.

Moore, Robert J. "The Civil Rights Advocate." In *Matthew J. Perry: The Man, His Times, and His Legacy*, edited by W. Lewis Burke and Belinda F. Gergel, 155–82. Columbia: University of South Carolina Press, 2004.

Moore, Winfred B., Jr., and Orville Vernon Burton, eds. *Toward the Meeting of the Waters: Currents in the Civil Rights Movement of South Carolina during the Twentieth Century*. Columbia: University of South Carolina Press, 2008.

Moorhead, James H. *World without End: Mainstream American Protestant Visions of the Last Things, 1880–1925*. Bloomington: Indiana University Press, 1999.

Morrison, Gayle. "Gregory, Louis George (1874–1951)." Bahá'í Encyclopedia Project website. Accessed November 17, 2014. http://www.bahai-encyclopedia-project.org/index.php?option=com_content&view=article&id=63:gregory-louis-george.

———. *To Move the World: Louis G. Gregory and the Advancement of Racial Unity in America*. Wilmette, Ill.: Bahá'í Publishing Trust, 1982.

Moses, Wilson J. *Alexander Crummell: A Study of Civilization and Discontent*. New York: Oxford University Press, 1989.

———. "The Lost World of the New Negro, 1895–1919: Black Literary and Intellectual Life before the 'Renaissance.'" *Black American Literature Forum* 21, nos. 1–2 (Spring–Summer 1987): 61–84.

Moss, Alfred A. *The American Negro Academy: Voice of the Talented Tenth*. Baton Rouge: Louisiana State University Press, 1981.

Mount, Guy Emerson. "A Troubled Modernity: W.E.B. Du Bois, 'The Black Church,' and the Problem of Causality." In *'Abdu'l-Bahá's Journey West: The Course of Human Solidarity*, edited by Negar Mottahedeh, 85–110. New York: Palgrave Macmillan, 2013.

National Park Service. "Atlanta Biltmore Hotel and Biltmore Apartments." National Park Service website. Accessed November 16, 2014. http://www.nps.gov/history/nr/travel/atlanta/text.htm#bil.

Newby, Idus A. *Black Carolinians: A History of Blacks in South Carolina from 1895 to 1968*. Columbia: University of South Carolina Press, 1973.

Niebuhr, H. Richard. *The Kingdom of God in America*. New York: Harper & Row, 1937.

Norman, Corrie E., and Don S. Armentrout, eds. *Religion in the Contemporary South: Changes, Continuities, and Contexts*. Knoxville: University of Tennessee Press, 2005.

Nugent, Walter. *Crossings: The Great Transatlantic Migrations, 1870–1914*. Bloomington: Indiana University Press, 1995.

Oldfield, John. "The African American Bar in South Carolina." In *At Freedom's Door: African American Founding Fathers and Lawyers in South Carolina*, edited by James Lowell Underwood and W. Lewis Burke, 116–29. Columbia: University of South Carolina Press, 2000.

O'Neill, Stephen. "Memory, History, and the Desegregation of Greenville, South Carolina." In *Toward the Meeting of the Waters*, edited by Winfred B. Moore Jr. and Orville Vernon Burton, 286–99. Columbia: University of South Carolina Press, 2008.

Pascoe, Peggy. *What Comes Naturally: Miscegenation Law and the Making of Race in America*. Oxford: Oxford University Press, 2009.

Patler, Nicholas. *Jim Crow and the Wilson Administration: Protesting Jim Crow in the Early Twentieth Century*. Boulder: University Press of Colorado, 2004.

Perry, Mark. "Robert S. Abbott and the *Chicago Defender*: A Door to the Masses." *Michigan Chronicle*, October 10, 1995. Accessed November 18, 2014. http://www.uga.edu/bahai/News/101095.html.

Power, J. Tracy. *I Will Not Be Silent and I Will Be Heard: Martin Luther King, Jr., the Southern Christian Leadership Conference, and Penn Center*. Columbia: South Carolina Department of Archives and History, 1993.

Rabbani, Rúhíyyih, ed. *The Ministry of the Custodians, 1957–1963*. Haifa, Israel: Bahá'í World Centre, 1992.

Randolph, Robert M. "James McBride Dabbs: Spokesman for Racial Liberalism." In *From the Old South to the New: Essays on the Transitional South*, edited by Walter J. Fraser Jr. and Winfred B. Moore Jr., 253–64. Westport, Conn.: Greenwood Press, 1981.

Rassekh, Farhad. "The Bahá'í Faith and the Market Economy." *Journal of Bahá'í Studies* 11, no. 3/4 (September–December 2001): 31–61.

Reed, John Shelton. *The Enduring South: Subcultural Persistence in Mass Society*. With a new afterword by the author. Chapel Hill: University of North Carolina Press, 1986.

Reed, Linda. *Simple Decency and Common Sense: The Southern Conference Movement, 1938–1963*. Bloomington: Indiana University Press, 1991.

Reid, Alfred S. *Furman University: Toward a New Identity*. Durham: Duke University Press, 1976.

———. "The Greenville County Council for Community Development: Furman and Greenville in Partnership in the 1930s." In *Proceedings and Papers of the Greenville County Historical Association*. Vol. 6, edited by Albert N. Sanders, 78–88. Greenville, S.C.: Greenville County Historical Association, 1981.

Rogers, George C., Jr. *The History of Georgetown County, South Carolina*. Columbia: University of South Carolina Press, 1970.

Rowe, David L. *God's Strange Work: William Miller and the End of the World*. Grand Rapids, Mich.: William B. Eerdmans, 2008.

Rutstein, Nathan. *Corinne True: Faithful Handmaid of 'Abdu'l-Bahá*. Oxford: George Ronald, 1987.

Saeidi, Nader. *Gate of the Heart: Understanding the Writings of the Báb*. Waterloo, Ont.: Wilfrid Laurier University Press, 2008.

———. *Logos and Civilization: Spirit, History, and Order in the Writings of Bahá'u'lláh*. Bethesda: University Press of Maryland, 2000.

Schaefer, Udo, Ulrich Gollmer, and Nicola Towfigh. *Making the Crooked Straight: A Contribution to Bahá'í Apologetics*. Oxford: George Ronald, 2000.

Schweiger, Beth Barton, and Donald G. Mathews, eds. *Religion in the American South: Protestants and Others in History and Culture*. Chapel Hill: University of North Carolina Press, 2004.

Sears, William. *Thief in the Night*. Oxford: George Ronald, 1961.

Smedley, Katherine. *Martha Schofield and the Re-Education of the South, 1839–1916*. Lewiston, N.Y.: Edwin Mellen Press, 1987.

Smith, Kenneth L., and Ira G. Zepp Jr. *Search for the Beloved Community: The Thinking of Martin Luther King, Jr*. Lanham, Md.: University Press of America, 1986.

Smith, Peter. "The American Bahá'í Community, 1894–1917: A Preliminary Survey." In *Studies in Bábí and Bahá'í History*. Vol. 1, edited by Moojan Momen, 85–223. Los Angeles: Kalimát Press, 1982.

———. "The Bahá'í Faith in the West: A Survey." In *Bahá'ís in the West*, edited by Peter Smith, 3–60. Los Angeles: Kalimát Press, 2004.

———. *An Introduction to the Bahá'í Faith*. New York: Cambridge University Press, 2008.

Snowden, Yates, and H. G. Cutler, eds. *History of South Carolina*. Vol. 5. Chicago and New York: Lewis Publishing Co., 1920.

Southern, David W. "Beyond Jim Crow Liberalism: Judge Waring's Fight against Segregation in South Carolina, 1942–52." *Journal of Negro History* 66, no. 3 (Autumn 1981): 209–27.

Stockman, Robert H. *'Abdu'l-Bahá in America*. Wilmette, Ill.: Bahá'í Publishing Trust, 2012.

———. "The Bahá'í Faith and American Protestantism." PhD diss., Harvard University, 1990.

———. *The Bahá'í Faith in America*. Vol. 1, *Origins, 1892–1900*. Wilmette, Ill.: Bahá'í Publishing Trust, 1985.

———. *The Bahá'í Faith in America*. Vol. 2, *Early Expansion, 1900–1912*. Oxford: George Ronald, 1995.

———. "United States of America." Bahá'í Library website. Accessed November 18, 2014. http://bahai-library.com/stockman_encyclopedia_usa.

———. "U.S. Bahá'í Community Membership: 1894–1996." *American Bahá'í*, November 23, 1996, 27.

Stricklin, David. *A Genealogy of Dissent: Southern Baptist Protest in the Twentieth Century*. Lexington: University Press of Kentucky, 2000.

Sullivan, Patricia. *Days of Hope: Race and Democracy in the New Deal Era*. Chapel Hill: University of North Carolina Press, 1996.

Taherzadeh, Adib. *The Child of the Covenant: A Study Guide to the Will and Testament of 'Abdu'l-Bahá*. Oxford: George Ronald, 2000.

———. *The Covenant of Bahá'u'lláh*. Oxford: George Ronald, 1992.

Tindall, George Brown. *The Emergence of the New South, 1913–1945*. Baton Rouge: Louisiana State University Press, 1967.

———. *South Carolina Negroes, 1877–1900*. Rev. ed. Columbia: University of South Carolina Press, 2003.

Toynbee, Arnold J. *Christianity among the Religions of the World*. New York: Scribner, 1957.

———. *A Study of History*. Vol. 5. London: Oxford University Press, 1939.

———. *A Study of History*. Vol. 7. London: Oxford University Press, 1954.

———. *A Study of History*. Vol. 8. London: Oxford University Press, 1954.

van den Hoonaard, Will. C. "Schopflocher, Siegfried." Bahá'í Library website. Accessed November 18, 2014. http://bahai-library.com/hoonaard_encyclopedia_siegfried_schopflocher.

Wacker, Grant. *Heaven Below: Early Pentecostals and American Culture*. Cambridge, Mass.: Harvard University Press, 2001.

Ward, Allan L. *239 Days: 'Abdul-Bahá's Journey in America*. Wilmette, Ill.: Bahá'í Publishing Trust, 1979.

White, John W. "The White Citizens' Councils of Orangeburg County, South Carolina." In *Toward the Meeting of the Waters*, edited by Winfred B. Moore Jr. and Orville Vernon Burton, 261–73. Columbia: University of South Carolina Press, 2008.

Whitfield, Bruce. *The Dawning-Place: The Building of a Temple, the Forging of the North American Bahá'í Community*. Wilmette, Ill.: Bahá'í Publishing Trust, 1984.

Whitfield, Stephen J. *A Death in the Delta: The Story of Emmett Till*. New York: Free Press, 1988.

Woods, Jeff. *Black Struggle, Red Scare: Segregation and Anti-Communism in the South, 1948–1968*. Baton Rouge: Louisiana State University Press, 2004.

Woodward, C. Vann. *Tom Watson: Agrarian Rebel*. New York: Oxford University Press, 1963. First published 1938.

Index

Page numbers in *italics* refer to illustrations.

Abbeville, S.C., 67–68
Abbeville (S.C.) Scimitar, 68
Abbott, Robert S., 127
'Abdu'l-Bahá, 14, 20, 24, 27, 42, 48, 87, 93, 105, 113, 138, 141, 194
   and Covenant: as Center of the Covenant, 10, 22, 57, 257n9; death, 106; on Guardianship and Houses of Justice, 106–8; on Hands of the Cause of God, 191; will and testament, 106–9, 112 (*see also* Bahá'í Administration)
   and house of worship, 46, 261n46 (*see also* Bahá'í house of worship: Wilmette, Ill.)
   in North America, 49–50, 56, 88–89, 94–95, 124–25, 147, 192
   and race, 146–47; on African civilizations, 49; on interracial harmony and world peace, 192; on interracial marriage, 49–50, 213–14; predicts racial violence, 211; on race in Washington, D.C., Bahá'í community, 28, 52–54; on racial imagery, 257n14
   and teaching, 55–56, 75–78 (*see also* Tablets of the Divine Plan)
   works: *Some Answered Questions*, 124; *Tablets of Abdul-Baha Abbas*, 124
   and world history, 209; on justice, 148, 193; predicts World War I, 56–57; predicts World War II, 132; on role of U.S., 149 (*see also under* Báb; Bahá'í Faith; Bahá'u'lláh)
   See also under specific individuals and places
Abercrombie, Charles, 218–19, 234, 247
Abercrombie, Lillie, 218–19, 234, 241
Abercrombie, Richard, 199–200, 218–19, 241
Africa, 1, 2, 4, 49, 96, 178, 185, 192, 200, 211, 244, 253n5
   decolonization, 192–93, 238
   in Seven Year Plan (1946–1953), 182, 185, 191–95
   in Tablets of the Divine Plan, 76
   in Ten Year Plan (1953–1963), 206, 207–8, 239
   See also specific countries
African Americans, 1
   accommodationism, 65–68
   in Augusta area, S.C./Ga., 97
   and Democratic Party, 176–77
   demography, 17, 135, 215
   elite, 16, 26–28
   emancipation, 10, 80
   and justice system, 40, 67–68, 97
   and mental health, 39–40
   migration, 40, 69, 71, 135, 153, 157, 173
   and politics of respectability, 35–37, 40–41
   and racial uplift, 65–68, 70, 83–90
   slavery, 96
   in Washington, D.C., 26–27
   See also Bahá'í Faith in United States: and African Americans; Civil rights movement; *specific individuals, organizations, and places*)
Afro-American Citizen (Charleston, S.C.), 33
Aiken, S.C., 71, 73, 96, 99, 102, 173, 215, 267n7
   See also Bahá'í Faith in Augusta area, S.C./Ga.
Alabama, 8–9, 36, 45, 58, 65, 93, 177, 228, 245, 246
   Birmingham, 176–77, 229
   Fairhope, 45–47
   Louis Gregory in, 117
   Selma, 231
   Tuskegee, 135
Alaska, 131, 240
Alexander, Agnes, 184, 187
Alexander, Mary, 24

Alexander, Will W., 74, 119
Allendale, S.C., 196
Allen University, 35, 71, 82, 120, 140, 185, 204
Allison, Bill, 216
Allison, Thelma, 216
American Negro Academy, 27
Anderson, Robert, 234–35
Anderson County, S.C., 71, 73, 78, 141, 158
   See also Bahá'í Faith in Greenville area, S.C.
Andrews, Mary Biggar, 122
Armageddon. *See* World War I: Battle of Megiddo (Armageddon)
Asheville, N.C., 93, 217, 223
Asia, 1, 4, 121, 168, 178, 195, 211
   decolonization, 238
   in Tablets of the Divine Plan, 76
   in Ten Year Plan (1953–1963), 206, 239
Atlanta, Ga., 70, 73, 98, 104, 122, 234
   Bahá'í Faith in, 49, 53, 79, 116–17, 167, 178, 196, 216
   crisis over National Spiritual Assembly's southern teaching strategy in, 150–52, 216
   See also Bahá'í Faith in United States: southern states
Audé, Susan, 252n8
Augusta, Ga., 14, 50, 91, 93
   economic development, 96, 98–100, *102*
   origins, 95–96
   in Reconstruction and Jim Crow eras, 96–98
   See also Bahá'í Faith in Augusta area, S.C./Ga.
Augusta (Ga.) Chronicle, 101, 105
Augusta (Ga.) Herald, 101
Australia, 2, 195, 239
   in Tablets of the Divine Plan, 76
Avery Normal Institute, 32–34, 70

Báb, 141
   and Covenant, 108, 206
   life and ministry, 4, 20; declaration of prophetic mission, 57, 130; on Greatest Name, 263n6; shrine, 194
   as promised one, 2, 6, 20, 57, 219, 257n11
   and world history, 2–3, 13, 148, 218, 254n7, 256n8; associated with U.S. history, 11 (*see also under* 'Abdu'l-Bahá; Bahá'í Faith; Bahá'u'lláh)
Bacot, Mary, 30–31
Bacote, Mattie, 222
Bacote, Paul, 222
Bacote, Robert, 222
Bagdadi, Zeenat, 125

Bagdadi, Zia
   in Augusta area, 124–25, 127–28
   in Chicago, 79, 104
Bahá'í Administration, 138, 149, 180, 194–95, 201, 205–6, 209, 244
   Auxiliary Boards, 195
   development: *Bahá'í Administration*, 124; consolidation during second Bahá'í century, predicted, 173; under Shoghi Effendi, 1920s–1930s, 91–92, 106–13; "World Order Letters," 112
   Guardianship, 11; no successor to, 238; origins of, 106–9
   Hands of the Cause of God, 11; development of, under Shoghi Effendi, 195, 238; origins of, 191–92; temporary collective leadership, assumed by, 238 (*see also specific individuals*)
   Houses of Justice (local and secondary): as "bedrock" of Universal House of Justice, 112; choice of temporary designation as "Spiritual Assemblies," 110; origins of, 42, 107, 109–10 (*see also* Bahá'í Faith in United States: Local Spiritual Assemblies; Universal House of Justice)
   International Bahá'í Council, 194
   International Convention, 206, 241
   National Convention, 109–10, 241
   National Spiritual Assemblies: in Africa, 195; in Alaska, 240; in Canada, Central America, and South America, 181–94; as electors of Universal House of Justice, 206, 241; in Europe, 182, 194 (*see also* National Spiritual Assembly, U.S.)
   origins and purpose: Covenant, 11–12, 22, 108, 197, 257n9; purpose, 112; Western political culture, contrasted with, 112, 168
   principles and practices, 111; collective decision-making, 8; local community organization, 7, 42; preference for minority, in cases of ties or appointed positions, 147, 273n27; women's equality, 89–90
   See also Bahá'í Faith in S.C.; Bahá'í Faith in United States; *specific individuals, institutions, and teaching plans*
Bahá'í Faith
   categorization, by scholars, 3–4
   growth and spread (worldwide), 1–2, 4, 129–32, 134, 169–70, 205–6, 238–40 (*see also* Tablets of the Divine Plan; *specific plans*)
   origins, 1–2, 4 (*see also* Báb; Bahá'u'lláh)

teachings and practices, 21–22, 29, 86–88; calendar, 257n12; Christianity, relationship with, 86–88; economics, 7, 22; harmony of science and religion, 186; house of worship, 261n46 (*see also* Bahá'í house of worship); individual search for truth, 89; Manifestations of God, 20–22, 83, 87–88, 123, 148–49, 177, 218; Nineteen Day Feast, 24, 257n12 (*see also* Nineteen Day Feast); obedience to government, 142; oneness of humanity, xiii, 2, 11, 24, 78, 83, 100, 103, 135, 142, 150, 169, 177, 214, 231; pilgrimage, 22, 27; prayer, 21; prohibition of clergy, 8; summarized, 86, 88; unity of religions, 37; women, 7 (*see also* Bahá'u'lláh, teachings of)

terminology, 15, 263n6

and world history, xi, 2–3, 13, 112–13, 146–49, 172–73, 207–11, 218, 256n8; "dark heart" of age of transition, 244–45; entry by troops, 209, 239–40, 243–44; Formative Age, 112; Lesser Peace, 173, 211; mass conversion, 209, 226; as possible universal religion (Toynbee), 254n7 (*see also under* 'Abdu'l-Bahá; Báb; Bahá'u'lláh)

See also specific individuals, institutions, and places

Bahá'í Faith in Augusta area, S.C./Ga., 7–8, 14, 30, 50, 55, 79, 91–93, *94*, 95, 100–105, *102*, 106–7, 133–36, 181, 199

Aiken, 55, 95, 101

Aiken County, 196–97

establishment and early development (1910–1930s), 100–105, 114–16, 120–28; 'Abdu'l-Bahá on, 102–3; Bahá'í Center, 124–27; Louis Gregory's first teaching trip, 30; first Local Spiritual Assembly, 123, 125, 142; as interracial community, 92, 126–28, 142; opposition to, 105, 127–28, 142, 188; as part of global movement, 110–11; Shoghi Effendi on, 112–13, 128; and Washington, D.C., compared, 127

in Nine Year Plan (1964–1973), 247

North Augusta, 10, 30, 55, 79, 94–95, 101, *102*, 103–4, 116, 121–25, 127–28, 136–37, 141–42, 155, 185, 188, 196–97, 216, 226; Local Spiritual Assembly, 156

in Seven Year Plan (1937–1944), 129, 136–37; change in Local Spiritual Assembly jurisdictions, 156–57; and expansion in S.C., 137, 139–41, 155–56

in Seven Year Plan (1946–1953), 183–85, 188, 196–97

in Ten Year Plan (1953–1963), 215–16, 226

See also Aiken, S.C.; Augusta, S.C.; Edgefield County, S.C.; Johnston, S.C.; North Augusta, S.C.; *specific individuals*

Bahá'í Faith in Beaufort area, S.C., 14, 199, 223–26, 225

first Local Spiritual Assembly of St. Helena Island, 222, 226, 240

in Nine Year Plan (1964–1973), 233, 247

See also Beaufort, S.C.; Penn Center; St. Helena Island, S.C.; *specific individuals*

Bahá'í Faith in Charleston area, S.C., 14, 44, 76, 79, 117, 181

Louis Gregory's first teaching trip, 30, 33–34, 45, 47, 85–86

in Nine Year Plan (1964–1973), 247

in Seven Year Plan (1937–1944), 129, 137–38, 169

in Seven Year Plan (1946–1953), 184, 187, 196

in Ten Year Plan (1953–1963), 215–16

See also Charleston, S.C.; *specific individuals*

Bahá'í Faith in Chicago, Ill., 103–4, 114, 124–25, 143, 195, 212

arrival and early growth: early community organization, 24, 42–43, 46; Ibrahim Kheiralla's classes, 18–19, 23, 42; source of pioneers to other localities, 41–43, 45; southern expatriates encounter Bahá'í Faith in, 43–44, 260n43

as interracial community, 49, 79, 127; 'Abdu'l-Bahá in, 49–50, 260n43; in Red Summer, 79, 127

pioneers and traveling teachers from, to S.C., 165, 186, 221, 248

See also Bahá'í house of worship: Wilmette, Ill.; Bahá'í National Convention, U.S.; Illinois: Chicago

Bahá'í Faith in Columbia area, S.C., 8, 14, 79, 81–82, 83–90, 116, 119–20, 181, *186*, 252n8

in Nine Year Plan (1964–1973), 247–48

in Seven Year Plan (1937–1944), 129, 139–42, 157, 167, 169, *170*

in Seven Year Plan (1946–1953), 172, 183–87, 196–97; first Local Spiritual Assembly, 184, 187; Irmo, 184; police suppression, 188

in Ten Year Plan (1953–1963), 215–16, 225–26

See also Columbia, S.C.; Lexington County, S.C.; Richland County, S.C.; *specific individuals*

Bahá'í Faith in Florence area, S.C., 14, 220–22, 226
   first Local Spiritual Assembly, 222, 240
   Lake City, 221–22, 225, 247, 252n8
   in Nine Year Plan (1964–1973), 247
   See also Darlington, S.C.; Florence, S.C.; Lake City, S.C.; specific individuals
Bahá'í Faith in Greenville area, S.C., 8, 14, 78, 199
   in Nine Year Plan (1964–1973), 244, 247
   in Seven Year Plan (1937–1944), 129, 140–41, 155–59, 162–67; first Local Spiritual Assembly, 159; selected as goal city, 157
   in Seven Year Plan (1946–1953), 172, 183–84, 187–89, 196–97, 248; city council, recognition by, 189; Ku Klux Klan violence, 188–89; struggling Local Spiritual Assembly, 179–81
   in Ten Year Plan (1953–1963), 215–20, 225–26, 232–37, 240–41; legal protections, 232–33; new Local Spiritual Assembly in Greenville County, 220, 240
   See also Anderson County, S.C.; Greenville, S.C.; specific individuals
Bahá'í Faith in South Carolina
   and civil rights movement, xiii–xv, 13–14 (see also Civil rights movement)
   and diversity, xvi, 3, 196–98, 206, 225–26, 240; class, 7, 127–28; religious liberty, 232–33; women, 7–8, 9; youth, xv–xvi, xviii, 199–200, 217–19, 225–26
   and interracialism, xii–xiv, 6–7, 129–30, 200–201, 223–24, 232–37, 240–42; interracial marriage, 233; and other reform movements, compared, 8–10; social equality, 8–10, 89, 165–67, 180, 233–37 (see also Interracialism)
   and Jim Crow, 13–14, 188–89 (see also Jim Crow)
   large-scale growth after 1968, xi–xviii; as largest religious minority, xi, xvii, 3
   music in, xi, 226
   and national Bahá'í movement, xi–xii, 12–13, 91–92, 249 (see also Bahá'í Faith in Chicago, Ill.: pioneers and traveling teachers from, to S.C.; Bahá'í Faith in Washington, D.C.: southern expansion: pioneers and traveling teachers from, to S.C.; Illinois, pioneers and traveling teachers from, to S.C.; New York: pioneers and traveling teachers from, to S.C.)

Nine Year Plan (1964–1973), 247–49; and Ten Year Plan (1953–1963), compared, 247
opposition, xiii–xiv, 9–10, 117–18, 127–28, 216–17, 219; FBI, 9, 165, 179; Ku Klux Klan, xiv, 9, 188–89
and Protestantism, xiii, 3, 8–10, 33, 37–38, 40–41, 75, 83–90, 138, 139, 187, 199 (see also Protestantism; specific individuals, denominations, and organizations)
Seven Year Plan (1937–1944), 129–30, 136–41, 151–52, 197; Regional Teaching Committee for N.C., S.C., and Ga., 156–58
Seven Year Plan (1946–1953), 172–73, 182–84, 197; Louis Gregory's absence, 189; Regional Teaching Committee for N.C., S.C., and Ga., 183–84, 188, 197
state convention, 198, 247–49
Ten Year Plan (1953–1963), 200–201, 223–26; Area Goals Committee for Fla., Ga., and S.C., 224–26; legal protections, 232–33; and previous plans, contrasted, 207, 215; results, 240–42; seasonal schools, 223–24, 225, 226
and worldwide Bahá'í movement, 10–13, 241–42
See also Bahá'í Faith in United States; Bahá'í Faith in specific localities; specific individuals, institutions, and teaching plans
Bahá'í Faith in United States
   and African Americans, 81, 135–36, 141–45, 192–93, 207–8, 213–15, 240–42, 249 (see also specific individuals and organizations)
   arrival, 1 (see also Bahá'í Faith in Chicago, Ill.: arrival and early growth)
   Bahá'í schools: Davidson, Mich., 112, 141, 196, 223; Geyserville, Calif., 112, 141, 157, 196, 223 (see also Green Acre Bahá'í School)
   and civil rights movement, xii–xv, 1, 5, 8–9, 13–14; in New Deal era, 136, 142, 148; in 1950s, 190–91, 200–201, 205, 211–15; in 1960s, 232–38, 243, 245–46, 248; relationship with Africa, 190–93, 207–9, 238; in World War I era, 55, 70, 75, 79–83, 127; in World War II era, 168–69 (see also Civil rights movement; specific states and cities)
   and Great Depression, effects of: on discourse, 121; on finances, 114; on teaching, 114–15 (see also New Deal; Seven Year Plan [1937–1944])
   growth and spread (nationwide), xi–xii, xv–xviii, 16–17, 18–19, 41–43, 129–32, 134–36,

249; Enterprise, Kan., 42 (*see also* Tablets of the Divine Plan; *specific teaching plans*)
and interracialism, 6–7, 12–13, 17, 75–76, 79–83, 129–30, 135–36, 231–32, 240–42; in *Advent of Divine Justice*, 146–52; interracial marriage, 50–51, 54, 213–14, 233; Race Amity Committee, 119; Race Amity Conventions, 79–81, 88, 135, 192; social equality, 51–54, 89, 165, 213–15 (*see also* Interracialism; *specific states and cities*)
and Jim Crow, 1, 12–13, 129–30, 135–36, 141–45, 147–48, 150–52 (*see also* Jim Crow; *specific states and cities*)
Local Spiritual Assemblies: annual election, 111; clarification of jurisdiction, 156; early local organizations, 42, 109; and teaching, 114–15 (*see also under* Bahá'í Administration: Houses of Justice; *specific places*)
and Protestantism, 5–7, 35–36, 40–41, 82, 83–90, 142–45, 214, 234–35, 256n8, 284n7; religious background of American Bahá'ís, 19, 256n8, 43 (*see also* Bahá'í Faith in S.C.: and Protestantism; Christianity: and Bahá'í Faith, relationship with; *specific individuals, denominations, and organizations*)
southern states: arrival of, 11, 16–17; described in Tablets of the Divine Plan, 58, 77–78; and development of national movement, 12–13, 46–47, 54, 129–31, 134–36; Fairhope, Ala., 45–47; growth and spread (regionwide), 41–47, 129–30, 135–36, 249; southern schools and colleges, 119–20, 149–50; southern teaching policy, 141–45, 147–48, 150–52, 162–67, 213–15 (*see also* Tablets of the Divine Plan; *specific teaching plans; specific places*)
and U.S. history, xiv–xv, 3–10, 146–49
See also specific individuals, institutions, and agencies
Bahá'í Faith in Washington, D.C., 14, 23–30, 33, 46, 47, 95, 115
and Augusta area, S.C./Ga., compared, 92, 127
and Charleston, S.C., compared, 35, 40–41
as interracial community, 17, 20, 23–29, 48–54, 59–60, 89, 101, 242; 'Abdu'l-Bahá's visits, 49–50, 192; first Race Amity Convention, 79–81; opposition from black elite, 27–28, 35–37, 40–41
Local Spiritual Assembly, 121
and southern expansion, 14, 17, 23, 44–45, 53, 58–59, 78, 119, 242; pioneers and traveling teachers from, to S.C., 101–3, 104, 121–22, 137, 158; Seven Year Plan (1937–1944), 135–36, 137, 142, 158; Seven Year Plan (1946–1953), 195, 197; Tablets of the Divine Plan, 58–59, 78
Working Committee, 28, 48, 58
Bahá'í house of worship
origins and purpose, 261n46
other locations: additional sites, 206, 239, 261n46; Ashgabat, Turkmenistan, 46, 261n46; Eliot, Maine (predicted), 94; Frankfurt, Germany, 206, 239; Kampala, Uganda, 239; Sydney, Australia, 239; Tehran, Iran, 206, 239
Wilmette, Ill., 43, 46, 110, 125, 206, 249, 261n46; contributions for, from Augusta area, S.C./Ga., 94, 102; Great Depression, effects of, 114, 132; linked to developments in administration and teaching, by Shoghi Effendi, 133–34; quartz for, mined in S.C., 140; in Seven Year Plan (1937–1944), 132–35, 140, 167, 169–71, *170–71*; in Seven Year Plan (1946–1953), 181, 191, 194, 196, 206 (*see also* Bahai Temple Unity)
Bahá'í National Convention, U.S., 105, 117, 119, 125, 130–32, 141, 145, 149, 181, 242, 247
apportionment of delegates by state, 198
of 1944, 168–71
of 1953, 206
origins, 111;
See also Bahá'í Administration: National Convention; Bahai Temple Unity: annual national convention; National Spiritual Assembly, U.S.
Bahá'í News, 145, 152, 166, 214
Bahá'í temple. *See* Bahá'í house of worship
Bahai Temple Unity, 46–47, 48, 57, 79, 106, 107, 110
annual national convention, 46, 48, 57, 104, 109, 111; of 1919, 76–78, 104; of 1922, 110 (*see also* Bahá'í National Convention, U.S.)
Executive Board, 46–47, 79, 104, 106, 109–10, 125, 261n48; dissolution, 110 (*see also* National Spiritual Assembly, U.S.)
Teaching Committee of Nineteen, 78, 87 (*see* National Teaching Committee, U.S.)
Bahá'í World, 126
Bahá'í World Center, 24, 52, 76, 79, 93, 109, 121, 194–95, 205–6
'Akká, 20, 22, 48, 194

Index   307

Bahá'í World Center—*continued*
    Haifa, 22, 24, 58, 106–10, 125, 137, 194, 206, 241–42
    Mount Carmel, 194, 206
    See also Báb: shrine; Bahá'u'lláh: shrine; Israel (Palestine)
Bahá'u'lláh, 15, 36, 138, 141, 187, 194, 213, 247
    and Covenant, 11, 22, 108, 257n9; administrative principles, 111; Hands of the Cause of God, 191; hereditary principle, 107; Houses of Justice, 42, 107, 112 (*see also* Bahá'í Administration)
    life and ministry, 4, 20–22, 123, 187; announcement of prophetic mission, 111, 193, 200, 206, 241; beginning of prophetic mission, 181, 193, 205 (*see also* Ridván, Festival of); Hidden Words, 21, 24–25; *Proclamation of Bahá'u'lláh*, 248; proclamation to rulers, 244; title, 88, 247, 263n6, 284n7; shrine, 22, 206
    as promised one, xi, 2, 6, 20, 21, 23, 87–88, 112, 158, 219, 221, 234; Kitáb-i-Íqán, 124
    teachings of, xi, 2, 29, 56, 77, 87, 121, 244; house of worship, 261n46 (*see also* Bahá'í house of worship); individual search for truth, 89; materialism, 210; Nineteen Day Feast, 24, 257n12 (*see also* Nineteen Day Feast); obedience to government, 4–5, 142; oneness of humanity, 2, 11, 51, 146; prohibition of clergy, 8, 89, 115 (*see also* Bahá'í Faith: teachings)
    and world history, xi, 2–3, 13, 148–49, 173, 177, 207, 209, 218, 254n7, 256n8; associated with Reconstruction, by Louis Gregory, 10–11 (*see also under* 'Abdu'l-Bahá; Báb; Bahá'í Faith)
Bahíyyih Khánum, 106
Baird, Nellie F., 104, 122
Baker, Dorothy Beecher, 179, 195
    in Atlanta, 149–51
    at intercontinental conference in Chicago, 207–9, 213, 215
Baptists, 37, 117, 141, 199, 218, 220–21, 226
    and Furman University, 9, 154–55, 235–37
    hegemony theory, 5–6
    and interracialism, 9, 82, 148
    and Jim Crow, 9, 153–55
    Morris Street Baptist Church, Charleston, S.C., 70
    New Tabernacle Fourth Baptist Church, Charleston, S.C., 34
    South Carolina Baptist Convention, 236–37
    Southern Baptist Convention, 65, 148
    Springfield Baptist Church, Greenville, S.C., 227
    West Greenville Baptist Church, Greenville, S.C., 220
    See also specific individuals and institutions
Barney, Alice Pike, 23
Barney, Laura Clifford, 23
Barnwell County, S.C., 65
Barton, Morgan, 123
Barton, Pawnee, 125
Bassett, John, 104
Batesburg, S.C., 174
Beaufort, S.C., 71, 267n7, 173, 223, 229
    See also Bahá'í Faith in Beaufort area, S.C.
Benedict College, 65, 120, 204
    and African American activism, 71, 82, 160
    and Bahá'í Faith, 120, 140, 185, 247
Bennettsville, S.C., 196
Benson, Joy Faily, 215–18, 225, 244
Benson, Richard, 215–17, 219, 225, 232, 244
Bethel Literary and Historical Society, 16, 27–28, 44, 50
Bevel, James, 234
Bidwell, Christine, 122, 137, 155–58, 187–88
    arrival in Greenville, 141
    and Local Spiritual Assembly, 179–81
    and race, 152, 162–63, *164*, 165, 167, 180
Bidwell, Thelma, *164*
Bidwell, William, 122, 155–58, 187–88
    arrival in Greenville, 141
    and Local Spiritual Assembly, 179–81
    and race, 152, 162–63, *164*, 165, 167, 180, 241
Black, Gail. *See* Fassy, Gail
Black Belt, 201, 215, 220
Blease, Coleman L., 64, 82
Blue Ridge Assembly, 73–75, 223–24
Bob Jones University, 203
Bobo, Eulalia Barrow, 199, 218–19, 226
Bodmer, Amelie, 137, 156
Booker T. Washington High School, 140
Boulware, Harold, 160, 202
Bower, Viola, 158, *164*, 179, 181
Bracey, Mary Anne, 101, 103
Brazil, 139
British Empire, 178
    See also United Kingdom
Brown, Horace, 248
Brown, Robert C., 35
Bruce, Roscoe Conkling, 36–37

Buchanan, Dorothy Thomas, 216
Byrd, Levi, 159–60
Byrnes, James F., 72–73, 176
    school equalization program, 202–3 (*see also* Jim Crow: in education and employment: public education)

Calhoun, John C., 99
California, 121
    Bahá'í Faith in, 23, 43, 56, 108, 112, 137, 157–58, 165, 195–96, 199, 218, 252n3
    Los Angeles, 6, 157, 195, 252n8
    San Francisco, 105, 178, 195
Callison, T. C., 204
Camelon, Virginia, 158
Camp Jackson. *See* Fort Jackson
Camp Wadsworth, 70
Canada
    early growth of Bahá'í Faith in, 110, 114
    Montreal, 57, 121
    separate National Spiritual Assembly for, 181, 194
    in Seven Year Plan (1937–1944), 131–32, 134, 146, 167–68
    in Seven Year Plan (1946–1953), 181, 183, 194
    and Tablets of the Divine Plan, 58, 76
    in Ten Year Plan (1953–1953), 240
Carroll, Richard, 65–70, 83, 89
Carter, Rex L., 232
Cartledge, Mabelle, 125
Cass, J. Kenneth, 163
Chapman, Viola, 226
Chappelle, William D., 71
Charleston, S.C., xvii, 14, 44, 59, 96
    in Cold War era, 173, 175, 177, 190–91, 202, 205, 215, 216
    in 1960s, 228–30
    in post–Civil War era, 30–35, 61, 63, 83, 97, 267n7
    Roper Hospital, 38
    in World War I era, 69–73, 118
    in World War II era, 157, 160
    See also Bahá'í Faith in Charleston area, S.C.
Charleston Air Force Base, 247
Charleston Navy Yard, 69, 173
Charleston (S.C.) News and Courier, 205
Charlotte, N.C., 50, 101
Chase, Thornton, 41–43
Cheraw, S.C., 159–60, 252n8
Chesterfield County, S.C., 159
Chicago Defender, 127

Chinese Americans, 150
Christianity, 6, 18, 77, 138, 155, 209
    and Bahá'í Faith, relationship with, xiv, xvii, 4, 15, 20–23, 36–37, 86–90, 105, 117, 124, 138, 214, 232–35, 256n5
    millennialism in, 56–57, 88, 243, 256n8 (*see also* Protestantism: millennialism in)
    and race, 1, 8–9, 53, 64, 221, 252n2
    See also Jesus Christ; Jim Crow: and Protestantism; Kingdom of God; *specific individuals, denominations, and organizations*
Civil rights movement, xii–xv, 5, 8–9, 176, 192, 200, 207, 238
    in Cold War era, 172–77, 190–93, 200–205, 226–27; *Briggs v. Elliott*, 201–5; *Brown v. Board of Education*, 201–4, 209, 227, 230; Little Rock crisis, 214
    in New Deal era, 142–43, 148, 152–55
    in 1960s, 201, 226–32, 235–37, 242; Black Power, 246; Civil Rights Act of 1964, 229–32, 233, 235, 246; direct-action protest, 227–31; Voting Rights Act of 1965, 231
    in 1970s, 227
    in Progressive era, 1, 18, 32, 51; Niagara Movement, 16
    in S.C., historiography of, 255n17
    in World War I era, 55, 68–75
    in World War II era, 159–62, 168–69
    See also Bahá'í Faith in United States: and civil rights movement; Interracialism; *specific individuals, organizations, government agencies, and places*
Civil War, U.S., 10, 11, 17, 32, 34, 96, 98
Claflin University, 34, 83, 120
Clarendon County, S.C., 191, 201–2, 204
Clapp, Moses E., 79–80
Clark, Della, 187
Clemson, S.C., 196, 247
Clemson College (Clemson University), 230
Cobb, James A., 18
Cobb, Stanwood, 121–23, 134
Cold War, 173, 178, 201, 203, 210–11, 244
    effects on S.C. (*see under* South Carolina; *specific localities*)
    effects on U.S. culture, 209–11
    See also Soviet Union; *specific conflicts*
Coles, Claudia Stuart, 44
Columbia, S.C., 14, 35, 39, 40, 86, 93, 120, 185, *186*, 283n54
    in Cold War era, 173, 175, 177, 188
    Masonic Temple, 161, 248

Columbia, S.C.—*continued*
  in 1960s, 228–30
  in post–Civil War era, 61, 65–66
  Wade Hampton Hotel, 185–86
  in World War I era, 70–71, 73, 76, 85
  in World War II era, 139–40, 157, 160–62
  See also Bahá'í Faith in Columbia area, S.C.; Richland County, S.C.
Columbia (S.C.) Record, 140, 185–86
Commission on Interracial Cooperation. *See* Interracial Commission
Communism, 9–10, 72, 210, 214
  anticommunism, U.S., 2, 9, 72, 82, 153–54, 161, 203–5, 210–11, 214, 228, 235, 275n60
  and Bahá'í Faith, 10, 142, 148, 165, 201, 210–11, 217
  and Christianity, 9
  in New Deal era, 142, 148, 153–54
  and post–World War II activism, 175, 177
  and Seven Year Plan (1946–1953) in Europe, 182
  See also Cold War; Interracialism: and Communism, accusations of; Soviet Union
Congregationalists, 18
  First Congregational Church, Washington, D.C., 80
CORE (Congress of Racial Equality), 227–28, 231
Crawford, Anthony, 67–68
Crawford, Lacey, 248
Crisis, 1, 50
Cuba, 138, 158
  missile crisis, 210
Culbertson, John Bolt, 234

Dabrowski, Luda, 158, 164–65, *164*, 179–80
Daily Record (Columbia, S.C.), 85
Daniel (prophet), 194
Daniel, Charles, 229
Daniels, Wilhelmina, 187
Dargan, George E., 190
Dargan, George Washington, 30
Darlington, S.C., 30–31, 71, 97, 189–90, 246, 247
  See also Bahá'í Faith in Florence area, S.C.
Davis, Bob, 65
Dealy, Adelaide, 45–46
Dealy, Paul, 45–46
Debs, Eugene V., 104
De Laine, J. A., 201
Democratic Party, 148, 160, 229, 231, 245–46
  and African Americans in New Deal coalition, 176–77
  and fall of Reconstruction, 31, 97
  interracialism in, 5
  and Jim Crow, 31, 51, 61–63, 98, 281n30
  primary elections, 160–61, 175–76
  Progressive Democratic Party (PDP), 161, 168, 175–76, 231
  States' Rights Democratic Party (Dixiecrats), 176–77
Denmark, S.C., 228
Diggett, Julia Elizabeth, 43–44
Dillon, S.C., xv, 247
Disfranchisement. *See under* Jim Crow
Dixiecrats. *See under* Democratic Party
Dixon, Charlotte Brittingham, 23
Dixon, Pearl, 139–40, 185, 187
Dorn, W.J.B., 203
Dorsey, Zenobia, 140
Doty, Henry "Harry" Archer, 44–45
Doty, Pearl Battee, 44
Du Bois, W.E.B., 1–3, 10, 16, 18, 93, 253n1
  and Bahá'í Faith, 1, 50, 253n2
  on "color-line," 1, 175
  and Communism, 2, 175
  Souls of Black Folk, 1
  and Southern Negro Youth Congress, 175
  See also Crisis; NAACP
Dudley, Alice, 187, 197
Dukes, Henrietta, 187
Dunning School, 62

Earle, Willie, 174–75, 217
Easterbrook, Pearl, 216
Eastland, James O., 203
Ebony, 248
  "*Ebony* reprint," xv, 285n9
Edgefield County, S.C., 62, 97, 121, 174
  See also Bahá'í Faith in Augusta area, S.C./Ga.
Egypt, 2, 48–49, 182, 192, 194
  Alexandria, 48
  Cairo, 24
Eisenhower, Dwight D., 203, 214, 217
Eliot, Maine, 124, 191
  See also Green Acre Bahá'í School
Ellis, Adrienne, 158
Elmore, George, 175
Emancipation Day, 59, 70, 226, 227
Enfield, N.C., 30
Entzminger, Jesse, 139, *186*, 187–88
Episcopalians, 23, 33
Esperanto, 125
Ethiopia, 49, 132

Europe, 56–58, 69, 103, 109, 130–31, 137, 168, 178, 185
  and Seven Year Plan (1946–1953), 182–83, 194
  and Ten Year Plan (1953–1963), 206
  See also specific countries

Fádil-i-Mázandarání, Mírzá Asadu'lláh (Jináb-i-Fádil), 104
Faily, John, 216–17
Faily, Junie, 216–18
Fairclough, Adam, 14
Farmer, Sarah J., 93
Farmers' Alliance, 62, 97
Fassy, Gail, 188–89
FBI (Federal Bureau of Investigation), 72, 203–4
  See also under Bahá'í Faith in S.C.: opposition
Fettig, Martha, 216, 225
Fisher, May, 137
Fisk University, 16, *19*, 33, 53, 117, 143, 273n22
Flack, Eva Lee. *See* McAlister, Eva Flack
Fletcher, Ailene, 122–23
Fletcher, Clay, 123
Florence, S.C., 14, 71, 73, 160, 220, 222, 229
  See also Bahá'í Faith in Florence area, S.C.
Florida, 58, 104–5
  Jacksonville, 45, 91, 104
  Miami, 122, 135, 141
  St. Augustine, 135, 164, 225
Ford, Virginia Allen, 158, 179, 188–89, 216
Fort Jackson, 71, 173, 188, 247
Frain, George Stevens, 125
Frain, Marie Kershaw, 122–28, 137
France, 24, 70–71, 77, 93, 182, 244
  See also French Empire
Frank, Leo, 98
Freedom Rides, 228, 248
  See also CORE
French Empire, 178
Friendship Junior College, 227–28
Frogmore, S.C. *See* St. Helena Island, S.C.
Furman University, 9, 154–55, 216, 235–37
  See also under Baptists

Gaffney, S.C., 246
Gammon Theological Seminary, 73
Gantt, Harvey, 230
Gassaway, M. H., 73
Geer, Bennett Eugene, 9, 154–55
George, Ebenezer, 30–33
George, Henry, 45
George, Mary Elizabeth, 30–33

George, Theodore, 30–33
Georgetown County, S.C., xvii, 63, 160, 222
  See also Louis G. Gregory Bahá'í Institute; Radio Bahá'í WLGI
Georgia, 9, 14, 44, 49, 53, 79, 96, 135, 188, 220, 228
  Bahá'í Faith in, 58, 79, 169, 183, 189, 225–26, 240
  Louis Gregory's first teaching trip in, 17, 30, 44–45, 95
  and Jim Crow, origins of, 97
  See also specific individuals, institutions, and localities
Georgia State College, 127
Germany, 24, 49, 91–92, 96, 122, 123, 177, 182, 266n1
  Nazi regime, 132, 161, 174, 177–78
  See also under Bahá'í house of worship: other locations
Getsinger, Lua, 18–20, 23
Gewertz, Gertrude, 163
GI Bill of Rights, 174
Gibson, Amoz, 3, 242
Gillespie, John Birks "Dizzy," 252n8
Glazener, Carolyn, 158, 165, 167, 179, 181, 216
Glenn, Celia, 185, *186*, 187
Glover, Claire. *See* Michaels, Claire Glover
Gray, Nellie, 19–20, 21
Great Britain. *See* United Kingdom
Great Depression, 114, 119, 121, 131–32, 159, 177
  See also under Bahá'í Faith in United States
Greatest Name of God, 59, *164*, *170–71*, 222
Green Acre Bahá'í School, 33, 111–12, 119, 139, 141, 189, 196, 223
  Margaret Klebs and, 93–95, *94*, 124
Greensboro, N.C., 227
  Bahá'í Faith in, 50, 158, 165, 167, 184
Greenville, S.C.
  as center of textile industry, 14, 64, 141, 155, 220
  in Cold War era, 173–75, 203, 215
  Greenville Memorial Auditorium, 234
  municipal airport, 227
  in New Deal era, 9, 152–55, 160
  in 1960s, 227–30, 235–37
  Phillis Wheatley Center, 234, *237*
  in Progressive era, 220
  Sterling High School, 159, 217, 228, 234–35
  in World War I era, 69, 78
  See also Bahá'í Faith in Greenville area, S.C.
Greenville County Council for Community Development, 9, 154–55

Index   311

Greenville (S.C.) News, 163, 184, 187, 203, 235
Greenwood County, S.C., 63, 65
Gregory, George, 32–34, 79, 118
Gregory, Louisa "Louise" Mathew, 50, 132, 189
Gregory, Louis G., 5, 23, 55, 127–28, 134–35, 142, 144–45, 184, 195, 202, 207, 216, 241, 248
  and 'Abdu'l-Bahá, 28, 48–50, 191; pilgrimage, 48–49
  as administrator of Bahá'í Faith, 48, 193, 261n48; member of Committee on Assembly Development, 179, 181; member of National Spiritual Assembly, 149, 151; member of planning committee for 1944 National Convention, 168–69, *170*; member of Race Unity Committee, 149–50
  discovery of Bahá'í Faith, 17–22, 45; opposition to conversion of, 35–37, 40–41
  early life, 16–18, *19*, 31–34; as member of black elite, 30; as political activist, 16, 18, 193; resignation from U.S. Treasury Department, 51
  final years, 189–93; Africa and African Diaspora, assessment of connection with, 191–93; as Hand of the Cause of God, 191–92
  marriage, 50–51, 89
  at nexus of Bahá'í teaching and interracial work, 75–76, 80–83; and S.C. NAACP, 70
  teaching trips: in 1910, 30, 33–34, 45, 47, 91–92, 95, 129–30, 136, 247; in 1915, 53, 57; in 1916, 59–60; in 1917, 70; in 1919–1921, 76, 78–79, 81–90, 120, 139, 159; in 1924, 117–18, 137; in 1931, 116; in 1934, 116–17, 143; in 1936 (Haiti), 132; in 1942, 140; in 1944–1945, 181, *186*, 189 (*see also specific states and localities*)
  and Washington, D.C., Bahá'í community, 23, 27–29, 44, 48–54, 242
  writings: "Brief Answer to Questions on the Fulfillment of Some Bible Prophecies Concerning This Day," 86–88; on harmony of religions, 37; on justice for oppressed peoples, 193, 201; on Reconstruction, 10–11; on Shoghi Effendi, 109
Gregory, Saint (the Illuminator), 77–78
Grimsley, Genelle, 222, 225
Grimsley, Lee, 222, 225
Gullah, 10, 223–26, 233
  and Reconstruction, 10–11, 223
  See also Avery Normal Institute; Bahá'í Faith in Beaufort area, S.C.; Bahá'í Faith in Charleston area, S.C.; Beaufort, S.C.; Charleston, S.C.; Georgetown, S.C.; Penn Center; *specific individuals*
Gulpaygani, Mirza Abu'l-Fadl, 24, 33

Haines Normal and Industrial Institute, 95
Hainsworth, Philip, 207–8
Hamburg, S.C., 96, 98
Hamburg Riot, 97
Hammond, Samuel, 246
Hampton, S.C., 229
Hampton, Wade, 99–100
Hampton Terrace Hotel, 100–102, *102*
Hanahan, S.C., 247
Hands of the Cause of God. *See* Bahá'í Administration: Hands of the Cause of God; *specific individuals*
Hannen, Joseph, 24, 25, 26, 44, 58–59, 115, 127
  in Augusta area, 101–3, 126
  and "Central Bureau for the South," 78
  and Louis Gregory, 21–22, 27–29, 33, 77
Hannen, Pauline Knobloch, 20, 24–29, *25*, 44, 127
  and Louis Gregory, 18, 20–22, 27–29, 45
Haney, Paul, 223
Harleston, Edwin A. "Teddy," 70–71, 73
Harris, Augustus, 127
Harris, Erwin, 70
Hawaii, 184, 187
Haygood, Nathaniel F., 71, 85, 90
Hayne, Eugene R., 34–35
Haynsworth, Clement Furman, 216–17, 281n30
Hearst, Phoebe Apperson, 23, 137
Hemingway, S.C., xii, 252n8
Hewlett, Emanuel M., 18
Heyward, Duncan C., 65
Highlander Folk School, 142
Hinton, James, 161, 205
Hoagg, H. Emogene, 137–38, 152, 158, *164*, 179–81
  and Guardianship, 108–9, 137
  on southern teaching policy in Greenville, S.C., 163–67
Hoffman, Emma B., 125
Hoffman, Vivian, 123
Holley, Horace, 155–56, 180–81, 194
Hollings, Ernest F., 228, 230
Holsapple-Armstrong, Leonora, 139
Honea Path, S.C., 64
Howard University, 16, 18, 26, 33, 50
Hulse, Frank, 101–2
Humphrey, Hubert, 245

Illinois, 71
	Chicago, 43, 49–50, 51, 93, 103, 227, 231, 245, 248
	pioneers and traveling teachers from, to S.C., 158, 165, 184–87, 216, 221, 248
	and Red Summer, 79, 127
	See also Bahá'í Faith in United States: Chicago, Ill.; Bahá'í house of worship: Wilmette, Ill.
Immigration and Nationality Act of 1965, 233
India, 109, 182, 227
	in Ten Year Plan (1953–1963), 2, 193, 205, 239
Interracial Commission (Commission on Interracial Cooperation), 8, 73–75, 80, 82, 223
Interracialism, 5
	and biracialism, contrasted, xiii
	and Communism, accusations of, 201, 203–5, 211, 214, 217, 228
	interracial marriage, 49–51, 213–14, 233; opposition to (see Jim Crow: miscegenation)
	in New Deal era, 142
	opposition, 8–10
	during Reconstruction, 10–11, 223
	social equality, 8–10, 62, 69–70, 75, 89, 175, 190, 212, 233
	as spiritual principle, 5, 12, 54, 83
	in World War I era, 55, 59–60, 69, 73–76, 79–82
	See also Bahá'í Faith in United States: and interracialism; Civil rights movement; Protestantism: and interracialism; *specific individuals and organizations*
Ioas, Leroy, 114–15, 195
	and challenges in Greenville, S.C., Bahá'í community, 164, 166, 180
	on teaching, 114–15, 134, 157
	See also National Teaching Committee, U.S.
Iran, xi, 1, 4, 20, 46, 109, 124, 169, 191, 210, 215, 239
	Bahá'í community, persecution of, 54, 238–39
	Bahá'í teachers, and U.S. community, 24, 42, 104 (*see also specific individuals*)
	in Seven Year Plan (1946–1953), 182
	Shiraz, 20, 130
	Tehran, 181, 193, 205, 239
	in Ten Year Plan (1953–1963), 206, 207
Iraq, 20, 241
	Baghdad, 194, 206, 241
Irvin, Robert, 101–4, 125
Isaiah (prophet), 177
Islam, 2, 4, 6, 20, 121, 133, 209, 215

Ahmadiyya sect, as possible universal religion (Toynbee), 254n7
al-Azhar University, 24
"entry by troops" in, 280n15
Greatest Name of God in, 263n6
millennialism in, 20
Muhammad, 218
Shia clergy, 20, 238
Sunni intellectuals, 'Abdu'l-Bahá and, 48
Israel (Palestine), 20, 103, 124, 193
	'Akká, 22
	Haifa, 22, 57
	during World War I, 51, 57–58, 76
	See also Bahá'í World Center
Italy, 93, 119, 137
	fascist regime, 132
	in Seven Year Plan (1946–1953), 182, 194
Ives, Mabel, 165–66

Jackson, Daisy. See Moore, Daisy King Jackson
Jackson, Edith Barrington King, 101, 124
Jackson, James U., 98–101, *102*
Japan, 132, 188
Japanese Americans, 150
Jenkins, Eloise Harleston, 70–71
Jesus Christ, xi, 18, 36, 77, 86–89, 112, 138, 203, 218, 284n7
	return, 6, 20, 23, 34, 88, 158, 218, 221, 234, 256n8
Jews, xiii, 5, 71, 82, 98, 220–21, 232–33
Jim Crow, xii–xiii, 59
	in education and employment: defense industries, 69; Dunning School, 62; federal employment, 51; labor movement, 8–9, 10; New South ideology, 91, 98–100; public education, xii–xiii, 64–65, 67, 201–3, 227, 230–31; textile industry, 32, 61, 64, 153, 155
	and gender, 61–65, 73
	legal aspects: disfranchisement, 31–32, 61–63, 67, 98, 161, 231; justice system, 64, 97; *Plessy v. Ferguson*, 32, 64; S.C. constitution of 1895, xii, 31, 63, 202; "separate but equal" doctrine, 32, 202
	miscegenation, 8–10, 62, 204, 214; antimiscegenation laws, 50–51, 64, 214, 233; Bob Jones Sr. on, 203; Richard Carroll on, 66; Citizens' Councils on, 214; "social equality" as euphemism for interracial sex, 9, 62, 66; (*see also* Interracialism: interracial marriage; Interracialism: social equality)

Index   313

Jim Crow—*continued*
  origins, 60–65, 97–98; Spanish-American War (War of 1898), 11
  post–World War II challenges to, 172–78; "massive resistance," 203–5, 213 (*see also* Civil rights movement; White Citizens' Councils)
  and Progressivism, 63–65, 67–68, 69, 98–100
  and Protestantism, xiii, 1, 3, 9, 29, 64–65, 74–75, 85–86, 141–45, 152–55, 161–62, 203
  spatial segregation, 7, 32, 63–64, 162–63, 171, 221, 276n65
  violence, 10, 63–64, 68–69, 228–31; Augusta area, Ga./S.C., 97; after *Brown* decision, 204–5; Georgetown, S.C., 63; Greenville, S.C., 153–55, 157; Lake City, S.C., 63; lynching, 64–68, 73, 85, 98, 174–75; Phoenix, S.C., 63; Red Summer of 1919, 71–73, 79–80; shifting white attitudes, 174–75
  See also under Bahá'í Faith in United States; Democratic Party; Republican Party
Johnson, Jack, 51
Johnson, James Weldon, 70, 72
Johnson, Lyndon B., 230–32, 245
Johnson, Ruth, 125
Johnston, Olin D., 160–61, 203, 228
Johnston, S.C., 121
  See also Bahá'í Faith in Augusta area, S.C./Ga.
Jones, Bob, Sr., 203
Jurney, David, 222

Kennedy, John F., 229, 273n27
Kennedy, Robert F., 245, 249
Kentucky, 43, 44, 58
Kershaw, Marie. *See* Frain, Marie Kershaw
Khan, Ali-Kuli, 163, 275n47
Kheiralla, Ibrahim George, 18, 22, 23, 42, 45, 263n6
King, Coretta Scott, 248
King, Martin Luther, Jr., 199
  assassination, 245, 248
  on "beloved community," 243
  on violence, 245
Kingdom of God, 20, 21–22, 57, 87–88, 90, 110, 112, 243, 256n8
Klebs, Margaret, 7–8, 91–92, 94, 100–105, 121, 125–26, 134, 137, 139
  and 'Abdu'l-Bahá, 94–95
  declining health, 123–24
  discovery of Bahá'í Faith, 93–94
  early life, 92–93, 266n1
  and Jackson family, 98, 100
Knobloch, Alma, 24
Knobloch, Amelia, 24
Knoblock, Fannie, 24
Koinonia Farm, 9
Korean War, 210, 220. *See also* Cold War
Krogius, Anna, 122
Ku Klux Klan, 72–74, 98, 105, 204, 228
  in New Deal–era Greenville, S.C., 153–54, 160
  See also under Bahá'í Faith in S.C.: opposition

Labor movement, 72, 104, 168, 173, 175
  in Alabama coal and iron region, 8–9
  in Charleston, S.C., 33–34, 175
  Food, Tobacco, Agricultural, and Allied Workers Union (FTA), 175
  in Greenville, S.C., 9, 152–53, 155, 234
  interracialism in, 5, 8–10, 142, 148, 152, 175, 229, 281n30
  National Textile Workers Union (NTWU), 153
  in New Deal era, 9, 142, 148, 152–53, 155
Lake City, S.C., 63
  See also Bahá'í Faith in Florence area, S.C.
Lake Mohonk Conference, 82–83
Landes, John H., 102
Latin America, 4, 178, 211
  in Seven Year Plan (1937–1944), 129–32, 134, 139, 167–69, *170–71*
  in Seven Year Plan (1946–1953), 181, 183, 194–95
  in Tablets of the Divine Plan, 76
  in Ten Year Plan (1953–1963), 239–40
  See also specific countries
Lawrence, Emma, 187
League of Nations, 132, 177
  League of Nations Union, 120
  Paris Peace Conference, 77
League of Women Voters, 81
Lexington County, S.C., 174, 184
  See also Bahá'í Faith in Columbia area, S.C.
Lighthouse and Informer (Columbia, S.C.), 161
Limestone College, 246
Lindsey, Cleo, 216
Lindsey, Estelle, 150–51, 216
Lindsey, Raymond, 150–51, 216
Linfoot, Charlotte, 137
Lohse, Adline, 158, 163, *164*, 179–81
Long, Eunice Grant, *186*, 187
Louis, Joe (Joe Louis Barrow), 199, 218

Louis G. Gregory Bahá'í Institute, xii, xvii
Louis G. Gregory Bahá'í Museum, xvii
Louisiana, 13, 58, 177
    New Orleans, 197, 228
Lowery, Ethel, *186*
Lowery, Irving E., 40, 83–90, *84*, 105, 145
Lutherans, 24
Lynch, Effird, 125
Lynching. *See under* Jim Crow: violence
Lytle, Alice Louise, 105

MacDonald, Josephine, 122
Manning, Richard, 69–70
Manning, S.C., 228
Marangella, Philip, 119–20
Marshall, Thurgood, 160, 202
Martin, Elizabeth Allison, 248, 273n22
Martin, J. Robert, 174, 235
Maryland, 23, 44, 58, 118
    Baltimore, 30, 44, 49, 58, 119, 135, 185
Massachusetts, 84, 186, 220
    Boston, 43, 70, 93, 104
McAlister, Eva Flack, 158, 165
McCain, James T., 227
McCormick, Marjorie, 184–86, 188
McKaine, Osceola, 161
McKay, Barney, 18
McKim, Lutie, 185, *186*
McLeod, Daniel, 232, 235
McNair, Robert, 246, 248
McNair, Ronald E., 252n8
Methodists, 34, 35, 83–84, 127, 161–62
    African Methodist Episcopal (AME) denomination, 50, 117, 139
    AME conference in S.C., on lynching, 66
    hegemony theory, 5–6
    and Holiness movement, 23
    and Interracial Commission, 74–75
    Morris Brown AME Church, Charleston, S.C., 34
    Northern Methodist denomination, 34–35
    Old Bethel Methodist Episcopal Church, Charleston, S.C., 35, 40
    Sidney Park Colored Methodist Episcopal (CME) Church, Columbia, S.C., 71, 85–86, 88, 90, 139
    Washington St. Methodist Church, Columbia, S.C., 161–62
    See also specific individuals and organizations
Mexico, 132, 181, 245

Meyer, Eugenie, 187, 197
Meyer, Zoe, 216
Michaels, Claire Glover, 123, 226
Michigan, 215–16, 233, 248
    Davidson, Bahá'í school in, 112, 141, 196, 223
    Detroit, 218, 219
Mickey, Edward, 118
Mickey, Richard, 69, 118
Mickle, Jennie, 139–40
Mickle, Maud, 139–40, 157, 169, 184
Middle East, 185, 191
Mississippi, 177, 203, 228, 230
Mitchell, Samuel Chiles, 82–83, 119
Moffett, Ruth, 165, 186–87, 221
Montgomery, Eugene A. R., 176
Montgomery, Louise Moore, 140, 185
Moore, Daisy King Jackson, 101–3, 122, 124, 127
Moore, Edward, 169, 185
Moore, Julia, 101, 103, 105
Moore, Louella, 139–40, 169–70, *170*, 185, *186*
Morris College, 117, 228
Morrison, Gayle, 5
Morse, Josiah, 82, 88, 119–20
Mothersill, Rachel, *164*
Murrah, P. Bradley, 217
Myrtle Beach, S.C., 173
    See also under Bahá'í Faith in Florence area, S.C.
Myrtle Beach Air Force Base, 247

NAACP (National Association for the Advancement of Colored People), 1, 9, 49–51, 72, 81–82, 89, 148, 160, 217
    in Cold War-era S.C., 175–76; and "massive resistance," 204–5; and school desegregation cases, 201–3
    in 1960s, 227, 229
    S.C. branches: Aiken, 71, 73; Anderson, 71, 73; Beaufort, 71; Charleston, 70–71, 73, 118, 160; Cheraw, 159–60; Columbia, 70–71, 73, 160; Darlington, 71; Florence, 71, 73, 160; Georgetown, 160; Greenville, 153–54, 160; Orangeburg, 71, 204; Sumter, 160, 227
    S.C. Conference, 159–62, 175–76, 201–2, 204–5, 229, 234–35, 246
    in World War I-era S.C., 70–73, 75, 160
    in World War II-era S.C., 159–62; and Isaac Woodard Case, 174
    See also Civil rights movement; *Crisis*; Du Bois, W.E.B

Nakhjavání, 'Alí, 207–8
National Spiritual Assembly, U.S. (National Spiritual Assembly of the Bahá'ís of the United States and Canada [1922–1948], of the United States [1948–])
   on formation of Local Spiritual Assembly in Augusta area, S.C./Ga., 123
   origins and development, 109–12, 114 (*see also* Bahai Temple Unity; Bahá'í Administration: National Spiritual Assemblies); annual election, 111, 198 (*see also* Bahá'í National Convention, U.S.)
   and Plans of Unified Action, 114
   and Seven Year Plan (1937–1944), 129–36, 168; appoints Committee on Assembly Development, 179, 181; appoints Race Unity Committee, 149; and pioneers in Greenville, S.C., 155–56, 180–81; role of National Spiritual Assembly, described in *Advent of Divine Justice*, 147–48; southern teaching policy during, 143, 145, 147–52; and United Nations, 178
   and Seven Year Plan (1946–1953): "Bahá'í Institute" program, 196–97; Canada, separate National Spiritual Assembly for, 181, 194; J. Waties Waring, correspondence with, 191
   and Ten Year Plan (1953–1963), 223, 226, 242; Alaska, separate National Spiritual Assembly for, 240
   and Nine Year Plan (1964–1973), 247; *Why Our Cities Burn*, 248
   See also specific agencies
National Teaching Committee, U.S., 114–15, 117
   and Seven Year Plan (1937–1944), 134–39, 157, 164, 166; sends pioneers to Greenville, 155–56, 180–81
   and Seven Year Plan (1946–1953), 183–84, 188
   and teaching methods: firesides, 115–16; pioneers, 134–35; study groups, 115–16; teaching campaigns, 116, 121
   See also Bahai Temple Unity: Teaching Committee of Nineteen; National Spiritual Assembly, U.S.
National Urban League, 81
Native Americans, xvi, 95–96, 150, 206
   in Ten Year Plan, (1953–1963), 239, 242
New Deal, 9, 10, 121, 130–32, 153–54, 159, 161, 173
   and African Americans in Democratic Party coalition, 176–77
   and interracialism, 142, 148, 175

Newman, I. DeQuincey, 246
News and Courier (Charleston, S.C.), 175
New South (ideology), 91, 98–100
New York, 70, 91, 93, 122, 123, 191, 245
   Bahá'í Faith in, 43, 46, 70, 76, 78 93, 104, 195, 212
   Lake Mohonk Peace Conference, 82–83
   pioneers and traveling teachers from, to S.C., 119, 158–59, 197
New York Times, 228
Nigeria, 244
Nineteen Day Feast, 112, 125, 242
   as interracial gathering, 28–29, 51, 54, 145, 150–51, 162, 164, 185, 188, 247
   origins and development of, 24, 112, 116, 257n12
Nine Year Plan (1964–1973), 243–44
   five-year youth program in U.S., 249
   intercontinental conferences (1967–1968), 244
   results, 249
Nixon, Richard M., 245–46, 281n30
North Augusta, S.C., 14, 173
   origins, 98–100, *102*, 121
   See also Bahá'í Faith in Augusta area, S.C./Ga.
North Carolina, 19, 24–6, 34, 44, 73, 101, 228
   African American population, 135
   Bahá'í Faith in, xvii, 58, 119, 132, 156–59, 183–84, 189, 248
   Louis Gregory in, 17, 30, 76, 79, 95, 117–18, 140
   See also specific individuals, institutions, and localities
Northern, Chauncey, 119–20

Ober, Harlan, 79
O'Neill, Agnes, 137
Orangeburg, S.C., 34, *71*, 82, 83, 176, 204, 228–30
   Bahá'í Faith in, 116, 120, 196
   Orangeburg Massacre, 246, 248, 284n6
Osborne, Alfred, 168
Ottoman Empire, 20, 52, 57

Paine College, 95
Palestine. *See* Israel (Palestine)
Palmer College of Chiropractic, 220–21
Palmetto Leader (Columbia, S.C.), 140
Palmetto Medical Association, 140
Pan-Africanism, 192
Parsons, Agnes, 79–80
Pellagra, 38–40
Pendleton, S.C., 122, 141, 247

Penn Center, 199, 223–24, 224–25, 226
    See also Bahá'í Faith in Beaufort area, S.C.; Beaufort, S.C.; Gullah
Pentecostals, 6–7
Perry, Matthew J., 234–35, 283n54
Persia. See Iran
Pickens, S.C., 174
Pinson, Josie, 184, 187, 197
Player, Almetta, 222
Pope, Pocahontas, 25–27, 257n14
Popular Front, 5
    See also Communism; New Deal
Populism (People's Party), 29, 97–98
Presbyterian College for Women, 93–94
Presbyterians, 93–94, 117
    First Presbyterian Church, Augusta, Ga., 98
Progressive Democratic Party (PDP), 161, 168, 175–76, 231
Progressivism, 7, 59, 61, 85, 90, 100
    See also Jim Crow: and Progressivism; specific individuals and organizations
Protestantism
    Baptist-Methodist hegemony theory, 5–6; diversity and dissent, 5–7
    and black accommodationism, 65–66
    and black respectability, 35–38, 40–41
    Cold War revival, 211; association of Communism, internationalism, interracialism, and Antichrist, 214, 234–35
    interracialism in, xiii, 5–10, 73–75, 154–55
    and Jim Crow, xiii, 1, 3, 9, 29, 64–65, 74–75, 85–86, 141–45, 152–55, 161–62, 203
    and materialism, 65–66, 210–11
    millennialism in, 21, 256n8; Millerites, 23, 257n11 (see also under Christianity)
    See also Christianity; Bahá'í Faith in S.C.: and Protestantism; Bahá'í Faith in United States: and Protestantism; specific individuals, denominations, and organizations

Race riots. See Jim Crow: violence
Radford, Donald, 125–26
Radio Bahá'í WLGI, xvii
Reconstruction, 36, 44, 161, 172, 223
    and education, 31, 34, 199, 223, 230; S.C. constitution of 1868, 31
    insurgency against and collapse, 26, 30–31, 34, 43, 61; Dunning School, 62; in Georgia, 96; in South Carolina, 96–97, 99, 267n7
    and interracialism, 5, 10–11, 231
    "Port Royal Experiment," 223 (see also Penn Center)
Red Summer of 1919, 71–73, 79–80
Remey, Charles Mason, 23–24, 104, 137, 158, 195
Republican Party, 16, 18, 79, 245
    and Jim Crow, 32, 51, 63
    and Reconstruction, 31, 96–97
Rexford, Orcella, 150
Reynolds, Annette, 246
Richland County, S.C., 160, 175, 215, 230–31
    See also Bahá'í Faith in Columbia area, S.C.; Columbia, S.C.
Ridván, Festival of, set as beginning of Bahá'í administrative year, 111
    "Most Great Jubilee," centenary celebration and conclusion of Ten Year Plan, 193, 199, 206, 240–41
Robinson, Annie Mae, 187
Robinson, Essie, 151–52
Rock Hill, S.C., 82, 228–29
    Bahá'í Faith in, 248
Rogers, Mabel, 102
Roman Catholics, xiii, 5, 98, 118
Romer, Annie, 184, 197
Roosevelt, Franklin D., 115, 176
Root, Martha, 104–5
Russia. See Soviet Union

Sample, Carlton, 125
Savages (friends of William and Christine Bidwell), 187
Savannah, Ga., 96, 101, 103
    Bahá'í Faith in, 37, 50, 122, 127
Savannah River Site, 173
Schofield Normal and Industrial School, 95, 102, 126
Schopflocher, Lorol, 121
Scott, Della, 126
Sego, Esther, 104, 121–22, 124, 126, 185
Segregation. See under Jim Crow
Sellers, Cleveland, 246, 284n6
Seven Year Plan (1937–1944)
    and Advent of Divine Justice, 146–52
    new goal of establishing one Local Spiritual Assembly in each goal territory, 156
    origins and scope, 129–36
    results, 167–71, 179
    and southern teaching policy, 141–45, 146–52
    and world situation, 130–32

Seven Year Plan—*continued*
   See also under Bahá'í house of worship: Wilmette, Ill.; National Spiritual Assembly, U.S.; National Teaching Committee, U.S.; Shoghi Effendi; *Bahá'í Faith in specific places*
Seven Year Plan (1946–1953)
   Africa Campaign, 192–95
   intercontinental conferences (1953), 193
   origins and scope, 172–73, 181–82
   results, 193–96, 205
   See also under Bahá'í house of worship: Wilmette, Ill.; National Spiritual Assembly, U.S.; National Teaching Committee, U.S.; Shoghi Effendi; *Bahá'í Faith in specific places*
Shoghi Effendi, 11, 15, 91, 116, 138, 180, 243
   appointment to Guardianship, 106–9
   death and succession, 238, 240
   and development of Bahá'í administration, 1920s–1930s, 110–13; *Bahá'í Administration*, 124; *The Dawn-Breakers*, 124; "World Order Letters," 112
   and development of institution of Hands of the Cause of God, 191–92, 195, 238
   on early election of Universal House of Justice, 109–10, 137
   early life, 107; title, 269n22
   on materialism, 146, 149, 209–13
   on proposed Seven Year Plan (1956–1963), 193–94, 205
   on Seven Year Plan (1937–1944), 129–34, 146–52; *Advent of Divine Justice*, 146–52, 162, 168, 209; goal of establishing one Local Spiritual Assembly in each goal territory, 156; on links among temple project, administration, and growth, 133–34; and pioneers in Greenville, S.C., 155–56; southern teaching strategy during, 143–45, 147–48, 150–52, 164–66; *World Survey of the Bahá'í Faith, 1844–1944*, 169
   on Seven Year Plan (1946–1953), 172–73, 178–79, 182–83, 193–96
   on Ten Year Plan (1953–1963), 205–15; "American Bahá'ís in the Time of World Peril," 209–12; on Communism, 210; new southern teaching strategy during, 213–15, 222, 237, 241; and race in U.S., 207–11, 226, 232, 238
   See also Bahá'í Administration; *specific individuals, localities, and teaching plans*

Shook, Glenn A., 186
Shultz, Henry, 96
Shumates (friends of Junie Faily), 218
Silver, Luther B., 219, 235
Simkins, Modjeska, 205
Smith, Hattie, 234
Smith, Terah, 150–51
Social equality. See under Bahá'í Faith in S.C.: and interracialism; Bahá'í Faith in United States: and interracialism; Interracialism
South Carolina
   in Cold War era, 173–77; effects of World War II, 177–78
   in colonial period, 95–96
   demographics, 61, 69, 135, 153, 157, 173, 215
   economy, 61–62, 173–74; textile industry, 61, 64, 70, 72, 103, 152–53, 154, 173, 196, 220, 229; textile industry, antebellum, 96, 98 (*see also* Greenville, S.C.: as center of textile industry; Jim Crow: in education and employment)
   government: General Assembly, 63, 64, 82, 161, 174, 176, 217, 230, 232, 252n8; "massive resistance," 204, 235; school equalization program, 202; State Law Enforcement Division (SLED), 204 (*see also* Jim Crow: legal aspects)
   in New Deal era, 152–53
   regions: Lowcountry, 30–31, 62–63, 96, 196, 204, 215; Midlands, 204, 215; Pee Dee, 30, 63, 159, 196, 220; Piedmont (Upstate), 32, 61, 63, 64, 67, 78, 95, 152–53, 196; Sea Islands, 223–24
   in World War I era, 68–75
   in World War II era, 159–62
   See also Bahá'í Faith in South Carolina; Civil rights movement; Jim Crow; *specific individuals, institutions, and localities*
South Carolina Hospital for the Insane (Lunatic Asylum), 37–40, 39, 86
South Carolina State University ("State College"), 82, 120, 204, 228
   See also Orangeburg, S.C.: Orangeburg Massacre
Southern Christian Leadership Conference (SCLC), 199, 234
Southern Conference on Human Welfare, 142
Southern Indicator (Columbia, S.C.), 83
Southern Negro Youth Congress, 175
Soviet Union, 72, 173, 178, 210–11, 244–45
   and Bahá'í Faith, 46, 182, 261n46

See also Cold War
Spartanburg, S.C., 70, 73, 219–20, 228–29, 234
  Bahá'í Faith in, 248
  as source of quartz for Bahá'í house of worship, 140
Star of the West, 58, 106, 108, 121, 125
State (Columbia, S.C.), 68, 140, 162, 185
States' Rights Democratic Party (Dixiecrats), 176–77
St. Helena Island, S.C., 199, 223–24
  See also Bahá'í Faith in Beaufort area, S.C.; Gullah; Penn Center
Stockman, Robert, 5
St. Stephen, S.C., 247
Summerton, S.C., 201
Sumter, S.C., 63, 83, 160, 173, 227–29
  Bahá'í Faith in, 116–18, 120

Tablets of the Divine Plan, 14, 55, 58–59, 75–78, 111, 173, 206
  as inspiration for Seven Year Plan (1937–1944), 129–30
  new phase of implementation, after end of World War II, 178
  and potential loss of "spiritual primacy" of U.S. Bahá'í community, 212
  See also 'Abdu'l-Bahá; Shoghi Effendi; specific teaching plans and places
Talbot, G. P., 103
Talbot, Louise Biggar, 103–5, 115, 122
Tennessee, 16, 33, 74, 122, 245
  Bahá'í Faith in, 44, 58, 117, 143, 219
  Memphis, 59, 135, 165–66
  Nashville, 53, 117, 167, 216, 248, 273n22; and development of southern teaching policy, 143, 145; first Local Spiritual Assembly, 117, 135, 143; Hermitage Hotel, 143
Ten Year Plan (1953–1963):
  call for "exodus" to U.S. goal cities, 212
  intercontinental conferences (1953), 205, 207–8, 215
  intercontinental conferences (1958), 238
  origins and scope, 205–8
  results, 238–40, 243
  and revised southern teaching policy, 213–15
  World Congress, 199–200, 206, 241
  and world situation, 206–12
  See also under National Spiritual Assembly, U.S.; Shoghi Effendi; *Bahá'í Faith in specific places*

Terrell, Mary Church, 35
Texas, 82, 161
  Bahá'í Faith in, 45, 58, 132
Thomas, Charles, 248
Thomas, Dorothy L., 216
Thomas, Helen, 248
Thompson, Emma, 138, 140
Thompson, Louise, 137–38, 140
Thomson, Ga., 97, 105
Thurmond, J. Strom, 174, 176–77, 203–4, 228
Tillman, Benjamin R., 62–63, 64–65
  and Hamburg Riot, 97
Timmerman, George Bell, 204, 214
Tinsley, Myrtis, 103
Toombs, Fannie Gadson, 126
Townes, Laura, 234
Toynbee, Arnold J., 254n7
True, Corinne Knight, 43, 46
Truman, Harry, 174, 176–78
Tucker, William, 217, 234
Tuskegee Institute, 36, 65, 70
Twine, Alonzo E., 47, 59, 83, 86, 88, 90, 197, 226
  early life, 33–35
  institutionalization, 37–41, 39, 118
Twine, Charles, 34
Twine, Joseph, 34
Twine, Phillipa, 34, 38

Uganda
  in Seven Year Plan (1946–1953), 193–95
  in Ten Year Plan (1953–1963), 205, 207–8, 238, 239
Ullrich, Marjorie, 187
Union, S.C., 187, 196–97
Unitarians, 90, 138
United Kingdom
  Bahá'í Faith in, 182, 194, 207, 238 (see also Ten Year Plan: Bahá'í World Congress)
  and World War I, 57–58
  See also British Empire
United Nations (UN), 177–78, 186, 192, 234
  Universal Declaration of Human Rights, 234–35
United States, government of, xiv, 2, 7, 27, 51, 53, 159, 173, 202, 210–11, 214, 227, 242, 273n27
  Congress, 72, 177, 190, 203; Civil Rights Act of 1964 and Voting Rights Act of 1965, 229–32; District of Columbia, oversight of, 26–27
  Justice Department, 204, 228
  Supreme Court, 281n30; on antimiscegenation statutes (1967), 233 (see also interracialism:

United States—*continued*
    interracial marriage; Jim Crow: miscegenation); *Brown v. Board of Education* (1954), 201–4, 209, 213–14, 227, 230; on desegregation of interstate travel (1960), 228; *Plessy v. Ferguson* (1896), 32, 64, 74, 202–3; on Texas's "white primary" (1944), 161
    See also individual officeholders
Unity Feast. *See* Nineteen Day Feast
Universal House of Justice, 2–3, 11, 106–10, 137, 194–95, 200, 206
    formation, 238, 241–42
    and local and national Spiritual Assemblies, 112
    on Nine Year Plan (1964–1973), 243–44, 248
    See also Bahá'í Administration: Houses of Justice; Nine Year Plan (1964–1973)
University of South Carolina, 82, 119, 186, 230, 234–35

Vail, Albert, 90
Vaughn, Joseph, 235–37
Vaughn, Villa, 158
Verdery, Ann McKennie, 103
Vietnam War, 210, 244–45, 247
    See also Cold War
Violence. *See under* Jim Crow
Virginia, 82, 119, 226, 228, 242
    Bahá'í Faith in, 24, 44–45, 54, 58, 117–19, 132, 140
    Colonial Beach, 54
    Fauquier County, 45
    Louis Gregory's first teaching trip, 17, 30
    Richmond, 30, 45, 119
Vogt, Dorothea, 122
Vogt, Elkin, 122
Von der Heydt, Grace, 216–17

Wallace, George, 245
Wallace, Sophie, 122
Walpole, Orie, 138
Walterboro, S.C., 196
Waring, Elizabeth Avery, 190–91
Waring, J. Waties, 160, 175–76, 190–91, 202
Washington, Booker T., 36, 255n2; as inspiration for black leaders in S.C., 65–67, 85, 89; speaking tour of S.C., 84
Washington, D.C., 18, 44, 73, 97, 119, 121, 158, 242
    as black intellectual capital, 16, 26–27, 36, 54
    civil rights movement in, 18, 202, 228, 229
    racial segregation in, 27, 50–51, 53

and Red Summer, 79
    See also Bahá'í Faith in Washington, D.C.; United States, government of
Washington Bee, 28, 36–37
Watchman and Defender (Timmonsville, S.C.), 83
Watson, Thomas E., 97–98, 105
Waynesboro, Ga., 121
    See also Bahá'í Faith in Augusta area, S.C./Ga.
Westendorff, Clarence W., 117–18, 137–38
West Germany. *See* Germany
West Virginia, 140
Wheaton College, 186
Wheeler, Alta, 139–40, 157, 169, 184, *186*
White, Walter, 174
White Citizens' Councils, 203–4, 214–15, 228
White supremacy. *See* Jim Crow
Wilder, Grace, 157–58, 164–65, *164*, 179–81
Williams, Bernice, 162–63, 170–71, *171*, 183, 216, 234, 236
    arrival in Greenville, S.C., 158–59
    and desegregation of city parks, 235
    and Local Spiritual Assembly, 179–80
Williams, Fannie, 222
Williams, Otis, 222
Williams, Roy, 162–63, 170–71, *171*, 183, 189, 216
    and 'Abdu'l-Bahá, 180
    arrival in Greenville, S.C., 158–59
    and Louis Gregory, 78–79, 120, 159
    and Local Spiritual Assembly, 179–81
Williamston, S.C., 158
Wilmington, N.C., 18, 24
    Bahá'í Faith in, 30, 76
Wilson, Woodrow, 51, 57
    childhood in Augusta, Ga., 98
Winnsboro, S.C., 174, 228, 248
    Bahá'í Faith in, 273n22, 248
Wise, Martina S., 125
Women's movement
    clubs, 35, 118, 125, 140
    interracialism in, 5, 148
    among Protestants, 6, 9, 74, 89, 138
    South Carolina Federation of Colored Women's Clubs, 67
Woodard, Isaac, 174
Works Progress Administration (WPA), 153
World Crusade. *See* Ten Year Plan
World War I, 8, 14, 17, 48, 52, 57–9, 65, 73, 90, 125, 135, 177, 203
    Battle of Megiddo (Armageddon), 56, 58 (*see also* Bahá'í World Center)

black activism during, 55, 60, 68–75, 85, 192
and international order, 76–77, 131, 132. *See also* Civil rights movement: in World War I era; Tablets of the Divine Plan; *specific places*
predicted by 'Abdu'l-Bahá, 56–58

World War II, 130–31, 161, 210, 242
and black activism in U.S. and Africa, 192
effects in S.C., 159, 172–74, 201
and international order, 172–73, 177–78
predicted by 'Abdu'l-Bahá, 132
See also Civil rights movement: in World War II era; Seven Year Plan (1937–1944); *specific places*

YMCA (Young Men's Christian Association), 8, 73–74, 103, 223
in Augusta, Ga., 104, 121–22, 126
York, Carrie, 25–27
York, Mildred, 19, 21
Young, Annette McNeely, 220–21
Young, Jordan, 220–21
YWCA (Young Women's Christian Association), 8, 74
in Augusta, Ga., 101
in Charleston, S.C., 190

LOUIS VENTERS is associate professor of history at Francis Marion University, where he teaches courses on African, African American, and southern U.S. history. A historic preservationist who has authored or coauthored a number of site studies and exhibits, he serves on the South Carolina Board of Review of the National Register of Historic Places and the South Carolina African American Heritage Commission. He lives in Florence with his wife and children.

www.ingramcontent.com/pod-product-compliance
Lightning Source LLC
Chambersburg PA
CBHW021848230426
43671CB00006B/313